Constructing a Criminal Case

Constructing a Criminal Case

An Integrative Approach to Criminal Law

Katherine Pang

Carolina Academic Press
Durham, North Carolina

Library of Congress Cataloging-in-Publication Data

Pang, Katherine.
Constructing a criminal case : an integrated approach to criminal law / Katherine Pang.
p. cm.
ISBN 978-1-59460-887-2 (alk. paper)
1. Criminal law--United States. I. Title.
KF9219.85.P36 2011
345.73--dc22 2010043262

Carolina Academic Press
700 Kent Street
Durham, NC 27701
Telephone (919)489-7486
Fax (919)493-5668
www.cap-press.com

Printed in the United States of America

Contents

Acknowledgments

I would like to thank all of the students who inspired me to encourage them to reach beyond their limitations and think about learning Criminal Law from a new perspective. I am so grateful to William (Pat) Hussey who served as a teaching assistant for many years and who contributed the hypothetical fact-patterns that used throughout this book. I am so blessed by my husband who supports me in my many diverse endeavors and who recognizes the gifts we have together.

Constructing a Case

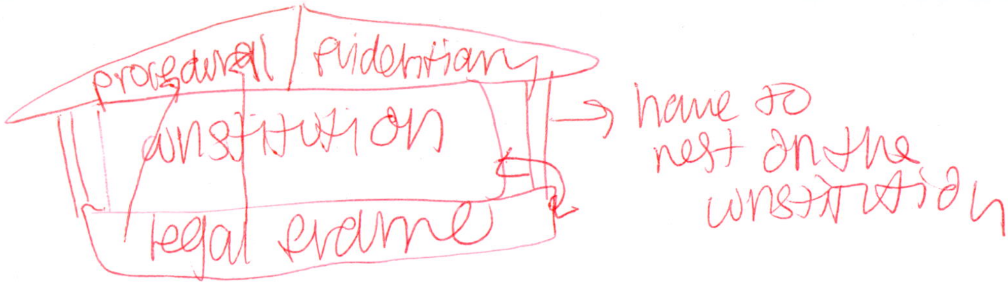

Did some violate the law

Chapter 1

The Integrative Model

Key Terms and Concepts

The Evidentiary Frame	Constitutional Frame
Bill of Rights	Constructivism
CDC Model	Cognitive Dissonance
Frames	Worldview
Integrative Model	Learning inductively
Criminal Law Frame	Criminal Procedure Frame

1.1 Introduction

When learning about criminal law, it is important to think about it in context. In other words, it is useful to ask yourself, "Why is it important that I know the elements of a particular crime?" or "How do I, as a law enforcement officer or a forensic specialist, think about the crime in the context of the criminal justice and legal system?" When studying criminal law, it is useful to start with an understanding of the other areas that impact criminal law such as constitutional law, criminal procedure, and evidence. For example, if you are a law enforcement officer you want your arrest to be successfully prosecuted so that the offender is convicted at trial. This requires an understanding of not only how to determine if the offender committed the crime, but also what evidence needs to be collected in the process and what rules of criminal procedure apply so that the case is not dismissed because of tainted evidence or a violation of the offender's constitutional rights. This textbook will help you in learning not only how to identify the elements of each crime but also how to think about that crime in the context of the different stages of the criminal and legal process. You will have the opportunity to analyze from the perspectives of law enforcement, forensics specialists, lawyers, and the other professionals who function to develop a criminal law case and to present it during the various stages of the trial process.

The integrative frame approach provides a good way to think about the context for learning about various crimes in criminal law and for understanding why learning the elements of each crime is important. The integrative frame approach or model begins with four distinct yet interrelated **frames** that serve as a lens through which you can think about criminal law and how to construct a case for a criminal trial. Understanding how to determine if an offender has committed a particular crime, such as manslaughter or burglary, requires learning the elements of those crimes. However, it is not enough merely to identify the elements of a crime because a prosecutor needs to prove each element of the crime at trial based on evidence relevant to proving the elements of the crime. Further, evidence can be excluded from trial because of violations of rules in both criminal procedure and evidence. Therefore, to better understand how to think about constructing a criminal case based on the elements of a crime it is important to learn how to integrate the substantive and procedural principles derived from, not only criminal law, but also constitutional law, criminal procedure, and evidence. The diagram below presents a visual depiction of the **Integrative Model**.

The Integrative Model

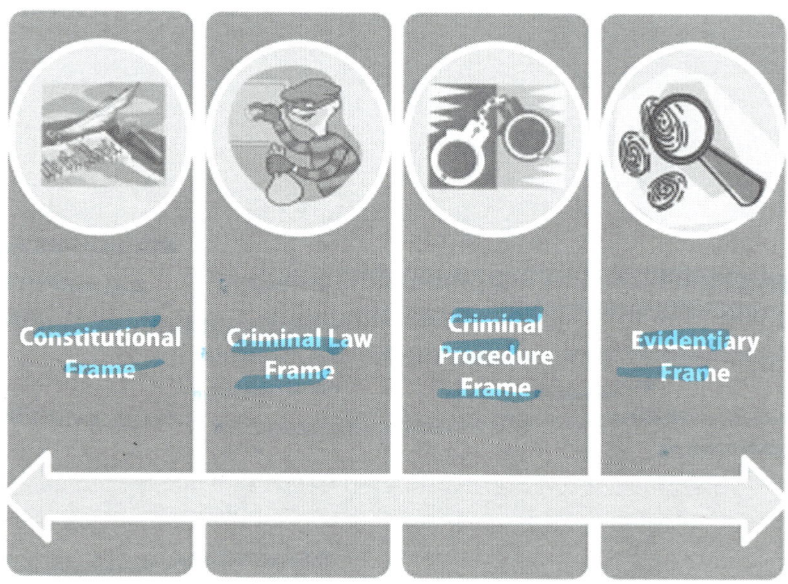

From an introductory perspective, a criminal trial is about a case—a case that starts with the alleged commission of a crime and the related charge(s) and ends with the verdict; albeit sentencing awaits and further decisions frequently depend on the appeal process. The premise, therefore, of the integrative frame model is that the four frames provide the structure for thinking about how to develop a successful case and how to analyze the various steps in the criminal trial process from a criminal law perspective. The four frames provide the context for learning the substantive and procedural content of criminal law while also recognizing the interconnectedness and interrelationships of criminal procedure, constitutional implications, and evidence. From this approach, you will develop skills that will facilitate logical thinking, analytical reasoning, and applied learning.

1.2 Learning the Frames

In the field of social psychology there is a theory known as **constructivism** which suggests that we categorize and structure our experiences based on how we view and understand the world. This is commonly referred to as a '**worldview**.' For example, how we perceive a crime is influenced by our experience, or lack of it, with a particular offense, with anyone we know who may have committed a crime, or with media sources, our friends' perspectives, and other influential factors. These influencing factors can be thought of as lenses and frames of understanding and interpretation. Think about a burglar. Do you think of a cartoon-type of character wearing a black mask and black tights? Do you think of someone breaking into a building at night? The thoughts that come to mind when you hear a word or think about it are your attempt to make sense of the word or topic through those lenses and frames that contribute to your ability to make sense of the word or topic and avoid confusion. Perceptions, views, beliefs, and opinions all fold into your interpretive understanding as you seek to assimilate new information into your existing knowledge databases. For example, what happens when you hear a word or are presented with a topic that is unfamiliar to you? You immediately seek to understand the word or topic by trying to make sense of it so as to process it and make meaning for yourself. If you did not do this, you would find yourself confused and agitated, in a state known as **cognitive dissonance**. Cognitive dissonance arises when you have a thought or idea or are confronted with a word or topic that does not fit with your views or ways of understanding. Since cognitive dissonance is uncomfortable, you want to avoid it, and you accomplish this by trying to understand it and make sense of it or by avoiding it. This is why you may avoid learning a new term or subject in one of your courses because you cannot make sense of this new information without a specific context or a particular application. As a result, you fail to process the information in a constructive manner at deeper levels, and you seek to learn the minimum—what is necessary for assessment recall, such as minimally passing an exam. In this scenario, you do not construct the necessary frames to establish the associations and connections to categorize the learning in such a way as to build expertise through application. Rather, your knowledge acquisition is without frames of reference that build depth of understanding for later use as you gain understanding in a variety of courses.

To develop meaningful and effective learning that translates to practical arenas outside of the classroom, such as the workplace and your profession, it is important to learn to contextualize the course content within the related frames. For example, when you read about the Fourth Amendment prohibitions on unlawful searches and seizures and the need for probable cause, how do you assimilate that information? The words, without context and a frame of reference lack concreteness, and therefore, the words do not make sense, and the information cannot be processed in a successful way. Examples of this might include questions like these: What does the Fourth Amendment state? How do you define 'probable cause'? How do you define a search and/or a seizure? If you take the time to think about the context of your education, then the integrative frame model will help you think inductively while your learning is further developed through exploration and experimentation. This type of framing will develop your ability to better regulate and manage your own learning because you begin to develop your metacognitive skills. Inductive learning, an active process where you learn to interact with the course content and apply it in relevant and personal ways, differs from a more passive learning process where the emphasis deviates from practical application. If you understand the context of a crime based on the integrative frame model, then you will develop the skills to create new crime and case scenarios and think about solutions and strategies that will demonstrate your understanding of the course material.

1.3 The Constitutional Frame

If you start from the perspective that learning criminal law and the elements of various crimes is important because a prosecutor cannot successfully prosecute a case and a defense lawyer cannot successfully defend a case if there are violations of constitutional rights, then the constitutional frame has relevance to your understanding of criminal law. The entire criminal trial process from the first offense to the final verdict is latent with constitutional issues. In order to successfully contextualize the importance of learning and knowing the elements of various crimes, it is necessary to view not only how criminal law relates to constitutional law but also to view how procedural and evidentiary issues interact in the criminal trial process. One way to visualize the constitutional frame's relationship to these topics is through the diagram below.

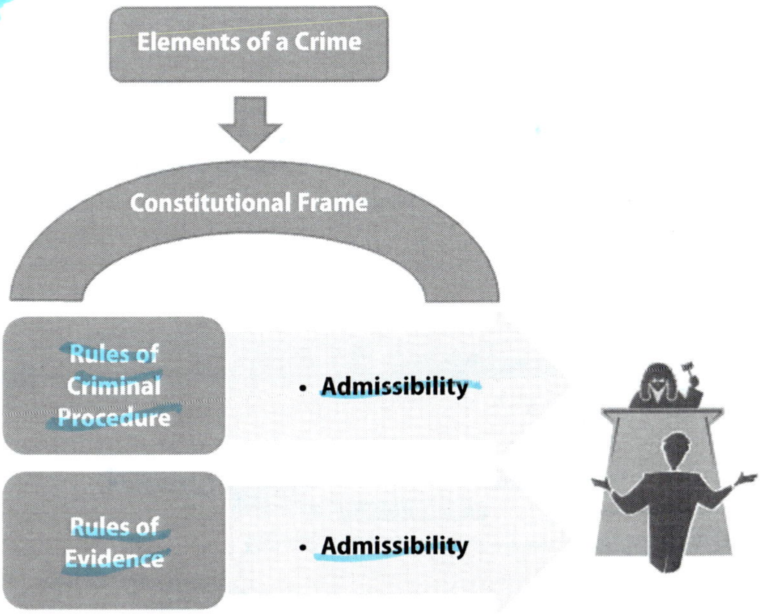

In thinking about the constitutional frame and its relationship to criminal law and the components in the criminal trial process, consider an illustration. If a prosecutor wants to prove an offender committed murder under the applicable state's penal code, the prosecutor will have to prove both the *mens rea* and the *actus reus* based on the actual evidence. The procedures and laws that govern the admissibility of evidence are based on constitutional concerns that seek to balance notions of due process and protection of an individual's right to privacy and security in one's home. When learning new course material in criminal law, it is useful to consider the textbook chapter and section titles and ask, "What are some of the constitutional concerns or issues that impact this particular subject matter?" If the reading is framed within a larger context, it is easier to spot important points and issues. A key point to remember in framing issues from a constitutional law perspective is that it is usually a balancing act between governmental action and individual rights. Many of the excerpted cases or abbreviated fact patterns in this textbook that serve to illustrate a particular point related to criminal law are also evidentiary or procedural issues. Understanding the larger constitutional frame allows you to ask questions. For instance, do the criminal law statutes or actions of law enforcement, for example, related to search and seizure, infringe on the constitutional rights and liberties granted to an individual by the U.S. (or even a state) Constitution? Many of these rights and liberties exist in the Bill of Rights and other amendments to the Constitution. Therefore, it is important to consider not only the specific language of the United States Constitution but also the Bill of Rights and other amendments to the Constitution.

The first ten amendments to the United States Constitution are known as the **Bill of Rights**. The Bill of Rights protects individuals against intrusive governmental action and is considered a limitation on the government's ability to act in certain ways. The United Stated Supreme Court, in several judicial decisions, has interpreted the Bill of Rights to protect what are known as liberties that are guaranteed to individuals in the United States Constitution. For example, these protections would include the First Amendment right to free speech and free press; the Fourth Amendment provides the right to be free from unreasonable search and seizure; and additional rights are granted under other amendments within the first ten amendments of the United States Constitution. For example, in the Fifth Amendment and the Fourteenth Amendment, there are due process clauses. The Due Process Clause in the Fifth Amendment pertains to actions by the Federal Government. The Due Process Clause in the Fourteenth Amendment pertains to actions by the states. Under the Due Process Clause neither the federal nor state governments may take a person's life, liberty, or property without due process of law. As you can imagine, the question as to what constitutes due process has been analyzed in numerous judicial opinions.

The key, therefore, to understanding the **constitutional frame** requires analyzing whether a government's act(s) infringe upon an individual's guarantee of rights and liberties as enumerated in the Constitution as well as the judicial decisions that have examined the government's infringement of those constitutional rights; and in so doing, these decisions have established precedent that will govern the interpretation of subsequent actions. Remember, the constitutional frame always requires several elements: (a) an understanding of the constitutional issues derived from the actual language of the Constitution and judicial precedent; (b) a balancing of individual constitutional rights and protections against governmental (i.e., law enforcement) actions; (c) a perspective for understanding Statutory provisions (i.e., privileges in evidence) and Supreme Court rulings that have created rules (i.e., the Exclusionary rule in criminal procedure). The constitutional frame is therefore a lens through which one can view issues of power, checks and balances, or governmental actions, and then understand them in the context of legislative intent and judicial precedent by assessing the impact on individual rights and liberties as guaranteed under the United States Constitution.

1.4 The Criminal Law Frame

Criminal law is the substantive foundation for determining the applicable crime(s) and identifying the relevant elements of the crime(s). As such, the **criminal law frame** emphasizes a focus on learning to extract the material elements of the crime and then determining the relationship of those elements to develop a strategy for the trial process. Chapter 3 details a process for identifying the crime(s) from the material facts so that the relevant elements of *mens rea* (if applicable), *actus reus*, causation, and any attendant circumstances are highlighted and assessed against the requirements for a particular crime(s) in the appropriate penal code; in this case the odel enal ode.

The criminal law frame is the lens through which determinations about relevance, materiality, and procedure are contextualized so that all strategic and tactical decisions pertaining to the trial process are logically connected to proving, disproving or asserting defenses, justification, or excuses pertaining to the crime measured, weighed, and established by either the prosecution or the defense. When the investigator or lawyer constructs a case, the elements of the crime provide the foundation for strategic and tactical decisions as to how to evaluate and analyze the facts of the case, how to determine evidentiary value, and how to develop a trial strategy. In Chapter 3, you will learn the statutory provisions of various crimes as categorized under the model penal code and selected state penal codes. Selected crimes against the person, crimes against property, and inchoate crimes will be deconstructed based on the material elements of the crime and identified according to determinations of association such as an element that signifies the *mens rea or actus reus*. Remember, in thinking about the criminal law frame it is important to ask, "What do the material facts reveal that will assist me in identifying the applicable elements of appropriate crime(s)?"

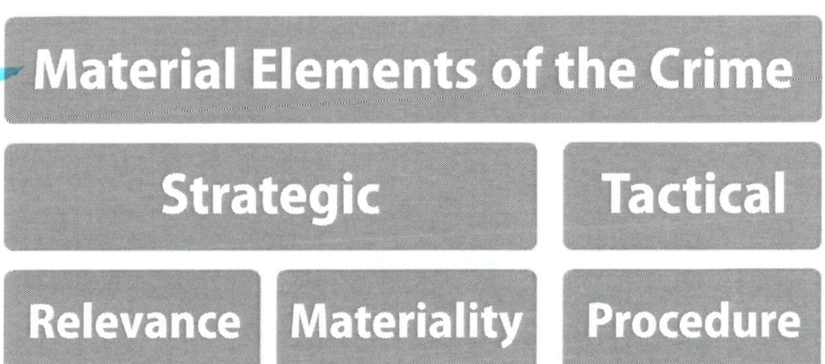

"What do the material facts reveal that will assist me in identifying the applicable elements of the appropriate crime(s)?"

Chapters 3 and 4 will teach you how to identify and extract material facts by using a construction-deconstruction connectionist (CDC) model that is activity-based; this will give you the opportunity to construct a hypothetical fact pattern that illustrates a particular crime or crimes from your knowledge of the elements of the crime(s) using a criminal law lens. **The CDC Model** teaches you how to identify the main points or principles of a crime from the language of the statute and "chunk" or "parse" them so as to facilitate learning bymaking associations and connections. This process of chunking and connecting content will enable you to apply the substantive statutory content with greater facility and speed, thereby helping you successfully learn the course material. The deconstruction and connection steps in the CDC model will be explained in Chapter 2.

1.5 The Criminal Procedure Frame

If criminal law is the substantive foundation for determining the applicable crime(s) and identifying the relevant elements of the crime(s), then criminal procedure is the process through which we evaluate the actions and decisions of the various players in the process such as law enforcement and social and judicial agencies. When using the criminal procedure frame, the first step is to consider the relevant constitutional amendments and overlay the constitutional lens. For example, we know that the Fourth Amendment protects against unlawful search and seizure. We also know that, according to the Fourth Amendment, no warrants shall issue but upon probable cause. Therefore, from a layered frame perspective, we can note constitutional implications that pertain to how we evaluate criminal procedure issues. We should investigate by asking questions like these: "Was the law enforcement officer correct in his/her decision to enter the house without a warrant?" or "Was there probable cause for the issuance of the warrant?" These questions require an evaluation of the facts as presented in a hypothetical fact pattern or a case from a criminal procedure frame perspective so as to stimulate questions such asthe following: "What are the requirements for probable cause?" and "Under what circumstances can a law enforcement officer enter a house without a warrant?" These questions can be answered by not only knowing how judicial decisions have interpreted these scenarios but also how the Courts have established precedent and how this precedent impacts the way we analyze subsequent actions in different fact patterns.

The **criminal procedure frame** not only intertwines with the constitutional law frame but it also interconnects with understanding the ways that courts have applied and interpreted constitutional provisions, state Codes of criminal procedure, and other court decisions (case law) or judicial precedent.

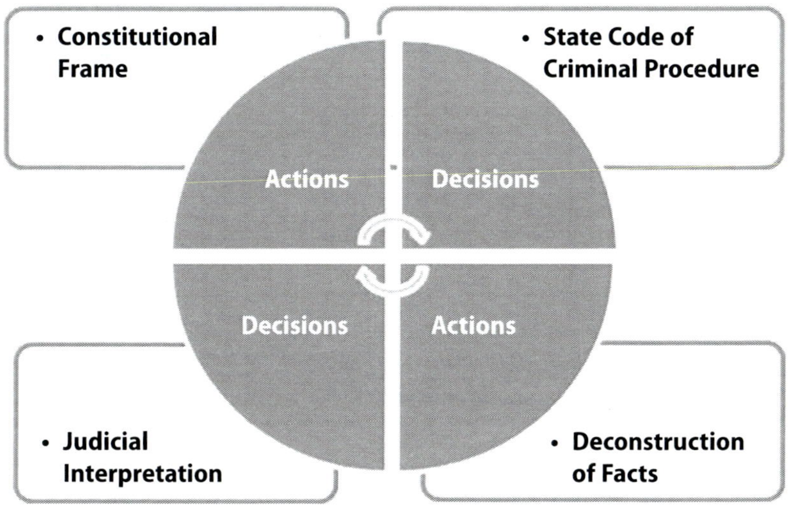

The criminal procedure frame is intertwined with the constituional frame, judicial interpretation, state codes of criminal procedure, and the deconstruction of facts.

For example, a state statute as depicted in a code of criminal procedure might state that a police officer may arrest an offender without a warrant when the offense is committed within his/her presence or within his/her view. The criminal procedure lens frames a perspective for analysis of the facts by highlighting that there are certain instances when an arrest can be made without a warrant. If you deconstruct the facts of the case, that is, extract and extrapolate the material facts (as we will learn in Chapter 3), and then identify issues based on a frame, you will be able to identify that the issue of "whether the arrest was valid" is a criminal procedure issue. The answer will be based on, in this example, a knowledge of the material elements of the code of criminal procedure. This process is very similar to the one used when deconstructing and analyzing facts under the criminal law frame. Remember the main purpose of the frames is to provide perspective so that you can identify all relevant issues from the 4-frames that comprise the integrative frame model.

1.6 The Evidentiary Frame

The evidentiary frame is the fourth frame in the integrative frame model. **The evidentiary frame highlights not only how you enter information** derived from the material facts into evidence for purposes of the trial; but how you actually present and use the information at trial. For example, if the defense contests the validity of an arrest warrant, you must ask yourself if the actual arrest warrant is admissible at trial. If the prosecution wants to use the testimony of an eyewitness who stated that "she saw the defendant enter the house," then, is that statement admissible at trial? The evidentiary frame allows you to review the facts to identify possible items of evidence as well as to make determinations about whether the prosecution or defense can use those items of evidence at trial. The Federal (or applicable state) Rules of Evidence, such as the hearsay rule, judicial notice, and expert testimony govern the admission and use of evidence in the criminal trial process. In many ways, you can think of the evidentiary frame as a bridge from the construction of the case to the presentation of the case. What is important to remember is that you can have a substantial amount of evidence, but if the collection of it violates a rule of criminal procedure or its relevancy is limited, the rules of evidence will serve as a barrier to its use in the courtroom. In constructing a case, the evidentiary frame allows you to evaluate the quality of the evidence from an admissibility perspective. If the evidence, for example, cannot be authenticated or a witness can only present third-hand testimony, the evidence may not be admissible, and from a criminal trial perspective, it is useless and is of no value in proving or disproving a case. The evidentiary frame enables us to ascertain whether the information gleaned from the material facts has probative value and whether you can move through the rules of evidence barrier that can keep us from presenting that information in the courtroom. This diagram presents a visual depiction of the evidentiary frame as part of the integrative frame model.

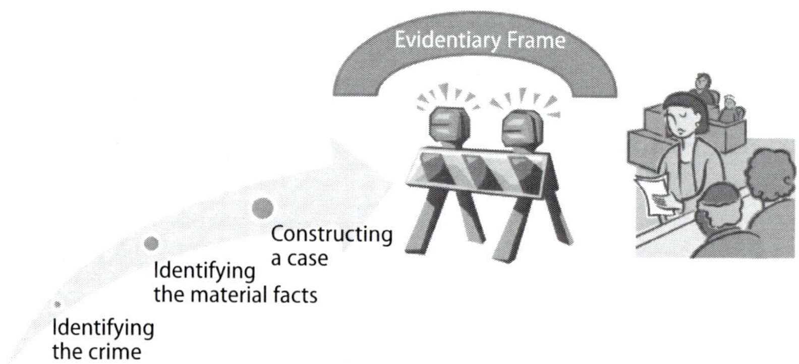

The key impact of the evidentiary frame is that it provides the opportunity to assess the viability of the evidence from a criminal trial process perspective. Often, in exploring issues pertaining to criminal law or criminal procedure or in identifying material facts, students fail to consider whether the evidence will ultimately be admissible in a criminal trial. As depicted in the illustration above, once you construct a case, you will face new obstacles that require you to determine how to use your evidence in presenting your case in the courtroom. The evidentiary frame allows you to move across the barrier between the existing evidence and the admissible evidence for proving or disproving your case.

1.7 The Criminal Trial Process

The criminal trial is an elaborate and complex web of procedures, rules, and strategies that begin with the events leading up to an arrest and end with adjudication. In most academic settings, you can enroll in courses in Criminal Law, Criminal Procedure, Constitutional Law, and Evidence, and, as you are now aware, these are the four frames that constitute the integrative frame model. In Criminal Law, for example, the emphasis is on learning the elements of the various crimes, as classified and defined by the Model Penal Code (or applicable state penal codes). Most criminal law courses will have you memorize the material elements of the crime as presented in the penal code or your textbooks and then use them to identify applicable crimes and develop analysis and reasoning from application to a hypothetical fact pattern. You will also learn, in most Criminal Law courses, to read court decisions and identify material facts, issues, and the court's reasoning and its holding. You may also be asked to construct arguments for both the prosecution and the defense according to the case scenario. These are very important skills for those who are thinking about law as a profession or those who will be involved in various aspects of the criminal justice system.

In learning about the criminal trial, it is important to think about the interconnectedness of the main contributing components. For example, a prosecutor cannot charge an alleged offender with a crime without believing or knowing that the material facts will constitute sufficient evidence that will be admissible at trial to prove the material elements of the crime. This requires an understanding of the statutory elements of the crime (criminal law), the collection and admission of the evidence (criminal procedure and evidence) and any issues that may present constitutional challenges to the use of the evidence or the violation of established rules of criminal procedure (constitutional law, criminal procedure, and evidence). As a student of the criminal justice system or the legal system, it becomes obvious that an integrated understanding of constitutional law, criminal law, criminal procedure, and evidence is necessary for learning about not only these subjects but also the criminal trial process itself and then developing the skills for constructing and deconstructing a case for trial. Once you learn the basic components for constructing a case in Chapter 2, you will learn how to identify elements of the crime in Chapter 3; construct and deconstruct a case in Chapter 4; identify applicable rules of criminal law in Chapters 5 through 12; identify applicable rules of criminal procedure in Chapter 13; identify applicable rules of evidence in Chapter 14; and then have the opportunity participate in a mock trial activity in Chapter 15.

1.8 Summary

There are many ways to learn about the various components of the criminal trial process and the substantive subjects, such as criminal law, criminal procedure, and evidence that are an integral part of that process. The purpose of this chapter was to familiarize you with a new way of thinking about the criminal trial by considering each of these central areas through frames that assist you in identifying material aspects of each area as well as contextualizing them for a richer and deeper understanding of the material. If you know that the constitutional frame will help you in learning about searches and seizures or that the criminal law frame will equip you to focus on extracting the material elements of a crime from the statute, then you will not only find it easier to perform required tasks, but you will remember more because you will see a meaningful connection. For example, if, when reading an excerpted case or a hypothetical fact pattern through the criminal law frame, you will know that manslaughter requires the *mens rea* of *reckless* and you will be able to interpret the facts knowing that you need to find indices of recklessness. If you are reading the same facts through a criminal procedure frame, and you know that the officer has a search warrant to search the offender's house and the officer searches the barn, 1000 feet away, you will recognize that you may have a Fourth Amendment problem that may result in the exclusion of any evidence. These frames not only provide you with perspective, but they contextualize the content so that you understand how the pieces fit together when constructing a case for trial.

1.9 Chapter Review Questions

The purpose of these questions is to provide you with an opportunity to think about the material presented in this chapter and to express your understanding in a well-reasoned explanation. This requires that you write in paragraph form and demonstrate your understanding of the course material through answers that are well-developed, well-structured, and sufficient in length to indicate a depth of understanding, integration, and synthesis of the chapter material.

1. What is the integrative frame model, and why is it helpful to you as a student? Provide specific reasons in your answer.
2. What is the relationship between the constitutional frame and the criminal procedure frame in the context of studying criminal law? Please be specific in your answer.
3. Provide an example of how the evidence frame relates to the criminal procedure frame.
4. How do the frames pertain to the criminal trial process?
5. What is most interesting to you from this chapter and why?

Chapter 2

Constructing a Case

Key Terms and Concepts

Precedent	Precedential Value	Main Components
The CDC Model	Constructing a Case	*Mens Rea*
Substantive Law	Case Law	*Actus Reus*
	Procedural Law	

2.1 Introduction

In many law-related subjects, such as criminal law, there are two main skill sets that are necessary for your success: learning the elements of the crimes and learning how to read judicial decisions or cases. Statutory law is law that is derived from legislative action. For example, the legislature of each state has enacted a penal code. The penal code sets forth the definitions and elements necessary to prove a crime. When a law enforcement officer wants to arrest someone for the commission of a particular crime, the officer must know the elements of the crime and must have sufficient evidence for a prosecutor to successfully bring charges and then construct a case in court. When a suspect is charged with a crime, and criminal proceedings are initiated, the case is then tried in a court of law with either a judge or a jury as the determiner of fact. In some instances the judge will not only determine what evidence is admissible but will also decide the outcome of the case. In other cases, the defendant may be entitled to a jury trial in which case the judge presides over the proceedings, but the jury determines the outcome of the case. In either instance, the case is "written-up" and a formal judicial opinion is issued and memorialized in writing as a judicial decision or "case," and this accounts for our use of the term **case law** or **judicial decision**. In order to learn how the law, or for purposes of criminal law, the statutory law (penal code) has been applied to a particular set of facts unique to a case, you will read cases. These cases, or judicial decisions, provide you with a summary of the key or material facts, the applicable law (statutory and even other previous cases—known as case law), the analysis or reasoning of the court, and the holding or determination. Therefore, the main parts of each case include the facts, the applicable law, the analysis or reasoning, and the final decision.

This chapter focuses on the concept of **constructing a case**. The idea of constructing a case is based on the premise that in order to understand how to read a case, one must learn how to construct a case. When you construct a case, you work in steps. The first step includes learning to identify the material facts that are relevant and necessary for proving the elements of the crime at trial. Many facts are presented during a trial, and the key is to learn how to find the material facts. For example, if I need to prove that John touched Susan, for purposes of proving an element of the crime of battery, does it matter if John wore a blue shirt or a black shirt at the time of the incident? The color of the shirt would not be a material fact, but where John stood, how far he was from Susan, with what part of his body he touched Susan, and where he touched her could all be material facts for proving the element of an "unlawful or unwanted touching." In reading a hypothetical fact pattern or facts of the case, you need to learn to focus on those facts that are material to proving the elements of the crime, not those facts that have no probative value.

The second step involves learning to apply the elements of the crime to the material facts so as to prove your case. This requires that you learn to integrate the material facts of the case with the elements of the crime; then you should develop a well-structured logical discussion of how the material facts can be used to prove each element of the crime. This is the skill of developing analytical reasoning and critical thinking. To simply state a fact, such as "John touched Susan" and then reach a conclusion that John committed assault shows faulty reasoning. In constructing a case, you must establish logical connections and develop analytical reasoning so that you demonstrate in your writing and in your oral arguments how the material facts can be used to prove each element of the crime. Learning how to establish logical connections and develop analytical reasoning is the third step in constructing a case, and we will discuss the components of this step later in the chapter. Finally, we will learn in this chapter how to use the construction-deconstruction connectionist model (CDC) to construct a case by reasoning all the way to a conclusion or an outcome.

2.2 Main Components

In constructing a case, you must first identify the main elements of the particular crime or crimes. Most crimes, other than strict liability crimes, or crimes that do not specifically express a culpable mental state, have a *mens rea* and an *actus reus*. The ***mens rea*** of a particular crime involves the mental state or culpability state of the defendant. The penal code in your state will have a chapter on the definitions of culpable mental states. Each state may use slightly different terminology, but each state will have a section that describes the required "mental state." We can, therefore, think of *mens rea* as the defendant's mental or culpability state. The ***actus reus*** is the act required by the particular statutory provision that defines the elements (or main components) of the crime. In many states, the penal code will have a provision that sets the requirements for criminal liability. The usual minimum requirement is that the defendant's conduct included a voluntary act or failed to perform some conduct required by a duty imposed by the law. In other words, it necessitates that the defendant "did something," and usually, it requires that the conduct/act was voluntary or failed to "do something" that the defendant had a "duty to do." If this confuses you, take a moment and think about what is required of you for purposes of constructing a case based on this last sentence. In reading the facts of the case, you must read the facts in the context of knowing the *mens rea* and *actus reus* for the crime so that you can identify the conduct or act to use in proving the *actus reus*. In addition, the issue of voluntariness is raised because if the defendant committed the conduct or act, but he did so because someone was pointing a gun to his head, or he was intoxicated or under some form of compulsion or duress, that changes the facts in the case. The idea of whether the defendant's conduct or act is voluntary now falls under factual determination to be established based on the material facts of the case. This requires that you read the facts not only to determine if the defendant committed the necessary *actus reus* but also to see if the facts support the concept that the conduct was voluntary. If the facts can be used to support an argument that the *actus reus* was involuntary, then depending on the particular elements of the crime, there may be an opportunity to either argue an affirmative defense or perhaps even find a justification that will negate criminal liability (we will discuss these concepts in Chapter 9).

In addition to learning how to identify the *mens rea* and *actus reus* for each particular crime, you must also learn how to find the "causation" element. In reading the definition for a crime in the penal code, you will often see that the *mens rea* and *actus reus* resulted in some action where some type of harm or injury occurred. For example, in the crime of assault there usually must be some physical injury to another person. In crimes in the category of homicide, there usually must be the killing of another human being. This requires that you learn to read the facts to determine not only if the defendant had the requisite mental state for the particular crime and whether the defendant committed the particular *actus reus* but also to determine if there is a connection between the *actus reus* and the result that is necessary in the statutory definition of the crime. You can see that this can become quite complex, and the easiest way to learn how to identify the elements (*mens rea* and *actus reus*) of a crime is to memorize the definition of the crime from the applicable state penal code.

Learning Activity

For each of the hypothetical fact patterns below, use the culpability mental states in your state penal or criminal code and identify the *mens rea*. If you were using the Texas Penal Code, for example, you would begin by finding the culpability states in the TPC, and you would then highlight the *mens rea* and the material terms that assist you in defining the *mens rea* in the context of a hypothetical fact pattern. For example, consider the following excerpts from the TPC:

> *Mens rea* [§6.03 (a)–(d)]
>
> (a) A person acts intentionally, or with intent, with respect to the nature of his conduct or to a result of his conduct when it is his conscious objective or desire to engage in the conduct or cause the result.
>
> (b) A person acts knowingly, or with knowledge, with respect to the nature of his conduct or to circumstances surrounding his conduct when he is aware of the nature of his conduct or that the circumstances exist. A person acts knowingly, or with knowledge, with respect to a result of his conduct when he is aware that his conduct is reasonably certain to cause the result.
>
> (c) A person acts recklessly, or is reckless, with respect to circumstances surrounding his conduct, or the result of his conduct when he is aware of but consciously disregards a substantial and unjustifiable risk that the circumstances exist or that the result will occur. The risk must be of such a nature and degree that its disregard constitutes a gross deviation from the standard of care that an ordinary person would exercise under all the circumstances as viewed from the actor's viewpoint.

> (d) A person acts with criminal negligence, or is criminally negligent, with respect to circumstances surrounding his conduct or the result of his conduct when he ought to be aware of a substantial and unjustifiable risk that the circumstances exist or the results will occur. The risk must be of such a nature and degree that the failure to perceive it constitutes a gross deviation from the standard of care that an ordinary person would exercise under all the circumstances as viewed from the actor's viewpoint.

Now use those key terms in the context of the fact pattern to determine the applicable *mens rea*.

1. Jason had just installed a supercharger in his 1991 Mustang 5.0, boosting the horsepower to well over 400. He picked up his girlfriend, and he was speeding through a residential neighborhood, hoping to impress her. He lost control of the car, skidding into a tree, and Jason's girlfriend was killed. What is the *mens rea*?
2. Aubrey was working three jobs, supporting her two kids and a husband while he finished school. After working an 18-hour day, she came home to find her husband engaged in sexual activity with a neighbor. Filled with rage, Aubrey went to the gun cabinet, chose a shotgun, and killed them both. What is the *mens rea*?
3. Paul found himself in a financial crunch and was becoming desperate. He borrowed his friend's shotgun, went to the local bank and proceeded to rob it. During the robbery, Paul was surprised by a guard. He pointed the shotgun at the guard and fired, killing him. What is the *mens rea*?
4. While driving along an expressway with three friends in her car, Anita chose to text another friend. Because Anita was distracted she allowed her car to drift into on-coming traffic, where a semi struck it. Two of her friends were killed. What is the *mens rea*?
5. Frank was enraged at his wife. He grabbed a shotgun which he had unloaded the night before, pointed it at her, and pulled the trigger. However, without Frank's knowledge, in preparing to go dove hunting, his son had loaded the gun a few hours earlier. The gun discharged, seriously injuring Frank's wife. What is the *mens rea*?
6. Mario operated a chop shop, where almost any part for any car could be had at rock-bottom prices. For an extra fee, Mario would steal a particular model and color so that the parts would match. Mario had an order for a red Viper and spotted one in the mall parking lot. Mario proceeded to steal it. He did not know that it was a sting car, and the police arrested Mario on the spot. What is *mens rea*?

2.3 The Crime

The penal or criminal code for each state will usually organize crimes based on particular category headings. For example, in Texas there is a category entitled "Offenses against the Person"[1] which includes crimes such as criminal homicide, sexual offenses, and assaultive offenses. In New York the category is "Offenses against the Person involving Physical Injury, Sexual Conduct, Restraint, and Intimidation"[2] and includes crimes such as homicide, sex offenses, and kidnapping. In Arizona there are separate categories for "Sexual Offenses"[3] and "Kidnapping and Related Offenses"[4]. Each of these narrower categories in Arizona has a list of specific crimes that are included in the relevant, particular category. In California, for example the larger category is "Crimes against the Person,"[5] and it includes nine chapters. Chapter 1 covers homicide, Chapter 3 covers kidnapping, Chapter 4 covers robbery, and Chapter 9 covers assault and battery. When learning the elements of a particular crime, it is useful to learn the crime in the context of its larger category. Learning the elements of each crime will also aid in finding the relationships between crimes, and finding similarities and differences that will aid your learning.

To help you understand how to think about the elements of a crime, you should examine a few crimes and the statutory wording of the crime by examining the language of the penal code. As we discovered above, several states categorize homicide within the larger category of crimes against the person. If you spend some time familiarizing yourself with the organization of your state penal (or criminal) code, it will be easier for you to find particular crimes as you proceed through your criminal law course. In many states, the penal code lists the crime of murder under the subcategory of homicide which is, in turn, included in the category of crimes against the person. To help you understand how to identify the elements of the crime of murder, you need to examine the specific wording from the state statutes, so we will look at Texas, California, and Florida (since we will revisit this crime in Chapter 5 where we can also examine the statutes of a few more States).

> *Texas*: A person commits an offense if he: (1) intentionally or knowingly causes the death of an individual; (2) intends to cause serious bodily injury and commits an act clearly dangerous to

---

1. Texas Penal Code, Title 5
2. New York Penal Code, Title H
3. Arizona Criminal Code, Chapter 14
4. Arizona Criminal Code, Chapter 13
5. California Penal Code, Title 8

> human life that causes the death of an individual; or (3) commits or attempts to commit a felony, other than manslaughter, and in the course of and in furtherance of the commission or attempt, or in immediate flight from the commission or attempt, he commits or attempts to commit an act clearly dangerous to human life that causes the death of an individual."[6]
>
> *California*: "Murder is the unlawful killing of a human being, or a fetus with malice aforethought"[7]
>
> *Florida*: "The unlawful killing of a human being: (1) When perpetrated from a premeditated design to effect the death of the person killed or any human being; (2) When committed by a person engaged in the perpetration of, or in the attempt to perpetrate, any: a. trafficking offense prohibited by Section 893.135(1), b. arson, c. sexual battery, d. robbery, e. burglary, f. kidnapping, g. escape, h. aggravated child abuse, i. aggravated abuse of an elderly person or disabled adult, j. aircraft piracy, k. unlawful throwing, placing, or discharging of a destructive device or bomb, l. carjacking, m. home-invasion robbery, n. aggravated stalking, o. murder of another human being, p. resisting an officer with violence to his or her person, q. felony that is an act of terrorism or is in furtherance of an act of terrorism; or (3) Which resulted from the unlawful distribution of any substance controlled under Section 893.03(1), cocaine as described in Section 893.03(2)(a)(4), or opium or any synthetic or natural salt, compound, derivative, or preparation of opium by a person 18 years of age or older, when such drug is proven to be the proximate cause of the death of the user, is murder in the first degree and constitutes a capital felony."[8]

Each of these statutory provisions defines the act of murder in the applicable state. As you can see, each of these definitions differs by various degrees, and each definition of murder has one or more requisite *mens rea* and one or more applicable *actus reus*. We will learn later in this chapter and in other chapters how to find the *mens rea* and *actus reus*. In the meantime, see if you can find them in the statutory provisions above by underlining the *mens rea* and circling the *actus reus* in your textbook. You may need to look at other sections in these state penal codes to find the requisite culpability states for that particular state. We will discuss how to do that later in this chapter, but you may want to try to find them on your own for now.

6. Texas Penal Code, Section 19.02(b)
7. California Penal Code, Section 187.
8. Florida Statutes, Title XLVI, section 782.04

2.4 The Facts

When you read a case (a judicial decision) you notice that the court's decision is directly related to how the court applies the law (the penal code, for example, and other relevant case decisions) to the facts of the particular case. This is also true when you are presented with hypothetical fact patterns where you must identify the material facts so that you can determine the applicable crime(s), and then develop reasoning and analysis that integrates the material facts with the elements of the crime so that you can reach a well-reasoned conclusion. You will have numerous opportunities to learn how to identify material facts by reading actual cases and hypothetical fact patterns. However, in order to identify material facts, you must know the elements of the crime(s) so that you can recognize the facts you will need to support an argument that the elements of the crime(s) can be proven by the material facts of the case. Try reading the facts from the case below and see if you can identify the material facts. Before you begin you will need to know the elements of the applicable crime(s). To assist you in this early stage of learning how to recognize material facts, the crime and the relevant sections of the penal code have been provided to you. Remember, this is just an excerpt from the case. If you want to read the case in its entirety, you will need to find it on the internet in the Court of Criminal Appeals of Texas Case Opinions.

Kosoul Chanthakoummane v. The State of Texas[9]

No. AP-75,794, Court of Criminal Appeals of Texas, April 28, 2010

Before you read the facts in the following section of the case, circle the main *mens rea* and the *actus reus* from the statutory language in this paragraph so that you have the facts you need to prove the elements of the crime of capital murder. Are there statutory sections that you need to look up based on the facts of the crime in order to prove the elements of capital murder under these facts?

Appellant was convicted in October 2007 of capital murder under Texas Penal Code Section 19.03(a). Section 19.03(a) which pertains to capital murder states that a person commits an offense if the person commits murder under Section 19.02(b)(1) and in 19.03(a)(2) (2) the person intentionally commits the murder in the course of committing or attempting to commit kidnapping, burglary, robbery, aggravated sexual assault, arson, obstruction or retaliation, or terroristic threat under Section 22.07(a)(1), (3), (4), (5), or (6). Section 19.02(b)(1) states that a person commits an offense if he: (1) intentionally or knowingly causes the death of an individual.

On Saturday, July 8, 2006, real estate agent Sarah Walker was murdered in the D. R. Horton model home where she worked in the "Craig Ranch" subdivision in McKinney, Texas. Appellant

9. On Direct Appeal from cause No. 380-81972-07 in the 380th District Court, Collin County.

was charged with intentionally and knowingly causing Walker's death while in the course of committing or attempting to commit robbery. On the morning of July 8, Walker's ex-husband, Randy Tate, went to Walker's residence in Frisco, Texas. Walker planned to work at the model home that day, so Tate picked up their son early that morning. While Tate was at Walker's residence, Walker showed him a new Rolex watch that she said she had purchased the previous day. Later that morning, Walker went to a Bank of America in Frisco. Still photographs taken from the bank surveillance video showed Walker wearing a watch and a ring at around 11:45 a.m. Walker's cousin, Jessica Allen, testified that Walker often wore ornate rings and a Tag Heuer watch that she had owned for several years. Another real estate agent, Mamie Sharpless, received a phone call at 9:40 a.m. that morning from a man who identified himself as "Chan Lee." The man told Sharpless that he found her phone number in a Keller Williams advertisement and that he wanted to look at a town house she had listed in the Craig Ranch subdivision. He said that he had just moved from North Carolina to the Dallas area, that he had graduated from the University of North Carolina at Charlotte, and that he worked for Texas Instruments. He said that he was calling from a phone booth at the 7-Eleven at Midway and Park and that he was staying in Room 245 at the "InTown Suites." When Sharpless asked him for a contact number, he said that he did not have a cell phone. The phone "cut off" before their conversation ended, so Sharpless tried to reach him by calling his hotel. Sharpless testified that she "called two InTown Suites, and one didn't have a [Room] 245, the other one did, but it just had a recording on it."

Sharpless arrived to show the town house between 11:30 a.m. and noon, and she brought her husband, Nelson Villavicencio, with her. As they sat in their car and waited, they saw a man drive by in a white Ford Mustang and park across from a D. R. Horton model home down the street. They observed the man getting out of the Mustang and starting to cross the street. They drove over to the man and asked him if he was "Chan Lee," and he replied, "No." Sharpless described him as a muscular man of Asian descent, about 5' 4" or 5' 5" tall, with a "buzz cut." She made an in-court identification of appellant as the man she saw that day, but explained that he was thinner with longer hair at the time of trial. As Sharpless and Villavicencio drove away, they noticed that the Mustang had Texas license plates. When Villavicencio drove to the end of the block, turned around, and drove back, the Mustang was no longer there. He then drove back to the town house so Sharpless could show it to another potential buyer. As Villavicencio looked out the bedroom window while Sharpless showed the town house, he observed Walker arrive in her Porsche Boxster. Walker parked her car across the street from the D. R. Horton model home and went inside. At that point, Villavicencio also saw a white Mustang parked on the street in front of the model home. Sharpless then finished showing the town house and they left between 12:30 and 1:00 p.m. As they left the subdivision, Sharpless also noticed a white Mustang parked in front of the model home. At about 12:30 p.m., Walker called her cousin, Jessica Allen. Allen testified that Walker was "in a really good mood" during their brief telephone conversation. They talked for about 15 minutes, then Walker "said someone had walked in and she'd call [Allen] back."

At approximately 1:10 p.m., Andy Lilliston and his wife came to look at the D. R. Horton model home. When they entered the model home, Lilliston thought that it appeared to have been "ransacked." He observed a large pool of blood in the dining room, where the sales desk was located. He followed a trail of blood into the kitchen, where he saw Walker lying face-up on the floor, with the upper half of her body covered in blood. Lilliston directed his wife to call 9-1-1, and they exited the model home. Lilliston ran into the street and flagged down a vehicle for help. He briefly went back inside the model home to check on Walker, but she did not display any signs of life. Lilliston then went back outside and waited for emergency personnel to arrive. When Texas Ranger A. P. Davidson arrived at the model home, he noticed signs of a struggle in the dining room. The desk was crooked, the desk chair was out of place, a plant stand was knocked over, and a potted plant was on the floor. A pair of women's shoes, a broken hair clip, and a broken earring was also on the floor. There was a trail of blood leading from the dining room into the kitchen. Walker's body was on the kitchen floor, and it appeared that she had multiple stab wounds. Davidson opined that Walker had been dragged by her feet from the dining room to the kitchen because the long skirt she was wearing was rolled up to her waistline. McKinney police officer Pete Copin discovered a bloody fingerprint on the deadbolt lock on the front door of the model home; however, he testified that there were "not enough individual characteristics for a positive identification." Copin further observed what appeared to be blood on the plant stand, on the ceramic tile in the entryway, on the wall next to the edge of the window beside the front door, and on the pull cord for the window blinds. It also appeared that there had been blood in the kitchen sink that had been washed or diluted with water. Copin collected blood swabs and other evidence from the scene for further testing.

When Walker's body was discovered, she was no longer wearing the watch and ring that she had been shown wearing earlier on the bank surveillance video. When the police searched Walker's residence after her death, they found her Tag Heuer watch. The police never located her Rolex watch, but they did find the box and the receipt for the Rolex watch in her residence.

William Rohr, the Collin County Medical Examiner who performed Walker's autopsy, testified that Walker sustained several blunt force injuries to her head. He opined that the blunt force injuries were the result of "several blows," and that they were consistent with Walker being struck in the face and head with the plant stand in the model home. Walker had multiple bruises on her face and head, a broken nose, and fractured teeth. She had some defensive wounds, including an excised wound on her left arm and a broken fingernail on her right hand. She suffered a total of 33 stab wounds, 10 of which penetrated vital organs and blood vessels. Rohr testified that any one of those 10 wounds could have been "pretty much immediately fatal." Walker also had a bite mark on the back of her neck that Rohr opined was inflicted "at or near her death." Rohr testified that he preserved this evidence by using a scalpel to excise the bite mark and surrounding area.

DNA analysis linked appellant to evidence from the crime scene. Appellant's DNA profile was consistent with the DNA obtained from Walker's fingernails, the window blind pull cords, the deadbolt lock and faceplate, and some of the swabs taken from the living room, kitchen, and entryway of the model home. The DNA analyst testified that only a "partial profile" was obtained from a swab taken from the kitchen sink because the DNA extracted from that swab "was of low quality and degraded quality." However, the set of genetic markers that she was able to detect in the partial profile "corresponded with the genetic markers observed in the DNA profile of [appellant]."

After receiving the results of the DNA analysis, police arrested appellant at his apartment on September 5, 2006. Texas Ranger Davidson testified that appellant owned a white Ford Mustang and that his apartment was located three miles away from the pay phones at Midway and Park. Davidson spoke to appellant's sister, who informed him that appellant had attended school in North Carolina and that he had moved from Charlotte to Dallas in February 2006. Davidson determined that appellant had filled out a lease application at an apartment complex near the InTown Suites on Trinity Mills. Davidson also discovered that appellant's bank account was overdrawn by $82.27 on the day before Walker's murder. Davidson testified that appellant was muscular and had a shaved head atthe time of his arrest. Officer Copin, who later photographed appellant to document his appearance, testified that he observed what appeared to be some healed cuts or scratches on appellant's hands and fingers.

Appellant was transported to the McKinney Police Department, where he was interviewed by Officer Randall Norton. Appellant at first denied ever being in McKinney in his white Mustang. Upon further questioning, he stated that his car had broken down at "a model house," that he knocked on the door but no one answered, that he took "like three or four steps" inside and asked if anyone was home but no one was there, and that he spoke to a man and a woman in a green or blue "Corolla or Camry" as he left. Next, he admitted that he went to the kitchen sink for a drink of water, but said that he "didn't know how to use the faucet because the hot water came out," so he left. He acknowledged that he had "old cuts" on his hands "from work," so it was possible that he could have been bleeding when he was inside the model home. He also acknowledged that he had sold some of his own property for cash at a pawn shop on Greenville Avenue, including a tape deck, a drill, and an inexpensive Kenneth Cole watch.

Forensic dentistry consultant Brent Hutson examined appellant and made impressions of his teeth. Hutson compared appellant's teeth to the bite mark on Walker's neck and found enough similarities that he was "unable to exclude [appellant] from that population of individuals that could have inflicted this injury." Hutson concluded "within reasonable dental certainty beyond a doubt" that appellant was responsible for the bite mark on Walker's neck.

Stop and Engage

As you can see, there are numerous facts within a case, and the challenge is to learn to identify those facts that you can use to prove each element of the crime. Not all facts are relevant or necessary in proving each element of the crime(s), and those irrelevant facts are known as immaterial facts. Now that you have read the facts from the case, what have you identified as the material facts? Since the defendant has been charged with capital murder, and capital murder requires the *mens rea* of "intentionally," what facts can you use to establish or prove the *mens rea*? Capital murder in this case also requires that the defendant had to be in the course of committing or attempting to commit robbery. In order to identify the material facts that you will need to use to prove the defendant in this case committed capital murder, you must know the elements (the *mens rea* and the *actus reus*) for the crime of robbery. You will need to know under Section 29.02 of the Texas Penal Code that "a person commits an offense if, in the course of committing theft as defined in Chapter 31 and with intent to obtain or maintain control of the property he (1) intentionally, knowingly, or recklessly causes bodily injury to another; or (2) intentionally or knowingly threatens or places another in fear of imminent bodily injury or death." When you read this statutory language, you note that in order to prove the elements of robbery you also need to prove the elements of theft. Section 31.03 of the Texas Penal Code provides the definition of theft and it is quite detailed, so you need to extract the relevant language which is "(a) A person commits an offense if he unlawfully appropriates property with intent to deprive the owner of property. (b) Appropriation of property is unlawful if: (1) it is without the owner's effective consent."

Learning Tip

You have probably noticed the complexity of the process of identifying material facts because you cannot recognize the facts you need for proof of the elements of the crime(s) unless you know the elements of the crime(s). In this case you need to know the elements for the crime charged, which is capital murder, but you cannot define capital murder—for purposes of this case—without knowing the elements of robbery, and you cannot know the elements of robbery without knowing the elements of theft. Therefore, before you even begin to try and identify the material facts of this case, you must have a list of the elements of the applicable crime(s). Now that you know the elements of the applicable crime(s), read back through the facts above, and, using three different color highlighters, color the facts that are necessary to prove the *mens rea* and *actus reus* for murder in one color, color the facts to prove robbery in another color, and color the facts to prove theft in the third color; then extract them and summarize them in a few short paragraphs. These short paragraphs can now be used as the material facts you will need to start to construct a well-reasoned analysis when you learn later how to integrate the material facts with the applicable rules of law to develop analysis and reach a conclusion.

2.5 Statutory Law

As you have learned previously, statutory law is that legislative law in your state that is relevant to criminal law. This is usually the penal code or the state criminal code. You have already looked at some language from the Texas Penal Code on capital murder, robbery, and theft. You examined this statutory law so that you could identify the *mens rea* and the *actus reus* for those particular crimes. You identified the *mens rea* and the *actus reus* for those crimes so that you could identify the material facts from the case example in the last section. Statutory law is very important for learning criminal law because without it, you would not know what elements are necessary to prove or disprove a particular crime. The prosecution wants to prove each element of a crime, and defense counsel wants to introduce evidence to create doubt about the defendant's actions and culpability state. Although you will learn about burdens of proof in another section in this chapter, for now, it is important to understand that without knowing what the law is—what the applicable statutes say—you cannot learn the elements of the crimes of criminal law.

Since we have looked at the language from the Texas Penal Code for capital murder, robbery, and theft, it may be useful to see if there are similarities and differences in the statutory language of these statutes for some other states. In the California Penal Code, there is no definition for capital murder; however, first degree murder in California seems to be very similar to capital murder in Texas. Section 189 of the California Penal Code states:

> All murder which is perpetrated by means of a destructive device or explosive, a weapon of mass destruction, knowing use of ammunition designed primarily to penetrate metal or armor, poison, lying in wait, torture, or by any other kind of willful, deliberate, and premeditated killing, or which is committed in the perpetration of, or attempt to perpetrate, arson, rape, carjacking, robbery, burglary, mayhem, kidnapping, train wrecking, or any act punishable under Section 206, 286, 288, 288a, or 289, or any murder which is perpetrated by means of discharging a firearm from a motor vehicle, intentionally at another person outside of the vehicle with the intent to inflict death, is murder of the first degree.

Stop and Engage

What are some of the similarities between capital murder in Texas and first degree murder in California? You will note that capital murder in Texas is applicable if the person is also committing or attempting to commit robbery. This language resembles the language for a charge of first degree murder in California. You will note the importance of using proper terminology and correct wording since you do not want to refer to first degree murder for Texas or capital murder for California.—The importance of learning precise wording cannot be overstated so that it becomes a part of your assignments, tests, and assessments.

Robbery in California is defined in Section 211 as "the felonious taking of personal property in the possession of another, from his person or immediate presence, and against his will, accomplished by means of force or fear." In reading this statutory definition, what question immediately comes to mind that must be answered in order to fully understand the definition? You need to know what the statute means by "force or fear." In Section 212, which immediately follows Section 211, it states that: "The fear mentioned in Section 211 may be either: (1) the fear of an unlawful injury to the person or property of the person robbed, or of any relative of his or member of his family; or, (2) the fear of an immediate and unlawful injury to the person or property of anyone in the company of the person robbed at the time of the robbery." Are there other words in Section 211 that may be problematic in understanding what is necessary to prove the elements of the crime? For example, what is a "felonious taking"? This may be an interpretative question that depends upon how previous California cases have interpreted these words. Judicial decisions or case law is important, because you need a working knowledge of how courts have interpreted certain statutory provisions and what certain words in statutes mean so that you know how to interpret those same words when seeking to identify the material facts to prove the elements of the crime.

2.6 Judicial Decisions

As you just read, judicial decisions or case law is very important in learning how to correctly interpret and understand the wording of statutory language, but it also plays a very important role in learning how to apply the statutory language to the particular facts of a case. Judicial decisions or case law is also important because it has **precedential value.** In constructing a case, a prosecutor must prove the elements of the crime(s) based on admissible evidence, and the material facts of the case. There is a difference between evidence and admissible evidence, and we will discuss this briefly in Section 2.9 of this chapter. Numerous procedural issues also arise in the criminal trial process. At any stage, the prosecutor or the defense may introduce a motion to a judge on numerous topics, such as the exclusion of particular evidence, the ability to access a particular witness, the need for additional forensic or expert assistance. In order to support the motion, the attorney may be required to provide legal support for the request, such as has this situation been encountered before, and, if so, how was it determined by the court? This is where the attorney would cite other relevant cases that support his/her argument and ultimately the request. For example, in the case we reviewed earlier to identify the material facts (*Kosoul Chanthakoummane v. The State of Texas),* we read this excerpt: "Granting or denying a motion for continuance is within the sound discretion of the trial court. *Wright v. State,* 28 S.W.3d 526, 532 (Tex. Crim. App. 2000). In order to establish an abuse of the trial court's discretion, an appellant must show that the denial of his motion resulted in actual prejudice. *Id.*" Notice how the court uses another case to support its right to grant or deny the appellant's motion for a continuance. The *Wright* case provides the **precedent** (the support or justification for the action) for the court's actions.

You will also note as you read cases that the court's analysis will often include references to other cases in support of the current court's determinations. For example, we can review some language from the same case we studied earlier, *Kosoul Chanthakoummane v. The State of Texas.*[10] In extracting some language from the court's reasoning and analysis we read:

> In support of his argument, appellant cites *Herrin v. State*, 125 S.W.3d 436 (Tex. Crim. App. 2002), a case in which this Court held that the evidence was legally insufficient to support Herrin's conviction for murder in the course of committing robbery or attempted robbery. In that case, the victim's wallet disappeared after the murder and there was no evidence directly linking Herrin to the missing wallet. Id. at 442. There was no evidence that Herrin knew the victim had any money in his wallet or that Herrin even knew whether the victim had his wallet with him. And the evidence showed that Herrin "had a balance of over $13,000 in his bank account, suggesting that he did not need money." Id. The Herrin case is distinguishable from the instant case. The watch and ring that Walker was shown wearing on the bank surveillance video would have been clearly visible to appellant. And the evidence showed that appellant's bank account was overdrawn on the day before Walker was murdered. In contrast to*Herrin*, the evidence in the instant case was such that the jury could reasonably infer that appellant murdered Walker in the course of committing or attempting to commit robbery. The evidence, viewed in the light most favorable to the jury's verdict, was legally sufficient to support appellant's conviction. Point of error four is overruled.

You will note that the appellant (the defendant's name on appeal) cited *Herrin v. State* to support an argument that the evidence was legally insufficient to support his conviction (which is what the Court in the language above refers to as "point of error four.") You will also note that the present court distinguishes the facts in *Herrin* from its facts when they state: "The Herrin case is distinguishable from the instant case. The watch and ring that Walker was shown wearing on the bank surveillance video would have been clearly visible to appellant. And the evidence showed that appellant's bank account was overdrawn on the day before Walker was murdered. In contrast to Herrin, the evidence in the instant case was such that the jury could reasonably infer that appellant murdered Walker in the course of committing or attempting to commit robbery."

---

10. No. AP-75,794; On Direct Appeal from cause No. 380-81972-07 in the 380th District Court, Collin County.

As you can see, it is necessary to learn not just the elements of the crimes, but then you must understand the material facts from the case or hypothetical fact pattern you are studying as well as learn how to identify factual differences or similarities with other cases so that you can cite them to support your arguments. The cases you cite should have substantially similar facts to the facts in your case for purposes of supporting the point you want to develop in your reasoning and analysis. The more similar the facts are to the facts of your current case, the greater the precedential value of that case to the judge. Judges do not want to ignore cases of precedential value because of the compelling concern that a judge's determination and ruling will be appealed and that the disregard of precedent could result in a reversal of the judge's opinion in the case.

2.7 Procedural Issues

As you learned in Chapter 1, it is important to think about criminal law in the context of the frames that are so important in learning how to construct a criminal case. In Chapter 1, you learned that understanding how to determine if an offender has committed a particular crime, such as manslaughter or burglary requires learning the elements of those crimes. However, it is not enough merely to identify the elements of a crime; a prosecutor needs to prove each element of the crime at trial based on evidence relevant to proving the elements of the crime. Further, evidence can be excluded from trial because of violations of rules of both criminal procedure and evidence. Therefore, to better understand how to think about constructing a criminal case based on the elements of a crime, it is important to learn how to integrate the substantive and procedural principles derived from not only criminal law but also constitutional law, criminal procedure, and evidence.

Criminal law is known as **substantive law** because it provides the "substance"—the statutory law and the case law—that governs the crimes that are applicable to the facts of the case. Criminal procedure and evidence have substantive laws as well, but they also contain numerous procedural requirements. The procedure specifies how we "do something." What are the methods by which we collect evidence? What is the process for arresting a suspect? In matters of **procedural law**, the question is: What are the steps, procedures, methods, and process that have to be followed so that violations of the procedural rules applicable to the case do not occur? When you read criminal law cases or fact patterns, you want to focus on the criminal law issues for purposes of criminal law, but you also want to note some of the procedural, evidentiary and constitutional issues; that is why it is important to remember the integrative model diagram from Chapter 1 and think about learning the substantive aspects of criminal law as they relate to the various frames that are a part of the criminal trial process.

2.8 Burden of Proof

In every criminal case, the prosecutor has the initial burden of proof. The burden of proof in every state begins with the prosecution having the burden of proving each element of the crime beyond a reasonable doubt. The prosecution's initial burden of proof is, therefore, known as "beyond a reasonable doubt." For example, Section 2.01 of the Texas Penal Code states this: "all persons are presumed to be innocent and no person may be convicted of an offense unless each element of the offense is proved beyond a reasonable doubt. The fact that he has been arrested, confined, or indicted for, or otherwise charged with, the offense gives rise to no inference of guilt at his trial." Section 1096 of the California Penal Code states the same idea this way:

> A defendant in a criminal action is presumed to be innocent until the contrary is proved, and in case of a reasonable doubt whether his or her guilt is satisfactorily shown, he or she is entitled to an acquittal, but the effect of this presumption is only to place upon the state the burden of proving him or her guilty beyond a reasonable doubt. Reasonable doubt is defined as follows: "It is not a mere possible doubt; because everything relating to human affairs is open to some possible or imaginary doubt. It is that state of the case, which, after the entire comparison and consideration of all the evidence, leaves the minds of jurors in that condition that they cannot say they feel an abiding conviction of the truth of the charge."

In New York, Section 2.01 states that "all persons are presumed to be innocent and no person may be convicted of an offense unless each element of the offense is proved beyond a reasonable doubt. The fact that he has been arrested, confined, or indicted for, or otherwise charged with, the offense gives rise to no inference of guilt at his trial." It appears that Texas and New York have the same language for the burden of proof. What are the burden of proof requirements in your state?

2.9 Evidence Issues

In constructing a case, we have discussed the importance of the various frames in Chapter 1. One of the main reasons for studying and learning criminal law is to enable you to identify the applicable crimes and then to determine the material elements of those crimes so that the case can be successfully prosecuted or defended during the criminal trial process. Think about the role of evidence; how does it fit in the criminal trial process? If you have the facts of a case, such as those set forth above in Section 2.4, what evidence would a prosecutor need to successfully prove each element of the crime? How would a defense attorney rebut such evidence? How would a criminal investigator or a forensics team handle such evidence to ensure its validity and reliability? These questions pertain to the evidence issues in the case. In addition to Federal Rules of Evidence, each state has its own statutory rules of evidence. In Illinois, for example, Article VIII of the Code of Civil Procedure sets forth some of the evidentiary rules. In Florida, Title VII, Chapter 90 contains the Evidence Code. Spend some time finding the evidence code or rules of evidence for your state and look at the various sections and issues of admissibility and inadmissibility.

In understanding the importance of evidence in the criminal trial process, think about the relationship between criminal law and criminal procedure. In criminal law, you learn the elements of various crimes so that you can identify what facts you need to prove or disprove the elements of those crimes. As you have learned, criminal law is substantive law. In criminal procedure, you learn what procedures and processes must be followed so as to avoid violating the constitutional rights of an individual and to prohibit jeopardizing the information (for example, a confession) or the physical evidence that may be searched or seized during a criminal investigation. Criminal procedure is procedural law. The exclusionary rule, which you will learn about in criminal procedure, provides a remedy when evidence is obtained in violation of rules of criminal procedure. In essence, the exclusionary rule prohibits evidence that is obtained in violation of rules of criminal procedure to be admitted as evidence—the evidence becomes inadmissible. This is why evidence issues are so important in thinking about the criminal trial process. Think about it this way—if you want to prove or disprove certain criminal charges (for example, a charge of manslaughter or burglary), how do you do that? You need to present evidence (testimony of witnesses, perhaps even testimony of the defendant, physical evidence, expert testimony, and other forms of evidence) to prove or disprove each element of the particular crime. If the evidence is inadmissible in court, then the evidence cannot be used to prove or disprove the elements of the crime. The rules of evidence provide both the substantive and procedural rules that guide law enforcement, forensic investigators, prosecutors and defense counsel in understanding when evidence is admissible and inadmissible. Therefore, understanding the connections between criminal law, criminal procedure, and evidence in the criminal trial process becomes of utmost importance.

2.10 Establishing Logical Connections

Establishing logical connections is a developed skill that requires practice. Developing an ability to think logically—that is to construct a case by taking it one sequential step at a time and thinking about relationships between material facts, the elements of the crime and how the facts can be applied to support the elements of the crime to prove or disprove the crime—is crucial to your success. In other words, you must seek to find causal relationships. For example, as we reviewed in Section 2.5, the crime of robbery in California is defined in Section 211 as "the felonious taking of personal property in the possession of another, from his person or immediate presence, and against his will, accomplished by means of force or fear." In order to prove that a person committed this crime, you would need to read the facts of the case and extract those facts that would support that (1) there was a felonious taking of (2) personal property that was (3) in the possession of another and that the felonious taking was (4) from his person or immediate presence and that it was (5) against his will and was (6) accomplished by means of force or fear. Now when you read the statutory language from the California Penal Code, you may not have thought about it in terms of six different steps that will require logical connections with the facts in order to prove each element of the crime. In addition, you also need to define the terms, such as "felonious taking" and "force or fear" in accord with the definitions in other sections of the penal code or, if none exist, then by examining how previous cases in your jurisdiction (state) have defined those terms so that you can use those definitions to support your application of those elements to the particular facts of your case.

When thinking about establishing logical connections, ask yourself if your sentences flow one from another in a progressive order (rather than jumping about from one thought to another in a disconnected manner) and whether there is a clear relationship between your ideas and your sentences. For example, in trying to prove a case of robbery using the language above from the California Penal Code, you would not want to first discuss "against his will" and then discuss "whether there was personal property" because those elements of the crime are out of order and if there is no felonious taking, which has not been discussed first, then the existence or non-existence of those other elements is not significant. Proving that there was a "felonious taking" is the first step, and if, by using facts, you can first prove that, then you can move to determining whether it was of personal property and establish the logical connections between the elements of the crime as you discuss them in a sequential and progressive manner. The goal is to make sure that the elements of the crime connect logically to the material facts of the case so that you capture all relevant information when you move to the next step of developing analytical reasoning to reason your way to a conclusion when examining a fact pattern or case.

2.11 Developing Analytical Reasoning

In order to develop analytical reasoning, you must first establish your logical connections. Remember, the goal, to make sure that the elements of the crime are logically related to the material facts of the case, ensures that you capture all relevant information when you move to the next step of developing analytical reasoning. This, in turn, helps you reason your way to a conclusion when examining a fact pattern or case. In essence, you construct a logical argument either for or against the applicability of the particular crime(s) to the facts of the particular case. You seek to use the material facts of the case to justify whether each element of the crime is applicable or inapplicable—thus, you construct a logical argument through the use of analytical reasoning. In order to be successful in developing analytical reasoning, you must first know the elements of the crimes. If you do not spend the time necessary to memorize the elements of the crime you will study in this course, you cannot use that knowledge to identify the material facts you will need to prove or disprove those elements, and you cannot see logical connections so as to build analytical reasoning. If you know the necessary elements of the crime for proof, then you can start to identify the material facts you need to use to prove those elements. This allows you to start from an issue statement, such as—"In this scenario, we need to determine if we can charge Joe with robbery." This is known as an issue statement—"We need to prove whether or not Joe is guilty of robbery." In order to prove or disprove this statement, we need to proceed by taking each element of the crime, one at a time and in order—as presented in the language of the code, and support each element by applying the relevant and material facts from the case through the use of reasoning and argument. In essence, you are developing a deductive argument because you are seeking to develop the logical connections between each element of the crime and the material facts of the case, and then, through your writing (the development of your sentences and paragraphs), you must demonstrate your reasoning and apply the elements of the crime to the facts of the case; in other words, you are revealing your thinking by explaining the logical connections and relationships through your writing. Developing analytical reasoning is the ability to demonstrate your understanding of the relationships (or the lack of relationships) between the elements of a particular crime and the material facts of a particular case, and then using those relationships to reason your way to a conclusion about those relationships—which ultimately will allow you to conclude whether or not "Joe is guilty of robbery."

2.12 Working within the Frames

As you read through and study the chapters in this textbook, be mindful of the various frames in the criminal trial process. The goal in this course is to learn the elements for the crimes we will study in Chapter 3, but you must think about those crimes in the larger context of the criminal trial process. As you memorize the elements of the crimes and apply them to hypothetical fact patterns, think about the evidence you would need to prove or disprove the crime, and the procedures by which law enforcement or forensics professionals would need to approach the collection of that evidence. Think about how lawyers—prosecutors and defense attorneys—would use the rules of evidence to argue for the admissibility or inadmissibility of a particular statement, expert examination, or contradictory testimony by character witnesses. Keep in mind that constitutional concerns woven throughout the criminal trial process exist—from the initial burden of proof to the right to a jury trial or invocation of the privilege against self-incrimination. It will help you in learning the principles of criminal law to remind yourself that you are not memorizing statutory language (the definitions and elements of particular crimes) in a vacuum but rather using academic discipline to learn the crimes so that you can be more effective in applying them as a law enforcement officer, a forensic specialist, an investigator, an attorney, or another important professional in the criminal justice system.

2.13 The CDC Model

In Chapter 4 you will learn how to identify and extract material facts by using a **construction-deconstruction connectionist (CDC) model** that is activity-based, so that you can construct a hypothetical fact pattern that illustrates a particular crime or crimes from your knowledge of the elements of the crime(s) using a criminal law lens. Basically, the CDC Model teaches you how to identify the main elements of a crime from the language of the statute and "chunk" or "parse" them so as to facilitate your learning by making associations and connections. This process of chunking and connecting content will enable you to apply the substantive statutory content with greater facility and speed and help you more successfully learn the course material.

The first step in the CDC model is the construction step. In the construction step, you find and assemble the necessary elements of the crime to prove the crime by creating a hypothetical fact pattern that uses the elements without using the exact words of the elements. In other words, you want someone to easily read the fact pattern and determine the applicable crime without making it too obvious by using the exact words from the statute. The construction step provides the means by which you use your knowledge of the material elements of the crimes to develop a deeper understanding of the elements of the crime and make meaning for yourself. This step will develop your identification and reasoning skills.

The second step requires deconstruction. Deconstruction is the extraction and identification of the material elements of the crime that are embedded in the previously constructed hypothetical fact pattern. The second step of deconstruction is analogous to reverse engineering where you work to identify the material facts that can be used to support an argument for the applicability of an element of a crime and linked to that element in the statutory language. The purpose of the deconstruction step is for you to demonstrate your understanding of the specific material elements of the crime based on the material facts of the hypothetical fact pattern. One method to use in deconstructing a hypothetical fact pattern or an actual case is to highlight, circle, or underline key words and sentences and then note their application and relevance to the applicable crime(s). You can think of it as a mapping process between your knowledge of the elements of the applicable crime(s) and each relevant and material fact. This step will develop your identification, reasoning, and critical thinking skills.

The third step flows from the mapping concept and is the connection step. In the connection step you learn how to use the relevant and material facts deconstructed in the second step and then specify their connections to the material elements of the crime(s). The connectionist step requires you to demonstrate your ability to perform illustrative connections—make the logical connections discussed in Section 2.10. One way to illustrate the connection between each element of the crime and the relevant and material facts is by annotating or formulating explanations to demonstrate your understanding of the connection—it is a step towards developing analytical reasoning through annotated explanations. By connecting the illustrative facts from a case to previously chunked and parsed elements of the crime(s), you develop logical coherence in your thinking which you can then use to draw inferences which illustrate the depth of your understanding. You will demonstrate your analytical reasoning through your written or verbal explanations. This step will develop your identification, reasoning, critical thinking, and analytical skills.

2.14 Summary

In this chapter we have examined the **main components** or elements of most crimes: the *mens rea* and the *actus reus*. We have also learned about the various aspects of building a criminal case in the context of the larger criminal trial process and the importance of working within the frames. As you may have noted, criminal law involves more than just memorizing the elements of certain crimes, although that is a very important step for success in this course; but it is also about learning how to use the knowledge of the statutory definitions of certain crimes and the elements of those crimes to explain the logical connection of those elements to particular facts and also to think logically about those connections. The goal for success in any course is to learn how to apply the learned material. In criminal law, the application of the statutory law—the definitions of crimes and the identification of *mens rea*, *actus reus*, and other material elements—is important for purposes of learning to develop analytical reasoning so that through your written or verbal explanations you can demonstrate an ability to make logical connections, illustrate causal relationships, and reason your way to an appropriate conclusion. This will require you to make a commitment to the first step of memorizing and understanding the definitions and elements of the various crimes from the applicable penal or criminal code. If you do not spend the time to learn the elements of the crimes, you will not be able to identify the relevant and material facts, and then you will not be able to demonstrate the logical connections or develop the reasoning to adequately explain the relationships that will lead you to answer the issue in the question or determine if the defendant is guilty of the criminal charges. There is no short-cut or easy way around learning the definitions and elements of the crime—it takes time and energy, but if you invest in your success, you will see how you can successfully develop the skills necessary to construct logical arguments and reason your way through solid analysis to an appropriate conclusion—and this skill is critical for anyone seeking to work as a professional in the criminal justice system.

2.15 Chapter Review Questions

The purpose of these questions is to provide you with an opportunity to think about the material presented in this chapter and to express your understanding in a well-reasoned explanation. This requires that you write in paragraph form and demonstrate your understanding of the course material through answers that are well-developed, well-structured, and sufficient in length to indicate a depth of understanding, integration, and synthesis of the chapter material.

1. Why is it important to identify the *mens rea* and *actus reus*? How does this step help you in learning about a particular crime?
2. What is the CDC Model, and how can it help you learn more effectively throughout this course? Please be specific in your answer.
3. Provide an example of how statutory law, procedural issues, and evidence issues are connected for purposes of understanding criminal law.
4. Explain, in your own words, how you can identify material facts by having a good knowledge of the elements of a particular crime?
5. What is most interesting to you from this chapter and why?
6. Use an internet search engine to find the website for the penal or criminal code in your state and find the definitions of the

culpable mental states; then write out the definitions in your own words.

7. Use an internet search engine to find the section in your state's penal or criminal code that pertains to capital murder or its equivalent. Then compare its language to the statutory language in this chapter for Texas, California, and Florida. How is it similar or different?
8. Break into small groups and discuss why it is important to have different degrees or types of homicide or murder. What are some policy reasons for these differences?
9. Break into small groups and create a hypothetical fact pattern based on a crime of your choosing using the construction step from the CDC model. Then pass that fact pattern to another group and see if they can use the second step in the CDC model to identify the correct crime.

Chapter 3

An Introduction to Selected Types of Crimes and Working with Fact Patterns and Cases

Key Terms and Concepts

Deconstruction	The Integrative Frame Model	Scaffold
Parsing	Inductive Process	Identification
Chunk and Connect	Relevance	

3.1 Introduction

Learning Tip

In this chapter you will focus on learning the substantive elements for a number of different crimes. One way to approach this chapter is to spend some time exploring the penal or criminal code for your state. It is very useful to read the table of contents and the section headings to learn how the various crimes are categorized and organized in your state. Identifying the correct crime or crimes to apply to the facts of a case is an important skill, and it can only be mastered by first learning the elements of the various crimes. While we will not cover every crime in this textbook, we will cover the main crimes under the most common sections of the penal codes of various states. When reading the definition of a crime, it is helpful to use a highlighter or a pen to circle, underline, or highlight the *mens rea* and *actus reus*. Take the time to identify the causal relationship between the various elements of the particular crime. Also, take the time to write a succinct definition of the crime and the material elements of the crime in a notebook so that you can memorize it and learn to apply it to facts as you read through cases and hypothetical fact patterns. Remember, there are no short-cuts to learning the definitions and elements of the crimes. If you start early and spend the time as you are reading to write out your own precise and correctly worded definitions to identify the elements of the crime, and to develop a study outline, it will be easier for you to successfully learn the course material.

3.2 Foundational Issues

One of the foundational issues in learning to define and identify the material elements of the various crimes is based on understanding how the crimes are organized in the penal or criminal code of your state. For example, in Florida, Title XLVI of the Florida Statutes is entitled "Crimes," and it is organized by chapter. You will note that it is categorized in terms of crimes that are generally related such as assault and battery in Chapter 784 and inchoate crimes and parties to crimes in Chapter 777. It is important when you read the various sections in this chapter to think about those crimes in the context of a higher level of organization. This is helpful in case you have an exam or assignment that asks you to identify and define two inchoate crimes. If you do not know that solicitation and attempt are both inchoate crimes, then you would not be able to correctly answer that question. Consider this example: In New York's penal code, inchoate offenses such as solicitation and attempt are referred to as Anticipatory Offenses in Part 3, Title G. Crimes such as robbery and larceny are categorized under Offenses Involving Damage to and Intrusion upon Property; this categorization is similar to the one used in this textbook where robbery is categorized as a crime against property. You can see that it is important to learning the crimes to take the time to understand how your state categorizes them, and the terms it uses which may be different from the way they are organized and described in other states.

Learning Tip

A second foundational issue is based on understanding how words are used in the statute. In Texas, for example, Section 30.02 of the Texas Penal Code defines burglary, in part, as someone—who does not have effective consent—entering a habitation or building (not then open to the public) with intent to commit a felony, theft, or an assault in the building or habitation. In order to make sense of this definition of burglary you would need to know: (a) what constitutes effective consent, (b) how is a habitation defined, (c) what type of act constitutes a felony, (d) what is the definition and what are the elements of the crime of theft, and (e) what is the definition and what are the elements of the crime of assault. If you just read the definition and do not take the time to deconstruct it—that is to break it into its component parts—then you cannot fully learn how to apply the definition to the facts of a case or a hypothetical fact pattern. Theft, in Texas, is defined in another part of the code—in Chapter 31 and more specifically in Sections 31.01 and 31.03—so you would need to read those definitions and then insert the applicable language into your reading of Section 30.02 which defines burglary. In certain instances you may need to find cases to provide greater clarity in understanding a particular term or phrase. For example, exactly what constitutes effective consent in Texas for purposes of negating a charge of burglary? This is an important question because the statutory language in Section 30.02 states that "a person commits an offense if, without the effective consent of the owner, the person...." Therefore, if you can establish that effective consent exists, continuing with the other elements of the crime is unnecessary since one of the elements of the crime has been successfully negated. This may require that you determine how Texas case law has interpreted "effective consent" in the crime of burglary by finding cases where this is discussed in detail so that you can use the courts' reasoning and analysis in determining whether effective consent is more of a factor in your particular case or whether it would classify as hypothetical fact pattern.

A third foundational issue closely related to the importance of adequately defining terms as you read the statutory language corresponds to the connections between certain types of crimes. This is also illustrated by the previous example where in order to prove the crime of burglary in Texas you need to determine that there was "intent to commit a felony, theft, or an assault," and this requires that you search the Texas Penal Code to find definitions for felony, theft, and assault. If you do not know how the code defines these terms, then you cannot determine if the elements for any one of these terms can be proven based on the facts of your particular case or hypothetical fact pattern. In order to know if these crimes or terms are further defined in the code you need to be familiar with the table of contents as well as the various categories and classifications within the table of contents. It was suggested earlier that you take some time to familiarize yourself with the organization of your state's penal or criminal code, and this is one of the main reasons why that task is important.

A fourth foundational issue of importance is consideration of the crime from both the prosecution's and defense's perspectives. The prosecution wants to prove that the defendant committed the crime, and its goal is to establish each element of the crime, beyond a reasonable doubt, based on the facts and evidence of the case. The defense wants to introduce evidence that will cast doubt on the prosecution's case so that the prosecution cannot successfully establish its burden of proof. The defense may also attempt to introduce evidence to mitigate a particular charge from a first degree to a second degree charge, for example, or even establish a defense or a justification. In Texas, for instance, if a defendant is charged with murder, under Section 19.02, the defendant may at the "punishment stage of the trial ... raise the issue as to whether he caused the death under the immediate influence of sudden passion arising from adequate cause. If the defendant proves the issue in the affirmative by a preponderance of the evidence, the offense is a felony of the second degree." It is important when reading Section 19.02 which begins in (a)(1) and (2) with definitions of adequate cause and sudden passion to understand where those definitions fit within the definition of murder. The definition of murder is really found in Section 19.02(b)(1), (2), or (3) and Sections (a)(1) and (2) and are for the defense to raise as an affirmative defense by a preponderance of the evidence to reduce the punishment for the charge of murder from the first to the second degree. The prosecution needs to prove the elements of murder as listed in Section 19.02(b)(1), (2), or (3) by the burden of proof required which is "beyond a reasonable doubt." If the defense can establish from the facts of the case that the defendant acted under the "immediate influence of sudden passion arising from an adequate cause" as those terms are defined in Section 19.02(a)(1) and (2) and as they have been interpreted by other cases (thereby establishing precedent), then the defense can raise an affirmative defense and the defense's burden of proof as set forth in Section 19.02(d) is "by a preponderance of the evidence." It is important not to be confused when reading the code and to determine that murder requires proving sudden passion arising from an adequate cause—it does not if you read the definition in 19.02(b)(1), (2), or (3). Rather, sudden passion arising from an adequate cause is an affirmative defense that can be raised by the defendant at the punishment stage to reduce the punishment—not negate the charge of murder.

These types of foundational issues are very important to successfully learning, understanding, and applying the language of the statute and the elements of the crime(s) to particular facts. If you hurry through a reading of the statute, you will mistakenly define murder in Texas as sudden passion resulting in murder, which is incorrect. If you do not take the time to carefully look-up and learn the definition of theft, it is possible that when reading the burglary definition, you will not be able to determine if there is a theft in the facts, and, therefore, if there is no assault and there is no felony, you will not be able to adequately discuss whether you can successfully prove the elements for the crime of burglary based on your facts. It is important not to skip important foundational issues because if you do, you will be learning incorrectly, and, therefore, you will not be able to properly answer your exam or assignment questions or correctly learn the information you need to be successful as a professional in your career in criminal justice.

3.3 Selected Types of Crimes

In the following chapters you will explore different selected categories of crimes and the types of crimes most common to those categories. You will also have the opportunity to see how some states categorize and define various crimes. The states that we will consider include Texas, California, New York, Illinois, and Florida You may find it helpful to note any differences or similarities in the categorization of different crimes by the various states in addition to noting how they compare with your home state. You may also find it useful to write out your own definition of each crime using the key words from the penal code and identify the *mens rea*, the *actus reus*, and causation elements. Remember, one way to learn the crimes is to note their category and identify similarities and differences among the different types of crimes within a category.

3.4 Deconstruction of the Crime

In the following chapters of this book, you will have the opportunity to practice identifying material facts, identifying issues, defining crimes, and analyzing hypothetical fact patterns. You will also have the opportunity to read court decisions and analyze specific cases, where you can also practice identifying material facts, rules of law (the applicable crimes and the corresponding statutory language), and the court's reasoning and analysis. One method that is very useful has been discussed in Chapter 2 and is the *construction-deconstruction connectionist model* which is referred to as the CDC model. A main component of this model is the notion of **deconstruction**. In deconstruction the emphasis is on **parsing** where you want to break-down the hypothetical fact pattern or the case into its component parts which primarily consist of:

- Material Facts
- Applicable crime(s) based on the material facts
  - A precise and specific definition of the crime(s)
  - The material elements of the crime(s)
    - *Mens Rea*
    - *Actus Reus*
    - Attendant Circumstances

Once you parse the material facts of the hypothetical fact pattern or the case then you can start to think about the applicable crimes and how to develop well-reasoned analysis that allows you to integrate the material facts with the material elements of the crime so as to reason through to a well-supported conclusion (decision). The deconstruction of the crime is grounded in the parsing method, and it provides a four-step methodology which is useful for analyzing a fact pattern:

1. Deconstruct the statute. Identify the material (relevant) elements. Isolate the elements of the crime and the culpability states.

2. Identify the relevant facts. This step usually requires deconstruction of the fact pattern into short, specific statements of fact, and then selecting those which are relevant to the statute.
3. Identify and discuss the relationships between the facts and the statute. Establish whether the facts either prove the crime or will provide a viable argument for the defense.
4. Perform an analysis which will produce a conclusion. Answer specifically: (1) How is *mens rea* satisfied? (2) How are elements of the crime satisfied? Conclusions belong at the end of this section.

Associated with the idea of deconstruction is another model of learning known as **the Integrative Frame Model (IFM)**, where the emphasis is on an **inductive process** so that learning is developed through exploration and experimentation that stimulates the development of metacognitive (self-regulated and self-facilitated) ability as contrasted with a more deductive method where exploration is constrained by a passive learning process. The IFM combines the cognitive processes of identification, reasoning, critical thinking, and applied analysis under the umbrella of metacognitive-driven and derived skills. This model emphasizes meaning-making and frame construction.

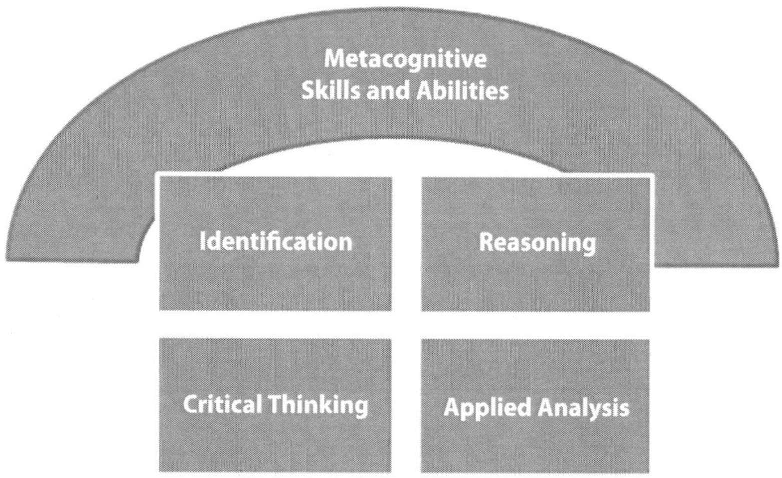

Understanding the different frames, discussed in Chapter 1, develops skills of adaptive transfer where you construct your own hypothetical fact patterns to demonstrate your understanding of the parsed rules of the law (the definitions of the crimes). Central to both the CDC and IFM models is the premise that you need to learn to **chunk and connect** facts and rules of law. This process of chunking and connecting content helps you apply what you have learned with facility, speed, and ease. In essence, the CDC model is an efficient way of organizing information for later retrieval since it is a form of parsing. From an effective learning perspective, you gain a better understanding of what you are learning since **relevance** emerges through connection of material facts with the material elements of the crime. Your ability to better understand the course content is generated through the activation of the chunked and parsed components of the course. This promotes meaning-making and contextual sense-making of the rules of law learned in this course.

If you think about criminal law as the substantive foundation for determining the applicable crime(s) and identifying the relevant elements of the crime(s), then you will have a context to build or **scaffold** your learning. If you think about criminal law as a lens through which you can extract the material elements of the crime and then determine the relationship of those elements to develop a strategy for developing well-reasoned analysis, you can understand the relevance of learning the statutory elements of the various crimes. By deconstructing the material facts of a hypothetical fact pattern and the applicable elements of the relevant crime(s) and by parsing it down into its component parts, you will develop skills of **identification**. For example, if the selected crimes against persons, crimes against property, or inchoate crimes are deconstructed based on the material elements of the crime, then you can use cognitive strategies of association by recalling that a particular element of the crime can be identified as the *mens rea* or *actus reus*. For example, you may want to ask, "What do the material facts reveal that will assist me in identifying the applicable elements of appropriate crime(s)?"

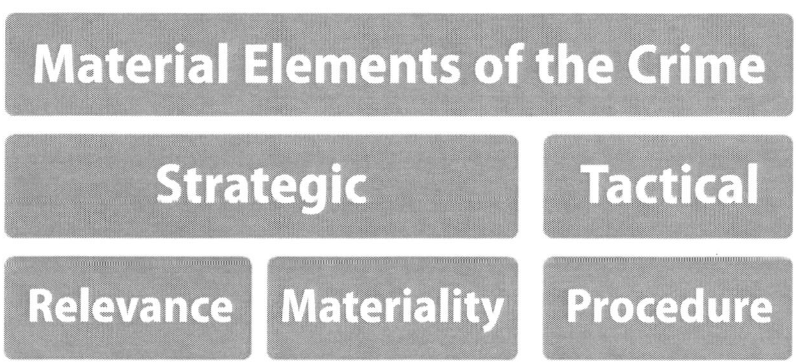

"What do the material facts reveal that will assist me in identifying the applicable elements of appropriate crime(s)?"

The following hypothetical fact pattern is a complex construction of several crimes. Since you have not yet learned the statutory definitions of crimes against the person or crimes against property or other crimes, you will note that it will be difficult for you to discern and identify the material facts in this fact pattern. Successful learning requires that you diligently learn the precise and specific definitions for the crimes and the material elements of the crimes so that when you read a fact pattern, you can "see" what facts are material and relevant for identifying applicable crimes.

Learning Activity

To illustrate the difficulty of identifying material facts without a solid foundation in the rules of law (the definitions and elements of the crimes), use a yellow highlighter to identify the material facts in this hypothetical fact pattern.

> At approximately 2:30 a.m., city police officer John Jay observed a vehicle traveling 68 mph in a 35 mph residential zone. Officer Jay turned on his emergency lights and began to pursue the vehicle. While in pursuit of the speeding vehicle, Officer Jay observed the driver weaving between lanes. In addition to the speeding and failure to stay in a lane, the driver sideswiped two parked cars. After approximately one-half mile, the driver drove into a ditch and stopped. Officer Jay unholstered his weapon and approached the vehicle. He instructed the driver to exit and lie face down on the ground. After the male driver complied, Officer Jay handcuffed the driver, stood him up, and walked him to the front of his patrol car.
>
> Officer Jay observed that the driver was emotionally distraught, and he had evidence of blood on one hand and on the sleeve of his shirt. Officer Jay did not smell alcohol on the driver's breath, and he observed that the pupils of the driver's eyes were normal. Officer Jay began to ask the man questions, regarding why he was out so late at night, where he was going, and why he was in such a hurry. Speaking almost incoherently, the driver informed the officer that he had been in a fight with a man in his living room, and that he had shot and killed the man. The driver informed the officer that the gun used to kill the man was lying on the passenger seat in the vehicle. Officer Jay went to the driver's vehicle and retrieved a handgun from the seat. The driver informed Officer Jay that the victim was still lying on the floor just beyond the front door of his residence. Officer Jay placed him under arrest for reckless driving and murder.
>
> Officer Jay radioed for help, and two other officers went to the driver's home address. All exterior doors were locked. Through the glass in the front door, officers could see a man lying on the floor, adjacent to a large clay urn which contained a small tree. There was a broken piece of the urn lying nearby.
>
> Officers forced open the door and, upon entering, confirmed that the man was dead. A pool of blood was observed near the victim's head, and a bloody area was observed on the victim's shirt, near his left shoulder. The victim's clothes were in disarray, and there was evidence of minor injuries to his face and hands, leading officers to conclude that the victim had been in a fight.

> Officers searched the driver's home, and, in a bathroom cabinet, found a large quantity of methamphetamine. In a desk drawer in the den, officers found a large quantity of cash, estimated to exceed $10,000. Three days later, the medical examiner described the cause of death as blunt force trauma to the rear of the head, consistent with striking his head on the clay urn. The bloody area on the man's shirt was caused by a bullet wound. The bullet had entered his body just below his collarbone and exited his body just above his shoulder blade.
>
> What crimes are applicable, and how would you analyze this fact pattern?

At this point you can only guess about the material facts, and you can only guess about potentially applicable crimes. Since guessing is not an effective method for success, make a note to come back to this fact pattern when you complete Chapter 12 and have a better understanding of the statutory definitions of various crimes.

3.5 Summary

There are four foundational issues in commencing your journey into understanding criminal law from an integrative frame perspective. One of the foundational issues is learning to define and identify the material elements of the various crimes based on understanding how the crimes are organized in the penal or criminal code of your state. A second foundational issue is based on understanding how words are used in the statute. A third foundational issue that is closely related to the importance of adequately defining terms as you read the statutory language is to also think about the connections between certain types of crimes. A fourth foundational issue is to think about the crime from both the prosecution and defense perspective. Remember, it is important to use the CDC Model and engage in deconstruction where the emphasis is on **parsing** where you want to break down the hypothetical fact pattern or the case into its component parts. Once you parse the material facts of the hypothetical fact pattern or the case, then you can start to think about the applicable crimes and how to develop well-reasoned analysis that allows you to integrate the material facts with the material elements of the crime so as to reason through to a well-supported conclusion (decision).

Chapter 4

Combining It All: Constructing and Deconstructing a Case

Key Terms and Concepts

Analysis	FIRAC Technique	Application
Reasoning	Analytical Reasoning	Call of the Question
Framed Issue	Conclusion	Analogy
	Westlaw and *Lexis*	

4.1 Introduction

In any law-related course the ability to coherently discuss the elements, rules, procedures, or principles that derive from statutory law or case law is foundational and fundamental to your success. The concepts of analysis and reasoning may seem difficult to grasp if you are not accustomed to explanatory writing. The ability to develop **analysis**—examining and evaluating relevant and material information, such as facts or definitions, for the purpose of developing well constructed logically flowing sentences—is critically important. The ability to develop **reasoning**—logical and coherent thinking that demonstrates your inferences and develops "argument" to reach a conclusion is also crucial. In legal reasoning and analysis, the **FIRAC technique**—facts, issues, rules of law, analysis, conclusion—which provides a methodology for developing well structured and logically progressive legal reasoning and analysis—is frequently used. When reading a case or hypothetical fact pattern you want to search for the:

- Material facts of the case (**Facts**)
- Issue or issues before the Court for decision (**Issues**)
- The rules of law that the judge is relying upon in issuing his or her decision (**Rules**)
- The judge's analysis and reasoning upon which he or she is issuing the decision (**Analysis**)
- The judge's decision (**Conclusion**)

In this chapter you will learn some of the basic techniques for developing well-reasoned analyses and then applying those techniques to constructing a case. Throughout this book you will have the opportunity to learn how to deconstruct and parse rules of law and then apply that strategy to analyze a hypothetical fact pattern or an actual case. This chapter will provide you with a continued opportunity to construct hypothetical fact patterns as well as deconstruct them so as to develop and practice your skills in legal analysis, legal reasoning, legal writing, and legal research.

4.2 Legal Analysis and Reasoning

In the following chapters, as you learn about the law, you will have the opportunity to develop legal analysis and reasoning in response to several hypothetical fact patterns. It is important to think about a strategy before reading a hypothetical fact pattern or working with the facts of a real case because without one you will be prone to the following common errors:

- Failing to develop an analysis in your answer.
- Starting your analysis with a conclusion; e.g., "Joe is guilty of manslaughter."
- Writing only conclusionary sentences (e.g., "Since Joe broke into the building, he is guilty of burglary"), and then either providing no analysis or explanation, or only providing a few sentences of general explanation. Conclusionary sentences are of no value because they provide no insights into the analysis process.
- Simply restating the facts rather than providing analysis
- Giving explanations and reasoning that are not precise, specific, explicit, and clear.
- Providing non-comprehensive answers; answers that did not address all of the issues.
- Failing to spend the time to thoroughly analyze each material fact, each element of the applicable crime(s), and then to integrate them into a substantive and detailed analysis that demonstrates explanatory reasoning and leads to a conclusion.

Learning Tip

When you read the facts of a case or a hypothetical fact pattern, there is a temptation to immediately form a conclusion and start your analysis from that conclusion. It is not that your conclusion is necessarily wrong but that you really cannot formulate a conclusion until you engage in the analytical reasoning process that allows you to apply the deconstructed elements from the applicable rules of law, procedure, etc., to the specific material facts. In addition, if you begin from a conclusionary frame, you do not provide yourself with opportunity to find all of the relevant issues since one issue may be paramount in your mind. Remember the goal of **analytical reasoning** is to demonstrate your "thinking," your "explanatory reasoning," and "your ability to integrate and synthesize information—to develop a persuasive 'argument.'" This process requires that you ask questions as you move through the facts of a case or hypothetical fact pattern—that you do not make assumptions nor draw conclusions that that do not flow logically from an exploration of the material facts in the context of the applicable rules of law. In learning to develop reasoning, you are learning to "explain information" and "articulate reasons" so as to provide support and justification for your conclusion.

In legal reasoning and analysis, the emphasis is on the application of the relevant and pertinent elements of the rules of law to the specific material facts. Legal reasoning and analysis is a skill that requires **application**—the ability to integrate and apply different components from different sets of information. Well-developed and constructed legal reasoning and analysis, therefore, requires a solid understanding of the applicable law as well as a solid grasp of the material and relevant facts of the case. As you will see when you have the opportunity throughout this textbook to analyze a hypothetical fact pattern or read a case, the issue or issues are not always readily apparent. Further in some hypothetical fact patterns, you are presented with a very broad **call of the question**; that is, what the question is asking you to answer—such as, "Of what crimes is Joe is guilty?" In other hypothetical fact patterns, there may be a **framed issue**, such as, "Is Joe guilty of felony murder?" When you are developing your legal reasoning and analysis, it is critical that you stay focused on the call of the question which may require that when you first read the fact pattern, you frame the issue(s) yourself. For example, if the call of the question is "Of what crimes is Joe is guilty?" then you want to begin your analysis with an issue statement that frames the crime, so you may start with "Based on the material facts, the first issue is whether Joe is guilty of felony murder." You would then define your crime and parse the material elements which would then allow you to begin your actual analysis—the application and integration of the elements of the crime of felony murder to the material facts so that you can then reason your way to a **conclusion**—an answer to the call of the question, or more specifically, the framed issue(s).

You will learn as you work through the material in this textbook and your course, that there are numerous sub-issues and subtleties that arise when discussing the application of legal principles. It is important that you learn to think about related issues and anticipate questions when you read through a hypothetical fact pattern. It is an acquired and learned skill to be able to spot issues, and this skill comes solely from your familiarity with the rules of law. If you do not know the specific and precise definition for a crime, how can you spot it in fact pattern? You also need to learn not to read beyond the facts or make assumptions that cannot be supported by the facts. For example, if the fact pattern says that "Joe struck Mary" but does not say with what, you cannot make an assumption as to what it was he used to strike her. If the fact that he used his hand, a pillow, or a wrench to strike Mary matters to the identification of the crime and the application of its material elements to the facts, then you need to state in your analysis something similar to this: "Since the facts do not state what Joe used to strike Mary and the definition of [insert crime] requires that he used his hand, we can, for purposes of this analysis, suggest that Joe used his hand so that we can proceed with our analysis." This type of wording demonstrates that you understand the definition of the crime well enough to know that the use of a hand is a material element and, further, it demonstrates that you are aware that the facts are silent on this issue. By crafting that sentence, you are showing an awareness of the law, its application to the facts (or lack thereof), and more importantly, that if you do not proceed under the notion that he used his hand, you will have nothing to discuss, and therefore, there would be no purpose to analyzing the fact pattern. This will make more sense as you proceed through the chapters in this book and learn more about the law and its application to hypothetical fact patterns.

Learning Tip

In certain instances you will have to reason by analogy. An **analogy** is a kind of similarity—where two situations (or fact patterns) will share common elements and patterns of relationships, but they are not identical. For example, if in one fact pattern Joe hits Mary on the head with a hammer, killing her, and in another fact pattern, he trips her and she hits her head on the floor and bleeds to death, there are very similar components, but the facts are not identical. This is important because we may find case law that supports a certain finding (conclusion) based on the first factual scenario, but in order to argue its application to the second factual scenario, we would have to argue by analogy. Using reasoning by analogy works best when the facts are substantially similar. The further apart the facts, the harder it is to effectively reason by analog since the counterarguments will derive from the factual differences. There is a saying in the law: "if you change one fact, you change the outcome"—so pay particular attention to the factual details of your hypothetical fact pattern or your case.

4.3 Effective Legal Writing

For many, effective legal writing is foreign and difficult. In courses other than law-related courses, you often do not have exposure to concepts of legal reasoning and analysis and to writing in a logical, progressive, scaffolding manner. Legal writing needs to be clear and concise, and it is different from other writing skills in that it requires a logical organization and progression of substantive legal thought. It is not uncommon for those who are new to legal writing to forget to use proper grammar, syntax, and style to communicate complex substantive principles in a well-organized manner. Legal writing requires choices regarding the use of words, sentence structures, and paragraph organization so that words are used economically and efficiently.

Some of the goals of effective legal writing include asking the following questions:

Success Tip

- Does my writing clearly communicate information?
- Is the writing clear and logical?
- Is the writing well-organized?
- Does my writing progress in a logical, sequential fashion?
- Does my writing include terminology that is verbose, unnecessary or convoluted?
- Does my writing have redundancies or internal inconsistencies?

It is important in effective legal writing that your analysis be organized in a logically consistent, progressive fashion, moving from basic information to more specific information. It is important, therefore, to use descriptive headers and subheaders where appropriate so that your document presents itself in a manageable order and reads easily, particularly if there are multiple issues. Beginning an analysis with a conclusion rather than a framed issue would not be wise in that the flow of a document moves you from the framed issue, to the definition of the crime(s), to the material elements of the crime(s), to the application and integration of the material elements of the crime(s), to the material and relevant facts—the analysis—to the conclusion.

The basic requirements for precision and simplicity in drafting are these elements:

- Accuracy
- Completeness
- Exactness
- Specificity and Precision

Simplicity and precision require that cumbersome complexities are replaced with short, to-the-point sentences. In effective legal writing you are also concerned with these basic rules of grammar:

Success Tip

1. Place a comma before a conjunction introducing an independent clause.
2. Do not join independent clauses by a comma, but rather use a semicolon.
3. Use a colon after an independent clause to introduce a list of particulars.
4. The number of the subject determines the number of the verb.
5. A participial phrase at the beginning of a sentence must refer to the grammatical subject.
6. Place statements in a positive form, and make definite assertions.
7. Use definite, specific, concrete language.
8. Omit needless words.
9. Avoid loose sentence style. Express coordinate ideas in a similar form. Parallel construction requires that expressions similar in content and function be stated in a similar manner; thus, it is important to keep related words and ideas together. It is also important to write in one tense, the present active tense.
10. Make sure the document is free of spelling errors! Spelling errors will cost you in the area of professionalism.

Remember, effective legal writing is very important for legal analysis and legal research. Legal analysis includes applying the rules of law to the facts of the situation. Legal analysis is the FIRAC method in action which emphasizes several specific facts:

Success Tip

- What needs to resolved or decided? This will assist you in framing the issues.
- Identify the issues one at a time; then, sort them and categorize them so you can organize the information.
- Once you have identified the issues and sorted through the facts, then analysis becomes easier and more effective.
- Analysis of the facts is critical. How are you analyzing the facts in the context of the rules of law?

4.4 Tips on Legal Research

Stop and Engage

You will note as you read through this textbook that there are many opportunities to "**Stop and Engage.**" These are places where you will be asked to use an internet search engine to find a code or specific rule of law. You will have the opportunity to read case excerpts and interact with the case by highlighting information and then answering specific questions. You may need to find related cases, or you may want to explore further for your own learning.

Statutory law is a primary authority and consists of constitutions, statutes, rules and regulations. Case law has great precedential value if the decision is from a court in the jurisdiction of the current litigation, and if the facts of the case are very similar to the facts of the current case you are investigating or researching. The authority that is cited to a court is very important. In the research process, you want to find primary authorities first before you use secondary authorities. Primary authority is the law itself. Secondary authority may be a legal encyclopedia or law review article. Any federal law such as the U.S.C. (the United States Code) is an important primary authority. The U.S.C.A., an annotated version of the U.S.C. Annotations, can be helpful in beginning the research process. The U.S.C.S. is the United States Code Service, and the annotations are more comprehensive than U.S.C.A. You will see numerous references to the U.S.C. as you read through this textbook.

Case law is also a very important part of legal research. It is important to learn how to find cases that are relevant to the current facts you are working with and then learn how to cite to the cases so that when you reference them, you do so correctly. A case citation may look like "23 P.2d 198 (2007)." This citation has the volume number (23), the reporter (Pacific 2nd.), the first page of the case is 198, and the year is 2007. Here are some current forms of citing to case reporters:

- The United States Reports is cited as (U.S.).
- The Supreme Court Reporter is cited as (S. Ct.).
- United States Courts of Appeals decisions are often reported in, the Federal Reporter which is cited as (F). There are also 2nd and 3rd series that are cited as (F.2d and F.3d).
- The United States District Court decisions are often published in the Federal Supplement and that is cited as (F. Supp.).

Remember, you will always have a volume number and a page number as part of your citation so a complete citation for the United States Reports would look like: 45 U.S. 121 (1965).State court decisions are published in 12 different regional reporters. The regional reporters are grouped by geographic location of states. When citing to case law you need to cite the case name, the volume number, the publication, the page number and the year of publication; for example, *Smith v. Jones* 134 F.2d 187 (1976). You may want to purchase the *Bluebook: A Uniform System of Citation* (referred to as the *Bluebook*) and published by the Harvard Law Review Association and the *ALWD Citation Manual: A Professional System of Citation* (referred to as *AWLD).*

You will see numerous case citations as you read through the chapters of this textbook, and you will want to note the court—is it the United States Supreme Court, a court of appeals, a district court, a federal court, or a state court—as well as the year of the case. It is important to know that just because a case is "old" does not mean that it is not important—it may still represent the "current thinking on an issue" and, therefore, have precedential value.

Computerized legal research is an important tool but should not totally replace research in an actual law library. Westlaw and Lexis are two important names in legal research. Westlaw is available at http://www.westlaw.com and Lexis is available at http://www.lexis.com, but you need a subscription to access these databases, so you may want to check with your school library to see if you have access. Using the internet is also a very useful way of accessing codes and cases as well as interpretative guides, but it is critical that you use only credible and reliable sources when surfing the web. Also, make sure you are very familiar with the definition of plagiarism, and never cut and paste information from another source to use as your own work.

4.5 Constructing a Case—Working Forward: Identifying the Crime

One of the important skills that you will develop in your course in criminal law is the ability to write a fact pattern and construct a case. In Chapter 2 you were introduced to the CDC model and the notions of construction and deconstruction. When you construct a fact pattern, the idea is to present sufficient facts so that a reader can identify the issues and then analyze the fact pattern using the applicable rules of law. However, in order to construct a fact pattern, you need to know the precise definition of the crime and the elements of the crime. For example, if you were to construct a fact pattern illustrative of the crime of capital murder under the Texas Penal Code, you would need to know the definition of the crime as it is stated in the TPC Section 19.03:

> A person commits an offense if the person commits murder as defined under Section 19.02(b)(1)[1] and: (1) the person murders a peace officer or fireman who is acting in the lawful discharge of an official duty.... .(2) the person intentionally commits the murder in the course of committing or attempting to commit kidnapping, burglary, robbery, aggravated sexual assault, arson.... .... (3) the person commits the murder for remuneration.... or employs another to commit the murder for remuneration.... (4) the person commits the murder while escaping or attempting to escape from a penal institution. (5) omitted (6) omitted (7) the person murders more than one person (A) during the same criminal transaction (B) omitted (8) omitted (9) omitted.

Since the crime of capital murder requires the commission of murder as stated in Section 19.02(b)(1), we need to know the definition in that sec-

1. §19.02 (b) (1): "A person commits an offense if he: (1) intentionally or knowingly causes the death of an individual;"

tion (see footnote 1 above). We can then parse the material elements of the crime to note that the *mens rea* is *intentionally* or *knowingly* and the *actus reus* must cause the death of an individual; however, to make sure it is a fact pattern for capital murder and not murder, we need to have one of the factual circumstances enumerated in Section 19.03 in our hypothetical fact pattern.

Learning Activity

Before you read our model hypothetical fact pattern below—stop and engage. Write your own fact pattern based on the definition of the crime and its material elements.

Hypothetical Fact Pattern

Model Answer

> Jill was a passionate pro-lifer. She believed that any abortion, for whatever reason, amounted to murder of an unborn child. In spite of her fervent participation in almost every demonstration, Jill watched with increasing dismay as, over the years, courts at every level rejected appeals based upon every conceivable argument and continued to affirm *Roe v Wade*. Finally, Jill decided that more violent protest was needed, and she targeted for attack clinics that performed abortions. Jill found a recipe for an easily formulated explosive, whose primary ingredients were fertilizer and diesel fuel. Jill prepared a moderate amount of the mixture, packed it into a large coffee can and placed the device near the rear door of the clinic. She had chosen an early morning hour for the attack, reasoning that no one would be inside. Jill used a cell phone attached to an igniter to cause the mixture to explode. The device detonated with much more force than Jill had expected, and the building was almost completely leveled. Later in the day, to her horror, Jill learned that two nurses, a doctor, and a custodian had arrived early for work, and all were killed.

Stop and Engage

Pick another crime and write another hypothetical fact pattern. Practice with several crimes until you are comfortable constructing a fact pattern. Give the fact pattern to your professor or other students in the class to see if they can identify the correct crime from the fact pattern.

Learning Tip

When you construct the fact pattern, try not to use "key words" from the definition of the crime. For example, do not use the specific word for the *mens rea* because that will make it too easy to identify the culpable mental state. Instead, describe facts that can be used to establish the applicable *mens rea*, such as "intentionally" or "recklessly" (under the Texas Penal Code). In addition, avoid specific words that are in the definition of the crime since the goal of constructing a fact pattern is to present facts that describe events that illuminate the necessary elements of the crime so as to support the identification and application of that crime in a well-reasoned analysis.

4.6 Deconstructing a Case — Working Backward: Connecting to the Facts

Deconstruction is discussed in numerous places throughout this textbook. Deconstruction requires that you parse the elements of the crime from its definition and that you identify the material facts of the case. Deconstruction is a crucial step in order to begin the integration and analysis of the elements of the crime with the material facts. You will have many opportunities to practice deconstruction in the subsequent chapters. Remember the **Four Step Process:**

> **Step 1:** Deconstruct the statute. Identify the material (relevant) elements. Isolate the elements of the crime and the culpability states.
> **Step 2:** Identify the relevant facts. This step usually requires deconstruction of the fact pattern into short, specific statements of fact, and then selecting those which are relevant to the statute.
> **Step 3:** Identify and discuss the relationships between the facts and the statute. Establish whether the facts either prove the crime or will provide a viable argument for the defense.
> **Step 4:** Perform an analysis which will produce a conclusion. Answer specifically: (1) How are the *mens rea* and *actus reus* satisfied? (2) How are the elements of the crime satisfied? Conclusions belong at the end of this section.

Learning Activity

Now engage a learning activity by reading the fact pattern below and using a yellow highlighter to identify the material facts. Once you have highlighted the material facts, make an itemized list of those facts and then check your work with the model answer below.

Hypothetical Fact Pattern

> Carl was an alcoholic. His family and all those who interacted with him regularly knew of his addiction, and for the most part did their best to avoid enabling his drinking. In spite of three prior DWI convictions, Carl was resolute, and he managed to consume large quantities of alcohol every day. One afternoon, Carl had been sitting at his favorite bar with two friends, had been drinking for several hours and was obviously drunk. One of the friends asked Carl for his car keys, and Carl complied. Shortly thereafter, Carl complained that he had run out of cigarettes, and

that he had a fresh pack in his car. He insisted that his friend loan him his car keys so that he could replenish. His friend gave Carl his keys. Carl could not find a fresh pack in his car, so he drove away, intending to go to the liquor store to buy more. On the way, he struck a motorcyclist. The cyclist died the next day. The coroner's report listed cause of death as blunt force trauma to his head. Carl was arrested.

Highlighted Material Facts

Model Answer

Carl was an alcoholic. His family and all those who interacted with him regularly knew of his addiction, and for the most part did their best to avoid enabling his drinking. In spite of three prior DWI convictions, Carl was resolute, and he managed to consume large quantities of alcohol every day. One afternoon, Carl had been sitting at his favorite bar with two friends, had been drinking for several hours and was obviously drunk. One of the friends asked Carl for his car keys, and Carl complied. Shortly thereafter, Carl complained that he had run out of cigarettes, and that he had a fresh pack in his car. He insisted that his friend loan him his car keys so that he could replenish. His friend gave Carl his keys. Carl could not find a fresh pack in his car, so he drove away, intending to go to the liquor store to buy more. On the way, he struck a motorcyclist. The cyclist died the next day. The coroner's report listed cause of death as blunt force trauma to his head. Carl was arrested.

Deconstruction of Facts

Make an itemized list of facts.

1. Carl was an alcoholic.
2. Family and friends were aware that Carl was an alcoholic.
3. Carl had three prior DWI convictions.
4. Carl drank large quantities of alcohol every day.
5. Carl was at a bar.
6. Carl was drinking with two friends.
7. Carl had been drinking for several hours.
8. Carl was obviously drunk.
9. One of his friends asked Carl for his car keys.
10. Carl gave his car keys to the friend.
11. Carl ran out of cigarettes.
12. Carl asked his friend for his keys.
13. The friend gave Carl his keys.
14. Carl could not find cigarettes in his car.
15. Carl entered his car and drove away.
16. Carl struck a motorcyclist with his car.
17. The motorcyclist died the next day.

Learning Activity

The deconstruction model of learning is important in the early stages of learning how to identify material elements and material facts. It is a useful method for learning how to approach the development of analysis and how to work your way through a hypothetical fact pattern or case. However, as you gain experience and expertise, you want to move away from writing exam, assignment, or other assessment answers using the CDC Model. You may want to use it to make notes on scratch paper or in a first draft of an assignment at home; eventually, however, you want to learn how to develop a sophisticated level of in-depth reasoning and analysis with the logical progression we discussed in previous sections of this chapter. Here is an opportunity to learn how to apply the CDC Model as well as to then develop an analysis based on a more sophisticated flowing analysis with the emphasis on application and integration.

There are three parts to this learning activity:

1. First, read this hypothetical fact pattern and then complete the following activities:
   - Use a highlighter to highlight the material facts
   - Write an itemized list of the material facts
2. Next, use the deconstruction-construction model to develop an analysis and a conclusion.
3. Finally, develop a more robust analysis that emphasizes integration and application.

Hypothetical Fact Pattern

> Rival gang members had been "dissing" each other for months, and members of both gangs knew that a turf fight in a parking lot was imminent. Kevin "borrowed" his father's shotgun and carried it with him to the fight, just to show that his gang would take whatever action necessary to protect their turf. At the fight, yelling and taunting escalated into pushing and shoving, and a rival gang member grabbed the barrel of Kevin's shotgun. The gun discharged, and the rival gang member was killed. The coroner ruled that cause of death was a fatal injury to the heart. Discuss the applicable crime(s).

Make sure to complete all three steps as listed above before you read the model answer.

First, read this hypothetical fact pattern, and then use a highlighter to identify the material facts.

Model Answer

Highlighted Material Facts

> Rival gang members had been "dissing" each other for months, and members of both gangs knew that a turf fight in a parking

lot was imminent. Kevin "borrowed" his father's shotgun and carried it with him to the fight, just to show that his gang would take whatever action necessary to protect their turf. At the fight, yelling and taunting escalated into pushing and shoving, and a rival gang member grabbed the barrel of Kevin's shotgun. The gun discharged, and the rival gang member was killed. The coroner ruled that cause of death was a fatal injury to the heart. Discuss the applicable crime(s).

Second, write an itemized list of the material facts

Itemized List of Material Facts

1. Gangs knew
2. Kevin borrowed the shotgun
3. Just to show he would take whatever action was necessary
4. A rival gang member grabbed the barrel of the gun
5. Gun discharged
6. Rival gang member was killed

Third, use the deconstruction-construction model to develop an analysis and a conclusion.

Deconstruction-Construction Illustration

This is an illustration of the deconstruction-construction model. This is a prototype that is useful to us as you move from novice to more advanced learner.

Based on the facts, it would appear that the most relevant crime is <u>homicide</u>. Homicide is a category of crime that includes different types of homicide. The overall difference in the types of homicide is the <u>*mens rea*</u>. The analysis will <u>deconstruct</u> the <u>relevant and material facts</u>, <u>deconstruct the elements of one of the crimes</u> of homicide (manslaughter), and <u>determine</u> whether the <u>relevant facts support the elements</u> of the crime of manslaughter.

Identification of <u>relevant and material facts</u>:

1. A street fight between two rival gangs was planned.
2. Kevin brought a loaded weapon to the fight.
3. A rival gang member grabbed the barrel of the weapon.
4. The weapon discharged.
5. The rival gang member was killed.

The main <u>elements of the crime</u> of manslaughter include these facts:

Mens Rea—recklessly

Actus Reus—a specific, voluntary act

Causation—death

Result (harm): death to a human being

Analysis:

In order to prove a *mens rea* of "recklessly" we can look to the fact that Kevin knew that bringing a loaded weapon to a gang fight was inherently dangerous, but he chose to ignore the risks. *Actus reus* is more difficult to match with the material and relevant facts. First, the act must be voluntary. In this case, there is no evidence to demonstrate that Kevin pulled the trigger of the weapon, or even that his finger was on the trigger or that he reflexively pulled the trigger when the weapon was grabbed by the victim. According to Samaha, when one act in a series of acts leading to harm is voluntary, the remaining acts need not be voluntary. Kevin voluntarily brought a loaded weapon into a dangerous situation; consequently, it is not necessary to demonstrate that the remaining acts were voluntary. Secondly, there must be a specific act that caused harm. The specific act that caused the harm was discharge of the weapon. This weapon was in Kevin's possession and control—whether the discharge was voluntary is irrelevant, as argued earlier. Causation is supported by the relevant fact that the victim died of a wound inflicted by Kevin's weapon.

Conclusion:

The relevant facts successfully correspond to the main elements of the crime of manslaughter.

Fourth, develop a more robust analysis that emphasizes integration and application.

Analysis Illustration

This is the type of answer you want to develop for future assignments and exams where the steps are implicitly stated and integrated into your analytical reasoning. This is a more advanced and analytically robust answer.

The issue is whether we can charge Kevin with a type of homicide; more specifically, the crime of manslaughter. Manslaughter, under the TPC is defined in the following way: "a person commits manslaughter if he recklessly causes the death of an individual." The main elements of the crime of manslaughter consist of a *mens rea* of recklessly, and an *actus reus* of an "act" that causes (causation) the result, which is the death of an individual. According to the TPC, Kevin knew that bringing a loaded weapon to a gang fight was inherently dangerous, but chose to ignore the risks. Although there are no facts that specifically demonstrate that Kevin pulled the trigger of the weapon, or even that his finger was on the trigger or that he reflexively pulled the trigger when the weapon was grabbed by the victim, we know that when one act in a series of acts leading to harm is voluntary, the remaining acts need not be voluntary. Kevin voluntarily brought a loaded weapon into a dangerous situation; consequently, it is not necessary to demonstrate that the remaining acts were voluntary. The act of bringing the gun to the gang fight resulted in its discharge which caused the harm. Causation is, therefore, supported by the relevant fact that the victim died of a wound inflicted by Kevin's weapon which leads us to conclude that Kevin may be charged with the crime of manslaughter.

Learning Tip

Notice that the analysis illustration contains a logically flowing analysis that is not chunked into separate component parts. Notice how the issue is stated up front. The crime is defined, and the elements are parsed for ease of application. The analysis contains an integration of the elements of the crime with the material facts and then ends with a conclusion that stems from the well-reasoned analysis.

4.7 Summary

You can see from the illustrations and examples in this chapter that it is impossible to either construct or deconstruct a hypothetical fact pattern without a solid knowledge of the rules of law. In this textbook, you will be exposed to numerous crimes and definitions based on different state statutes. Regardless of the state, the essential task is for you to learn the crime and its definition so that you can parse its material elements. This takes time and energy. You cannot learn the number of crimes in this textbook in a day or hours before an exam. You must spend time reading them, understanding the meaning of the words, learning to paraphrase them with specificity and precision so that you can use them accurately in the development of a well-reasoned analysis in answer to questions and issues raised in a hypothetical fact pattern or case. You will have many opportunities to write your own paraphrased definitions of crime, practice identifying the *mens rea* and *actus reus*, as well as practicing the development of analytical reasoning. If you do not take the time to "stop and engage" and consider the "learning tips," you will find it difficult to succeed in your criminal law course. It is important to practice and commit the time so that you can learn how to apply this knowledge in your profession and in your career.

Chapter 5

Crimes Against the Person

Key Terms and Concepts

Crimes against the Person	Malice	Involuntary Manslaughter
Criminal Homicide	Malignant Heart	Voluntary Manslaughter
	Felony Murder	

5.1 Introduction

"**Crimes against the person**" is a common name for a category of crimes that includes homicide, sexual crimes, battery, assault, and other crimes that result in death or physical injury to a human being. Consider how the following states categorize and group crimes against the person:

Texas—Title 5 of the Texas Penal Code: Offenses against the Person

Chapter 19—Criminal Homicide
Chapter 20—Kidnapping and Unlawful Restraint
Chapter 20A—Trafficking of Persons
Chapter 21—Sexual Offenses
Chapter 22—Assaultive Offenses

California—Title 8 of the California Penal Code: Of Crimes against the Person

Chapter 1—Homicide
Chapter 2—Mayhem
Chapter 3—Kidnapping

Chapter 3.5—Hostages
Chapter 4—Robbery
Chapter 5—Attempts to Kill
Chapter 6—Assaults with Intent to Commit Felony, Other Than Assaults with Intent to Murder
Chapter 8—False Imprisonment
Chapter 9—Assault and Battery

New York—Title H Penal Code: Offenses against the Person involving Physical Injury, Sexual Conduct, Restraint and Intimidation

Article 120—Assault and Related Offenses
Article 125—Homicide, Abortion and Related Offenses
Article 130—Sex Offenses
Article 135—Kidnapping, Coercion and Related Offenses

Florida—Title XLVI Crimes

There is no specific heading related to crimes or offenses against the person. You will note that there are three chapters that appear to contain the types of crimes that are categorized by other states as crimes or offenses against the person. Included in that list are the following:

Chapter 782—Homicide
Chapter 784—Assault; Battery; Culpable Negligence
Chapter 787—Kidnapping; False Imprisonment; Luring or Enticing a Child; Custody Offenses

Illinois—Title III, Part B: Offenses Directed against the Person

Article 9—Homicide
Article 10—Kidnapping and Related Offenses
Article 11—Sex Offenses
Article 12—Bodily Harm
Article 12A—Violent Video Games
Article 12B—Sexually Explicit Video Games
Article 14—Eavesdropping

Stop and Engage

How are crimes or offenses against the person categorized in your state? Are there similarities and differences you can easily identify based on the categorization of these crimes by the various states? How does this assist you in learning the different types of crimes within the category? As you learn about some of these crimes, remember to write a clear and concise definition for each crime based on the statutory language and identify the *mens rea* and *actus reus*.

5.2 Criminal Homicide

When you begin to learn and study the various types of crimes, it is very important to learn the precise definitions. **Criminal homicide,**

Learning Tip

in many states, including Texas, includes a number of different types of crimes that all pertain to the ultimate death of an individual. Although you may think of "criminal homicide," or "homicide," synonymously with "murder," the terms may have different meanings and different definitions depending upon the language in your particular state statute. This emphasizes the importance of **not** using synonymous terms or mixing terms but learning and memorizing the very specific terms and definitions used in your particular state and the states you are studying in your criminal law course. For example, in Title 5, Chapter 19, Section 19.01 of the Texas Penal Code the section heading titled "Types of Criminal Homicide" tells you that there are different types of criminal homicide included under the *category* of criminal homicide, but criminal homicide is not a particular crime unto itself. The crimes included in Section 19.01 are listed in sub-section (b) and include murder, capital murder, manslaughter, and criminally negligent homicide. These four crimes are all examples of criminal homicide. This illustrates the importance of learning the categorization for types of crimes as well as the precise names and definitions for the crimes. On an exam, for instance, it would be best to refer to criminal homicide (in Texas) as a category under which murder or manslaughter falls as a particular and specific crime rather than discussing criminal homicide as a specific crime by itself.

5.2.1 Murder

In order to better understand the types of crimes that some of the states categorized under criminal homicide, it is useful to analyze some specific language from the state statutes. As stated above, in Texas there are four types of crimes in the category of criminal homicide. In California, in Title 8, Chapter 1, the heading is "Homicide." Section 187(a) enumerates one of the major types of crimes under the category heading of "Homicide" and that crime is murder. The other sections in Chapter 1 of Title 8 include 188 which defines malice as it pertains to understanding the *mens rea* described in Section 188; Section 189 which differentiates between first degree and second degree murder; and other sections pertaining to burden of proof and punishment. Therefore, it appears that in Chapter 1 of Title 8, one of the stated crimes, murder, is found in Section 187(a). For precision and accuracy purposes, you would want to state that in California, the category of homicide includes the crime of murder which is defined in Section 187(a) as "the unlawful killing of a human being, or a fetus, with malice aforethought." The *mens rea* is "malice aforethought" and the *actus reus* is the "unlawful killing" and the result is the death of a human being or a fetus. This is an example of how you would define the crime of murder and parse out (or identify) the elements of the crime of murder from the California Statute.

The difficult question arises in how you define "malice aforethought?" Some clarification is provided in Section 188 which takes the definition a bit further:

> Such malice may be express or implied. It is express when there is manifested a deliberate intention unlawfully to take away the life of a fellow creature. It is implied, when no considerable provocation appears, or when the circumstances attending the killing show an abandoned and malignant heart. When it is shown that the killing resulted from the intentional doing of an act with express or implied malice as defined above, no other mental state need be shown to establish the mental state of malice aforethought. Neither an awareness of the obligation to act within the general body of laws regulating society nor acting despite such awareness is included within the definition of malice.

Stop and Engage

When you read this definition, what is apparent to you?

- Malice may be express or implied
- The section defines both express and implied malice
- Express malice requires a deliberate intention to take away life
- Implied malice requires no considerable provocation, and circumstances surrounding the killing must show an abandoned or malignant heart
- If the killing resulted from the intentional doing of an act with express or implied malice, then no other mental state (or *mens rea*) is required because express or implied malice = malice aforethought (which is the stated *mens rea* in Section 187(a) for the definition of murder)
- Further, the definition also tells us what is not included in the definition of malice: the person does not need an awareness of an obligation to act, nor does it matter if the person acted despite such awareness.

Learning Tip

Even after reading this definition, crucial questions still remain unanswered that must be resolved before you can develop a complete definition for murder under the California Penal Code. For example, we know the definition for express and implied malice, but how is "malice" defined? We cannot simply use our own definition or look the word up in a dictionary. We need to first see if the term is defined elsewhere in the penal code. This is the reason that at the start of your course in Criminal Law you will find it useful to peruse the table of contents of the penal code(s) you will be studying, and look around to see where you can find different definitions and types of crimes. In the California Penal Code there is no title or chapter that is labeled "General Definitions" or "Definitions." There is a heading named "preliminary provisions" and this would be a good place to see if there are any definitions for terms. If you open that section in the California Penal Code and read through it, you will note that Section 7 contains definitions, and one of those definitions is in Section 7, item 4, where you read, "The words "**malice**" and "maliciously" import a wish to vex, annoy, or injure another person, or an intent to do a wrongful act, established either by proof or presumption of law." Now that you have found a definition for malice, you can use that definition for further interpreting how express and implied malice are used in the definition of murder in Section 187(a). Take a moment and use the various definitions to write out a more detailed definition of murder that incorporates the fullness of the various words.

Another example also presents itself in the above definition. If you cannot establish express malice from the facts of the case, and you need to determine whether you can establish implied malice from the facts of the case, you need to know what constitutes an "abandoned or malignant heart" (Section 188). In *People v. Thomas* 41 Cal.2d 470, 480 (1953) the court wrote "that [**malignant heart**] is shown when, as here, the defendant for a base, antisocial motive and with wanton disregard for human life, does an act that involves a high degree of probability that it will result in death. By his own admissions defendant's conduct demonstrates that he was not averse to endangering life for the sake of the sexual pleasure it gave him. Only a person with an abandoned and malignant heart could value the attainment of that pleasure more highly than human life." What are some other acts that would demonstrate a malignant heart?

In New York, homicide is defined in Section 125 of the penal code as "conduct which causes the death of a person or an unborn child with which a female has been pregnant for more than twenty-four weeks under circumstances constituting murder, manslaughter in the first degree, manslaughter in the second degree, criminally negligent homicide, abortion in the first degree or self-abortion in the first degree." From that definition, it is apparent that New York has two categories of murder: murder in the first degree and murder in the second degree in addition to manslaughter in the first and second degree and criminally negligent homicide. Murder in the first degree is defined in Section 125.27 and requires "intent to cause the death of another person" and the killing of a certain classification of person, or the commission of the killing was in a certain location, or the killing had certain attenuate circumstances as delineated further in the Section. Use a search engine to find Section 125.27 and identify some of the additional requirements for a first degree murder. Manslaughter in the first degree is defined in Section 125.20 and states "when with intent to cause serious physical injury to another person, he causes the death of such person or of a third person" whereas manslaughter in the second degree which is defined in Section 125.15 states, "he recklessly causes the death of another person." Based on the definitions, what differences do you see in the *mens rea* between first and second degree manslaughter? What do you think the *mens rea* is for "crim-

Stop and Engage

inally negligent homicide" in New York? Read Section 125.10 in the New York Penal Code to find your answer. You will note at this point, as in the states illustrated so far, and in most states, there is a general category for homicide, but homicide includes a number of different crimes that result in the death of an individual. This underscores the importance of extreme precision in your use of terminology as well as your need to specify with precision the type of crime and the requisite *mens rea* and *actus reus*.

In Florida, in the category of homicide in Chapter 782 of Title XLVI of the Florida Statutes, you will find the crimes of murder, excusable homicide, attempted felony murder, manslaughter and other crimes that result in the death of an individual. In Section 782.04(1)(a) murder is defined as "the unlawful killing of a human being when perpetrated from a premeditated design to effect the death of the person killed or any human being or 2. when committed by a person engaged in the perpetration of, or in the attempt to perpetrate, any: a. trafficking offense prohibited by Section 893.135; b. arson, c. sexual battery, d. robbery, e. burglary, f. kidnapping, g. escape, h. aggravated child abuse, i. aggravated abuse of an elderly person or disabled adult, j. aircraft piracy, k. unlawful throwing, placing, or discharging of a destructive device or bomb, l. carjacking, m. home-invasion robbery, n. aggravated stalking, o. murder of another human being, p. resisting an officer with violence to his or her person, q. felony that is an act of terrorism or is in furtherance of an act of terrorism; or 3. Which resulted from the unlawful distribution of any substance controlled under Section 893.03(1), cocaine as described in Section 893.03 (2)(a)4., or opium or any synthetic or natural salt, compound, derivative, or preparation of opium by a person 18 years of age or older, when such drug is proven to be the proximate cause of the death of the user, is murder in the first degree and constitutes a capital felony, punishable as provided in Section 775.082." Identify the *mens rea* for murder in this Section 782.04(1)(a). In order to do this, you need to explore what constitutes an unlawful killing and how the Courts have defined premeditated design. If you read further in the statute, you note that murder is also defined in Section 782.04(1)(b)(2) as "the unlawful killing of a human being, when perpetrated by any act imminently dangerous to another and evincing a depraved mind regardless of human life, although without any premeditated design to effect the death of any particular individual, is murder in the second degree and constitutes a felony of the first degree, punishable by imprisonment for a term of years not exceeding life or as provided in Sections 775.082, 775.083, or 775.084." What is the *mens rea* for murder in this Section 782.04(1)(b)(2)? Can you find more than one?

As you continue to explore the penal codes in various states, you will note the complexity of the definitions. It is not enough to identify the *mens rea* and the *actus reus*, but you also need to know how the courts have defined the *mens rea*. In other words, what facts are necessary to support a finding of "premeditated deign" or "a depraved mind regardless of human life?" For purposes of writing an analytical essay answer to a fact pattern question, you not only need to know the elements of the specific crime, but you need to know the material facts for proving or disproving the elements of the specific crime.

Stop and Engage

- What do I know at this point?
  - Different crimes exist within the category of homicide
  - Different states have different names for crimes and different definitions for them
  - It is important to name the type of crime specifically and define it precisely
  - There are different degrees of murder and manslaughter. The type of degree (first and second) is dependent upon the *mens rea* and *actus reus* as defined in the statute
- What are the most common types of homicide?
  - Murder
  - Manslaughter
  - Criminally negligent homicide or negligent homicide
- What is the major difference between murder in the first degree and murder in the second degree?
  - Murder in the first degree usually requires a more stringent *mens rea*; such as premeditation or malice aforethought
  - Murder in the first degree usually requires a certain set of circumstances that involve another felony or an extreme act of cruelty (the *actus reus*)

5.2.2 Degrees of Murder

In Massachusetts, Chapter 265, Section 1 defines first degree murder as "murder committed with deliberately premeditated malice aforethought, or with extreme atrocity or cruelty, or in the commission or attempted commission of a crime punishable with death or imprisonment for life." Second degree murder is defined as "murder which does not appear to be in the first degree is murder in the second degree." Michigan delineates first degree murder in Section 750.316 as "(a) perpetrated by means of poison, lying in wait, or any other willful, deliberate, and premeditated killing. (b) committed in the perpetration of, or attempt to perpetrate, arson, criminal sexual conduct in the first, second, or third degree, child abuse in the first degree, a major controlled substance offense, robbery, carjacking, breaking and entering of a dwelling, home invasion in the first or second degree, larceny of any kind, extortion, kidnapping, vulnerable adult abuse in the first and second degree under section 145n, torture under section 85, or aggravated stalking under section 411i. (c) A murder of a peace officer or a corrections officer committed while the peace officer or corrections officer is lawfully engaged in the performance of any of his or her duties as a peace officer or corrections officer, knowing that the peace officer or corrections officer is a peace officer or corrections officer engaged in the performance of his or her duty as a peace officer or corrections officer." Note, the *mens rea* in both Massachusetts and Michigan emphasize some form of premeditation. You will also note that first degree murder is connected to certain circumstances such as murder committed during the commission of another type of crime or involving a certain category of person. Again, this exemplifies the importance of knowing the specific requirements of the statute so that you know what to look for when reading a fact pattern. Does your state make a distinction between first and second degree murder? If so, identify that the distinction?

5.2.3 Manslaughter

What is the major difference between **voluntary and involuntary manslaughter**? First, you need to determine if the statute in your state distinguishes between the two. Second, the answer usually depends upon the stated *mens rea*. In Texas, Section 19.04 only mentions manslaughter, and defines it as recklessly causing the death of an individual. However, Texas, as well as some other states, also includes the crime of criminally negligent homicide where the *mens rea* is "criminal negligence." Although some commentators and authors may suggest that involuntary manslaughter is the equivalent of criminally negligent homicide, you must remember the importance of using the correct terms as stated in the penal code for your state as well as understanding how the courts in your state have interpreted those sections in the penal code. Involuntary manslaughter usually carries a less stringent *mens rea* than voluntary manslaughter, evidenced by the terms "voluntary" and "involuntary." In involuntary manslaughter, the death is usually accidental and unintended even though it usually the results from some act of negligence or gross negligence that demonstrates a disregard for human life. Since involuntary manslaughter can result from a reckless or criminally negligent act, it is often equated with criminally negligent homicide. Can you think of an example of a fact pattern that would illustrate involuntary manslaughter?

Stop and Engage

Section 125.20 of the New York Penal Code defines manslaughter in the first degree as the death of a person if there was intent to cause serious physical injury but a death results. Manslaughter in the second degree is defined in Section 125.15 as recklessly causing the death of another person. You will note that in many states the *mens rea* for voluntary manslaughter or manslaughter in the first degree (depending upon the classification in the state statute) falls under the description of "reckless." In Ohio in Section 2903.03, voluntary manslaughter requires "the influence of sudden passion or a sudden fit of rage which is brought on by serious provocation occasioned by the victim that is reasonably sufficient to incite the person into using deadly force that knowingly causes the death of another." The *mens rea* for voluntary manslaughter in Ohio, based on this statutory language, would appear to be "knowingly," but the circumstances must be very specific such as those brought on by "serious provocation ... that are reasonably sufficient to incite." In order to understand how to define and interpret those words, you would need to understand how the Ohio courts have used them in deciding cases. One definition of involuntary manslaughter in Ohio, found in Section 2903.04(A) is defined as causing a death that is the proximate result of committing or attempting to commit a felony. Ohio also has reckless homicide, defined in Section 2903.041 which requires the reckless death of another as well as negligent homicide, in Section 2903.05, where the *mens rea* is negligence. You can see that it can become very confusing since different states use different classifications and specify a different *mens rea* for different crimes. You cannot generalize that all manslaughter requires a certain *mens rea* or that certain facts would prove second degree manslaughter since not all states recognize degrees or types of manslaughter. You can, however, try to recognize some of the major differences and think about some general points, but you should always check your state statute, learn the types of crimes, and learn the specific requirements.

Learning Tip

- What major differences between voluntary manslaughter and involuntary manslaughter and/or first degree manslaughter and second degree manslaughter exist?
  - Voluntary manslaughter and/or first degree manslaughter often requires a reckless *mens rea* and some act that results in death
  - Involuntary manslaughter or manslaughter in the second degree usually requires an unintended death and more of a negligent *mens rea*. However, you will note that in New York, "reckless" is the *mens rea* for second degree manslaughter, and in Texas "reckless" is the *mens rea* for manslaughter (without distinction between degree or voluntary or involuntary). This, again, underscores the importance of using the specific terms from the statutes and learning the precise requirements.

Case Example: Practice Opportunity

Read the following case excerpt and use a yellow highlighter to identify the material facts of the case; use a blue highlighter to note the relevant statutory language; use a pink highlighter to note the alleged crime; and use a green highlighter to note the Court's application of the law to the facts of the case, to highlight the Court's analysis.

State of Kansas v. Mardoqueo Gutierrez (2007)

In the Supreme Court of the State of Kansas
No. 94,317

1. When the sufficiency of evidence is challenged in a criminal case, the standard of review is whether, after review of all the evidence, viewed in the light most favorable to the prosecution, the appellate court is convinced that a rational fact finder could have found the defendant guilty beyond a reasonable doubt.

2. Aggravated burglary is defined in K.S.A. 21-3716 as "knowingly and without authority entering into or remaining within any building ... in which there is a human being, with intent to commit a felony ... therein." As used in that statute, the phrases "entering into" and "remaining within" refer to legally distinct factual situations. The entering into element is satisfied when the evidence shows that a defendant crossed the plane of a building's exterior wall. Remaining within refers to a defendant's presence in the building's interior after any entering into, authorized or unauthorized, has been accomplished.

3. Both unauthorized entering into and unauthorized remaining within may be present in a single burglary or aggravated burglary case. Neither is necessarily instantaneous.

4. To commit a burglary or aggravated burglary, a defendant's formation of intent to commit a felony in a building must, at some point, coexist with an unauthorized entering into the building or an unauthorized remaining within it. It is not necessary, however, to prove remaining within burglary or aggravated burglary to show that the intent to commit a felony was precisely contemporaneous with any withdrawal of a defendant's authority to be inside the building.

5. On the record of this case, the evidence was sufficient to support defendant's conviction of aggravated burglary.

6. Attempted voluntary manslaughter is a legally viable crime in Kansas.

We granted his petition for review on two issues: the sufficiency of the evidence against him on aggravated burglary and the legal viability of the crime of attempted voluntary manslaughter.

Factual and Procedural Background

Luz Gutierrez had obtained a protection from abuse order against defendant, her estranged husband, because of a May 23, 2004, incident in which he grabbed her by the neck and choked her until she nearly lost consciousness. Defendant also was arrested and charged with domestic battery in municipal court in

Emporia. On the afternoon of July 20, 2004, defendant appeared in the municipal court and entered into a diversion agreement in the domestic battery case. Although the agreement prohibited him from having contact with Luz, he left the municipal court and drove to her new apartment—the address of which he had obtained from a mutual friend. He parked his truck a block away so that Luz would not see him.

Luz had just arrived home from picking up her daughters when she heard a knock at her door. She was expecting a representative of a shelter to stop by, but when she answered the door, she saw defendant. He told Luz that they had to talk; the testimony is conflicting on whether he then pushed his way into the apartment or was permitted to enter when Luz stepped back from the door. Luz told defendant she had nothing to say to him and asked him to leave. Defendant demanded that Luz drop all the charges against him. When she responded that she would not, the two argued; Luz called defendant names. In addition, defendant saw marks on Luz that he believed were evidence of her physical relationship with another person. Defendant eventually told Luz that, if she was not going to withdraw the domestic battery charge, he "might as well kill her."

Defendant grabbed Luz by the throat, threw her to the floor, and squeezed hard for 15 to 20 seconds. His testimony indicated he stopped choking Luz either because he saw her eyes flutter or because he looked up and saw their children watching. In any event, Luz lost consciousness. When she awoke, her children were crying and shaking her.

Defendant, who had fled on foot, flagged down a friend a few blocks away, and got into the friend's car. Defendant said he had killed Luz and asked the friend to call 911. The friend drove defendant back to Luz' house, where police and an ambulance had already arrived. Defendant turned himself in to police. Defendant denied any intent to kill Luz. He also eventually testified at trial that he had seen a knife sitting out on a counter in Luz' apartment, but there was no suggestion that Luz threatened him with it or otherwise made a move toward it. Luz ultimately testified that there was no knife and that she did not and could not defend herself. Police found no weapons at the scene other than a butter knife under a pile of dishes in a sink.

Defendant was charged with attempted first-degree murder; aggravated burglary based on the underlying felony of attempted first-degree murder; and violation of a restraining order. Near the close of the State's case at trial, the district judge permitted the State to amend its aggravated burglary charge to rely on an underlying intent to commit first-degree murder rather than attempted first-degree murder. Defense counsel objected but did not articulate any specific prejudice that would result from the amendment.

The defense moved for judgment of acquittal at the close of the State's case, arguing the evidence of premeditation and intent to kill was insufficient. The district judge denied this motion.

The jury was instructed on the elements of attempted first-degree premeditated murder and lesser-included offenses, including Instruction No. 6 on attempted voluntary manslaughter in accord with PIK Crim. 3d 55.01 and PIK Crim. 3d 56.05. The instructions defined heat of passion in accord with PIK Crim. 3d 56.04(e).

The first part of Instruction No. 8 on the crime of aggravated burglary was based on PIK Crim. 3d 59.18 and told the jury the State must prove:

> "1. That the defendant knowingly entered or remained in a building, to-wit: [Luz' apartment];
>
> "2. That the defendant did so without authority;
>
> "3. That the defendant did so *with the intent to commit murder in the first degree*, a felony therein;
>
> "4. That there was a human being, to-wit: Luz Gutierrez, at the residence ... ; and
>
> "5. That this act occurred on or about the 20th day of July, 2004, in Emporia, Lyon County, Kansas." (Emphasis added.)

It then set out the elements of premeditated first-degree murder.

Sufficiency of the Evidence on Aggravated Burglary

When the sufficiency of evidence is challenged in a criminal case, the standard of review is whether, after review of all the evidence, viewed in the light most favorable to the prosecution, the appellate court is convinced that a rational fact finder could have found the defendant guilty beyond a reasonable doubt. *State v. Morton*, 283 Kan. 464, 474, 153 P.3d 532 (2007) (quoting *State v. Kesselring*, 279 Kan. 671, 679, 112 P.3d 175 [2005]; *State v. Beach*, 275 Kan. 603, Syl. ¶2, 67 P.3d 121 [2003]).

Aggravated burglary is defined in K.S.A. 21-3716 as "knowingly and without authority entering into or remaining within any building ... in which there is a human being, with intent to commit a felony ... therein." Defendant insists that any intent to commit the felony of attempted voluntary manslaughter was not concurrent with either unauthorized entry into Luz' apartment or unauthorized refusal to leave it. Rather, the heat of passion or sudden quarrel motivating defendant's throttling of Luz arose later in time.

This argument requires three logical components. Defendant first asserts that the phrases "entering into" and "remaining within" refer to legally distinct factual situations. He is at least partially correct on this specific point. See *State v. Mogenson*, 10 Kan. App. 2d 470, 701 P.2d 1339, *rev. denied* 238 Kan. 878 (1985); *State v. Brown*, 6 Kan. App. 2d 556, Syl. ¶4, 630 P.2d 731 (1981). The entering into element of a burglary or aggravated burglary is satisfied when the evidence shows that a defendant crossed the plane of a building's exterior wall. Remaining within refers to a defendant's presence in the building's interior after any entering into, authorized or unauthorized, has been accomplished.

Defendant is incorrect, however, on the two other components of his argument.

First, he also asserts that "entering into" and "remaining within" are inevitably mutually exclusive, *i.e.*, that both cannot be present in a single case, because remaining within requires initial entry to be authorized. This is not so. The paradigmatic example of remaining within may occur when (a) a defendant's initial entry into a building was authorized; (b) authority is later withdrawn; and (c) defendant nevertheless stays inside the building. But such a fact pattern is not essential. A defendant who is unauthorized to enter into a building may continue to be unauthorized while he or she remains within, unless the person or entity empowered to grant permission has decided upon a change in defendant's status. It also is conceivable that a defendant who is unauthorized to enter into a building may be granted permission to remain within and then be subject to later revocation of that permission. Defendant also is incorrect in insisting that either entering into or remaining within must necessarily be instantaneous. In fact, both entering into and remaining within may take longer than a mere moment. Certainly, remaining within connotes at least briefly continuous behavior.

The facts of this case are very similar to those that faced the Court of Appeals in *Mogenson*, 10 Kan. App. 2d at 470. Paul Mogenson was charged with, *inter alia*, aggravated burglary based on an aggravated battery of the victim. There was a dispute about whether Mogenson's initial entry was authorized. The victim testified that she did not give him permission to come in. Mogenson and the victim's son said the son had unlocked the door for Mogenson, and then the victim had demanded that Mogenson leave. Instead, an argument and the battery ensued. On appeal, Mogenson challenged the district judge's decision to instruct the jury on both entering into and remaining within. The Court of Appeals affirmed, stating that an instruction in the alternative was proper on this evidence. 10 Kan. App. 2d at 473. It also discussed the timing of intent formation, approving the district judge's statement to the jury that "intent must exist at the time the defendant entered the house or at the time he remained in the house in the course of the argument." 10 Kan. App. 2d at 475-76.

The panel stated: "[T]he [defendant's] formation of intent to commit aggravated battery [on his wife] must have existed at the time his authority to be in the house was terminated or after he remained in the house without authorization." Because the "evidentiary record conclusively establishe[d] that the argument ensued after defendant was ordered out of the house ... the requisite intent was present during the course of argument, a time when defendant's authority had terminated." 10 Kan. App. 2d at 476. We have previously favorably discussed and consistently applied the holding of *Mogenson*. See, *e.g.*, *State v. Bowen*, 262 Kan. 705, 709, 942 P.2d 7 (1997) (analogizing to *Mogenson* to hold intent, absence of authority must be concurrent); *State v. Skelton*, 247 Kan. 34, 49, 795 P.2d 349 (1990) ("[t]he intent to commit a felony therein may be formulated after a defendant is within a structure, but the unlawful act of remaining without authority must concur with the criminal intent to commit a felony or theft to satisfy the statute's elements"). To support a conviction for aggravated burglary, the intent to commit a felony and the unauthorized entering into or remaining within must at some point in time coexist. *Bowen*, 262 Kan. at 709 (citing *Mogenson*, 10 Kan. App. 2d at 472-76). It is not necessary, however, to prove "remaining within" burglary or aggravated burglary to show that the intent to commit a felony was precisely contemporaneous with any withdrawal of a defendant's authority to be inside the building.

Here, viewing all the evidence in the light most favorable to the prosecution, although a rational fact finder may not have been able to conclude defendant was guilty beyond a reasonable doubt of aggravated burglary based on evidence of unauthorized entry contemporaneous with the heat of passion or sudden quarrel necessary for voluntary manslaughter, the evidence was adequate to support defendant's formation of the necessary intent while he remained in Luz' apartment without authority. Once she told him to leave, an expression of sentiment defendant admits occurred, his presence was unauthorized even if previously permitted. Evidence of development of defendant's intent to commit a felony at any point between Luz' expression that he was unwelcome and his departure from the apartment was legally sufficient to support the aggravated burglary conviction.

Attempted Voluntary Manslaughter

Defendant's second argument is that the crime of attempted voluntary manslaughter based on sudden quarrel or heat of passion is an impermissible legal fiction. In his view, one cannot intend to do an act that is defined by impulse and lack of reflection. This argument raises a question of law subject to unlimited appellate review. See *State v. Sexton*, 232 Kan. 539, 542, 657 P.2d 43 (1983) (function of court to determine whether statute, combination of statutes proscribes certain conduct as criminal). K.S.A. 21-3403(a) defines voluntary manslaughter as "the intentional killing of a human being committed ... [u]pon a sudden quarrel or in the heat of passion." K.S.A. 21-3301(a) provides that an attempt is "any overt act toward the perpetration of a crime done by a person who intends to commit such crime but fails in the perpetration thereof or is prevented or intercepted in executing such crime."

Defendant concedes that many Kansas cases recognize the crime of attempted voluntary manslaughter, but correctly notes that no Kansas court has squarely addressed the issue he raises. See, *e.g.*, *State v. Flores*, 283 Kan. 380, 153 P.3d 506 (2007) (defendant, a minor, pleaded guilty to felony murder, attempted voluntary manslaughter; issue whether case should have remained in adult, juvenile court); *State v. Gayden*, 281 Kan. 290, 130 P.3d 108 (2006) (defendant convicted of six felonies, including attempted voluntary manslaughter; issue whether double jeopardy properly raised through illegal sentence motion); *State v. Dixon*, 252 Kan. 39, 41-49, 843 P.2d 172 (1993) (defendant appealed attempted first-degree murder conviction; issue whether evidence warranted instruction on attempted voluntary manslaughter as lesser included offense). At least one of our sister jurisdictions appears to be in a similar position. See *Stice v. State*, 799 P.2d 1204 (Wy. 1990) (defendant pleaded guilty to attempted voluntary manslaughter; untimely appeal permitted where district court had failed to inform defendant of maximum penalty for that crime; issue whether error harmless).

Here, defendant relies on an Illinois Court of Appeals case, *People v. Stevenson*, 198 Ill. App. 3d 376, 555 N.E.2d 1074 (1990). In that case, defendant Stephen Stevenson had telephoned the home of his ex-paramour and her husband and had threatened to kill the husband. In the early hours of the next day, Stevenson came to the house, ready to fight. When the husband refused to come outside, Stevenson threw a brick through a window, kicked in a door, and stabbed the husband in the chest. Although seriously injured, the husband recovered; Stevenson was convicted of, *inter alia*, attempted murder.

On appeal Stevenson noted that, in a prosecution for murder, a mitigating state of mind such as intense passion or an unreasonable belief that one's actions were justified is an affirmative defense that, once raised by the evidence, must be disproved by the State. See 198 Ill. App. 3d at 383 (citing *People v. Reddick*, 123 Ill. 2d 184, 526 N.E.2d 141 [1988]). Therefore, he asserted, in cases of attempted murder, the State should have a similar duty to disprove the existence of a sudden and intense passion such as that arising from his jealousy of his ex-paramour's husband; and a mitigating state of mind that would reduce murder to voluntary manslaughter should reduce attempted murder to attempted voluntary manslaughter.

The Illinois court ultimately determined Stevenson's failure to raise the issue at trial resulted in waiver. 198 Ill. App. 3d at 383. Nevertheless, it added that Stevenson's argument was unpersuasive because, under Illinois' statutory definitions, no such thing as attempted voluntary manslaughter could exist:

"[T]here can be no [attempted voluntary manslaughter] in cases where the alleged mitigating state of mind is a sudden and intense passion. The intent to commit an offense contemplates deliberation. Voluntary manslaughter resulting from a sudden and intense passion, however, precludes any deliberation, but can be found only where the passion engendered is sufficient to deprive a defendant of his self-control. One cannot intend such passion." *Stevenson*, 198 Ill. App. 3d at 384 (citing *People v. Weeks*, 86 Ill. App. 2d 480, 230 N.E.2d 12 [1967]).

We note that New York has reached the same conclusion under its statutes. See *People v. Brown*, 21 A.D.2d 738, 249 N.Y.S.2d 922 (1964) *overruled on other grounds People v. Jackson*, 49 A.D.2d 680, 370 N.Y.S.2d 739 (1975); see also *People v. Martinez*, 81 N.Y.2d 810, 811-12, 595 N.Y.S.2d 376, 611 N.E.2d 277 (1993) (settled law that attempted manslaughter in the first degree is nonexistent crime); but see *People v. Foster*, 19 N.Y.2d 150, 278 N.Y.S.2d 603, 225 N.E.2d 200 (1967) (no reversal required where defendant pleaded guilty to attempted manslaughter in compromise with prosecution). Alabama, Massachusetts, Maine, Nevada, and Wisconsin have done likewise. See *Westbrook v. State*, 722 So. 2d 788, 792 (Ala. Crim. App. 1998) (person cannot attempt to kill as result of heat of passion; "If he attempts to kill that person, then he intends to cause that person's death. If he intends to cause that person's death, then he is guilty of attempted murder, not attempted manslaughter"; specific intent to take life not essential element of manslaughter); *Commonwealth v. Hebert*, 373 Mass. 535, 537-38, 368 N.E.2d 1204 (1977) (attempted voluntary manslaughter logically impossible, factually indistinguishable from assault with intent to kill); *State v. Howard*, 405 A.2d 206, 212 (Me. 1979) ("Because of the discrepancy in culpable mental states between criminal attempt on the one hand and manslaughter on the other, the proffered crime of "attempted manslaughter" is a logical impossibility"; voluntary manslaughter defined as "recklessly" or with "criminal negligence" causing death of another.); *Curry v. State*, 106 Nev. 317, 319-20, 792 P.2d 396 (1990) ("One cannot logically specifically intend to act pursuant to a spontaneous, unanticipated, and therefore, truly irresistible passion"; voluntary manslaughter general intent crime; thus attempted voluntary manslaughter cannot exist.); *State v. Carter*, 44 Wis. 2d 151, 155-56, 170 N.W.2d 681 (1969) (because intent not an element of manslaughter, attempted manslaughter does not exist).

However, a majority of the jurisdictions weighing in on this question have specifically rejected the argument defendant makes. See *State v. Barnes*, 162 Ariz. 92, 93, 781 P.2d 69 (Ct. App. 1989) (conviction for attempted heat-of-passion or sudden quarrel manslaughter based on intentional, knowing action to cause death not prohibited); *People v. Van Ronk*, 171 Cal. App. 3d 818, 824-25, 217 Cal. Rptr. 581 (1985) ("There is nothing illogical or absurd in a finding that a person who unsuccessfully attempted to kill another did so with the intent to kill which was formed in the heat of passion or which arose out of an honest but unreasonable belief in the necessity of self-defense."); *Taylor v. State*, 444 So. 2d 931, 934 (Fla. 1983) ("it is not a logical impossibility for the crime of attempted manslaughter to exist in situations where, if death had resulted, the defendant could have been found guilty of voluntary manslaughter," *i.e.*, where sufficient evidence present of intent to kill); *Anthony v. State*, 274 Ind. 206, 212, 409 N.E.2d 632 (1980) (while there can be no crime of attempted reckless homicide, "since both murder and manslaughter can be proved by evidence of the knowing or intentional killing of another human being, ... the crime of attempted manslaughter does exist under our present statutes"; culpability requirement satisfied); *State v. Harper*, 205 La. 228, 229-31, 17 So. 2d 260 (1944) (attempted voluntary manslaughter recognized as offense, given specific intent requirement); *Cox v. State*, 311 Md. 326, 331-34, 534 A.2d 1333 (1988) (specific intent required for both attempt, voluntary manslaughter); *Peo-*

ple v. Genes, 58 Mich. App. 108, 110, 227 N.W.2d 241 (1975) (because offense of voluntary manslaughter requires proof of intent to take life, voluntary manslaughter can be attempted); *State v. Jernigan*, 139 N.M. 1, 7-8, 127 P.3d 537 (2005) (by statute, voluntary manslaughter requires proof of general intent; however, if conduct qualifies as second-degree murder committed with sufficient provocation, specific intent crime defined; under limited circumstances, involving provocation, voluntary manslaughter also may be specific intent crime); *State v. Rainey*, 154 N.C. App. 282, 286-88, 574 S.E.2d 25, *rev. denied* 356 N.C. 621, 575 S.E.2d 520, 521 (2002) (because essential element of voluntary manslaughter intent to kill, attempted voluntary manslaughter cognizable offense); *Com. v. Garner*, 314 Pa. Super. 566, 569, 461 A.2d 302 (1983) (attempted voluntary manslaughter exists under Pennsylvania law); *State v. Ruane*, 912 S.W.2d 766, 783 (Tenn. Crim. App. 1995), *disapproved on other grounds State v. Williams*, 977 S.W.2d 101 (Tenn. 1998) (recognizing attempted voluntary manslaughter as lesser included offense of attempted murder; offense requires intent to kill); *Ex parte Buggs*, 644 S.W.2d 748, 750 (Tex. Crim. App. 1983) (element of intent essential to prove voluntary manslaughter; attempted voluntary manslaughter classified as lesser include offense of attempted murder); *State v. Norman*, 580 P.2d 237, 239-40 (Utah 1978) *overruled on other grounds State v. Standiford*, 769 P.2d 254 (Utah 1988) (no offense of attempted "reckless" manslaughter exists; however attempted manslaughter under "extreme mental or emotional disturbance" recognized as specific intent crime); see also *State v. Holbron*, 80 Hawaii 27, 45, 904 P.2d 912 (1995) (attempted manslaughter recognized by statute; see Hawaii Rev. Stat. §707-702[2] [1993 & 2006 Supp.]).

In Kansas, as in Illinois and New York, an attempt requires specific intent. Kansas does not recognize attempted felony murder, *State v. Robinson*, 256 Kan. 133, Syl. ¶1, 883 P.2d 764 (1994); attempted involuntary manslaughter, *State v. Gayden*, 259 Kan. 69, Syl. ¶2, 910 P.2d 826 (1996); *State v. Shannon*, 258 Kan. 425, Syl. ¶3, 905 P.2d 649 (1995); *State v. Collins*, 257 Kan. 408, Syl. ¶4, 893 P.2d 217 (1995); or unintentional but reckless second-degree murder under K.S.A. 21-3402(b); *State v. Clark*, 261 Kan. 460, 466-67, 931 P.2d 664 (1997); *Shannon*, 258 Kan. at 429. In other words, we have recognized in other circumstances that it is logically impossible to attempt to commit an unintentional act. Yet, in Kansas, unlike in Illinois and New York, voluntary manslaughter is a specific intent offense. See K.S.A. 21-3403(a) (defining voluntary manslaughter); *State v. Burrow*, 221 Kan.

745, 749, 561 P.2d 864 (1977) (involuntary manslaughter distinguished from voluntary manslaughter by the lack of intent to kill); *State v. Conley*, 6 Kan. App. 2d 280, 286, 627 P.2d 1174, *rev. denied* 229 Kan. 671 (1981) (voluntary manslaughter is specific intent crime; requires intent to kill); compare *Stevenson*, 198 Ill. App. 3d at 383 (citing 38 Ill. Rev. Stat. §9-2[a] [1985] [defining voluntary manslaughter as: "A person who kills an individual without lawful justification commits voluntary manslaughter if at the time of the killing he is acting under a sudden and intense passion resulting from serious provocation"]); N.Y. Penal Law §§125.115, 125.20 (McKinney 2004) (neither first- nor second-degree manslaughter require an intent to kill).

A defendant can form intent to kill without premeditation, without reflection, on impulse, while enraged or provoked, but, in order to support a conviction of voluntary manslaughter, that essential element of intent must be present. Moreover, if a defendant has formed the necessary intent, it is not logically impossible for him or her to attempt and fail to carry it out, that is, to engage in an overt act toward the accomplishment of an intentional crime. See *State v. Graham*, 275 Kan. 831, 836-40, 69 P.3d 563 (2003); *State v. Hedges*, 269 Kan. 895, 905-06, 8 P.3d 1259 (2000). For these reasons, we reject defendant's argument on this issue. Attempted voluntary manslaughter is a valid crime in Kansas.

We make one additional parting observation. The *Stevenson* decision from Illinois also is less than persuasive because it focuses on the inability of a defendant to intend the passion inherent in voluntary manslaughter. The appropriate inquiry is not whether a defendant intends passion, but whether he or she intends to kill. In both Kansas and Illinois, the conduct proscribed by the voluntary manslaughter statute, as a homicide, is not the passion. It is the killing. The existence of heat of passion or sudden quarrel, arising from severe provocation, reduces what would otherwise be murder to voluntary manslaughter. See *State v. Guebara*, 236 Kan. 791, 796, 696 P.2d 381 (1985).

Affirmed.

Stop and Engage

Now that you have highlighted key parts from this case, complete the following activities:

- Identify the main issue(s) in this case.
- Write a concise summary of the material facts.

- Paraphrase the relevant statutory language with precision and accuracy.
- Write a concise summary of the court's reasoning.
- Write a concise explanation as to how and why the court reached its decision—its holding.

5.2.4 Felony Murder

Finally, as you have seen most states recognize murder, manslaughter, and negligent homicide as crimes within the category of homicide. Some states also recognize the crime of felony murder. Felony murder has also been associated with other classifications of homicide where the *actus reus* is the commission of a felony and the *actus reus* results in a death. In **felony murder,** the *mens rea* does not need to be intentional or even reckless; in fact, in felony murder, the focus is on the *actus reus*—the commission of a felony—and not on the *mens rea*. In other words, in many states, if a person commits a felony, and a death results, he/she can be charged with felony murder which often carries penalties and punishments similar to first degree murder. See if you can find felony murder in penal codes for Connecticut, California, Colorado, Florida, Georgia, Massachusetts, or Rhode Island. Is it called felony murder or is it classified under a different name? In *Commonwealth v. Padgett*, 44 Mass. App. Ct. 359 (1998) the court held that in order to establish felony murder, the defendant must have participated in a felony that was inherently dangerous where a homicide occurred within the course of committing the felony, and the death was the consequence of the commission of the felony. In *State v. Cobbs*, 203 Conn. 4 (1987), the court held that the death was caused in the course of and in furtherance of the felony. In *State v. Villani*, 491 A. 2d 976 (R. I. 1985), the court held that under Section 11-23-1 of the Criminal Offenses in Rhode Island that felony murder is a type of homicide that requires the perpetration of one of the enumerated offenses listed in the statute that includes arson, rape, burglary, kidnapping, and others. Felony murder in Rhode Island, for example, is the equivalent of first degree murder without the requirement of proving the *mens rea* of premeditation or deliberation beyond a reasonable doubt. Rhode Island illustrates the point, as does the statutory language and court decisions of many other states, that it is not the *mens rea* that matters but rather the *actus reus* for proving felony murder.

Case Example: Practice Opportunity

Read the following case excerpt and use a yellow highlighter to identify the material facts of the case; use a blue highlighter to note the relevant statutory language; use a pink highlighter to note the alleged crime; and use a green highlighter to note the court's application of the law to the facts of the case, to highlight the court's analysis.

In the Matter of E.B.M.

Memorandum No. 2-04-201-CV (2005)

The evidence showed that on February 13, 2004, at approximately 10:45 p.m., Lindsay Roberts left her pickup truck running while she was inside the Quick-Sak convenience store. Appellant stole Roberts's pickup truck and proceeded down White Settlement Road. When Appellant approached the intersection with Churchill Road, he collided with a vehicle driven by Philip Andress, who died as a result. After the accident, Appellant fled the scene and was arrested a short time later. At the time of the accident, Appellant was driving without headlights, and his speed was calculated to be between 61 and 63 mph in a 35 mph zone. Appellant submitted to a blood test at the hospital and was found to have a blood alcohol level of 0.11 percent.

Appellant urges this court to adopt an interpretation of the definition of felony murder set forth in*section 19.02(b)(3) of the Texas Penal Code* as excluding unauthorized use of a vehicle as an underlying offense. n5 As support for his argument, Appellant contends that he has found no Texas case upholding a conviction for felony murder based upon unauthorized use of a motor vehicle as the underlying offense.

> Under the felony murder statute, a person commits an offense if he commits or attempts to commit a felony, other than manslaughter, and in the course of and in furtherance of the commission or attempt, or in immediate flight from the commission or attempt, he commits or attempts to commit an act clearly dangerous to human life that causes the death of an individual. Section 19.02(b)(3).

Appellant argues that the trial court erred in denying his request for a jury instruction regarding the lesser-included offenses of manslaughter and criminally negligent homicide.

A two-step test applies when assessing whether a charge on a lesser-included offense should be given.*Threadgill v. State,* 146 S.W.3d 654, 665 (Tex. Crim. App. 2004); *Feldman v. State,*71 S.W.3d 738, 750 (Tex. Crim. App. 2002). The first step is to determine whether the offense is actually a lesser-included offense of the offense charged.*Threadgill,* 146 S.W.3d at 665. The second step of the test requires that the record contain some evidence that would permit a rational jury to find that the defendant is guilty only of the lesser offense. *Id.*; *Feldman,* 71 S.W.3d at 750. There must be some evidence from which a rational jury could acquit the defendant of the greater offense while convicting him of the lesser-included offense.*Threadgill,* 146 S.W.3d at 665. The evidence must establish the lesser-included offense as a valid rational alternative to the charged offense. *Id.*

Criminally negligent homicide is a lesser-included offense of felony murder when the intended felony is other than an underlying assaultive offense. *See Jones v. State,* 100 S.W.3d 1, 6 (Tex. App.–Tyler 2002, pet. ref'd) (citing *Kuykendall v. State,* 609 S.W.2d 791, 797-98 (Tex. Crim. App. [Panel Op.] 1980), overruled on other grounds by *Cook v. State,* 858 S.W.2d 467, 469-70 (Tex. Crim. App. 1993)). Additionally, because manslaughter and criminally negligent homicide differ only in the required *mens rea,* manslaughter is a possible lesser-included offense of felony murder. *Id.*

Because manslaughter and criminally negligent homicide can be lesser-included offenses of felony murder, we must determine whether there is some evidence that would permit a rational jury to find that the defendant is guilty only of the lesser offense. Manslaughter requires proof that the defendant acted recklessly, that is, that he consciously disregarded a substantial risk of which he was aware.*Jones,* 100 S.W.3d *at 6*; *see* Texas Penal Code Section *6.03(c)*. Criminally negligent homicide requires proof that the defendant acted with criminal negligence, that is, that he ought to have been aware of a substantial and unjustifiable risk that the result would occur. *Jones,* 100 S.W.3d *at 6*; *see* Texas penal Code Section *6.03(d)*, *19.05(a)*.

Appellant contends that there was no evidence that he intentionally or knowingly caused the death of Andress, the driver of the other vehicle. Therefore, he argues that the*mens rea* of criminally negligent homicide and manslaughter "more closely relate to the actual actions of the Appellant than the offense for which he was ultimately convicted, felony murder."

In felony murder, the culpable mental state for the act of murder is supplied by the mental state accompanying the underlying felony. *Salinas v. State,* 163 S.W.3d 734, 741 (Tex. Crim. App. 2005); *Rodriquez v. State,* 548 S.W.2d 26, 28-29 (Tex. Crim. App. 1977). In the instant case, it is undisputed that Appellant intentionally operated Roberts's vehicle without her effective consent, thereby intentionally committing the underlying offense of unauthorized use of a vehicle.*See* Texas Penal Code Section *31.07(a)*. In reviewing the record, we have found no evidence that Appellant acted recklessly or with criminal negligence in this regard, nor has Appellant cited any such evidence in his brief. Therefore, we conclude that Appellant was not entitled to a lesser-included offense instruction. We overrule Appellant's fifth point. Having overruled all of Appellant's points, we affirm the trial court's judgment.

Stop and Engage

Now that you have highlighted key parts from this case, complete the following activities:

- Identify the main issue(s) in this case.
- Write a concise summary of the material facts.
- Paraphrase the relevant statutory language with precision and accuracy.
- Write a concise summary of the court's reasoning.
- Write a concise explanation as to how and why the court reached its decision—its holding.

5.3 Rape and Sexual Conduct

In many states rape and crimes related to sexual conduct are classified as "sex crimes." Identify the major classification in your state and find some of the associated crimes. In Indiana, for example, the classification is "sex crimes" and some of the types of crimes are "rape," "criminal deviate conduct," and "child molesting" (Indiana Code, Section 35-42-4). In Texas, the classification is "sexual offenses," and some of the crimes include: continuous sexual abuse of a young child or children, homosexual conduct, public lewdness, and indecent exposure (Title 5, Chapter 21 of the Texas Penal Code). Note that rape is not included in that classification. Where would you find rape in the Texas Penal Code? The classification for rape falls under sexual assault in Section 22.011 under the general classification of Assaultive Offenses (Chapter 22). Sometimes you need to search around to find a particular crime, which is a good reason for familiarizing yourself with the general categories of crimes and some of the crimes in those categories as an important initial step before learning the specific crimes. In California, you will find these types of crimes in Title 9, labeled "crimes against the person involving sexual assault, and crimes against public decency and morals." The crimes of rape and carnal abuse of children can be found in Chapter 1 of Title 9. Is there another place in Title 9 where you can find other sex offenses? Take a look at Chapter 5.5, for example. What are some of those types of crimes? In Florida's Chapter 794 of Title XLVI, the crime identified is sexual battery. Sexual battery is defined specifically in Section 794.011. Could this crime in Florida be considered the equivalent of the crime of rape in Indiana or sexual assault in Texas? Identify the necessary *mens rea* and *actus reus* for these three crimes based on the language in the state statute.

Learning Tip

It is helpful to examine some of the state statues and identify the *mens rea* and the *actus reus*. It is also important to identify the necessary factual circumstances as enumerated in the statutory language so that when you read a fact pattern you know what material facts must be present for you to develop analytical reasoning to support the applicable criminal charges. In California, for example, we can find rape defined in this way in Section 261:

> (a) Rape is an act of sexual intercourse accomplished with a person not the spouse of the perpetrator, under any of the following circumstances:
>
> (1) Where a person is incapable, because of a mental disorder or developmental or physical disability, of giving legal consent, and this is known or reasonably should be known to the person committing the act. (2) Where it is accomplished against a person's will by means of force, violence, duress, menace, or fear of immediate and unlawful bodily injury on the person or another.
>
> (3) Where a person is prevented from resisting by any intoxicating or anesthetic substance, or any controlled substance, and this condition was known, or reasonably should have been known by the accused.
>
> (4) Where a person is at the time unconscious of the nature of the act, and this is known to the accused. As used in this paragraph, "unconscious of the nature of the act" means incapable of resisting because the victim meets one of the following conditions:
>
> (A) Was unconscious or asleep.
>
> (B) Was not aware, knowing, perceiving, or cognizant that the act occurred.
>
> (C) Was not aware, knowing, perceiving, or cognizant of the essential characteristics of the act due to the perpetrator's fraud in fact.
>
> (D) Was not aware, knowing, perceiving, or cognizant of the essential characteristics of the act due to the perpetrator's fraudulent representation that the sexual penetration served a professional purpose when it served no professional purpose.
>
> (5) Where a person submits under the belief that the person committing the act is the victim's spouse, and this belief is induced by any artifice, pretense, or concealment practiced by the accused, with intent to induce the belief.
>
> (6) Where the act is accomplished against the victim's will by threatening to retaliate in the future against the victim or any other person, and there is a reasonable possibility that the perpetrator will execute the threat. As used in this paragraph, "threat-

ening to retaliate" means a threat to kidnap or falsely imprison, or to inflict extreme pain, serious bodily injury, or death.

(7) Where the act is accomplished against the victim's will by threatening to use the authority of a public official to incarcerate, arrest, or deport the victim or another, and the victim has a reasonable belief that the perpetrator is a public official. As used in this paragraph, "public official" means a person employed by a governmental agency who has the authority, as part of that position, to incarcerate, arrest, or deport another. The perpetrator does not actually have to be a public official.

(b) As used in this section, "duress" means a direct or implied threat of force, violence, danger, or retribution sufficient to coerce a reasonable person of ordinary susceptibilities to perform an act which otherwise would not have been performed, or acquiesce in an act to which one otherwise would not have submitted. The total circumstances, including the age of the victim, and his or her relationship to the defendant, are factors to consider in appraising the existence of duress.

(c) As used in this section, "menace" means any threat, declaration, or act which shows an intention to inflict an injury upon another.

Stop and Engage

Based on the California statutory language, identify the *mens rea* for this crime. What are a few of the required elements of the crime? What importance does the concept of "consent" play in this crime?

How does Texas define sexual assault?

Sec. 22.011. SEXUAL ASSAULT.

(a) A person commits an offense if the person:

(1) intentionally or knowingly:

(A) causes the penetration of the anus or sexual organ of another person by any means, without that person's consent;

(B) causes the penetration of the mouth of another person by the sexual organ of the actor, without that person's consent; or

(C) causes the sexual organ of another person, without that person's consent, to contact or penetrate the mouth, anus, or sexual organ of another person, including the actor; or

(2) intentionally or knowingly:

(A) causes the penetration of the anus or sexual organ of a child by any means;

(B) causes the penetration of the mouth of a child by the sexual organ of the actor;

(C) causes the sexual organ of a child to contact or penetrate the mouth, anus, or sexual organ of another person, including the actor;

(D) causes the anus of a child to contact the mouth, anus, or sexual organ of another person, including the actor; or

(E) causes the mouth of a child to contact the anus or sexual organ of another person, including the actor.

(b) A sexual assault under Subsection (a)(1) is without the consent of the other person if:

(1) the actor compels the other person to submit or participate by the use of physical force or violence;

(2) the actor compels the other person to submit or participate by threatening to use force or violence against the other person, and the other person believes that the actor has the present ability to execute the threat;

(3) the other person has not consented and the actor knows the other person is unconscious or physically unable to resist;

(4) the actor knows that as a result of mental disease or defect the other person is at the time of the sexual assault incapable either of appraising the nature of the act or of resisting it;

(5) the other person has not consented and the actor knows the other person is unaware that the sexual assault is occurring;

(6) the actor has intentionally impaired the other person's power to appraise or control the other person's conduct by administering any substance without the other person's knowledge;

7) the actor compels the other person to submit or participate by threatening to use force or violence against any person, and the other person believes that the actor has the ability to execute the threat;

(8) the actor is a public servant who coerces the other person to submit or participate;

(9) the actor is a mental health services provider or a health care services provider who causes the other person, who is a patient or former patient of the actor, to submit or participate by exploiting the other person's emotional dependency on the actor;

(10) the actor is a clergyman who causes the other person to submit or participate by exploiting the other person's emotional dependency on the clergyman in the clergyman's professional character as spiritual adviser; or

(11) the actor is an employee of a facility where the other person is a resident, unless the employee and resident are formally or informally married to each other under Chapter 2, Family Code.

Stop and Engage

Based on the Texas statutory language, what is the *mens rea* for this crime? Identify a few of the required elements of the crime. What importance does the concept of "consent" play in this crime? How does it compare with the California crime of rape?

In New York, "sex offenses" are in Article 130. What are some of the crimes under this classification? Sexual misconduct (130.20), rape in the first, second, and third degree (130.35, 130.30, and 130.25), criminal sexual act in the first, second, and third degree (130.50, 130.45, 130.40), forcible touching (130.52), and other enumerated crimes.

What is sexual misconduct?

> A person is guilty of sexual misconduct when:
>
> 1. He or she engages in sexual intercourse with another person without such person's consent; or
>
> 2. He or she engages in oral sexual conduct or anal sexual conduct with another person without such person's consent; or
>
> 3. He or she engages in sexual conduct with an animal or a dead human body.

What is rape in the first degree?

> A person is guilty of rape in the first degree when he or she engages in sexual intercourse with another person:
>
> 1. By forcible compulsion; or
>
> 2. Who is incapable of consent by reason of being physically helpless; or
>
> 3. Who is less than eleven years old; or
>
> 4. Who is less than thirteen years old and the actor is eighteen years old or more.

What is a criminal sexual act in the first degree?

> A person is guilty of criminal sexual act in the first degree when he or she engages in oral sexual conduct or anal sexual conduct with another person:
>
> 1. By forcible compulsion; or
>
> 2. Who is incapable of consent by reason of being physically helpless; or
>
> 3. Who is less than eleven years old; or
>
> 4. Who is less than thirteen years old and the actor is eighteen years old or more.

Stop and Engage

Determine the *mens rea* and *actus reus* for each of these crimes. Are there any particular factual circumstances that are material to proving the elements of these crimes? Identify the similarities and differences of the crimes.

One of the most challenging issues in evaluating sex crime cases is the issue of what constitutes consent and whether effective consent existed. A related issue would be whether one can withdraw consent after consent is granted and sexual activity has commenced. These questions are not answered in the state penal codes, and they are not easily answered by the courts.

Case Example: Practice Opportunity

Consider the facts from the following case. Use a yellow highlighter to note the material facts related to the issue of whether consent was present and whether the consent was withdrawn at any point.

Maloud Baby v. State of Maryland

No. 225, September Term, 2005
Court of Special Appeals of Maryland

Factual Background

At trial, the complaining witness, Jewel L., testified that, at the time of the incident at issue, she was an eighteen-year-old student at Montgomery College. On the night of December 13, 2003, accompanied by her best friend, Lacey, she went to the McDonald's Restaurant located in Montgomery Village. Appellant, Lacey's younger brother and her boyfriend at the time were all friends. When Jewel and Lacey were about to leave, appellant, who was sixteen years old at the time, prevailed upon Jewel to give him and a friend, Mike, a ride in her Chevrolet Cavalier, which she had owned for approximately seven months. Mike and another person identified as a "Hispanic boy" were passengers in the back seat of the car. When the group arrived at its destination, a community center believed by them to be the site of a party, they discovered there was no party. The Hispanic boy alighted from the vehicle and left the group.

During the return trip to McDonald's Restaurant, the complainant complied with appellant's request to park briefly near an apartment complex, thereafter proceeding back to the restaurant.

The complainant complied with appellant's second request to stop at another location in a townhouse development near the McDonald's Restaurant, where all of the passengers alighted from Jewel's car and proceeded toward a clearing between two townhouses. As appellant and Mike smoked marijuana, they discussed the possibility of getting a hotel room, noting that the boys were too young, but the girls could get a room. Upon their arrival at McDonald's, Lacey left the group to join a friend, after which the complainant agreed to drive appellant and Mike to a residential neighborhood where she parked her car. The complainant complied with the request of appellant and Mike to sit between them on the back seat of her car. Mike put her hand down in his pants and asked her "to lick it." Appellant then asked her to expose her breasts; when she did not comply, he fondled her breast with his hand. After Jewel acquiesced to the boys' insistence that they stay ten more minutes, she found herself on her back with appellant removing her jeans and Mike sitting on her chest, attempting to place his penis in her mouth. After she told them to stop, the pair moved her around so that her body was up in appellant's lap as he held her arms and Mike tried to insert his penis in her, but briefly inserted it into her rectum by mistake. After Mike again tried to insert his penis in the complainant's vagina, appellant inserted his fingers in her vagina. After appellant exited the car, Mike inserted his fingers, then his penis into her vagina. Mike then got out of the car and appellant got in. Appellant told Jewel that it was his turn and, according to the complainant, the following transpired:

> Q. [ASSISTANT STATE'S ATTORNEY]: And what else did he say?
>
> A. He, after that we sat there for a couple seconds and he was like so are you going to let me hit it and I didn't really say anything and he was like I don't want to rape you.
>
> Q. So when Maouloud said I don't want to rape you, did you respond?
>
> A. Yes. I said that as long as he stops when I tell him to, then—
>
> Q. Now, that he could?
>
> A. Yes.
>
> Q. Did you feel like you had a choice?
>
> A. Not really. I don't know. Something just clicked off and I just did whatever they said.
>
> Q. Now when you told [appellant] if I say stop, something like that, you have to stop. What did he do after you spoke those words?
>
> A. Well he got on top of me and he tried to put it in and it hurt. So I said stop and that's when he kept pushing it in and I was pushing his knees to get off me.
>
> Q. You were on your back and he was on top of you?
>
> A. Yes.
>
> Q. Did he stop pushing his penis into your vagina?
>
> A. Not right away.

> Q. About how long did he continue to put his penis into your vagina?
>
> A. About five or so seconds.
>
> Q. And then what happened?
>
> A. And that's when he just got off me and that's when Mike got in the car....

Jewel testified that appellant continued for five or ten seconds, but she did not believe that he had ejaculated.

She testified that, as the trio proceeded back to McDonald's, appellant asked her to "jack him off," but, although she refused, she did give him her telephone number. After obtaining Lacey's cell telephone number from appellant, Jewel called her and said she was okay and would be there (at McDonald's) in a couple of seconds. Mike parked the car across the street from McDonald's and hugged Jewel before he and appellant departed. Thereafter, the complainant drove Lacey to Shoppers Food Warehouse, where they met Jewel's mother and then proceeded to Lacey's house after helping Jewel's mother to shop. Upon arriving at Lacey's house, the complainant responded in the negative to inquiries about what was wrong from Lacey's brother, but related what had happened to Lacey's mother. After the police were called, Jewel went to the hospital to be examined. Testifying on behalf of the State was Boston College Professor of Nursing Ann Burgess, whose expert testimony was offered to explicate to the jury the rape trauma syndrome, a condition associated with post-traumatic stress disorder. Appellant had filed a motion *in limine* to exclude her testimony.

The following hypothetical was presented to Burgess by the prosecutor:

> Here's the hypothetical. Please, Doctor, assume that you have a young woman who was socializing with her best friend and she met two male acquaintances through other social contacts and she thought both of these people were harmless. Assume now that she found herself alone in a parked car with these two young men. Assume please that she was tricked into going into the backseat of the car, supposedly to have a conversation, look at a book or a magazine. However, assume that instead of having that conversation, the two men grabbed her, held her down and forced her to submit to multiple sexual acts, including sexual intercourse.

Dr. Burgess attributed complainant's failure to resist and failure to immediately report the incident and giving her home telephone number to her assailant to behavior consistent with the rape trauma syndrome.

Lacie S. testified that she and Jewel dismissed the suggestion by appellant and Mike that they get a hotel room as "normal teen talk" and that Jewel had said that she told them to stop and they did not.

Forensic nurse examiner Tracey Eichelberger testified that her examination of the complainant on the morning after the alleged rape revealed a small laceration in the vaginal and in the anal area. Dr. Julia Lojoie, upon examination of medical photographs, described one of the lacerations as a centimeter long and the other as one and one half centimeters. Karolyn Omarksky found no semen or sperm on vaginal and anal swabs taken from the complainant. Appellant's testimony, although at variance in material respects from that of complainant, was surprisingly consistent. He was sixteen years old and a student in the eleventh grade at the time of the incident. The complainant agreed to drive appellant, Mike and a Spanish boy to a party. After the Spanish boy left them, they discovered there was no party. On their return trip, the complainant parked her car in a residential neighborhood and they all got out. Appellant and Mike smoked marijuana and suggested getting a hotel room, given that the girls were old enough to rent a room. When they began discussing sex, appellant produced three condoms. Lacey told the others that she did not want to accompany them. After driving Lacey back to the McDonald's Restaurant, the complainant drove to a residential area and parked her car. Jewel climbed into the back seat between appellant and Mike, whereupon the latter put the complainant's hand in his pants. After the complainant refused appellant's request to expose her breasts, Mike asked appellant for a condom and told him to get out of the car. After waiting outside of the car for approximately fifteen or twenty minutes, Mike emerged from the car and said that he "just hit that," an expression connoting that he had had sex with the complainant. Appellant then related his version of what occurred when he entered the complainant's car:

> Q. When you got in the car, what, if anything, did you say or do?
>
> A. I asked her if she was going to let me have sex with her.
>
> Q. What exactly did you say?
>
> A. I said, "Are you going to let me hit that?"
>
> Q. And what does that mean to you, "Can I hit that?"
>
> A. Have sex.
>
> Q. What, if anything, did she say?
>
> A. She said yes, as long as I stop when she says to.

And then I said, "I'm not going to rape you."

Q. Did you feel that was permission?

A. Yeah, I thought that that was permission.

Q. Why did you say "I don't want to rape you"?

A. Just to, because she said, "Stop when I say to," just to tell her that. It's kind of like to confirm the permission.

Appellant took out a condom and put it on. Jewel laid down on the back seat. Appellant placed himself between her legs and tried to put his penis in. He testified that the following occurred:

Q. What did you do with your penis?

A. I tried to put it in.

Q. Do you know where it was touching or what happened to it?

A. No. After I tried to put it in once, it wouldn't go in. I didn't feel nothing there.

Q. What happened? What did she say or do?

A. And then she sat up. She was like, "It's not going to go in," and that's when, after she sat up and said "It's not going to go in," that's when I took off the condom and I put it in my pocket and then knocked on the window for Michael to come in.

Q. Who said, "It's not going to go in?" You or her?

A. She did.

Q. When she sat up, what did that mean to you?

A. That meant stop.

Q. Did she say "Stop"?

A. No, she didn't. She just sat up.

Q. And you took that to mean stop?

A. Yeah.

Q. When she sat up, did you try to put it in again?

A. No, I didn't.

According to appellant, he stopped immediately and never ejaculated when the complainant sat up. According to appellant, after Mike drove Jewel's car back to McDonald's, she gave appellant her telephone number and hugged Mike as she got out of the car. Thereafter, Jewel and Lacey drove away. At the conclusion of the evidence, the trial judge instructed the jury as follows regarding evidence of "consent" to negate a charge of sexual assault and the force required to sustain a conviction for rape:

The amount of force necessary depends upon the circumstances, and no particular amount of force is required but it must be sufficient to overcome the resistance of the victim. You must be satisfied that the victim either resisted and that this resistance was overcome by force or threat of force or that the victim was prevented from resisting by force or threat of force. The victim must have resisted to the extent of her ability at the time unless her resistance or will to resist was overcome by force or fear that was reasonable under the circumstances. Finally, "consent" means actually agreeing to the sexual act rather than merely submitting as a result of force or threat of force.

Stop and Engage

Based on the facts, what are your thoughts about whether effective consent was present and whether consent was withdrawn?

Now read an excerpt from the Court's analysis:

In the case at hand, the question posed by the jury was, "If a female consents to sex initially and, *during the course of the sex act* to which she consented, for whatever reason, she changes her mind, and the ... man continues until climax, does the result constitute rape?" Factually equating the parties' "different interpretations of the jury's question" to *Battle,* the State points out that counsel for appellant urged the court to respond that no rape, under the hypothetical, occurred because the prosecutrix had consented to the "male penetration" and the prosecutor was under the impression that the jury was asking whether consent could be withdrawn. The court, expressing the view that the question, as posed, was a factual hypothetical that the jurors wanted the court to answer, rather than finding the facts for themselves. I am unable to answer this question as posed," was the trial judge's response. "Please reread the instructions as to each element and apply the law to facts as you find them." The State, in its brief, urges that "this phrase is remarkably similar to the ambiguous phrase "during the course of the action" that the Court of Appeals found ambiguous in *Battle v. State*, 287 MD. 675 (1980)." We disagree. The plain meaning of the jury's words, "during the sex act," leads one ineluctably to conclude that the reference was to the act of intercourse. By contrast, a much broader connotation is conveyed by "during the course *of the action*." More importantly, if there had been initially any cause for confusion, it certainly should have been cleared up when the jury submitted the second note the following morning: "If at any time, the woman says stop, is that rape?"

The victim's change of mind, posits the State, could have just as probably referred to the "various sexual acts that took place prior to vaginal penetration by Baby, which included attempted fellatio, anal penetration, and the touching of her breasts and vagina; just prior to penetration by Baby; or after penetration." The State then argues that the jury's query regarding "the man continuing until climax" and the facts that neither appellant nor the prosecutrix testified that appellant had ejaculated or that he had engaged in any sort of "back and forth motion" during the penetration is support for the court's duty to reply to the jury's question because reaching a climax was not part of the evidence in the case. (Citing*Brogden v. State*, 384 Md. 631 (2005)).

The State appears to suggest that lack of absolute certitude regarding the jury's inquiry renders it ambiguous. We are not persuaded that the law imposes such a standard as a condition of requiring a response to the jury's inquiry. The mere fact that the initial question referred to the sex act, rather than, as premised by the State, during the various sexual acts, would certainly indicate that the jury was not referring to foreplay or other acts incidental to coitus or anal intercourse. Moreover, the State's argument that absence of testimony that appellant engaged in any sort of "back and forth" motion or ejaculated is "not part of the evidence in the case" misses the point. The question, as posed by the jury, did not assume, as a fact in evidence, that appellant had achieved a climax. A fair interpretation of the jury's question is that it was an inquiry as to the legal effect of a withdrawal of consent *subsequent to* penetration, and prior to climax.

Stop and Engage

Identify the central issue in this analysis. What is the court's reasoning? Use the internet to find the case with the citation above, and then read the entire case for a better understanding of the issues, the court's reasoning, and its holding.

5.4 Assault and Battery

In many states, battery and assault are not specifically enumerated as the crime of "battery" and the crime of "assault." In Texas, for example, Chapter 22 pertains to "Assaultive Offenses" and in Section 22.01, the title is "Assault." However, you will find something interesting when reading Section 22.01(a)(1) which states the following:

> (a) A person commits an offense if the person:
> (1) intentionally, knowingly, or recklessly causes bodily injury to another, including the person's spouse;

Compare the previous section to Section 22.01(a)(2) which states this:

> (a) A person commits an offense if the person:
>
> (2) intentionally or knowingly threatens another with imminent bodily injury, including the person's spouse;

You will note a significant difference. In Section 22.01(a)(1), there must be bodily injury. In Section 22.01(a)(2) there is a threat of imminent bodily injury. The difference is in (a)(1) there is bodily injury and in (a)(2) there is a threat. In Texas, both (a)(1)—bodily injury and (a)(2)—threat of imminent bodily injury are classified as the crime of "assault." In states which distinguish between the crime of "assault" and the "crime of "battery," this distinction is made:

> Battery requires physical contact that results in bodily injury
>
> Assault requires a threat of imminent bodily injury—there does not need to be physical contact or what some statutes and courts refer to as a "touching."

If you continue to read the remainder of Section 22.01(a) in the Texas Penal Code, you will see in (a)(3) that an assault (Texas terminology) is also committed if:

> (a) A person commits an offense if the person:
>
> (3) intentionally or knowingly causes physical contact with another when the person knows or should reasonably believe that the other will regard the contact as offensive or provocative.

In (a)(3) the requirements are physical contact (which in some states would lead us to name this battery rather than assault), but the additional requirement which distinguishes this Section (a)(3) from (a)(1) is that the person "knows or should reasonably believe that the other will regard the contact as offensive or provocative." In order to establish the elements for (a)(3), you would need to find in the facts indicators that demonstrate that the defendant knew what the victim would consider to be offensive or provocative.

Learning Tip

- What do you know at this point?
  - Although Texas does not distinguish between the crime of assault and the crime of battery, a slight distinction is made—and the difference is "bodily injury" versus a "threat of imminent bodily injury."

California does distinguish between the crimes of assault and battery. Section 240 defines assault as "an unlawful attempt, coupled with a present ability, to commit a violent injury on the person of another." Section 242 defines battery as "any willful and unlawful use of force or violence upon the person of another." In reading the statutory language, what is the key difference between the two crimes? In a battery, the use of force or violence (i.e., physical contact or touching) occurs, and in an assault there is an attempt with a present ability but no actual injury (i.e., contact or touching). California helps us see once again that the primary difference between an assault and a battery is that with assault there is no "physical contact, touching, use of force" just the threat of the use of force or the present ability to use that force.

In New York, the penal code in Article 120 labels the crimes contained therein as "Assault and Related Offenses." New York has assault in the first, second, and third degree. They also have a crime of menacing in the first, second, and third degree as well as reckless endangerment in the first and second degree, among other enumerated crimes. Section 120.10 defines assault in the first degree in this way:

> A person is guilty of assault in the first degree when:
>
> 1. With intent to cause serious physical injury to another person, he causes such injury to such person or to a third person by means of a deadly weapon or a dangerous instrument; or
>
> 2. With intent to disfigure another person seriously and permanently, or to destroy, amputate or disable permanently a member or organ of his body, he causes such injury to such person or to a third person; or
>
> 3. Under circumstances evincing a depraved indifference to human life, he recklessly engages in conduct which creates a grave risk of death to another person, and thereby causes serious physical injury to another person; or
>
> 4. In the course of and in furtherance of the commission or attempted commission of a felony or of immediate flight therefrom, he, or another participant if there be any, causes serious physical injury to a person other than one of the participants.

Note that in first degree assault, physical injury must result; we may infer that this means that some kind of physical contact or touching occurs. Does that appear to meet the criteria for what some states would label as "battery?" Remember, this illustrates the importance of using proper terminology. If you were analyzing a fact pattern under New York law with facts that would satisfy the criteria of Section 120.10, you would want to properly label the crime first degree assault rather than referring to it as the crime of battery. Notice the statutory language of assault in the third degree in New York:

> 120.00 Assault in the third degree.
>
> A person is guilty of assault in the third degree when:
>
> 1. With intent to cause physical injury to another person, he causes such injury to such person or to a third person; or
>
> 2. He recklessly causes physical injury to another person; or
>
> 3. With criminal negligence, he causes physical injury to another person by means of a deadly weapon or a dangerous instrument.

Note that there still must be some type of physical injury. One of the primary differences between first degree assault and third degree assault in New York is the *mens rea*. Identify the *mens rea* for first degree assault in New York. Determine the *mens rea* for third degree assault. Are there different *mentes rea* even within the degree of assault? Specificity is crucial at this step. The differences in *mentes rea* are meaningful because in order to prove the elements of the crime, you need to identify the material facts that will support the applicable *mens rea*. For example, in a fact pattern to support a charge of assault in the third degree under Section 120.00(2), you would need to establish that the person was reckless whereas in 120.00(3), you would need to establish that the person was criminally negligent. These two *mentes rea* differ in degree, and "reckless" is a higher level than criminal negligence. You would need more stringent facts to support "reckless" than you would to support criminal negligence. What are some facts that would support a charge under Section 120.00(2) versus a charge under Section 120.00(3)?

Learning Tip

You will note from the statutory language in some of these states that you can have an assault without a battery, but you usually cannot have a battery without an assault. This explains why many people refer to "**assault and battery**" as one charge. However, since we are considered with specificity and precision in our use of terminology and our labeling of criminal activity, you want to make sure to use the proper terminology as set forth in the applicable state statute. Below you will have a practice opportunity to read about one of the more important issues in determining whether a person "committed a touching" or an "unlawful or unwanted touching" for purposes of finding a battery.

Case Example: Practice Opportunity

Read the following case excerpt, and use a yellow highlighter to identify the material facts of the case; use a blue highlighter to note the relevant statutory language; use a pink highlighter to note the alleged crime; and use a green highlighter to note the court's application of the law to the facts of the case: to highlight the court's analysis. Before you begin, find Virginia Code Section 18.2-57 "Assault and Battery" using an internet search engine and read it fully.

Perkins v. Commonwealth of Virginia

12 Va. App 7 (1991)

Cary Randall Perkins was convicted of assault and battery in violation of Virginia Code 18.2-57. On appeal he challenges the sufficiency of the evidence. Finding the evidence sufficient, we affirm.

Viewed in the light most favorable to the Commonwealth, the evidence established that on November 19, 1997, the defendant was a teacher and coach at Marion Senior High School in Smyth County. The defendant is deaf and speech-impaired, and he communicates primarily by lip reading. He knew the fourteen-year-old victim through her boyfriend, but was neither her teacher nor coach. During a break from an algebra class, the victim was in the hallway getting a drink of water when the defendant asked her to come into his classroom. He inquired how she was doing in her algebra class and offered her assistance if she needed it. She returned to class, but about ten or fifteen minutes later, the defendant asked her to step into the hall. There, he showed her a picture of his former girlfriend and stated "how much he missed her and wanted to be with her." The victim returned to class. When class was over, the victim again saw the defendant in the hallway. He asked her how she did in algebra, and she told him she got a "B." The defendant asked where she was going and she said, "to the front of the school." The defendant replied, "I am too, so I will walk with you." As they walked down the hall, the victim testified the defendant "put his hand up under my hair on the back of my neck and started stroking it with his fingertips and said, 'It turns you on, don't it?'" The victim responded, "No, not by you" and jerked her head away. The victim understood his comment to mean "something sexual." She said the touching "scared" and "upset" her. The defendant placed his hand on her neck under her hair a second time and said, "Are you horny yet?" The victim said no, jerked her head away, and told him to stop. The victim told her mother and boyfriend about the incident the day after it happened. After the boyfriend talked to the defendant, the defendant went to the victim's class and motioned for her to come to the door. The victim stood in the doorframe. The defendant said that "he was sorry for what he had done and he didn't mean anything by it" and that he considered her like a little sister. He also said that he knew she would be at the school for three more years, her boyfriend would not, and if she ever needed anyone to talk to or look up to, "he would always be there. And he told me he was sorry again."

The defendant testified that on the date of the offense the victim appeared "down." The victim was walking ahead of him on his right side. In order to speak with her, he placed his hand on her neck to get her to face him; he said, "[t]he first time I grabbed her I was trying to get her to look at me." The defendant testified that when he asked the victim, "What is turning you on?," he meant, "What is bothering you?" He touched her neck again when she failed to turn around. He claims he did not hear her tell him to stop and she never turned around. The defendant initially denied saying anything about being "horny." He then testified, however, that if he did say it, it would have related to his former girlfriend, not the victim. He claims the incident was a miscommunication or misunderstanding. The defendant admits that he touched the victim. He contends, however, that the evidence was insufficient to prove that he intended to harm her. The defendant also argues that the court erroneously relied on the tort definition of assault and battery in concluding that a reasonable teacher would have known that the second touching was unwanted. We disagree.

An assault and battery is the unlawful touching of another. See *Gnadt v. Commonwealth*, 27 Va. App. 148, 151, 497 S.E. 2d 887, 888 (1998). Assault and battery is "the least touching of another, willfully or in anger." Roger D. Groot, Criminal Offenses and Defenses in Virginia 29 (4th. ed. 1998). The defendant does not have to intend to do harm; a battery may also be "done in a spirit of rudeness or insult." Id. (footnote omitted). The touching need not result in injury. See Gnadt, 27 Va. App. at 151, 497 S.E. 2d at 888. A touching is not unlawful if the person consents or if the touching is justified or excused. See id.; Groot, supra, at 30 ("an intentional touching which was not justified or excused is a battery"). The victim did not consent to the touchings. She jerked her head away when the defendant first touched her on the nape of her neck under her hair. No evidence suggested that the victim consented to the first touching. Her reaction to that touching removed any doubt that she consented to being touched. The court found that the second touching was "unauthorized and unwelcome and unwarranted." Even though a victim does not consent to the touching, it may be lawful if justified or excused. See Groot, supra, at 30 (examples include public authority, domestic authority, and crime prevention). The defendant claims the court failed to consider that he needed to touch the victim so she would turn to face him and he could read her lips. He asserts that his disability justified touching her so he could communicate with her.

The defendant said, "I usually just touch someone's shoulder to get them to make eye contact so I can understand them." He claimed that he touched the nape of the victim's neck under her hair twice because she was walking fast. The trial court found that the "touching of the neck was not in the ordinary course for [the defendant] to get the attention of someone that he wanted to communicate with." The trial court also found that "[t]here was no need for disciplinary or other control." Under the circumstances presented, the defendant's touching was neither excused nor justified. The fact finder, who determines the credibility of the witnesses and the weight accorded their testimony, may accept or reject the testimony in whole or in part. See *Bridgeman v. Commonwealth*, 3 Va. App. 523, 528, 351 S.E. 2d 598, 601 (1986). The defendant testified that he meant, "what is bothering you?" when he asked the victim, "what is turning you on?," that he was trying to get the victim's attention by touching her, and while he denies he used the word "horny" when speaking to her, if he did, he was talking about his former girlfriend. The trial court found the victim's testimony credible. It was entitled to disbelieve the defendant's self-serving testimony and to conclude that he was lying to conceal his guilt. See *Speight v. Commonwealth*, 4 Va. App. 83, 88, 354 S.E.2d 95, 98 (1987) (en banc).

For the foregoing reasons, we affirm the conviction of assault and battery. Affirmed.

Stop and Engage

Now that you have highlighted key parts from this case, complete the following activities:

- Identify the main issue(s) in this case.
- Write a concise summary of the material facts.
- Paraphrase the relevant statutory language with precision and accuracy.
- Write a concise summary of the court's reasoning.
- Write a concise explanation as to how and why the court reached its decision—its holding.

5.5 Fact Pattern Deconstruction Examples

Here are practice opportunities to learn to deconstruct the material facts. Read the following fact pattern and use a yellow highlighter to highlight the material facts of the case and a blue highlighter to note the key word from the facts that identify the applicable crime.

Example A

Jason had just installed a supercharger in his 1991 Mustang 5.0, boosting the horsepower to well over 400. He picked up his girlfriend, and he was speeding through a residential neighborhood, hoping to impress her. He lost control of the car, skidding into a tree, and killing his girlfriend.

Now answer the following questions:

- What is the applicable crime?
- What is the *mens rea* for that crime?
- What is the *actus reus* for the crime based on the material facts?

Model Answer to Example A

Jason had just installed a supercharger in his 1991 Mustang 5.0, boosting the horsepower to well over 400. He picked up his girlfriend, and he was speeding through a residential neighborhood, hoping to impress her. He lost control of the car, skidding into a tree, and killing his girlfriend.

- The crime is manslaughter.
- The *mens rea* is "reckless"—speeding through a residential neighborhood.
- The *actus reus* is "lost control of the car, skidding into the tree."

Here are some additional opportunities to practice deconstructing fact patterns. For all of the following examples, read the following hypothetical fact pattern and note the possible applicable crimes in the margins; then use a yellow highlighter to identify the material facts of the case.

Example B

Aubrey was working three jobs, supporting her two kids and a husband while he finished school. After working an 18-hour day, she came home to find her husband engaged in sexual activity with a neighbor. Filled with rage, Aubrey went to the gun cabinet, chose a shotgun and killed them both.

Example C

Paul found himself in a financial crunch and was becoming desperate. He borrowed his friend's shotgun, went to the local bank and proceeded to rob it. During the robbery, Paul was surprised by a guard. He pointed the shotgun at the guard and fired, killing him.

Example D

While driving along an expressway with three friends in her car, Anita chose to text another friend. Because she was distracted, Anita allowed her car to drift into on-coming traffic, where a semi struck it. Two of her friends were killed.

Now answer the following questions:

- What is the applicable crime?
- What is the *mens rea* for that crime?
- What is the *actus reus* for the crime based on the material facts?

5.6 Summary

"Crimes against the person," a common name for a category of crimes that include homicide, sexual crimes, battery, assault, and other crimes, classifies these acts that result in death or physical injury to a human being. When you begin to learn and study the various types of crimes, it is very important to learn the precise definitions. Criminal homicide, in many states includes a number of different types of crimes that all pertain to the ultimate death of an individual. Although, you may think of "criminal homicide" or "homicide" synonymously with "murder," the terms may have different meanings and different definitions depending upon the language in your particular state statute. In many states rape and crimes related to sexual conduct are classified as "sex crimes." One of the most challenging issues in evaluating sex crime cases is the issue of what constitutes consent and whether effective consent was present. A related issue is whether one can withdraw consent after consent has been granted and sexual activity has commenced These points are not answered in the state penal codes, and they are not easily answered by the courts. In many states, codes do not specifically enumerate battery and assault as the crime of "battery" and the crime of "assault." You will note from the statutory language in some of these states that you can have an assault without a battery, but you usually cannot have a battery without an assault. This explains the common reference to "assault and battery" as one charge. However, since we are concerned with specificity and precision in our use of terminology and our labeling of criminal activity, you want to make sure to use the proper terminology as set forth in the applicable state statute.

5.7 Chapter Review Activities

Below, you will find several hypothetical fact patterns that require you to answer specific questions. Make sure to identify the issues and answer the questions. Apply the appropriate law(s) and develop in-depth reasoning and analysis to reach your conclusions. Your final assignment is comprised of a drafting activity which will require some thinking "outside of the box."

Hypothetical Fact Pattern I

Art and Paul, both seniors at Ivory Tower University, have known each other since freshman year when they were assigned to room together in North Hall. They made something of an odd couple. Art was compulsively neat, and he liked everything to be orderly and predictable. He tended to follow routines, like always getting up at the same time every day, eating the same thing for breakfast, and brushing his hair and teeth and shaving in exactly the same order every day. Paul was very different from Art. Spontaneous and fun-loving, he was known to break the dorm rules and curfews. His side of the room was always a mess, with dirty clothes scattered over the floor. Although they did not choose to be roommates after freshman year, Paul and Art remained good friends and shared the same circle of friends and acquaintances at ITU.

Sophomore year, Paul started dating Cathy. Cathy shared Paul's fun-loving spirit, and they spent the summer between sophomore and junior year on a cross-country bus tour of America, going nowhere in particular. Junior and senior year, Cathy and Paul shared an apartment, and Art was a frequent guest. Art knew that Paul was completely in love with Cathy, and that he planned to propose to her after graduation. He also knew that Cathy did not feel the same way about Paul. At the beginning of their senior year, Cathy increasingly confided in Art that she needed to settle down and become more serious, and though she loved Paul, she was frustrated by his lack of ambition and did not see them sharing a future together. At some point, as Cathy and Art's discussions became more intimate, they both realized that romantic sparks were beginning to fly. One night, when Paul was away for the weekend, Art ended up spending the night with Cathy at her apartment.

When Paul returned from his weekend away, he sensed something different between him and Cathy. After he pressed her, she finally confessed that she was not in love with him anymore, that she was in love with Art, and that she had spent the night with Art in their bed. Paul fell into a deep depression and stopped eating or going to class. Cathy moved out. The spring semester was almost at an end, and Paul was now in danger of failing to graduate. He decided that the only way out would be to end his life. He bought a gun.

A few weeks later, desperate and heartsick, Paul was wandering around campus thinking about how his life had been ruined by Art and Cathy, especially by Art. About 2:30 on a beautiful Thursday afternoon in the spring, with students out milling around the quad, playing Frisbee and studying in the sun, the contrast between the nice weather outside and the terrible way he felt inside only made Paul feel worse. He saw a couple sitting on a park bench, arms wrapped around each other. Was that Art and Cathy? It looked like them. Now he was mad. Something had to be done. He pulled out the gun, waving it around wildly. "Stop me!?" He yelled, "For goodness sake, someone stop me!?" Then he started pulling the trigger, again and again, until all five chambers of the gun were empty.

The coroner and crime scene reports later indicated that three of the bullets had lodged in the wooden back of the park bench. Two hit the young man in the chest, fatally wounding him. He was not Art, and the young woman he was with was not Cathy. In fact, Art and Cathy never dated after the one night they spent together. At the time of the shooting, Art was following his regular routine of exercising at the gym, a routine he had followed every Tuesday and Thursday between 2:00 and 3:30 p.m. since his freshman year, something that Paul had often teased him about.

The police took Paul into custody, and he gave a statement to the police saying that when he pulled the trigger, he did not know what he was doing. He was not aiming for anything in particular. He just wanted to end all the pain.

You are the prosecutor in a jurisdiction that follows the Texas Penal Code but understand that the model penal code, and common law principles are also applicable with respect to mental states, causation, and criminal homicide.

(A) Discuss the possible homicide charges that you could bring against Paul, and the different theories upon which those charges would be based, as well as the factual inferences that would support each charge.

(B) After discussing the different charges that could reasonably be supported by the facts and inferences from the facts, state what your charging decision would be, and explain what criminal policies support your charging decision and why they support it.

Hypothetical Fact Pattern II

Tito was an amazingly strong professional wrestler, weighing almost 300 pounds. He also physically abused his wife, Angela. The beatings became worse, until Angela could no longer hide her injuries from her sister, Rosa. At first Rosa tried to get Angela to go to the police, but Angela refused. Rosa then called their brother, Carlos and asked him to help her confront Tito, assaulting him if needed to "teach him a lesson." Carlos reluctantly agreed, and he bought a baseball bat at the sporting goods store. While Carlos was waiting for Tito at the gym, Rosa called his cell phone and told him that Angela had finally gone to the police. Carlos went home without seeing Tito. Discuss any applicable crimes and develop a well-reasoned analysis to reach a conclusion in response to your framed issue(s).

Hypothetical Fact Pattern III

Carlos had just passed his 19th birthday when he attended an extended-family party in his honor. Over the past two years, he and his two younger brothers established themselves as neighborhood fences, where other youths who had committed thefts or robberies could dispose of the fruits of their crimes at heavily discounted process from even street values. Carlos and his brothers asked no questions and always paid in cash. In the weeks following his birthday party, Carlos noticed a decline in the volume of stolen goods brought to him for fencing. Upon investigation, Carlos discovered that a rival had begun a similar operation in his neighborhood, and this rival was paying a higher reward for similar goods. Carlos was shocked to learn that his cousin, Ramon, was running the operation. Carlos told Ramon that he couldn't allow competition, and he would "take care of business" to preserve his territory. Ramon mocked Carlos, which angered him, and as days passed, Carlos' anger intensified, so when he saw no signs of Ramon closing his operation, Carlos vowed to follow through. He approached Ramon with a baseball bat in hand and threatened Ramon. Ramon dismissed the challenge, saying in effect that Carlos would not hurt a family member. In response, Carlos swung the bat, striking Ramon just above the ear, killing him instantly. Upon investigation, the medical examiner ruled that Ramon had died from blunt force trauma to the head. Discuss the relevant crimes.

Hypothetical Fact Pattern IV

Joel's passion was his Corvette Stingray. He spent almost all of his disposal income on customizing the exterior paint, the interior upholstery, special suspension, and a turbo charger that drastically increased the engine's horsepower. Joel derived great pleasure in cruising past local hangouts, revving the engine, and releasing the clutch so that the rear tires spun with a great deal of noise and smoke. Joel would then speed away for several blocks, turn around, and repeat the process. It was July Fourth weekend, and crowds at the hangouts, parks, and other public attractions were exceptionally heavy. Joel was cruising, looking for someone to impress with his car, when he saw a group of friends in the parking lot of a local deli. Joel cruised slowly by, gunned the engine and, accompanied by the noise of the engine and smoke from the tires, sped away. In Joel's path were two teenagers who were walking across the street in the middle of the block. Joel did not see them. Both were killed by the impact. Discuss the relevant crimes.

Hypothetical Fact Pattern V

Arthur's car could be charitably described as a wreck. Many areas of the body had rusted through, the interior upholstery was simply gone, and many of the electrical systems had to be coaxed to operate. The tread had long since disappeared from the tires; Arthur had simply ignored the distinctive noise of the wear bars. It was raining lightly one afternoon as Arthur drove to work, so the streets were wet, and in some areas, small puddles had formed. As Arthur approached an intersection, a rider on a motorcycle turned into Arthur's lane. Arthur applied his brakes, but the tread-less tires hydroplaned in the moisture; Arthur lost control of his car and collided with the motorcycle. The rider died the next day at the hospital. The medical examiner concluded that the cause of death was massive injury to several internal organs.

Drafting Activity

Please draft a section for the Texas Penal Code (or the code of your state or a state that does not have a provision for the crime of) voluntary manslaughter into the category of homicide.

Chapter 6

Crimes Against Property

Key Terms and Concepts

Theft	Robbery	Burglary
Define and Interpret	Arson	Robbery

6.1 Introduction

In many states, crimes against property will be found in different sections of the penal code. Crimes against property may include arson, robbery, burglary, theft, and other crimes that involve the destruction of personal or real property. In California, for example, Title 13 lists crimes against property, and it includes among the enumerated crimes arson, burglary, forgery, larceny, embezzlement, and false pretenses. California's code, in Chapter 12 of Title 12, lists crimes that pertain to the unlawful interference with property. As you will see by the headings, they provide useful guidance for understanding how the state categorizes and groups certain crimes. In the Illinois Criminal Code, Part C pertains to "Offenses Directed Against Property," and it includes, among others, theft, deception, robbery, burglary, and arson. In Florida, however, there is no general category for crimes against property. If you look at the various chapter headings in Title XLVI, "Crimes" of the Florida Statutes, you will see burglary and trespass listed together in Chapter 810, arson and criminal mischief listed together in Chapter 806, while theft, robbery, and related crimes are found in Chapter 812. How are crimes against property categorized and listed in your state? Find the section in your state criminal or penal code that pertains to offenses against property and see what crimes are listed under that heading. You will probably find at least some of the crimes already listed above since these are well known

Stop and Engage

crimes against property. For purposes of better understanding the elements of the more common crimes against property, we need to examine them in more detail in the following sections.

6.2 Theft

The crime of **theft** usually involves an act that deprives an owner of property without the owner's consent. Theft, in many instances, requires a "taking," an "appropriation" of the property of another. In Texas, for example, theft is defined in Chapter 31. Before you read any further, use an internet search engine to find Chapter 31 in the Texas Penal Code. What do you notice? Section 31.01 contains a significant number of definitions pertaining to terms such as "deception," "deprive," "appropriate," and "effective consent." Why is this important? Remember, we do not want to bring our everyday understanding of words to interpret legal terminology. In fact, we do not want to use an ordinary dictionary to interpret legal words. We need to first search the penal code to see if it provides definitions for terms used in these various sections—and sometimes these definitions are not in the particular section but in the "General Provisions." In Texas, Chapter 1 contains the General Provisions and Section 1.07 contains a number of definitions for terms used in the code. This is the reason you want to familiarize yourself with the layout of the penal code of your state or the state code you are using, so that you know where to find important information, such as definitions for terms. If there are no specific definitions for the words and legal terms in a code section, then you need to use case law to determine how the courts for that state (jurisdiction) have interpreted the legal terms and words in the relevant code section. You also may want to consult a legal dictionary to provide some further guidance and understanding of specific legal terms.

Explain the significance of Section 31.01 of the Texas Penal Code in understanding the crime of theft. Theft in the Texas Penal Code is defined in Section 31.03, which delineates it as follows:

> (a) A person commits an offense if he unlawfully appropriates property with intent to deprive the owner of property.
>
> (b) Appropriation of property is unlawful if:
>
> (1) it is without the owner's effective consent;
>
> (2) the property is stolen and the actor appropriates the property knowing it was stolen by another; or
>
> (3) the property in the custody of any law enforcement agency was explicitly represented by any law enforcement agent to the actor as being stolen and the actor appropriates the property believing it was stolen by another.

Learning Tip

Note the use of the words "appropriates" and "effective consent." When you read statutory language, it is important to read slowly and carefully through the words and to stop and ask, "Does this word need a definition?" "Is there a definition for any of these terms in this section of the code?" "Could there possibly be definitions for any of these terms in other sections of the code?" Do not presume that you know how to define words, such as "effective consent." Not only do you need to use the definitions provided in the code, but if no definitions are available, you need to find case law to understand how the courts in the jurisdiction have interpreted the terms. Why is this important? When you read a fact pattern, how will you analyze the facts by applying the appropriate code section and discussing whether the facts support the elements of the crime if you do not know how **to define and interpret** the elements of the crime? Since we have definitions for "appropriate," "deprive," and "property" in Section 31.01, we can now read Section 31.03(a):

> A person commits an offense if he unlawfully appropriates [= brings about a transfer or purported transfer of title to or other nonpossessory interest in property, whether to the actor or another; or acquires or otherwise exercise control over property other than real property] property [= real property; tangible or intangible personal property including anything severed from land; or a document, including money, that represents or embodies anything of value] with intent to deprive [= to withhold property from the owner permanently or for so extended a period of time that a major portion of the value or enjoyment of the property is lost to the owner; to restore property only upon payment of reward or other compensation; or to dispose of property in a manner that makes recovery of the property by the owner unlikely] the owner of property.

However, we cannot stop at this point since Section 31.03(b) provides further insight on the meaning of "unlawfully appropriates" as used in Section 31.03(a) by stating the following:

> Appropriation of property is unlawful if:
>
> (1) it is without the owner's effective consent;
>
> (2) the property is stolen and the actor appropriates the property knowing it was stolen by another; or
>
> (3) the property in the custody of any law enforcement agency was explicitly represented by any law enforcement agent to the actor as being stolen and the actor appropriates the property believing it was stolen by another.

Before you become too confused, review your original definition of theft in Section 31.03(a), "A person commits an offense if he unlawfully appropriates property with intent to deprive the owner of property." Since the "unlawfully appropriation of property" is a key to understanding the crime, you must insert Section 31.03(b) into 31.03(a), as we did above in reading Section 31.03(a), with the definitions supplied in Section 31.01. We would now read Section 31.03(a) in this way:

> A person commits an offense if he **unlawfully appropriates property** [unlawfully appropriates property under 31.01 = to bring about a transfer or purported transfer of title to or other nonpossessory interest in property, whether to the actor or another; or to acquire or otherwise exercise control over property other than real property + **31.03(b) = without the owners effective consent and "without effective consent" is found in Section 31.01**] = consent that is induced by deception or coercion; given by a person the actor knows is not legally authorized to act for the owner; given by a person who by reason of youth, mental disease or defect, or intoxication is known by the actor to be unable to make reasonable property dispositions; given solely to detect the commission of an offense; or given by a person who by reason of advanced age is known by the actor to have a diminished capacity to make informed and rational decisions about the reasonable disposition of property [this is where you know need to also refer to the definition of **deception** in Section 31.01] with intent **to deprive** the owner of property [and in Section 31.01 "deprive" means to withhold property from the owner permanently or for so extended a period of time that a major portion of the value or enjoyment of the property is lost to the owner; to restore property only upon payment of reward or other compensation; or to dispose of property in a manner that makes recovery of the property by the owner unlikely.

Unfortunately, we are not finished, since Section 31.03(c) provides further interpretive insights into how to support a claim of the unlawful appropriation of property. You can see that it is not sufficient to define theft as "a person commits an offense if he unlawfully appropriates property with intent to deprive the owner of property (Section 31.03(a)) since you cannot adequately apply the elements of that crime to a fact pattern or to the facts of a case without a further understanding of the meaning of "**unlawfully appropriates**," "**property**," and "**deprive**," and these words have interpretive clarifications and definitions in other sub-sections which require you to know the meaning of "**without effective consent**" as well as "**effective consent**" and "**deception**." The enormity of the task of interpreting and applying statutory language to fact patterns should become obvious to you. As you can probably guess, this takes substantial time and effort, and it cannot be accomplished in a few minutes or hours of preparation or study for an exam or test, or the completion of a homework assignment. The greatest assistance comes in taking the time when first reading the statutory language to make sure you find necessary definitions and interpretations, substituting them into the specific language of the crime so that you can learn it in its fullness, and then applying it correctly to a fact pattern or the discussion of a case analysis. You may also want to write your own paraphrase (using precision and specificity) for the statutory language so that you have a "working definition" for a reference when preparing a study outline or for class discussions.

Here is one example of a paraphrase for Section 31.03(a) of the Texas Penal Code crime of theft:

> Theft is the acquiring or exercising control over the property of another or bringing about or purporting to bring about a transfer of the title or a nonpossessory interest in the property either to the person committing the theft or to another of real property or tangible or intangible property or documents or money or anything that represents something of value without the owner's effective consent with the intent to deprive (withhold the property permanently or for an extended period of time so that a major portion of the enjoyment of the property is lost or to dispose of the property so that recovery of the property is unlikely) the owner of the property.

You can see that the paraphrased definition of theft above includes most of the language from the definitions of "appropriate," "deprive," "property" and "effective consent." It is not complete, but it covers the major points of the meaning of those words which are very important to a further understanding of the crime of theft. You will also note that there are still numerous factual determinations that are necessary when applying the elements of the crime and the definition of the crime to a specific set of facts. Some questions that you might ask to determine those facts are these: "What is control?" "What is an extended period of time?" "Has a major portion of the enjoyment of the property been lost?" "Is recovery unlikely?" These are the types of factual determinations you need to identify and discuss (wrestle with) when you are analyzing a fact pattern and writing a well-reasoned analysis.

How Would You Analyze This Fact Pattern?

> Isadora, a crack addict, worked part-time at a local fast food café that did not pay her nearly enough to support her addiction. She supplemented her wages by stealing. Isadora discovered that security at local flea markets was almost non-existent, and vendors were easily distracted. She found stealing from these vendors relatively easy—just waiting for an opportune time was all that was needed. One Sunday afternoon, Isadora stopped at a vendor who offered coins and other collectibles. Samples were displayed on a make-shift table, so Isadora waited until the vendor was occupied with another shopper, and she scooped up a handful of coins, stuffed them into her pocket,

and casually walked away. She walked to her car in the parking lot, placed the coins inside, locked the doors, and prepared to return to the selling area to find other victims. Unfortunately for Isadora, an off-duty policeman hired by the flea market was in an adjacent booth and saw her pocket the coins. He followed her to her car, and after she had placed the coins in her car, he arrested her for theft.

A Method for Analysis

- What is the crime? In this case we are analyzing this fact pattern in terms of the crime of theft. You may have fact patterns with multiple crimes.
- What is the definition for the crime of theft? You might find it helpful to jot the definition down on scratch paper if this were an exam, or write it out in full if this was homework or another type of assignment.
- What are the material elements of the crime of theft?
  - Unlawful appropriation
  - Of property
  - Without effective consent
  - With intent
  - To deprive the owner
  - Of the property
- Highlight, circle, or underline the material facts that you will use to argue for or against the applicability of the crime of theft to the facts. For example:

Isadora, a crack addict, worked part-time at a local fast food café that did not pay her nearly enough to support her addiction. She supplemented her wages by stealing. Isadora discovered that security at local flea markets was almost non-existent, and vendors were easily distracted. She found stealing from these vendors relatively easy—just waiting for an opportune time was all that was needed. One Sunday afternoon Isadora stopped at a vendor who offered coins and other collectibles. Samples were displayed on a make-shift table, so Isadora waited until the vendor was occupied with another shopper, and she scooped up a handful of coins, stuffed them into her pocket, and casually walked away. She walked to her car in the parking lot, placed the coins inside, locked the doors, and prepared to return to the selling area to find other victims. Unfortunately for Isadora, an off-duty policeman hired by the flea market was in an adjacent booth and saw her pocket the coins. He followed her to her car, and after she had placed the coins in her car, he arrested her for theft.

- Develop your analysis by applying the elements of the crime to the material facts of the case in a well-reasoned discussion (analysis).
- Reach a conclusion based on your well-reasoned analysis.

A Model Analysis

The issue is whether Isadora can be charged with the crime of theft under the Texas Penal Code. In Section 31.03(a), theft is defined as the unlawful appropriation of property with intent to deprive the owner of the property. Here are the key elements: (1) unlawfully appropriation of property and (2) intention to deprive.[1] The Penal Code defines "unlawful" appropriation as bringing about a transfer or purported transfer of title to or other nonpossessory interest in property or otherwise exercising control over the property if it occurred without the owner's "effective consent." Note, that explicit consent (written or oral permission) is not required. In Section 1.07(11), the TPC defines consent as "assent in fact, whether express or implied."[2] A reasonable person doctrine must be used to understand "implied" consent. Body movements, gestures, or eye contact are among the behaviors that a reasonable person might understand to be "consent" to engage in any questionable behavior. In this case, we must determine if Isadora brought about a transfer of the title of the property or otherwise exercised control over the property, the coins. When Isadora scooped up a handful of coins, stuffed them in her pocket, and casually walked away, the question is, did she at that point unlawfully appropriate the property? Isadora further walked to her car in the parking lot, placed the coins inside, and locked the doors. These facts tend to support the claim that Isadora was exercising control of the property without the owner's effective consent. The vendor took no action or engaged in any behavior which would indicate to Isadora that she had permission to take custody of the coins. Consequently, a reasonable person would understand that Isadora did not have consent, whether explicit or implied. However, we must also consider whether Isadora had intent to deprive the owner of the property, the coins. When Isadora placed the coins in her car and then locked the doors, it is arguable that she intended to drive away with them, permanently depriving the owner of his property. Based on these facts, it would appear that the police-

1. Notice that there is no *mens rea*. If the elements of the crime are satisfied, mental state of the offender is irrelevant.

2. § 1.07 (19) also defines effective consent as it applies to a third person. Clearly, there was no third person in this fact pattern, so this Section of the TPC is not appropriate.

man was wise in his decision to follow her until she made her intention obvious, and then he arrested her for theft. Since the facts appear to support a claim of unlawful appropriation of tangible property (the coins) with intent to deprive the owner of that property, I would conclude that Isadora can be charged and she is likely guilty of the crime of theft.

Opportunity for Further Practice

The discussion so far has been based on the definition of theft in the Texas Penal Code. How does Florida, for example, define the crime of theft in Section 812.014?

> (1) A person commits theft if he or she knowingly obtains or uses, or endeavors to obtain or to use, the property of another with intent to, either temporarily or permanently:
>
> (a) Deprive the other person of a right to the property or a benefit from the property.
>
> (b) Appropriate the property to his or her own use or to the use of any person not entitled to the use of the property.

Learning Tip

When you read this definition, what words require further interpretation and definition; Look at the phrase "obtains or uses"—does it need further interpretation or definition? In Section 812.012, several definitions are listed that pertain to the sections within Chapter 812 pertaining to "theft, robbery, and related crimes." A helpful tip is to look at the chapter or category heading in which the specific crime is grouped, and then review the sections or parts of that chapter or category to see if there is a definitions section that may apply to that category. Section 812.012(3) defines "obtains or uses" in this way:

> (a) Taking or exercising control over property; (b) Making any unauthorized use, disposition, or transfer of property; (c) Obtaining property by fraud, willful misrepresentation of a future act, or false promise; (d) 1. Conduct previously known as stealing; larceny; purloining; abstracting; embezzlement; misapplication; misappropriation; conversion; or obtaining money or property by false pretenses, fraud, or deception; or 2. Other conduct similar in nature.

Property is defined in Section 812.012(4) in the following way:

> Anything of value, and includes: (a) Real property, including things growing on, affixed to, and found in land; (b) Tangible or intangible personal property, including rights, privileges, interests, and claims; (c) Services.

What words have not been defined or interpreted by other terms in this Chapter 812?

- Deprive

- Appropriate the property
- Temporarily
- Anything of value

Once again you can see that you will need to know how the courts in Florida have interpreted these words when analyzing a case involving theft. Consider the following case.

Case Example: Practice Opportunity

Read the following case excerpt, and use a yellow highlighter to identify the material facts of the case; use a blue highlighter to note the relevant statutory language; use a pink highlighter to note the alleged crime; and use a green highlighter to note the court's application of the law to the facts of the case, to highlight the court's analysis.

Nooe v. State of Florida

892 So. 2d 1135 (2004)

The defendant appeals from his conviction for grand theft of over $100,000, a first degree felony, and his sentence of 35 months imprisonment followed by 25 years probation. The charge arose out of financial irregularities which occurred at the Rape Crisis Center of Volusia County, Inc., (Center) while the defendant served as its executive director. The defendant raises two primary issues on appeal, the first relating to the denial of his motions for judgment of acquittal. The second asserts he is entitled to a new trial because of the prejudicial admission of evidence and improper closing argument by the prosecutor. We conclude this appeal presents but one meritorious issue. Did the State prove a grand theft felony of the first degree, or does the evidence establish only a grand theft felony of the second degree? The defendant was charged by amended information with one count of grand theft over $100,000, a first degree felony.

The defendant argues that the trial court erred in denying his motions for judgment of acquittal because the State failed to prove that: (1) he was involved in any theft, or (2) if there was a theft, that it amounted to over $100,000. The defendant maintains that all the evidence showed was that the Center may have been mismanaged during his tenure as executive director but not that criminal conduct had occurred.

Before addressing the evidence, analysis of the omnibus theft statute, section 812.014, Florida Statutes, is necessary. This statute includes a variety of offenses related to unlawful appropriation of property, including larceny, obtaining by false pretenses and misappropriation. *Crawford v. State*, 453 So. 2d 1139

(Fla. 2d DCA 1984). *See also Thomas v. State*, 584 So. 2d 1022 (Fla. 1st DCA 1991). In particular, the theft statute provides:

> A person commits theft if he or she knowingly obtains or uses, or endeavors to obtain or to use, the property of another with intent to, either temporarily or permanently: (a) Deprive the other person of a right to the property or a benefit from the property.

§812.014(1)(a), Fla. Stat. In defining "obtains or uses," the theft chapter provides in pertinent part:

> "Obtains or uses" means any manner of:....
>
> [1] [c]onduct previously known as stealing; larceny; purloining; abstracting; *embezzlement*; misapplication; misappropriation; conversion; or obtaining money or property by false pretenses, fraud, or deception.... §812.012(2)(d)1, Fla. Stat. (emphasis added).

In certain types of thefts, such as larceny or false pretenses, criminal intent must be formed at the time of the original taking. *State v. Siegel*, 778 So. 2d 426 (Fla. 5th DCA 2001) and *Szilagyi v. State*, 564 So. 2d 644 (Fla. 4th DCA 1990), hold that when the crime is larceny, the State must prove that the defendant knowingly obtained or endeavored to obtain the property of another, with intent to deprive the owner of property, and the State must prove that the felonious intent existed at the time of the taking. In considering this prosecution under section 812.014, this Court considers whether the evidence presented by the State was legally sufficient to establish any of the traditional common law offenses embraced within the statutory definition of theft. *Crawford*, 453 So. 2d at 1141.

The defendant initially argues that no competent evidence of a theft from Florida's Department of Health (Department) or the Center was presented. The defendant points out that the Department's representative, Nancy Linehan, had no independent knowledge that the defendant unlawfully took sums from the Department during the period charged in the amended information. Linehan, however, testified that the Department disbursed $70,125.65 during the time period alleged in the information to the Center based on invoices submitted by the Center through the defendant, its executive director, invoices which reflected the monies were being used for rape education programs but which other evidence, including the defendant's own admission made during an investigation, established had been falsified. The defendant's claim on appeal that his "admission or confession" was insufficient to support his conviction because corpus delicti was not established is without merit.

The State introduced the actual invoices labeled as "falsified" as well as the testimony of Michele Jones, the assistant director of the Center during the defendant's tenure. Jones testified that the defendant had knowingly signed and submitted fraudulent invoices to the Department for rape education programs which had never been conducted. The defendant thus obtained $70,125.65 from the State, Department of Health, by false pretenses, fraud or deception.

The defendant seems to assert something akin to a "Robin Hood" defense, that as executive director of the not-for-profit Center, he could not be guilty of theft of money from a State agency, perhaps because some of the money he obtained may have actually been used for good works, albeit not those good works for which he represented the monies would be used. We categorically reject the defendant's contention that as executive director of the not-for profit Center he could not, working in his director capacity, have effected a theft of funds from a State agency. A corporation, whether for profit or not-for-profit, operates through its officers and agents. *See Browning v. State*, 133 So. 847 (Fla. 1931). Further, the jury could have easily found that in acquiring this money the defendant had the requisite criminal intent which would support a theft conviction. *See Brewer v. State*, 413 So. 2d 1217 (Fla. 5th DCA 1982). This is particularly true given the evidence that the defendant wrongfully used money belonging to the Center (see discussion *infra*). While the State did not adduce evidence directly tracing the entire $70,125.65 into the defendant's own pockets, in a prosecution under section 812.014, the State needed only show that the defendant obtained the property of the Department with the intent to either temporarily or permanently deprive that entity of its right to the property. The fact that the defendant obtained the money from the Department through false pretenses while serving as executive director of the Center does not detract from the criminality.

The defendant erroneously relies on *Davis v. State*, 424 So. 2d 875 (Fla. 1st DCA 1982) for the proposition that "felonious intent" was not established. In *Davis*, a city manager's conviction for grand theft in regard to money issued to him by the city comptroller for mileage and per diem expenses for a convention to which the city manager did not himself drive, was reversed. The appellate court pointed out that the evidence did not show that the defendant knew the monies he received included money for mileage and further failed to show that the defendant used expense money for anything other than a proper municipal purpose. Contrast that situation to the evidence presented in this case. Much, if not all of the $70,125.65 received from the Department was not used for its intended purpose, rape prevention education programs. As further discussion will show, there was direct evidence reflecting that at least some of this money was used for improper purposes such as personal expenses and personal payments to employees. While the State adduced overwhelming evidence showing that the defendant had committed a theft from the Department, the question exists as to whether the State established the offense of grand theft of over $100,000, a first degree felony. Section 812.014 (2), Florida Statutes, provides in relevant part: (2)(a)1. If the property stolen is valued at $100,000 or more:.... the offender commits grand theft in the first degree, punishable as a felony of the first degree, as provided in Section 775.082, s. 775.083, or s. 775.084. (b)1. If the property stolen is valued at $20,000 or more, but less than $100,000;.... the offender commits grand theft in the second degree, punishable as a felony of the second degree, as provided in s. 775.082, 775.083, or s. 775.084.

Section 812.012(9) defines "Value" for the purpose of the theft statute and provides in relevant part: (c) Amounts of value of separate properties involved in thefts committed pursuant to one scheme or course of conduct, whether the thefts are from the same person or from several persons, may be aggregated in determining the grade of the offense. Thus, if one scheme or course of conduct is involved, the takings could be combined to reach the $100,000 threshold, even if multiple victims are involved. The defendant relies on *State v. Diaz*, 814 So. 2d 466 (Fla. 3d DCA 2002), in arguing that the annual contracts between the Center and the Department, whereby grants were disbursed to the Center, were separate and distinct and that the thefts during each annual contract period could not be aggregated. In *Diaz*, the defendant was charged with first degree grand theft in connection with 23 individual invoices he had submitted to Dade County over a period of 11 months for landscaping work in connection with Hurricane Andrew repairs. Each invoice was for specific foliage for a specific area. The defendant successfully moved to dismiss the charge as to 22 of the invoices which were outside the five year statute of limitations for grand theft. The appellate court affirmed over a strong dissent by Judge Cope. The majority rejected the State's claim that all 23 invoices were part of a common scheme to defraud the county and should be treated as a continuing offense within the five year statute of limitations. The majority explained that the theft statute "is silent on the issue of continuing offenses, with no suggestion that the legislature intended to make grand theft a continuing offense" 814 So. 2d at 467. The majority held that "[e]ach invoice was a separate taking, concluding the specific work requested in each county purchase order." *Id.*

The monies taken from the Department could properly be aggregated so that a theft of $70,125.65 was established. Likewise, theft of Center funds could be aggregated with the takings from the Department, given that some of the grant money obtained from the Department was misappropriated by the defendant from the Center for the defendant's and Michele Jones' personal use. The State adduced evidence that the defendant wrote 11 checks totaling $3,535.94 on the Center account made payable to his ex-wife ostensibly for her "insurance." While the defendant was entitled to insurance as part of his benefits package, the president of the Center's Board of Directors at the time the defendant was hired testified that the defendant was never told anything which would have justified these payments out of Center checking funds. The defendant signed 18 checks totaling $5,830 to pay Jones' husband's IRS debt, once again an expense of a personal nature which had not been knowingly authorized for payment by the Board. The defendant also approved a "loan" totaling $4,500 out of Center funds to Jones for personal expenses. There was evidence, including the defendant's own admission to investigators, that he charged personal expenses on Center credit cards though it appears that the sums involved were relatively modest, approximately $2,500. These sums amount to $16,365.94 and combined with the monies obtained from the Department by fraudulent invoices, total $86,491.59. The State, in order to meet the $100,000 threshold, sought additionally to rely on a $23,545.76 federal tax lien which arose due to the defendant's failure to remit employee payroll tax withholding to the IRS over an 18 month period.

The State contends that substantial competent evidence was adduced that the Center had specifically sought and received grant money from the State which money was earmarked for payment to the IRS of the Center's payroll taxes/withholding but which the defendant did not use for such designated purpose. The State relies on the testimony of Carol Pozella in this regard. Pozella testified over objection regarding grants obtained by the Center by way of the Victims of Crime Act (VOCA). She testified based on grant documents and was permitted to testify from VOCA grant application forms of the Center which contained columns reflecting money claimed by the preparer to have already been spent to pay the social security and income tax obligations of Center employees. Pozella's testimony was used to explain the income tax and social security tax reimbursement provisions of the VOCA grant forms but not to place a final figure on the precise amounts involved in this case. The problem with Pozella's testimony regarding the VOCA grants and documents is that while she understood VOCA grant forms, she was allowed to testify regarding the content of Center documents which were not prepared by her and which were not introduced into evidence by the records custodian. It does not appear that the State had these documents authenticated through a subsequent witness affiliated with the Department or Center. Accordingly, it was error to allow Pozella to testify based on the contents of these documents and her testimony in this regard was not competent to show that the defendant had, on behalf of the Center, expressly sought and obtained grant money based on his representation that said money was earmarked for payment of the $23,545.76 due the IRS.

Michelle Jones testified that VOCA grant money was designed to cover IRS payments but it is not clear from her testimony that the defendant, in obtaining this money, had fraudulently represented that such payments had been or would be made. The admissible evidence adduced by the State did not exclude the defendant's reasonable hypothesis of innocence that mismanagement of Center finances resulted in his failure to transmit funds to the IRS. Indeed, there was evidence presented in the State's case that while the defendant served as executive director, an expansion of the Center was undertaken to other locations in the county. Additional employees were hired, additional facilities were set up and the Center's administrative offices were transferred from Daytona Beach to Ormond Beach. Substantial raises were given to employees. The defendant had indicated to the IRS that the Center did not have enough money to pay everything. There was no direct evidence that the defendant, rather than transmitting the $23,545.76 to the IRS, misappropriated the money. The circumstantial evidence as regards the failure to remit payment of the payroll taxes to the IRS is entirely consistent with non-criminal financial mismanagement. We analogize this case to *Benitez v. State*, 852 So. 2d 386 (Fla. 3d DCA 2003), where the Third District reversed a grand theft conviction because the State's evidence was not inconsistent with the defendant's reasonable hypothesis of innocence on the issue of felonious intent. The evidence showed that the defendant ran into unforeseen problems with a home renovation project and it failed to establish that the defendant had acted with an intent to deprive the homeowners of their money. Because we conclude the State failed to equate non-payment of the monies to the IRS with the defendant's theft of the $23,545.76, the defendant was entitled to a judgment of acquittal as to that element of the prosecution. The evidence then, at most, would reflect theft of $86,491.59, and not an amount in excess of $100,000. The defendant's theft conviction accordingly must be reduced to grand theft, a felony of the second degree ($20,000–$100,000). We have thoroughly reviewed the record and find no abuse of discretion in connection with the denial of the defendant's motion for new trial. *See Woods v. State*, 733 So. 2d 980 (Fla. 1999)

The conviction for grand theft, a felony of the first degree, is reversed and the cause remanded to the trial court with directions to reduce the conviction to grand theft, a second degree felony, and to re-sentence the defendant. Affirmed.

Stop and Engage

Now that you have highlighted key parts from this case, complete the following activities:

- Identify the main issue(s) in this case.
- Write a concise summary of the material facts.
- Paraphrase the relevant statutory language with precision and accuracy.
- Write a concise summary of the court's reasoning.
- Write a concise explanation as to how and why the court reached its decision—its holding.

Further Study

Find the definition for theft in your state penal or criminal code. Which terms require definition and interpretation? How would you paraphrase your state's definition of theft using precision and specificity? How does your state's definition of theft differ from that of Florida or Texas?

6.3 Robbery

Robbery is defined differently by different states, and in some instances, is considered the crime of larceny with the added element of a threat of violence. Some define robbery as the taking of money or goods by force or intimidation or with the intent to permanently deprive the owner of the property. You will note that in a general discussion of robbery, there may be questions, such as, how does robbery differ from larceny? How is robbery different from theft? So, in order to answer these questions, you must have a good understanding of the definition of each of the crimes and then note how they are similar and different from other crimes in the same or a related category. This is important for purposes of analyzing a fact pattern since it will not always be obvious from the facts what crime has been committed, and the responsibility to be able to identify the material facts of the case so that you can consider them in the context of the definitions of possible applicable crimes and then discuss how those crimes may or may not be applicable based on those material facts lies with you. Consider this very simple example:

Fact Pattern Example

> Paul is visiting Susan at her apartment. While Susan is preparing some snacks in the kitchen, Paul takes a gold ring from Susan's night table and places it in his pocket. When Susan brings the snacks from the kitchen, Paul picks up the knife to slice some cheese and points the knife at Susan, commanding her to take off her gold necklace. Susan, shaking with fear, takes off the necklace and hands it to Paul. Paul runs out of the apartment and heads to the train station where he catches a train to another state. Paul can be charged with what crime(s)?

In order to answer the question posed in this fact pattern, you need to be very familiar with the definitions and elements of various crimes since the "call of the question" is "Paul can be charged with what crime(s)?" How would you answer this question?

- First, highlight the material facts.

  Paul is visiting Susan at her apartment. While Susan is preparing some snacks in the kitchen, Paul takes a gold ring from Susan's night table and places it in his pocket. When Susan brings the snacks from the kitchen, Paul picks up the knife to slice some cheese and points the knife at Susan, commanding her to take off her gold necklace. Susan, shaking with fear takes off the necklace and hands it to Paul. Paul runs out of the apartment and heads to the train station where he catches a train to another state.

- Second, based on the material facts, how many crimes can you identify?

This is where you will have a problem if you do not know the definitions of the crimes and the elements of those crimes. Based on the crimes you have studied so far, what crimes are possibly applicable? As of now, it appears that the crime of theft may be applicable, but in order to determine if other crimes are applicable, you need to know the definitions of other crimes. So, place a bookmark on the fact pattern, and we will return to it after we learn about robbery by reviewing the definition of the crime in a few state penal codes.

How is robbery defined in New York?

> Article 160: Robbery is forcible stealing. A person forcibly steals property and commits robbery when, in the course of committing a larceny, he uses or threatens the immediate use of physical force upon another person for the purpose of:
>
> 1. Preventing or overcoming resistance to the taking of the property or to the retention thereof immediately after the taking; or
>
> 2. Compelling the owner of such property or another person to deliver up the property or to engage in other conduct which aids in the commission of the larceny.

In order to understand the definition of robbery, you need to know the definition of larceny. Larceny is found in Article 155, and it includes various sections from 155.00 to 155.45. Section 155.05 defines larceny at length and has many sub-parts and definitions, so it would be helpful to use an internet search engine to find it and read it in detail. Here is an excerpt for purposes of forming a working definition for robbery.

> A person steals property and commits larceny when, with intent to deprive another of property or to appropriate the same to himself or to a third person, he wrongfully takes, obtains or withholds such property from an owner thereof.
>
> 2. Larceny includes a wrongful taking, obtaining or withholding of another's property, with the intent prescribed in subdivision one of this section, committed in any of the following ways:
>
> (a) By conduct heretofore defined or known as common law larceny by trespassory taking, common law larceny by trick, embezzlement, or obtaining property by false pretenses;
>
> (b) By acquiring lost property.
>
> A person acquires lost property when he exercises control over property of another which he knows to have been lost or mislaid, or to have been delivered under a mistake as to the identity of the recipient or the nature or amount of the property, without taking reasonable measures to return such property to the owner;
>
> (c) By committing the crime of issuing a bad check, as defined in section 190.05;
>
> (d) By false promise.

How would you write your own definition for robbery under the laws of New York? Here is one paraphrased definition:

> A person forcibly steals property and commits robbery when, with intent to deprive another of property, he wrongfully takes, obtains, or withholds such property from an owner by threats of the immediate use of physical force for the purpose of the taking of property or by the compelling of the owner of such property or another person to deliver up the property.

If you read the paraphrased definition above carefully, you would note that some of the language from the crime of larceny has been inserted into the definition since robbery requires an act of larceny. Based on the definition of robbery in New York, could you also charge Paul with robbery? Based on what material facts?

Before we analyze the fact pattern and identify the appropriate crimes, it is helpful to review the definition of robbery in a few other states. How is robbery defined in Texas? Robbery is found in Title 7, Offenses against Property, and more specifically in Chapter 29. Use an internet search engine to find Chapter 29 of the Texas Penal Code. You will note that Chapter 29 has a number of different sections, and it starts with definitions in Section 29.01. Remember to always find definitions and read them to assist you in interpreting the words in the definition of the crime since you do not want to use your own definition or understanding to interpret legal terms. Robbery is specifically defined in Section 29.02 in this way:

> (a) A person commits an offense if, in the course of committing theft as defined in Chapter 31 and with intent to obtain or maintain control of the property, he:
>
> (1) Intentionally, knowingly, or recklessly causes bodily injury to another; or
>
> (2) Intentionally or knowingly threatens or places another in fear of imminent bodily injury or death.

In Texas, in order to fully understand the definition of robbery, you would need to refer to the crime of theft and insert the elements of theft into the definition of robbery. Do you notice that in New York, robbery requires that there be the commission of larceny, and in Texas, robbery requires the commission of theft? What about California? In the California Penal Code, robbery is found in Title 9, Crimes against the Person, and it is found in Chapter 4, Sections 211-215. Use an internet search engine to find the crime of robbery in the California Penal Code. In Section 211, robbery is defined in the following terms:

> The felonious taking of personal property in the possession of another, from his person or immediate presence, and against his will, accomplished by means of force or fear.

Notice that in California, robbery does not include another crime. You would not need to refer to theft (as in Texas) or larceny (as in New York). How is robbery defined in Florida? Robbery is found in Title XLVI, Chapter 812, and specifically in Section 812.13. Use an internet search engine to find the crime of robbery in the Florida statutes. In Florida, robbery is defined in this way:

> The taking of money or other property which may be the subject of larceny from the person or custody of another, with intent to either permanently or temporarily deprive the person or

> the owner of the money or other property, when in the course of the taking there is the use of force, violence, assault, or putting in fear.

Notice that in Florida, the crime of robbery refers to larceny, and therefore, you need to review the definition of larceny in order to understand the definition of robbery. Larceny is generally defined as the unlawful taking of another's property with the intent to deprive the owner of its use. Therefore, in Florida, in order to establish the crime of robbery, you would need to have facts that support the unlawful taking of money or property of another with intent to either permanently or temporarily deprive the person or the owner of the money or other property, when, in the course of the taking, there is the use of force, violence, assault, or putting in fear.

Before we return to Paul and Susan (our hypothetical fact pattern), we will review one more state. Ohio defines robbery in Section 2911.02 in this detail:

> (A) No person, in attempting or committing a theft offense or in fleeing immediately after the attempt or offense, shall do any of the following:
>
> (1) Have a deadly weapon on or about the offender's person or under the offender's control;
> (2) Inflict, attempt to inflict, or threaten to inflict physical harm on another;
>
> (3) Use or threaten the immediate use of force against another.

Once again, as in Texas, Ohio refers to the crime of theft in its definition of robbery. Theft in Ohio is defined in Chapter 2913.02 in the following way:

> (A) No person, with purpose to deprive the owner of property or services, shall knowingly obtain or exert control over either the property or services in any of the following ways:
>
> (1) Without the consent of the owner or person authorized to give consent;
> (2) Beyond the scope of the express or implied consent of the owner or person authorized to give consent;
> (3) By deception;
> (4) By threat;
>
> (5) By intimidation.

How would you write a definition for robbery in Ohio? One example is:

> No person, with the purpose to deprive the owner of property or services, shall inflict, attempt to inflict, or threaten to inflict physical harm on another or use or threaten the immediate use

of force against another to knowingly obtain or exert control over either the property or the services.

Now that we have reviewed the law for robbery in several states, we can return to the "call of the question" in the hypothetical fact pattern—Paul can be charged with what crime(s)? Remember, we left off with the second bullet point question—how many crimes can you identify from the material facts? Based on your knowledge of the definitions of crimes discussed in this chapter, what crimes are applicable to Paul's actions? Once you have identified the crimes based on the material facts, you can now prepare a model answer by applying the elements of the crimes to the material facts and developing a well-reasoned analysis and then answering the "call of the question." For purposes of this model answer, we will use the law of Texas. You can write your own model answer using the applicable laws from your state.

Model Answer

The issue under this fact pattern is to determine what crimes Paul has committed based on the facts. In reading the fact pattern, we note that while Susan is preparing some snacks in the kitchen, Paul takes a gold ring from Susan's night table and places it in his pocket. At this point we may have sufficient facts to discuss the crime of theft. In Texas, theft is defined as the unlawful appropriation of property with intent to deprive the owner of that property. The Texas Penal Code (TPC) further defines unlawful appropriation as taking the property without the owner's consent. When Paul takes the gold ring from Susan's night stand and places it in his pocket while she is in the kitchen, he is taking the property of another without consent. Paul's placing of the ring in his pocket is indicative of his intent to deprive the owner of the property. It would, therefore, appear that the elements of the crime of theft are satisfied by the facts.

When Susan brings the snacks from the kitchen, Paul picks up the knife to slice some cheese and points the knife at Susan and commands her to take off her gold necklace. Susan, shaking with fear, takes off the necklace and hands it to Paul. Paul runs out of the apartment and heads to the train station where he catches a train to another state. At this point, we may have sufficient facts to discuss the crime of robbery. In Texas, robbery is defined as, in the course of committing theft there is intent to obtain or maintain control of property with either the *mens rea* of intentionally or knowingly threatening or placing another in fear of imminent bodily injury or death. Under the TPC, a person acts intentionally, or with intent, with respect to the nature of his conduct or to a result of his conduct when it is his conscious objective or desire to engage in the conduct or cause the result. A person acts knowingly, or with knowledge, with respect to the nature of his conduct or to circumstances surrounding his conduct when he is aware of the nature of his conduct or that the circumstances exist. A person acts knowingly, or with knowledge, with respect to a result of his conduct when he is aware that his conduct is reasonably certain to cause the result. When Paul picks up the knife, he is demonstrating an act of intent that would satisfy the *mens rea* of "intentionally" since it is his conscious desire to engage in the conduct, and he points the knife at Susan when he commands her to take off her necklace. At the point that Paul forces Susan, who is shaking with fear, to take off her necklace and hand it to him so that he can run out of the apartment, he is exhibiting not only the commission of a theft, the unlawful appropriation of property with intent to deprive the owner of that property, which is a required part of the definition of robbery, but he is also intending to maintain control of the property as he heads to the train station to catch a train to another state. It is evident from the facts that the intentional use of the knife to command Susan to hand over the necklace and Susan's shaking with fear satisfy the elements of knowingly threatening or placing another in fear of imminent bodily injury or death since Paul could immediately use the knife to commit bodily injury or even kill Susan. Based on this analysis, it would appear that we could also charge Paul with the crime of robbery under the TPC. In answer to the call of the question, we can charge Paul with the crimes of theft and robbery under the TPC.

6.4 Arson

Arson, as you can imagine, pertains to acts that involve fires or explosions that result in physical injury or harm. Many states have numerous degrees of arson. Rhode Island, for example, has seven different degrees of arson listed in Section 11-4-2. In Washington State, arson in the first and second degree and then reckless burning in the first and second degree as well as malicious mischief in three degrees are all listed in Chapter 9A.48. For purposes of this section, we will examine the definition of arson in a few states and see how we can develop some working definitions for the crime as well as identify the material elements of the crime.

In Title 13, Chapter 1, of the California Penal Code, arson is defined in Section 451 in this way:

> A person is guilty of arson when he or she willfully and maliciously sets fire to or burns or causes to be burned or who aids, counsels, or procures the burning of, any structure, forest land, or property.

Based on the definition of arson in California, what material elements comprise the crime? What is the *mens rea*? The definition states that "a person is guilty of arson when he or she willfully and maliciously.... In order to know how to interpret the *mens rea* you need to know the meaning of "maliciously." In Section 450, definitions that apply to the crimes in Title 13, Chapter 1, are given, and one of those definitions is found in Section 450(e) where "maliciously" is defined as follows:

> A wish to vex, defraud, annoy, or injure another person, or intent to do a wrongful act, established either by proof or presumption of law.

Learning Tip

Note, however, that the definition of the crime in Section 451 states "willfully and maliciously." We have the definition for "maliciously" in Section 450 right above Section 451; however, no definition is provided for "willfully" in Section 450? What step do you take at this point? You read through the rest of Chapter 1 of Title 13 to see if there is a definition—and in this case there is no definition. Do you stop and just use your own interpretation for "willfully," or do you look it up in an online dictionary? No. Remember, you learned that most state penal or criminal codes have a general definitions section and/or a section that defines states of culpability or mental states. In California, if you search through the Table of Contents of the California Penal Code, you will note that there are "Preliminary Provisions" in Section 2-24. Here, you have to think strategically, and use inductive reasoning. No heading exists for "general provisions," but "preliminary provisions" would serve a similar purpose, so you need to search through those sections. In Section 7 of the "Preliminary Provisions," you read this: "The following words have in this code the signification attached to them in this section, unless otherwise apparent from the context," and in 7.1, you find a definition for "willfully."

> The word "willfully," when applied to the intent, with which an act is done or omitted, implies simply a purpose or willingness to commit the act, or make the omission referred to. It does not require any intent to violate law, or to injure another, or to acquire any advantage.

Now that you have a definition for willfully and maliciously, you can proceed with interpreting the definition of the crime of arson under Section 451. We have identified the *mens rea* as willfully and maliciously, so now we need to find the *actus reus*. The *actus reus* is "sets fire to or burns or causes to be burned any structure, forest land, or property." The *actus reus* can also be "aids, counsels, or procures the burning of any structure, forest land, or property." Therefore, based on the definition of "a person willfully and maliciously causes to be burned an individual," can you charge the person with the crime of arson? The answer is no because an individual is not a structure, forest land, or property. To further understand the complete meaning of the crime of arson as defined in Section 451, you also need to know the definition for "structure," "forest land," and "property." These terms are all defined in Section 450. Use an internet search engine to find and read the definitions for these terms. At this point, you can create a precise and specific paraphrase of the California crime of arson.

Practical Application

Write a precise and concise paraphrase of the crime of arson based on the California Penal Code.

Arson, under the Texas Penal Code is found in Chapter 28 and is defined more specifically in Section 28.02(a) in this way:

> A person commits an offense if the person starts a fire, regardless of whether the fire continues after ignition, or causes an explosion with intent to destroy or damage:
>
> (1) any vegetation, fence, or structure on open-space land; or
> (2) any building, habitation, or vehicle:
>
> (A) knowing that it is within the limits of an incorporated city or town;
>
> (B) knowing that it is insured against damage or destruction;
>
> (C) knowing that it is subject to a mortgage or other security interest;
>
> (D) knowing that it is located on property belonging to another;
>
> (E) knowing that it has located within it property belonging to another; or
>
> (F) when the person is reckless about whether the burning or explosion will endanger the life of some individual or the safety of the property of another.
>
> (a-1) A person commits an offense if the person recklessly starts a fire or causes an explosion while manufacturing or attempting to manufacture a controlled substance and the fire or explosion damages any building, habitation, or vehicle.
>
> (a-2) A person commits an offense if the person intentionally starts a fire or causes an explosion and in so doing:
>
> (1) recklessly damages or destroys a building belonging to another; or
>
> (2) recklessly causes another person to suffer bodily injury or death.

> (b) It is an exception to the application of Subsection (a)(1) that the fire or explosion was a part of the controlled burning of open-space land.
>
> (c) It is a defense to prosecution under Subsection (a)(2)(A) that prior to starting the fire or causing the explosion, the actor obtained a permit or other written authorization granted in accordance with a city ordinance, if any, regulating fires and explosions.

Based on this definition, what is the required *mens rea*? Is it different depending upon the *actus reus*? It appears in Section 28.02(1) or 2(a)-(e) that no required *mens rea* is present—that the person must start a fire with "intent to destroy or damage;" whereas in 2(f) the *mens rea* is "recklessly." At this point, you want to refresh your recollection of the definitions for the culpable mental states. Where are these listed in the Texas Penal Code? If you review the table of contents, you will find them in Chapter 6, and specifically, in Section 6.03. "Recklessly" is defined in this way:

> A person acts recklessly, or is reckless, with respect to circumstances surrounding his conduct or the result of his conduct when he is aware of but consciously disregards a substantial and unjustifiable risk that the circumstances exist or the result will occur. The risk must be of such a nature and degree that its disregard constitutes a gross deviation from the standard of care that an ordinary person would exercise under all the circumstances as viewed from the actor's standpoint.

What else do you need to know to form a proper understanding of the definition of arson in Section 28.02? Do you need to know how the Texas Penal Code defines "habitation," "building," and "property?" Would you refer to the general provisions in Chapter 1 and the definitions in Section 1.07 first, or would you see if Chapter 28 lists any definitions specifically connected to the crimes listed therein? You always want to see if definitions specifically related to your crime are defined in the same chapter or section as that crime before you look for definitions in the general provisions or general definition section that is applicable to the entire code. You always want to use the narrower and more specifically related definitions and provisions in your interpretation. In this instance, there are definitions in Section 28.01 which is entitled "Definitions; in this chapter ..." and since the definition of arson, in Section 28.02, is in Chapter 28, you would want to use the definitions in Section 28.01 before using definitions from or in place of any definitions in the general definitions in Section 1.07. Remember to always make sure you look to see if definitions for each word in the crime are listed rather than using your own understanding or using a generic dictionary to search for a definition. Never presume that you know how to define a word in the code, even a word as simple as "building" or "habitation." The definitions of these types of words can be crucial to a proper interpretation of a crime and to the applicability of the elements of the crime to a particular set of facts. Many cases have been based on how these words are interpreted and applied to the facts of a particular case.

Case Example: Practice Opportunity

Read the following case excerpt, and use a yellow highlighter to identify the material facts of the case; use a blue highlighter to note the relevant statutory language; use a pink highlighter to note the alleged crime; and use a green highlighter to note the court's application of the law to the facts of the case, to highlight the court's analysis.

Scruggs v. The State of Texas

Court of Appeals of Texas, 14th District (May 20, 2010)

In 2003, Penny Thompson rented a farmhouse near Grandview, Texas where she met appellant who was working as a handyman on the house. Thompson's relationship with appellant soured and she made plans to move out of the house. On the day of the fire, Thompson, along with several friends and relatives, began moving Thompson's possessions out of the house. Appellant arrived at the house and told Thompson to remove all of her belongings because he was "going to torch the place." According to several witnesses, when Thompson began packing her things, appellant became agitated and began hitting his head against the walls of the house. Two of Thompson's sons attempted to calm appellant by escorting him outside. Appellant, however, failed to calm down and returned to the house. He walked into the kitchen, grabbed a piece of paper, walked into the dining room, lit the paper, and threw it onto a folded roll-a-way mattress positioned next to an interior wall. As he threw the paper onto the mattress, appellant said, "See, Penny, I told you I'd do it." When the mattress caught fire, appellant walked into a nearby bathroom and picked up a plastic bucket used to catch water draining from the sink. Appellant returned to the dining room, said, "Here, I'll help," and threw the contents of the bucket onto the mattress. When the liquid reached the fire, the flames immediately engulfed the mattress and spread to the nearby wall. Thompson's sons attempted to roll the mattress out of the house, but were unable to move it past the living room. Thompson remembered that a propane tank was being stored in the living room and warned everyone to evacuate the house. After everyone was safely outside, an explosion occurred and the house was engulfed in flames. Appellant turned to Thompson as they watched the house burn and said, "You're next." Appellant was subsequently arrested and convicted of arson.

In a single issue, appellant challenges the legal and factual sufficiency of the evidence to support his conviction. When reviewing legal sufficiency, we view all the evidence in the light most favorable to the verdict and then determine whether a rational jury could have found the essential elements of the crime beyond a reasonable doubt. *Hooper v. State*, 214 S.W.3d 9, 13 (Tex. Crim. App. 2007). The jury, as the trier-of-fact, is the sole judge of the credibility of witnesses. *See Moreno v. State*, 755 S.W.2d 866, 867 (Tex. Crim. App. 1988). The jury chooses whether to believe all or part of a witness's testimony. *See id.* We do not engage in a second evaluation of the weight and credibility of the evidence, but only ensure the jury reached a rational decision.

In a factual sufficiency review, we consider all the evidence in a neutral light. *Prible v. State*, 175 S.W.3d 724, 730-31 (Tex. Crim. App. 2005). The evidence may be factually insufficient in two ways. Id. at 731. First, when considered by itself, the evidence supporting the verdict may be so weak that the verdict is clearly wrong and manifestly unjust. *Id.* Second, where the evidence both supports and contradicts the verdict, the contrary evidence may be strong enough that the beyond-a-reasonable-doubt standard could not have been met. *Id.* In conducting a factual sufficiency review, we must employ appropriate deference so we do not substitute our judgment for that of the fact finder. *Jones v. State*, 944 S.W.2d 642, 648 (Tex. Crim. App. 1996). Our analysis must consider the evidence appellant claims is most important in allegedly undermining the jury's verdict. Appellant argues that the evidence is legally and factually insufficient to support his conviction because the evidence only proves that appellant caused a fire to the mattress, but that he did not intend to destroy the house. A person commits arson if the person starts a fire, regardless of whether the fire continues after ignition, or causes an explosion with intent to destroy or damage any building, habitation, or vehicle. Tex. Penal Code Ann. art. 28.02(a)(2) (Vernon Supp. 2009). A person commits arson with specific intent to damage or destroy a building, habitation, or vehicle if it is the person's conscious objective or desire to engage in the conduct or cause the result. *Beltran v. State*, 593 S.W.2d 688, 689 (Tex. Crim. App. 1980); *Prejean v. State*, 704 S.W.2d 119, 121 (Tex. App.–Houston [1st Dist.] 1986, no pet.). While intent may not be inferred from the mere act of burning, it may be inferred from the defendant's acts, words, and conduct.

In this case, the jury may have inferred that appellant intended to damage or destroy the house based on the following evidence: Appellant was agitated and told Thompson to remove all her possessions because he was "going to torch the place." After lighting the mattress on fire, appellant said, "See, Penny, I told you I'd do it."Appellant threatened Thompson after the house was engulfed in flames. Appellant made no attempt to stop the fire other than pouring the unknown liquid, which accelerated the fire. Viewing the evidence in the light most favorable to the verdict, we conclude that a rational trier-of-fact could have found beyond a reasonable doubt that appellant had the specific intent to damage or destroy the house when he started the fire.

In arguing that the evidence is factually insufficient, appellant argues that when he poured the unknown liquid he was attempting to douse the fire. He further contends that he helped Thompson's sons attempt to remove the burning mattress from the house. With regard to the unknown liquid, each of the witnesses at trial testified that the water pressure in the house was so low there would have been no time to fill a bucket with water. They also testified that the bucket appellant took from the bathroom was used to collect waste from the bathroom sink. The waste included water and any other chemical used in the sink. Further, each of the witnesses testified that appellant did not aid Thompson's sons in their attempt to remove the mattress from the house.

Viewing the evidence in a neutral light, we conclude that the evidence is not so weak that the jury's verdict is clearly wrong and manifestly unjust or that the verdict is against the great weight and preponderance of the evidence. Appellant's issue is overruled. The judgment of the trial court is affirmed.

Stop and Engage

Now that you have highlighted key parts from this case, complete the following activities:

- Identify the main issue(s) in this case.
- Write a concise summary of the material facts.
- Paraphrase the relevant statutory language with precision and accuracy.
- Write a concise summary of the court's reasoning.
- Write a concise explanation as to how and why the court reached its decision—its holding.

6.5 Burglary

When you think of the crime of burglary, do any other crimes come to mind? For example, you may think that burglary and robbery are the same or similar crimes. What about criminal trespass and its relationship to the crime of burglary; or theft and its relationship to burglary?

Learning Tip

Once you start to learn the definitions of various crimes and you are able to identify the material elements of those crimes, you begin to develop greater expertise and understanding. This development in your learning and critical thinking skills prompts you to start thinking about relationships between crimes and to start learning to note the similarities and differences. This is an important skill because when you read a fact pattern, the question will not always identify the applicable crimes. Often, while reading a fact pattern for the first time, you start to think about applicable crimes. You should make a note of those crimes, define those crimes and the material elements on scratch paper, and then re-read the fact pattern to identify the material facts of the case in order to assess whether you have correctly identified the material facts of the case.

For example, this is how the Florida code defines burglary in Chapter 810, Section 810.02:

> For offenses committed after July 1, 2001, "burglary" means:
>
> 1. Entering a dwelling, a structure, or a conveyance with the intent to commit an offense therein, unless the premises are at the time open to the public or the defendant is licensed or invited to enter; or
> 2. Notwithstanding a licensed or invited entry, remaining in a dwelling, structure, or conveyance:
>
> a. Surreptitiously, with the intent to commit an offense therein;
>
> b. After permission to remain therein has been withdrawn, with the intent to commit an offense therein; or
>
> c. To commit or attempt to commit a forcible felony, as defined in Section 776.08.

What is required for a prosecutor to prove the crime of burglary under this Florida statute? Remember that the prosecutor must prove **all** elements of the crime **beyond a reasonable doubt** (that is the standard of proof). In order to identify the elements of the crime, you need to **"parse"** (analyze the sentences and break them down into their component parts).

- What is the first element?
  - Entering a dwelling, a structure, or a conveyance
- What is the second element?
  - It must be a wrongful entry since some entries (such as a licensed or invited entry as permissible unless they violate (2)(a)-(c))

- What is the third element?
    - With the intent to commit an offense therein

Learning Tip

Remember as well that you do not want to use your own definitions or interpretations of words so you need to see if words such as "dwelling" or "structure" have specific definitions in the statute. In this instance, you would refer to Section 810.011, entitled "Definitions—as used in this chapter," to find definitions for "structure," "dwelling," "conveyance," and "in the course of committing." The punishment associated with the burglary depends upon whether the burglary is in the first, second or third degree, and this is determined by the "offense that is committed therein."

Stop and Engage

Based on the definition of burglary in Florida, how is it different from the crime of "Trespass in Structure" as defined in Section 810.08? Use an internet search engine to find this statute, and then parse the definition of the crime to determine how it differs from the crime of burglary. Can you commit the crime of trespass in structure but not burglary? Can you commit the crime of burglary but not commit the crime of trespass in structure? Now, think about three similar fact patterns that proceed from a simple to a more complex analysis. When you read the fact patterns, note the crimes that come to mind, then write the definitions for those crimes, parse the elements, and see what crimes are applicable based on the changing facts. Make sure to note the subtle changes.

Practical Applications

- Joe enters Mary's backyard to retrieve his cat that has climbed up a tree in her yard? Can you charge Joe with a crime(s), and, if so, what crime(s)?
- Joe enters Mary's backyard to retrieve his cat that has climbed up a tree in her yard, and once he has the cat and is leaving her yard, he sees her new pink bicycle and decides to take the bicycle back to his house. Can you charge Joe with a crime(s), and, if so, what crime(s)?
- Joe watches his cat run into Mary's backyard and sees the cat hide in the basket on the handlebars of Mary's new pink bicycle that is parked in the carport. He decides to enter her yard to retrieve his cat and take her new pink bicycle. He enters the yard and rides the bike back to his house with his cat still in the basket. Can you charge Joe with a crime(s), and, if so, what crime(s)?

Now that you have identified the applicable crime for each fact pattern, what is the difference between the second and third fact pattern? In the crime of burglary, what is the required *mens rea*, and when does it need to be formed? The critical difference between theft and burglary in the Florida Statutes is that for the crime of burglary, the person must "enter a dwelling or a structure **with the intent to commit an offense therein**"—the intent must be formed prior to entering the dwelling or structure whereas with theft (under Section 812.014) the person knowingly obtains or uses the property and the intent is formed at the time of the act, not necessarily prior to it. You will note in reading the headings for the types of crimes in Chapter 810 that there are many forms of trespass including "trespass in structure or conveyance" and "trespass on property other than structure or conveyance." For trespass on "property other than a structure or conveyance" a person must be one who is not authorized, licensed, or invited to be on the property and willfully enters upon or remains in any property. These are the types of subtle differences that you will only notice if you spend the time not only learning the definitions of the crimes and the material elements but parsing those definitions so that you can be aware of the specific and precise requirements of the crime. If you do not note these subtle differences, it will be very difficult to correctly identify and discuss the correct crime in a fact pattern analysis.

Before we move onto inchoate crimes, we will review a few more state statutes for the crime of burglary so that you can develop more experience finding differences and similarities. In Texas, burglary and criminal trespass are grouped together in Chapter 30. In Section 30.02 defines burglary like this:

> (a) A person commits an offense if, without the effective consent of the owner, the person:
>
> (1) enters a habitation, or a building (or any portion of a building) not then open to the public, with intent to commit a felony, theft, or an assault; or
>
> (2) remains concealed, with intent to commit a felony, theft, or an assault, in a building or habitation; or
>
> (3) enters a building or habitation and commits or attempts to commit a felony, theft, or an assault.

Based on this definition of burglary, what are the main elements of the crime?

- Enter a habitation or a building—not then open to the public
- With intent to commit a felony, theft, or an assault

Stop and Engage

Does the person need to enter the habitation or the building with the intent as in Florida? Does the Texas Code provide definitions for some of these terms? What are some of the factual questions you would need to resolve when analyzing a fact pattern to determine if a person committed the crime of burglary in Texas? Some of these factual questions may need to be addressed:

- Does the person have "effective consent?"
  - How does the code or the courts define "effective consent?"
- How is "enter" defined in the code?

- How is habitation or building defined in the code?
- How do you determine that the building was "not then open to the public?" What facts support or contradict this element?
- How do you prove intent to commit a felony, theft, or assault?
- How do you prove, based on the facts, the person had the intent before the "entry?"

Learning Tip

As you can see, knowing the definition of the crime and parsing its elements is a crucial first step, but if you do not know the precise and specific definition of the words used in the definition of the crime, you will not have an accurate definition. Further, once you have an accurate definition, you now need to think about questions that are implicit in the definition, such as the ones above, and decide how you will answer those questions based on the material facts of the case or hypothetical fact pattern. It is the ability to develop more complex critical thinking and analytical reasoning skills that will facilitate your ability to develop a well-reasoned answer to a case or hypothetical fact pattern.

In New York, the crime of burglary is grouped under "Offenses involving damage to and intrusion upon property" in Title I with burglary specifically defined in Article 140. As in Florida, New York groups the crime of burglary into several different degrees. Burglary in the first degree is defined in Article 140.30 in this way:

> A person is guilty of burglary in the first degree when he knowingly enters or remains unlawfully in a dwelling with intent to commit a crime therein, and when, in effecting entry or while in the dwelling or in immediate flight therefrom, he or another participant in the crime:
>
> 1. Is armed with explosives or a deadly weapon; or
>
> 2. Causes physical injury to any person who is not a participant in the crime; or
>
> 3. Uses or threatens the immediate use of a dangerous instrument; or
>
> 4. Displays what appears to be a pistol, revolver, rifle, shotgun, machine gun or other firearm; except that in any prosecution under this subdivision, it is an affirmative defense that such pistol, revolver, rifle, shotgun, machine gun or other firearm was not a loaded weapon from which a shot, readily capable of producing death or other serious physical injury, could be discharged.

Stop and Engage

Identify the *mens rea* for the crime of burglary in New York. Identify the *actus reus*. Are there other elements that will need to be established by applying them to the specific facts of the case? If so, what are some of those other elements? As with Florida and Texas, does the person need intent before entering or remaining in a dwelling? What words do you need to further define to specifically and precisely understand the definition of burglary? Are there specific factual issues that arise from some of those definitions? If so, how will you resolve them when analyzing a fact pattern?

In California, burglary is classified in the category of "Crimes against property" in Title 13 and specifically defined in Chapter 2, Section 459 as:

> Every person who enters any house, room, apartment, tenement, shop, warehouse, store, mill, barn, stable, outhouse or other building, tent, vessel, as defined in Section 21 of the Harbors and Navigation Code, floating home, as defined in subdivision (d) of Section 18075.55 of the Health and Safety Code, railroad car, locked or sealed cargo container, whether or not mounted on a vehicle, trailer coach, as defined in Section 635 of the Vehicle Code, any house car, as defined in Section 362 of the Vehicle Code, inhabited camper, as defined in Section 243 of the Vehicle Code, vehicle as defined by the Vehicle Code, when the doors are locked, aircraft as defined by Section 21012 of the Public Utilities Code, or mine or any underground portion thereof, with intent to commit grand or petit larceny or any felony is guilty of burglary.

Do you need to spend some time consulting some other sections of the California Penal Code and also finding some specific code definitions for the terms used in this definition? What are the material elements for the crime of burglary in California?

- Entry into one of the enumerated structures, vehicles, etc.
- With intent to commit grand or petit larceny

In order to prove the crime of burglary in California, you also need to prove intent to commit the crime of grand or petit larceny. This requires that you analyze the facts to determine if you can prove grand or petit larceny as described in Title 13, Chapter 5, Sections 484-502.9.

Case Example: Practice Opportunity

Here is a practice opportunity. Read the following case excerpt, and use a yellow highlighter to identify the material facts of the case; use a blue highlighter to note the relevant statutory language; use a pink highlighter to note the alleged crime; and use a green highlighter to note the court's application of the law to the facts of the case, to highlight the court's analysis.

Drew v. State of Florida

Supreme Court of Florida, No. SC95785 (2000)

On July 14, 1997, at approximately 11 p.m., Polk County Sheriff's Deputy James Orgic observed Terrell Curtis Drew and his codefendant, Willie D. Wright, in the vicinity of Mack Lewis Auto Sales. Orgic testified that Drew was carrying a lug wrench at the time and was using it to remove lug nuts from a vehicle. Drew admitted that he took the lug nuts from a brownish-red Chevrolet parked behind the Auto Sales business and that with the assistance of his co-defendant; he had removed the missing tires from the car. Subsequently, Drew and Wright were charged by information with petit theft, possession of burglary tools, and burglary of a conveyance in violation of sections 812.014(3), 810.06 and 810.02(4), Florida Statutes (1997), respectively. Drew filed a motion to dismiss the burglary and possession of burglary tools charges, asserting that the undisputed material facts as set out above did not constitute a prima facie showing of guilt on these charges. The trial court denied this motion and the case proceeded to trial. At trial, Drew did not dispute that he had removed tires from the car. Instead, his attorney contended that on these facts, Drew could not be found guilty of burglary or of possession of burglary tools.

At common law, burglary was defined as breaking and entering the dwelling house of another at night with the intent to commit a felony therein. The underlying purpose of the crime of burglary was to punish the forcible invasion of a habitation and violation of the heightened expectation of privacy and possessory rights of individuals in structures and conveyances. See Presley v. State, 61 Fla. 46, 48, 54 So. 367 (1911). As Sir William Blackstone once explained: "[burglary] has always been looked upon as a very heinous offense: not only because of the abundant terror that it naturally carries with it, but also as it is a forcible invasion of that right of habitation, which every individual might acquire in a state of nature." 4 William Blackstone, Commentaries on the Laws of England 223 (1769). In 1962, a definition of burglary was approved by the drafters of the Model Penal Code that closely resembled the common law crime:

> (1) Burglary Defined. A person is guilty of burglary if he enters a building or occupied structure, or separately secured or occupied portion thereof, with purpose to commit a crime therein, unless the premises are at the time open to the public or the actor is licensed or privileged to enter. It is an affirmative defense to prosecution for burglary that the building or structure was abandoned.

Model Penal Code, §221.1(1), at 60-61 (1980). The commentary to this section explains that this definition attempted to restate the original reach of the crime:

> The needed reform [of the offense of burglary] should take the direction of narrowing the offense to reflect more appropriately the distinctive situation for which it was originally de-

> rived. The offense has thus been limited in the Model Code to the invasion of premises under circumstances especially likely to terrorize occupants. Most of the extensions of the offense that have been added by legislation over the years have been discarded. Model Penal Code, §221.1 cmt. 2, at 67.

Of course, burglary of a conveyance was unknown at common law and is not included as part of the 1962 Model Penal Code definition of burglary as set out above. Rather, burglary of a conveyance is a creature of statute. In Florida, burglary is defined in a way largely consistent with the Model Penal Code but expanded to include conveyances:

> Burglary means entering or remaining in a dwelling, a structure, or a conveyance with the intent to commit an offense therein, unless the premises are at the time open to the public or the defendant is licensed or invited to enter or remain.

§810.02(1), Fla Stat. (1997). Section 810.011(3), Florida Statutes (1997), defines conveyance as "any motor vehicle, ship, vessel, railroad car, trailer, aircraft, or sleeping car." In addition, "'to enter a conveyance' includes taking apart any portion of the conveyance." §810.011(3), Fla. Stat. (1997). This Court construed the statutory definition of entry of a conveyance in Von Edwards v. State, 377 So. 2d 684 (Fla. 1979), and, based upon that construction, rejected a claim that the statutory definition of burglary was unconstitutionally vague or overbroad. In rejecting the claim of overbreadth we accepted the State's proffered interpretation of the statute:

> The state responds that the word "therein" in section 810.02(1) requires that when the entering of a conveyance is committed, there must be intent to commit an offense "therein," citing State v. Dalby, 361 So. 2d 215 (Fla. 2d DCA 1978). Thus, the legislative intent is that the removal of a portion of the conveyance must be to facilitate the commission of an offense within the conveyance. Thus the statute does not seek to punish as burglary conduct which should be treated as larceny. We agree.

Subsequently, in State v. Stephens, 601 So. 2d 1195 (Fla. 1992), we held that burglary of a conveyance can be proven even when the underlying offense intended to be committed is the stealing of the conveyance itself. See id. at 1196. Relying on the common English usage of the word "therein," this Court held "[t]he use of the word 'therein' plainly indicates that the crime of burglary can exist if the defendant formed an intent to commit a crime 'in that place.'" Id. at 1196 (emphasis added). Moreover, we explained:

> We believe the district court's error in this case was based on a misconception of the temporal sequence usually involved in burglaries of conveyances. Such a burglary is complete the moment the defendant enters or remains within the vehicle with the requisite intent. Even if the defendant changes plans and decides not to steal the vehicle, the crime of burglary still would exist.

Id. at 1197 (emphasis added). Importantly, in Stephens, we observed that the district court had erred in any reliance on the Fifth District's holding in Hankins that the removal of hubcaps was insufficient to constitute a burglary of a conveyance, because "[o]bviously, there was no 'entering or remaining in' the conveyance in that instance." Id. at 1196. Hence, we tacitly approved the holding in Hankins in our analysis.

Other cases have also declined to find that facts similar to those herein could be characterized as a burglary. The Fourth District recently considered this issue in Jones v. State, 763 So. 2d 1101 (Fla. 4th DCA), review granted, 760 So. 2d 948 (Fla. 2000), where the defendant appealed a conviction for burglary based solely upon the removal of hubcaps and lug nuts from the wheels of an automobile. On appeal, the court reversed the burglary conviction, relying on our decision in Von Edwards and the statement therein that "the legislative intent is that the removal of a portion of the conveyance must be to facilitate the commission of an offense within the conveyance." Id. at 1102 (quoting Von Edwards, 377 So. 2d at 685) (emphasis added). Based on this language from Von Edwards, the Jones court concluded that the removal of a wheel, tire, hubcap, or lug nut, or any combination thereof, from the outside of a conveyance, cannot constitute burglary because "[u]nder those circumstances there is no 'intent to commit an offense therein,' i.e., within the vehicle."3 See id. at 1103. The court also noted that Word did not address the requirement discussed by this Court in State v. Stephens, 601 So. 2d 1195 (Fla. 1992), that the offense must be capable of being committed within the vehicle. See Jones at 1103.

Of course, we have already noted the Fifth District's holding in Hankins that the removal of hubcaps alone did not constitute a burglary. In an opinion by Associate Judge Parker Lee McDonald, the Hankins court explained:

> The gravamen of the offense of burglary, whether of a conveyance or otherwise, is a nonconsensual entry with the intent to commit an offense within; the purpose of the statute is to punish an invasion of the possessory property rights of another in structures and conveyances. The definition of "en-

tering a conveyance" in Section 810.011(2) does not obviate the necessity for alleging facts in support of an intent to commit an offense therein.

Similarly, in R.E.S. v. State, 396 So. 2d 1219 (Fla. 1st DCA 1981), the court held that the sole act of siphoning gasoline from a car was not a burglary. There, the court reasoned that the cases upholding convictions for burglary of automobiles involved entry into a compartment of a vehicle which can be entered wholly or partially by a person. See id. at 1220.

On the other hand, a number of Florida cases have considered "entry of a conveyance" in other contexts and have applied a more expansive meaning to "entry." For example, the Second District held in Word that the removal of a tire from a motor vehicle constituted a burglary. Other cases have reached seemingly similar results. See, e.g., Braswell v. State, 671 So. 2d 228, 229-30 (Fla. 1st DCA 1996) (holding that reaching into the bed of a pickup truck to remove a secured item within the truck was an entry); Greger v. State, 458 So. 2d 858, 860 (Fla. 3d DCA 1984) (holding that the loosening and removal of bolts and nuts from the protruding motor at the stern of the boat constituted an entry for purposes of the burglary statute); State v. Harvey, 403 So. 2d 630, 630 (Fla. 2d DCA 1981) (holding that defendant's loosening of the bolts in the engine compartment underneath the car with the intent to remove the alternator was sufficient to constitute an entry); Bragg v. State, 371 So. 2d 1082, 1083 (Fla. 4th DCA 1979) (holding it was proper to convict the defendant of burglary for opening the hood of a vehicle with intent to remove the battery).

Other jurisdictions with burglary statutes similar to Florida's have also construed their statutes in a manner similar to our analysis in Von Edwards. For example, the Texas statute defines burglary of a vehicle as follows:

> A person commits an offense if, without the effective consent of the owner, he breaks into or enters a vehicle or any part of a vehicle with intent to commit any felony or theft.

Tex. Penal Code Ann., §30.04(a) (Vernon Supp. 2000). Further, as in Florida, the Texas Penal Code defines "enter" as "to intrude any part of the body or any physical object connected with the body" into the motor vehicle or a part thereof. Id. §30.04(b)(1)-(2). Based on this statute, the Texas Court of Criminal Appeals has held that the removal of tires and hubcaps alone is insufficient to constitute an entry under the Texas burglary statute. See Griffin v. State, 815 S.W.2d 576 (Tex. Crim. App. 1991). There, the court emphasized that the focus of the inquiry as to burglary should be on the "breaking of" or removing of things from an enclosed or interior area:

> Because "enter" is defined exactly the same for burglary of a building or habitation as it is for burglary of a vehicle, the element of intrusion into a building or habitation under § 30.02 should be of the same nature as intrusion into a vehicle under § 30.04. Stealing a mailbox or a window shutter attached to the side of a house would not be entry so as to constitute burglary. Similarly, stealing a hood ornament or antenna attached to the outside of a vehicle would not be entry so as to constitute burglary of a vehicle. Tires and hubcaps are analogous to these examples, because no entry of any part of the vehicle is effected. Contrast the taking of something from inside the trunk, inside the hood, or from the interior of the vehicle. There must be a "breaking of the close" to have entry in the sense long established for burglary. The protection is to the interior or enclosed part of the described object, be it a house, a building or a vehicle. Cf. Galemore [v. State, 61 S.W.2d 519 (1933)], where opening a door and looking in is not burglary because there is no entry. Taking items attached to the outside of the vehicle, house, or building that does not reflect an entry into an interior or enclosed part of the described object in order to steal does not constitute the offense of burglary. Since the burglary of a vehicle statute evolved from the "regular" burglary statutes, the interpretation of entry should be consistent. Therefore, we hold that taking the hubcaps or tires that are attached to the outside of the car, when no entry into any enclosed portion of the car is made to effectuate that taking, is not burglary of a vehicle. Id. At 579.

In California, the burglary statute provides: "Every person who enters any ... vehicle ... when the doors are locked ... with intent to commit grand or petit larceny or any felony is guilty of burglary." Cal. Penal Code, § 459 (West. 1999). In People v. Young, 57 Cal. Rptr. 2d 12 (Cal. Ct. App. 1996), the court held that the removal of headlights from a parked car did not constitute a burglary:

> Unlike the car's interior or its trunk, headlamp housings can be "entered" without regard to whether the car is locked, and we view the theft of headlights the same as we would the theft of windshield wipers or hubcaps. These are thefts (or attempted thefts) or auto tampering or acts of vandalism, not burglaries.

Id. at 14. In its opinion, the court relied upon its earlier holding in People v. Toomes, 306 P.2d 953 (Cal. Ct. App. 1957), wherein it was explained that an essential purpose of section 459 was to make it a more serious offense to break into the interior of a car as opposed to tampering with or removal of exterior parts unconnected with entry into the vehicle itself. See id. at 14. As in Texas, the focus of the California decisions in analyzing the entry requirement is on whether the defendant entered an interior section of a vehicle.

In our decisions in Von Edwards and Stephens we have recognized that Florida's burglary statute provides that taking apart any portion of a conveyance constitutes an entry. However, we have explained that the offense of burglary requires more than an entry, and there must also be proof of the requisite statutory intent to commit a crime within the conveyance. In this way the statute cannot be used to punish as burglary "conduct which should be treated as larceny." Von Edwards at 685. For example, in Hankins, as in this case, the State attempted to show that the removal of the hubcaps was the act constituting the entry as well as the crime intended to be committed therein. Although the Hankins court concluded that the removal of the hubcaps did not constitute an entry, it further explained that "[c]learly, the theft of hubcaps from an automobile wholly fail[ed] to establish a prima facie case of intent 'to commit an offense therein.'" 376 So. 2d at 286. The Fourth District in Jones similarly held that the removal of the hubcaps does not constitute a burglary because "[u]nder those circumstances, there is no 'intent to commit an offense therein' i.e., within the vehicle." 763 So. 2d at 1103. As noted above, some courts have applied the statutory definition of entry as if that was all that was required to prove a burglary. As was noted in Jones, it appears the Word court failed to consider our holding in Von Edwards when it held in a conclusory fashion that the "theft of the wheels and tires removed from the automobile supply sufficient evidence of his intent to commit an offense after entering the automobile by taking apart or removing the wheels and tires." Word, 711 So. 2d at 1241. Clearly, the Word court relied on the same act to satisfy both requirements of the statute, an illegal entry as well as the intent to commit a crime within the conveyance. This analysis is inconsistent with our reasoning in Von Edwards and Stephens. In fact, as explained by comment 3(c) to section 221.1 of the Model Penal Code, "[t]he word 'therein' in Subsection (1) of the Model Penal Code provision ... requir[es] that the intent be to commit an offense after the entry has been effected." Arguably, in some of the other cases, the courts did consider whether the entry was merely to facilitate the commission of an offense within the vehicle. For instance, in Bragg, lifting a hood (entry) may be seen as different from the act of actually removing the engine (the crime intended to be committed). Similarly, in Braswell, defendant's sticking his hand into the bed of the pickup truck (entry) may be distinguished from the removal of the object (the crime intended to be committed). Although such distinctions will ordinarily not present a problem because usually the conduct supporting the entry and the crime to be committed therein are easily identifiable and exclusive of each other, courts must be careful not to end the analysis once it is determined that an entry has occurred. As noted above, such a limited analysis would render meaningless that portion of the burglary statute requiring intent to commit an offense within the vehicle.

In other words, a proper analysis of the offense of burglary must focus both on the act constituting the entry and the intent to commit an offense therein. The language of the burglary statute, as drafted by the Legislature, requires both an entry and the requisite intent to commit a crime within the conveyance. Therefore, it follows that the crime must be one that is capable of being committed within or inside the vehicle. Moreover, it naturally follows that an entry into a vehicle without the requisite intent to commit a separate crime therein is not a burglary. Thus, while the actual penetration into any interior or enclosed area may constitute an entry, including the removal of a portion or part of one of these areas or compartments, intent to remove an object or commit an unauthorized act therein after the entry has occurred must also be established to satisfy the intent required to commit a crime.

This interpretation naturally follows from our previous pronouncement of the legislative intent that "the removal of a portion of the conveyance must be to facilitate the commission of an offense within the conveyance ... [and] not seek to punish as burglary conduct which should be treated as larceny." Von Edwards, 377 So. 2d at 685. Moreover, such a construction renders more meaningful the overall scheme of the burglary statute and Judge McDonald's observation in Hankins that the "definition of 'entering a conveyance'... does not obviate the necessity for alleging facts in support of an intent to commit an offense therein." 376 So. 2d at 286. It inherently follows from this interpretation that those acts deserving of a burglary conviction should be distinguished from those that constitute a criminal larceny, such as the removal of an antenna, hood ornament, or hubcap from a vehicle.

At issue in this case is whether the act of removing hubcaps or tires from a vehicle in and of itself constitutes a burglary. The Second District in Drew (tires) and State v. Word, 711 So. 2d 1240 (Fla. 2d DCA 1998) (tires) held that there was a burglary

> while the Fifth District in Hankins (hubcaps) held there was not. Based on the purpose and history of the offense of burglary at common law and our interpretation of the burglary statute, we hold that the sole act of removal of hubcaps or tires from a motor vehicle, while Mack Lewis, the owner of Mack Lewis Auto Sales, testified that three tires were missing from the car when he arrived that night after being notified of the incident by the police clearly constituting an act of criminal larceny, does not constitute a burglary.

Stop and Engage

Now that you have highlighted key parts from this case, complete the following activities:

- Identify the main issue(s) in this case.
- Write a concise summary of the material facts.
- Paraphrase the relevant statutory language with precision and accuracy.
- Write a concise summary of the court's reasoning.
- Write a concise explanation as to how and why the court reached its decision—its holding.

6.6 Summary

In many states crimes against property will be found in different sections of the penal code. Crimes against property may include: arson, robbery, burglary, theft, and other crimes that involve the destruction of personal or real property. The crime of theft usually involves an act that deprives an owner of property without the owner's consent. Theft, in many instances, requires a "taking," an "appropriation" of the property of another. Robbery is defined differently by different states, and in some instances is considered the crime of larceny with the added element of a threat of violence. It is also defined by some as the taking of money or goods by force or intimidation or with the intent to permanently deprive the owner of the property. Arson, as you can imagine, pertains to acts that involve fires or explosions that result in physical injury or harm. Many states have numerous degrees of arson. Burglary is difficult to define with reference to a specific statutory definition, but perhaps you can formulate one so that you remember the general elements and how it differs from other crimes in this chapter.

6.7 Chapter Review Activities

Analyze the fact pattern by identifying the relevant facts and elements of a crime, and determining what crime is appropriate for each actor. Be sure to write in clear, well-reasoned sentences. Note as well that there may be crimes that you have learned in previous chapters, so think of the crimes of this chapter as well as crimes learned in previous chapters. Reasoning, writing style, and clarity are important factors in these activities.

Hypothetical Fact Pattern I

Tim had just been fired from his job, "for no reason" according to Tim. Angry, Tim decided to burn the building down. He called his friend Scott, told him what had happened, and asked permission to borrow his truck so that he could take a load of pallets to his job and set them on fire. Scott agreed, and together they loaded a stack of old wooden pallets into Scott's truck. Tim drove to the location of his former job. A security guard stopped him at the gate and asked what he was doing. Tim replied that he was delivering some pallets to the company, and the guard let him in. He drove to the back of the building where he unloaded the pallets, piling them next to the building. He poured charcoal lighter fluid on the pile, lit it with a match, and then Tim drove back to Scott's house.

Hypothetical Fact Pattern II

Todd was going duck hunting. He had cleaned his 20 gauge, bought an extra box of shells, and gathered up his camouflage jacket and boots. Ignoring the various "No Trespassing" and "Keep Out" signs posted around Jim Sweeny's pasture, Todd drove his truck onto the property and parked near a large pond. Just as Todd was settling in among the reeds, Jim Sweeny discovered Todd, became angry, threatened Todd with bodily harm, and ordered Todd off his property. Todd tightened his grip around his shotgun, thought better of it, got into his truck and left.

That night, in the bar, Todd was still angry as he described his experience earlier that day to Juan and Kevin. The conversation turned to revenge, and Todd asked Juan and Kevin to help him burn down Jim Sweeny's barn. Both agreed to help. The following afternoon, as Todd and Kevin were preparing to leave to carry out their plan, Juan called Todd and told him he had changed his mind and would not participate. Todd and Kevin proceeded without Juan, driving onto Jim Sweeny's property. They stopped near the barn, poured gasoline around the outside walls, and set it on fire. Todd and Kevin drove away quickly. The barn burned to the ground.

Unknown to Todd and Kevin, Jim Sweeny's two grandchildren were playing in the barn, became trapped by the flames, and died. The coroner ruled cause of death of both children to be smoke inhalation.

Hypothetical Fact Pattern III

Ramon was in the processes of customizing his car. He really wanted a set of 22", three spoke, polished aluminum wheels with ultra-low profile tires, but he could not afford the $1,500 per wheel price. Ramon discovered that the exact wheels and tires that he wanted were stored in an open area behind the auto parts store, protected by only a high fence and a padlocked gate. Ramon borrowed bolt cutters and a truck from a friend, and late one night he drove into a parking area behind the store. He cut the padlock on the gate, went into the storage area and tossed a set of wheels and tires onto the truck. As he was preparing to leave, a security guard surprised Ramon, ordering him to stop. Ramon struck the guard on the head with the bolt cutters and fled in the truck. The security guard was not seriously injured. Identify the crime(s) for which Ramon might be culpable. Be sure to parse the elements and correlate with the relevant facts before you reach a conclusion.

Chapter 7

Parties to a Crime and Vicarious Liability Crimes

Key Terms and Concepts

Actor	Accessory before the Fact
Principal in the First Degree	Accessory after the Fact
Principal in the Second Degree	Accomplice
Model Penal Code	Respondeat Superior

7.1 Introduction

In the commission of a crime and criminal activity, there is often more than one "actor" or defendant. In certain instances, several people are involved in committing the crime—for example, in bank robberies, several people decide to engage in the criminal activity. In burglary or robbery, several people may be party to the crime. To further complicate matters, if more than one person plays a role, the people involved in the criminal activity may have different roles to play or may be involved in the criminal activity at different times. For example, someone may assist in the planning of the crime but not actually participate in the crime itself. Someone else may wait outside while the crime is committed and then drive the vehicle for the person or persons who committed the crime. Another person may supply a safe house where the person or persons who committed the crime may hide to avoid capture and prosecution. As you can see, not all people involved in criminal activity are involved in the same part or at the same time in the commission of the crime. Therefore, it is important to note how to identify and categorize the various people who may be involved in the entire scope of the criminal activity from pre-planning to past-commission.

7.2 Parties to a Crime

Although every state has specific requirements, we can generally categories the parties to criminal activity in the following ways:

- Principal in the first degree
- Principal in the second degree
- Accessory before the fact
- Accessory after the fact
- Accomplice

These terms are derived from the **Model Penal Code** (MPC) which was developed by the American Law Institute to provide a model statute that the states could use for guidance in developing their individual penal or criminal codes. Several definitions can be derived under the MPC:

- A Principal in the First Degree is the person who commits the crime. The principal in the first degree has the requisite *mens rea* and commits the necessary act(s).
- A Principal in the Second Degree assists in the commission of the crime in the presence of the principal of the first degree. This assistance may be actual or constructive. For example, a principal in the second degree may be the "getaway driver" or a "lookout."
- An Accessory Before the Fact is not actually present for the criminal activity (either actually or constructively) but is one who urges, counsels, solicits, etc. the Principal of the First Degree in the commission of the criminal activity.
- An Accessory After the Fact is one who aids another in avoiding the consequences of the criminal activity. The person who intentionally assists another, with knowledge of his/her criminal activity, to avoid arrest, prosecution, trial, conviction, etc. An accessory after the fact must engage in his/her intentional actions after the completion of the criminal activity. If the activities of assistance occur prior to the completion of the criminal activity then the proper categorization for this person is Principal in the Second Degree.
- An Accomplice is a person who provides physical assistance, psychological encouragement or omits to perform his/her duty to act. An accomplice must have the requisite *mens rea* for the crime and assist the Principal in the First Degree in the commission of the criminal activity. An accomplice's conduct or the omission of required conduct (such as an on-duty police officer's failure to intervene in criminal conduct) must be proven to assist in the

commission of the criminal activity, and the degree or amount of assistance is not relevant.

- A person is an accomplice of another person in the commission if: (a) with the purpose of promoting or facilitating the commission of the offense, he (i) solicits such other person to commit it, or (ii) aids or attempts to aid such other person in planning/committing it, or (iii) having legal duty to prevent commission, fails to make proper effort; or (b) his conduct is expressly declared by law to establish his complicity. (MPC Section 2.06(3)).
- Unless otherwise provided by the Code or by the law defining the offense, a person is not an accomplice in an offense committed by another person if: (a) he is a victim of that offense; or (b) the offense is so defined that his conduct is inevitably incident to its commission; or (c) he terminates his complicity prior to the commission of the offense and (i) wholly deprives it of effectiveness in the commission of the offense; or (ii) gives timely warning to the law enforcement authorities or otherwise makes proper effort to prevent the commission of the offense. (MPC Section 2.06(6)).

Stop and Engage

Use an internet search engine to find how California classifies the parties to a crime (hint, you will find it in Section 30-33). How does Florida classify parties to a crime (see Chapter 777)? How does Texas classify its parties (see Section 7.01)? What are the similarities and differences? In Massachusetts, for example, accessories before the fact are defined in Chapter 274, Section 2, in this way:

> Whoever aids in the commission of a felony, or is accessory thereto before the fact by counseling, hiring or otherwise procuring such felony to be committed shall be punished in the manner provided for the punishment of the principal felon.

An accessory after the fact is defined in Chapter 274, Section 4, like this:

> Whoever, after the commission of a felony, harbors, conceals, maintains or assists the principal felon or accessory before the fact, or gives such offender any other aid, knowing that he has committed a felony or has been accessory thereto before the fact, with intent that he shall avoid or escape detention, arrest, trial or punishment, shall be an accessory after the fact.

What is the difference between an accessory before the fact and an accessory after the fact under Massachusetts law?

Case Example: Practice Opportunity

Read the following case excerpt and use a yellow highlighter to identify the material facts of the case; use a blue highlighter to note the relevant statutory language; use a pink highlighter to note the alleged crime; and use a green highlighter to note the court's application of the law to the facts of the case: to highlight the court's analysis.

State of Maine v. Chamroeun Pheng

791 A.2d 925 (2002)

Chamroeun Pheng appeals from a judgment of the Superior Court (Cumberland County, Fritzsche, J.) following a jury verdict of guilty on the charge of aggravated assault, Class B, 17-A M.R.S.A. §208(1)(A) (1983). Pheng contends that the court erred in giving the jury an accomplice liability instruction and that there was insufficient evidence to support the verdict. Because the accomplice liability instruction was proper and the evidence is sufficient, we affirm.

The victim in this case, a senior at Portland High School, was severely beaten by a group of youths. When the Portland police found him on the evening of September 5, 2000, the victim was bleeding and unconscious. He was transported to a hospital by ambulance, where he remained for several days. Because of his injuries, the victim missed the first quarter of his senior year in high school and could not eat solid food for several months. Thus, there was no question at trial that an aggravated assault causing serious bodily injury had been committed upon the victim. The issue for trial was the extent of Chamroeun Pheng's involvement. That issue was significantly disputed. Based on the evidence construed most favorably to the jury's verdict, the jury could have reasonably found the following: While bicycling home on the evening of September 5, 2000, the victim came upon a group of people partying near a gazebo adjacent to Front Street in Portland. There he recognized several high school acquaintances, including Pheng, whom he had known for several years. While speaking with Pheng and several others, the victim was hit from behind by a hard object wielded by someone other than Pheng. The victim then fell to the ground and several people began kicking him. The victim saw and felt Pheng kick him in the face and chest. Another witness testified that Pheng had indicated that he was angry with the victim because of something the victim had said to Pheng's brother. Over Pheng's objection, the court instructed the jury on an accomplice liability theory. The jury returned a verdict of guilty. Following the imposition of a sentence of seven years to the Department of Corrections with all but four years suspended and a period of probation of three years, plus a restitution order, Pheng brought this appeal.

A person may be guilty of a crime as a principal if, with the requisite mental state, he engages in the physical acts which constitute the crime. 17-A M.R.S.A. §§32, 34 (1983 & Supp. 2001). To convict a person of aggravated assault as a principal, the State must prove, beyond a reasonable doubt, that the person intentionally, knowingly or recklessly caused serious bodily injury to another person. 17-A M.R.S.A. §208(1)(A). Where a group of individuals attacks a person and, as a result of the kicks and blows struck in their collective attack, the victim sustains serious bodily injuries, then each of those persons who actually participated in the physical attacks which collectively caused the serious bodily injury may be guilty of aggravated assault. *See Cox v. State*, 242 Ga. App. 334, 528 S.E.2d 871, 875 (Ga. Ct. App. 2000) (participant in group attack "criminally responsible for the injuries inflicted by all parties to the crime even if he personally delivered only one blow"); *State v. Thomas*, 210 Neb. 298, 314 N.W.2d 15, 18 (Neb. 1981) (holding defendant responsible for victim's injuries because defendant participated in the group beating of the victim). To sustain an aggravated assault conviction, a particular individual among the group of attackers need not be identified as the one who struck the blows that were the particular cause of the victim's serious bodily injury. Because Pheng was identified as one of the attackers, kicking the victim in the chest and the face, and because the victim indisputably sustained serious bodily injuries from the attack, there is sufficient evidence to support finding Pheng guilty of aggravated assault as a principal.

The defense contends that the instruction on the accomplice liability alternative should not have been given, as the evidence, which Pheng contested, supported only his liability as a principal. A person may be guilty of a crime as an accomplice if, with the intent that the crime be committed, the person aids, or agrees to aid, or attempts to aid another in the planning or commission of the crime. 17-A M.R.S.A. §57(3)(A) (1983); Maine Jury Instruction Manual §6-31 (4th ed. 2001).

Although mere presence at the scene when a crime is committed is not sufficient to establish accomplice liability, once presence is proven, accomplice liability may attach upon the State's proof of any conduct promoting or facilitating, however slightly, the commission of the crime. *State v. Kaler*, 1997 ME 62, P7, 691 A.2d 1226, 1229; *State v. Libby*, 435 A.2d 1075, 1077 (Me. 1981). Accomplice liability may attach if a person, intending that a crime be committed, aids by actively furnishing advice and encouragement. *See State v. Flint H.*, 544 A.2d 739,

742 (Me. 1988). An overt act of assistance or actual physical participation in the commission of the crime is not required.

The court correctly instructed the jury that mere presence at the scene of a crime is not sufficient for accomplice liability to attach. In this case, the jury could have determined that the principal attacker was the unknown individual who began the attack by striking the victim in the back with a hard object and knocking him to the ground. The jury could have concluded that Pheng then joined and supported this attack, with Pheng's kicks to the victim's chest and face being indicative of Pheng's intent that the collective result of the attack upon the victim, initiated by another, be serious bodily injury, thus constituting aggravated assault. With this view of the evidence, the court's accomplice liability instruction was proper.

Judgment affirmed.

Stop and Engage

Now that you have highlighted key parts from this case, complete the following activities:

- Identify the main issue(s) in this case.
- Write a concise summary of the material facts.
- Paraphrase the relevant statutory language with precision and accuracy.
- Write a concise summary of the court's reasoning.
- Write a concise explanation as to how and why the court reached its decision—its holding.

7.3 Vicarious Liability

The notion of vicarious liability and liability for the actions of another is normally found in civil actions, such as torts. In criminal law, we discuss vicarious liability in the context of whether a corporation can be liable for the acts of its agents and in connection with notions of ***respondeat superior*** ("let the master answer"). For example, Section 7.22(a) of the Texas Penal Code states:

> If conduct constituting an offense is performed by an agent in behalf of a corporation or association and within the scope of his office or employment, the corporation or association is criminally responsible for an offense defined: (1) in this code where corporations and associations are made subject thereto.

Stop and Engage

What are some of the factual determinations you would need to make in order to prove a crime under Section 7.22(a)?

- Was the conduct performed by an agent?

- Was the conduct performed on behalf of the corporation?
- Was the conduct within the scope of the agent's office or employment?
- What kind of criminal offense is the corporation or association criminally liable for in connection with this section?

Hypothetical Fact Pattern: Practice Opportunity

Read the following hypothetical fact pattern and note the possible applicable crimes in the margins; then use a yellow highlighter to identify the material facts of the case.

> Scott, a middle manager for a medium-sized public corporation, was also responsible for Corporate Citizenship, where each year a team headed by Scott would select one or two civic organizations and provide financial support. There was no budget for this assistance. Scott devised a scheme where, during the year as a condition of growth and promotion, all employees were required to enter various lotteries and betting pools for athletic events. Winners collected a token sum, and the majority of the pool was used to fund the corporate giving. The corporation received tax benefits for these contributions. Some employees became increasingly unhappy with this forced contribution, eventually filing a complaint with the Department of Human Resources. The department contacted the local district attorney who filed charges of criminal theft against Scott, his citizenship team, and the officers of the corporation.

Once you have read the fact pattern and highlighted the material facts, see whether the crimes you identified when you first read the fact pattern can be supported by the material facts. If so, write out a definition of the applicable crime(s) and then begin your analysis by integrating the material facts with the material elements of the applicable crime(s) to reason your way to a conclusion.

Model Answer

> There are two key issues in this case: (a) whether the employees were coerced into participating in the various lotteries and betting pools and (b) whether this activity constitutes theft under the Texas Penal Code. A further issue is whether Scott's team and the corporation in general can be severally culpable.
>
> In connection with the coercion issue, employees who did not participate were informed that they would not be considered for job growth and associated wage increases. Those who did participate in the lotteries enjoyed job security and continued career development, with financial rewards. It can reasonably be argued that Scott had devised a system, tacitly supported by the company, where employees believed they had no choice but to contribute, constituting coercion. An ensuing issue, then,

> is whether the forced participation in the pools constitutes theft. In Section 31.03 (a), the Texas Penal Code defines theft as unlawfully appropriating property[1] "with intent to deprive the owner of property." Further, in Section 31.03 (b), the TPC defines unlawful appropriation as occurring "without the owner's effect consent." The fact pattern asserts that the owners of the property (the employees) were deprived of certain sums of money, so the issue becomes whether they gave "effective consent." In Section 31.01 (3) (A), the TPC is clear: "Consent is not effective if (A) induced by deception or coercion;" It has been previously argued that the employees were coerced into contributing, and Section 31.03 of the TPC consequently defines the action in these circumstances as theft.
>
> Culpability is the remaining issue. Specifically, was the corporation criminally responsible for Scott's actions? The TPC specifies that a person must be an agent "acting in behalf of the corporation ..." Clearly, Scott was acting for the benefit of his corporation. In addition to local good will enjoyed by the corporation because of its benevolence to civic organizations, the fact pattern asserts that the corporation was receiving tax benefits.
>
> The remaining issue is whether Scott was acting as an agent for the corporation. In Section 7.21 (1), the TPC defines an agent: "Agent means a director, officer, employee, or other person authorized to act in behalf of a corporation or association." It can be argued that Scott and his team were given authority to administer the Corporate Citizenship program without corporate oversight because there is no evidence that the company was involved. Scott designed the system to fund the program through employee contributions, and he and his team unilaterally selected the civic organizations to receive company contributions. Therefore, it is reasonable to conclude that Scott was an agent acting in behalf of his company. In this analysis, the elements of the crime of theft have been supported by evidence, and the culpability of the corporation has been established by the relevant facts. Consequently, both Scott and his company are criminally liable for theft.

Colorado and California also have corporate criminal liability based on notions of *respondeat superior*. In section 7 of the California Penal Code, the term "person" includes a corporation. Many of the laws pertaining to vicarious liability are found in the California Corporate Criminal Liability Act and also in Section 387 of the California Penal Code) where it states the following:

1. "Property" in this case is money, defined in TPC §31.01 (5) (C).

(a) Any corporation, limited liability company, or person who is a manager with respect to a product, facility, equipment, process, place of employment, or business practice, is guilty of a public offense.... if that corporation, limited liability company, or person does all of the following:

(1) Has actual knowledge of a serious concealed danger that is subject to the regulatory authority of an appropriate agency and is associated with that product or a component of that product or business practice.
(2) Knowingly fails during the period ending 15 days after the actual knowledge is acquired, or if there is imminent risk of great bodily harm or death, immediately, to do both of the following:

(A) Inform the Division of Occupational Safety and Health in the Department of Industrial Relations in writing, unless the corporation, limited liability company, or manager has actual knowledge that the division has been so informed. Where the concealed danger reported pursuant to this paragraph is subject to the regulatory authority of an agency other than the Division of Occupational Safety and Health in the Department of Industrial Relations, it shall be the responsibility of the Division of Occupational Safety and Health in the Department of Industrial Relations, within 24 hours of receipt of the information, to telephonically notify the appropriate government agency of the hazard, and promptly forward any written notification received.

(B) Warn its affected employees in writing, unless the corporation, limited liability company, or manager has actual knowledge that the employees have been so warned. The requirement for disclosure is not applicable if the hazard is abated within the time prescribed for reporting, unless the appropriate regulatory agency nonetheless requires disclosure by regulation.

In Colorado, Section 18-1-606 pertains to criminal liability of business entities and states this:

(1) A business entity is guilty of an offense if:

(a) The conduct constituting the offense consists of an omission to discharge a specific duty of affirmative performance imposed on the business entity by law; or

(b) The conduct constituting the offense is engaged in, authorized, solicited, requested, commanded, or knowingly tolerated by the governing body or individual authorized to manage the affairs of the business entity or by a high managerial agent acting within the scope of his or her employment or in behalf of the business entity.

In reading further in the same section, you will note that there are definitions for "agent" and "business entity." Further in Section 18-1-607 it makes this statement:

> A person is criminally liable for conduct constituting an offense which he performs or causes to occur in the name of or in behalf of a corporation to the same extent as if that conduct were performed or caused by him in his own name or behalf.

This definition is stated in Section 281 of the Delaware Criminal Code:

> An organization is guilty of an offense when:
>
> (1) The conduct constituting the offense consists of an omission to discharge a specific duty of affirmative performance imposed on organizations by law; or
>
> (2) The conduct constituting the offense is engaged in, authorized, solicited, requested, commanded or recklessly tolerated by the board of directors or by a high managerial agent acting within the scope of employment and in behalf of the organization; or
>
> (3) The conduct constituting the offense is engaged in by an agent of the organization while acting within the scope of employment and in behalf of the organization and:
> a. The offense is a misdemeanor or a violation; or
>
> b. The offense is one defined by a statute which clearly indicates a legislative intent to impose such criminal liability on an organization.

Stop and Engage

Are there any commonalities among the statutes of these states? Does your state have provisions related to the criminal liability of organizations or business entities or provisions that impose criminal liability on an organization or business entity for the acts of its agents or employees? Use an internet search engine to find some of these provisions.

7.4 Criminal Responsibility for the Conduct of Another

A similar topic to vicarious liability and criminal liability for the acts of another is the topic of criminal responsibility for the conduct of another. In Texas, for example, Section 7.02(a) states this:

> A person is criminally responsible for an offense committed by the conduct of another if: (3) having a legal duty to prevent commission of the offense and acting with intent to promote or assist its commission, he fails to make a reasonable effort to prevent commission of the offense.

What are the essential elements of this crime? The best method to identify the essential elements of the crime is to parse the definition:

- A legal duty
- Prevent the commission of the offense
- Acted with intent
- To promote or assist its commission
- Fails to make a reasonable effort
- To prevent the commission of the offense

Now that we have a workable definition, we can use a practice opportunity to analyze a fact pattern with several issues that draw upon the above as well as other material you have learned in previous chapters.

Hypothetical Fact Pattern: Practice Opportunity

Read the following hypothetical fact pattern and note the possible applicable crimes in the margins; then, use a yellow highlighter to identify the material facts of the case.

Hypothetical Fact Pattern

Sergeant John Hightower was a tough, non-nonsense, ex-Marine street cop who welcomed an assignment to patrol the roughest area of town. He had been on the force for 22 years, working his way up from patrolman to sergeant. Over the years, he had refused several opportunities for promotion because he would be less involved in "catching the bad guys." He had never found it necessary to fire his sidearm, but he used his baton, his fists, his taser, and his handcuffs liberally. Sgt. Hightower had the highest rate of closure by confession in the department. He was often asked to be a training officer, where rookie patrolmen would ride along with him and learn the "real" job of being a cop. Late one night, while driving down a busy street with a rookie in the car, Sgt. Hightower saw two men he recognized as neighborhood thugs. They were walking quickly down the sidewalk with a third man between them. The three were walking unusually close together, and Sgt. Hightower suspected a shake-down was in progress. He turned his patrol car around, stopped near the curb, got out of the car, and confronted the three men. The rookie also exited the patrol car and stood nearby. Sgt. Hightower asked the three men where they were going and received a mumbled response. He noticed that the man in the middle had been roughed up, as evidenced by a black eye and blood coming from his nose and lower lip. He asked again for identification and received no response. Sgt. Hightower gripped his baton and struck one of the men

> behind the knee, causing him to fall to the ground. He then kicked the man in the back. The other man attempted to flee, and Sgt. Hightower struck him across the shoulder with the baton, breaking his collar bone. He then kicked the second man in the face, knocking out several teeth. The rookie cop realized that he was witnessing an assault, but he did nothing to intervene.

Once you have read the fact pattern and highlighted the material facts, see whether the crimes you identified when you first read the fact pattern can be supported by the material facts. If so, write out a definition of the applicable crime(s) and then begin your analysis by integrating the material facts with the material elements of the applicable crime(s) to reason your way to a conclusion.

Model Answer

There is no doubt that the rookie cop was caught in a dilemma. On the one hand, the assault was being committed by a fellow officer, and there is a Code of Silence among most law enforcement personnel which prevented the rookie from exposing the possible unlawful actions of a fellow officer. On the other hand, the rookie was a sworn officer of the law, and because of this status, he had a duty to take action to stop the assault.

The legal issue is whether the rookie officer is criminally responsible for an assault committed by another officer. First among the issues is whether an assault occurred, or whether Sgt. Hightower was justified in his actions. Section 22.02 (a) (1) of the TPC defines assault: "A person commits an offense if the person (1) intentionally, knowingly, or recklessly causes bodily injury to another...." Notice the breadth in *mens rea*: all levels of culpability are included except negligently. The fact pattern asserts that Sgt. Hightower swung his baton with the conscious objective of disabling through injury both men that he had confronted. Therefore, an argument could be formed that Sgt. Hightower acted intentionally (having a conscious objective to injure), but a secondary argument of knowingly (being aware that his actions will cause harm) would also satisfy the required *mens rea*.

The fact pattern also asserts that both men struck by Sgt. Hightower's baton suffered injury. (When Sgt. Hightower struck the two men with his baton, he satisfied the *actus reus* of assault.) The first fell to the ground because of a blow to the knee, and the second man suffered a broken collar bone and missing teeth. Unless Sgt. Hightower can demonstrate that his actions were justified, he is guilty of assault. In Subchapter B of Chapter 9, the Texas Penal Code provides several justifications for actions which cause injury to another person. The most relevant of them are

> Necessity (Section 9.22)[2] and Self Defense (Section 9.31)[3]. In both of these justifications, the person taking action was responding to a threat. There is no evidence in the fact pattern that either of the men threatened Sgt. Hightower; they were simply unresponsive to his questions. One of the men attempted to flee, which is inconsistent with threatening behavior. Both the *mens rea* and *actus reus* of assault have been satisfied, and there is no justification for his actions. Sgt. Hightower is consequently guilty of assault. The remaining issue is whether the rookie officer is also guilty of assault. The TPC specifies that if a person has "a duty to act," he can be criminally responsible if he takes no action. Upon graduation from the Academy, the rookie took an oath to uphold the Constitution and to enforce the law. He was therefore a sworn officer, with authority and duty to enforce law. In this case, he witnessed an assault in progress and having a duty to act, should have intervened to prevent further injury. Because he did nothing, Section 7.02 (a) of the TPC establishes that the rookie officer is "criminally responsible for an offense committed by the conduct of another." He is also guilty of assault.

7.4.1 Parental Liability

An issue that surfaces in the discussion of criminal liability for the acts of another is parental liability for the acts of minors. In Nevada, for example, the following is stated in Section 41.470 of the Nevada Revised Statutes:

> 1. Except as otherwise provided in NRS 424.085, any act of willful misconduct of a minor which results in any injury or death to another person or injury to the private property of another or to public property is imputed to the parents or guardian having custody and control of the minor for all purposes of civil damages, and the parents or guardian having custody or control are jointly and severally liable with the minor for all damages resulting from the willful misconduct.

In West Virginia Section 55.77A-2 states the following:

> The custodial parent or parents of any minor child shall be personally liable in an amount not to exceed five thousand dollars for damages which are the proximate result of any one or a combination of the following acts of the minor child:

2. Generally the actor believes that he must avoid imminent harm.
3. Generally the actor must use force to protect himself from another's use of force.

> (a) The malicious and willful injury to the person of another; or
> (b) The malicious and willful injury or damage to the property of another, whether the property be real, personal or mixed; or
> (c) The malicious and willful setting fire to a forest or wooded area belonging to another; or
> (d) The willful taking, stealing and carrying away of the property of another, with the intent to permanently deprive the owner of possession.
>
> For purposes of this section, "custodial parent or parents" shall mean the parent or parents with whom the minor child is living, or a divorced or separated parent who does not have legal custody but who is exercising supervisory control over the minor child at the time of the minor child's act.

In Florida, parents may be liable for willful destruction or theft of property under Section 741.24, and in Illinois, parents may also be liable for willful or malicious property damage or personal injury under Section 115-3 of the criminal code. Does your state have parental criminal liability laws for certain acts of minor children? Use an internet search engine to find them and compare them to those discussed in this chapter.

7.4.2 Spousal Relationships

Another interesting emerging area in the discussion of criminal responsibility for the acts of another pertains to the spousal relationship. This case will provide you with an opportunity to practice your case briefing, identification of issues, and analysis skills.

Case Example: Practice Opportunity

Here is a practice opportunity: read the following case excerpt and use a yellow highlighter to identify the material facts of the case; use a blue highlighter to note the relevant statutory language; use a pink highlighter to note the alleged crime; and use a green highlighter to note the court's application of the law to the facts of the case; to highlight the court's analysis. You may need to use an internet search engine to look-up some of the references to the crimes so that you have the applicable definitions.

People v. Wallace

123 Cal.App.4th 144 (2004)

> One summer evening in Fresno, Anthony LeRoy Wallace's wife of two months, Arlissa Pointer Wallace, caught him smok-

ing crack cocaine, called him a crack head, and told him to leave the house she had bought six or seven years before the marriage and had refinanced shortly after the marriage. Although she had kept the house in her name, Wallace presumably had acquired a small community property interest through mortgage payments with community property funds.

Instead of leaving, however, Wallace began tearing up the house. Frightened, Pointer kept her distance from him as she opened the living room curtains in the hope a neighbor might see and call the police. He kept breaking things. Twice she dialed 911, but twice she hung up, fearing things would get much worse if he knew she had called. He left before the police arrived. She told a police officer that the only thing he had not broken in the house was his own stereo and that everything else in the house belonged to her. A couple of hours later, alerted by a neighbor to "incredible pounding, very, very loud noise" from the house, police officers found Wallace inside the house breaking things again. Only after he challenged three armed and uniformed officers to fight did they subdue him with a taser and arrest him.

At trial, an expert witness testified to over $9,000 of damage to the house and to over $6,000 of damage to the furniture and furnishings. A jury found Wallace guilty of felony vandalism and of two misdemeanors—being under the influence and resisting, delaying, or obstructing an officer ("resisting")—[123 Cal.App.4th 147] and found two assault with a deadly weapon priors true as both serious felony priors and prison term priors.

Wallace argues that as a matter of law he cannot be guilty of vandalizing either community property or his spouse's separate property inside the marital home. In the published portion of our opinion, we will reject his argument and embrace the emerging rule imposing criminal liability on a spouse for intentionally causing harm to property in which the other spouse has an interest, whether the property is individual or marital, whether the harm occurs outside or inside the marital home. In the nonpublished portion of our opinion, we will address his numerous other arguments and grant relief as to two. In the first, the evidence showed, and the prosecutor argued, that Wallace committed two acts of resisting, but the record shows neither an explicit election by the prosecutor nor a unanimity instruction by the court, so we will order the resisting conviction stricken from the judgment. In the second, the court miscalculated Wallace's presentence custody credit and failed to award him the presentence conduct credit to which he was entitled, so we will modify the judgment accordingly. Otherwise we will affirm the judgment.

The question before us is whether a spouse can be guilty of vandalizing community property and the other spouse's separate property inside the marital home. Wallace asks us to answer that question in the negative on the basis of "the common law rule that a person's home is his or her castle" and the language in the vandalism statute that a vandal can deface, damage, or destroy only property that is "not his or her own." The Attorney General asks us to answer that question in the affirmative, arguing that vandalism is not a crime that threatens property rights only in a particular place, that the criminal law protects each owner's interest in community property against nonconsensual damage by the other, and that Pointer's separate property suffered most of the harm anyway.

In *People v. Kahanic* (1987) 196 Cal. App. 3d 461 [241 Cal. Rptr. 722], we held that the vandalism statute applies to community property on the rationale that the "essence of the crime is in the physical acts against the ownership interest of another, even though that ownership is less than exclusive." (*Id.* at p. 466.) Citing *Kahanic*, a proposed vandalism instruction from the Judicial Council's Task Force on Jury Instructions requires proof that the accused "did not own the property" or "owned the property with someone else. However, Wallace argues that with the vandalism in *Kahanic* occurring outside the marital home the case is inapposite to the issue here whether "the common law rule that a person's home is his or her castle" precludes criminal liability for vandalizing property in one's own home. He analogizes that issue to the question whether a person can burglarize his or her own home and notes the California Supreme Court relied on the common law rule to hold that the burglary statute applies only to "a person who has no right to be in the building." He argues that as one can neither burgle nor trespass in one's own home; neither can one vandalize property in one's own home.

Wallace's argument ignores three key differences between vandalism, on the one hand, and burglary and trespass, on the other. First, one can commit vandalism anywhere but one can commit burglary and trespass only by entering into a specific place. Second, one cannot commit vandalism without defacing, damaging, or destroying property, but one can commit burglary and trespass without harming any [123 Cal.App.4th 149] property at all. Third, the harm that vandalism by a spouse necessarily inflicts to community property or to the other spouse's separate property ousts the other spouse of his or her ownership interest in a way that neither burglary nor trespass necessarily does. Together, those differences foil Wallace's endeavor to broaden to vandalism the rule that applies to burglary and trespass.

Instead, on the question before us, we broaden our holding in *Kahanic* to embrace the emerging rule imposing criminal liability on a spouse for intentionally causing harm to property in which the other spouse has an interest, whether the property is individual or marital, whether the harm occurs outside or inside the marital home. (see, e.g., *Jackson v. United States* (D.C. 2003) 819 A.2d 963, 964-967 (*Jackson*) [spouse [123 Cal.App.4th 150] criminally liable for harm to marital property at marital home under statute prohibiting harm to property "not his or her own"]; *State v. Superior Court* (Ct. App. 1997) 188 Ariz. 372 [936 P.2d 558, 559] [spouse criminally liable for harm to joint tenancy property of both spouses under statute prohibiting damage to "property of another person"]; *State v. Coria* (2002) 146 Wn. 2d 631 [48 P.3d 980, 981-985] (*Coria*) [spouse criminally liable for harm to community property at marital home under statute prohibiting damage to "property of another"]; *Hughes v. State* (Alaska Ct.App. 2002) 56 P.3d 1088, 1094-1095 [spouse criminally liable for harm to marital property at marital home under statute prohibiting damage to "property of another"]; *Ginn v. State* (2001) 251 Ga.App. 159 [553 S.E.2d 839, 840, 842] [spouse criminally liable for harm to marital property at marital home under statute prohibiting damage to "any property of another"]; *State v. Sevelin* (Ct.App. 1996) 204 Wis.2d 127 [554 N.W.2d 521, 522-523] [spouse criminally liable for harm to marital property at marital home under statute prohibiting damage to "any physical property of another"]; *State v. Zeien* (Iowa 1993) 505 N.W.2d 498, 498-499 [spouse criminally liable for harm to marital property at marital home under statute prohibiting damage to property "by one who has no right to so act"]; *People v. Schneider* (App.Ct. 1985) 139 Ill. App. 3d 222 [487 N.E.2d 379, 379-381, 93 Ill. Dec. 712] [spouse criminally liable for harm to marital property under statute prohibiting damage to "any property of another"]; but see *Horn v. State* (Ala.Crim.App. 2004) ___ So. 2d ___ [2004 Ala. Crim. App. LEXIS 88, 2004 WL 924682] [spouse not criminally liable for harm to marital property under statute prohibiting "damages to property"]; *State v. Powels* (Ct.App. 2003) 2003 NMCA 90, 134 N.M. 118 [73 P.3d 256, 257-259] [spouse not criminally liable for harm to marital property under statute prohibiting damage to "any real or personal property of another"]; *People v. Person* (N.Y.App.Div. 1997) 239 A.D.2d 612 [658 N.Y.S.2d 372, 373] (*Person*) [spouse not criminally liable for harm to marital property under statute prohibiting damage to property of another person]; see generally Lutz & Bonomolo, *My Husband Just Trashed Our Home; What Do You Mean That's Not a Crime?* (1997) 48 S.C. L.Rev. 641, 651 ["[W]hen a husband destroys property that he owns jointly with his wife, not only does he destroy his property, which he may have a right to destroy, but he simultaneously destroys his wife's undivided one hundred percent interest in the property, which he does not have a right to destroy."]; cf. Carpenter, *Of the Enemy Within, The Castle Doctrine, and Self-Defense* (2003) 86 Marq. L.Rev. 653, 693 ["The innocent cohabitant still has an identifiable interest in the protection that the sanctuary might offer and should not be denied its safe harbor because someone else may share in its possession. [Footnote.]"].) [4] Accordingly, we answer in the affirmative the question before us and [123 Cal.App.4th 151] hold that a spouse can be guilty of vandalizing community property and the other spouse's separate property inside the marital home.

The judgment is affirmed.

Stop and Engage

Now that you have highlighted key parts from this case, complete the following activities:

- Identify the main issue(s) in this case.
- Write a concise summary of the material facts.
- Paraphrase the relevant statutory language with precision and accuracy.
- Write a concise summary of the court's reasoning.
- Write a concise explanation as to how and why the court reached its decision—its holding.

7.5 Summary

In the commission of a crime and criminal activity, there is often more than one "actor" or defendant. In certain instances, several people may be involved in committing the crime—for example, in bank robberies several people may engage in the criminal activity. In burglary or robbery, there may be several parties to the crime. In criminal law, we discuss vicarious liability in the context of whether a corporation can be liable for the acts of its agents and in connection with notions of ***respondeat superior*** ("let the master answer"). A similar topic to vicarious liability and criminal liability for the acts of another is the topic of criminal responsibility for the conduct of another which may include parental liability for the acts of minor children as well as spousal liability for the acts of a spouse.

7.6 Chapter Review Activities

Analyze the fact pattern, identifying the relevant facts and elements of a crime and determining what crime is appropriate for each actor. Be sure to write in clear, well-reasoned sentences. Note as well that you may need to refer to crimes that you have learned in previous chapters, so think of the crimes of this chapter as well as crimes learned in previous chapters. Reasoning, writing style, and clarity are important factors in this activities.

Hypothetical Fact Pattern I

Scott, a middle manager for a medium-sized public corporation was also responsible for Corporate Citizenship, where each year a team headed by Scott would select one or two civic organizations and provide financial support. There was no budget for this assistance. Scott devised a scheme where, during the year as a condition of growth and promotion, all employees were required to enter various lotteries and betting pools for athletic events. Winners collected a token sum, and the majority of the pool was used to fund the corporate giving. The corporation received tax benefits for these contributions. Some employees became increasingly unhappy with this forced contribution, eventually filing a complaint with the Department of Human Resources. The department contacted the local district attorney who filed charges of criminal theft against Scott, his citizenship team, and the officers of the corporation.

Hypothetical Fact Pattern II

Sergeant John Hightower was a tough, non-nonsense, ex-Marine street cop who welcomed an assignment to patrol the roughest area of town. He had been on the force for 22 years, working his way up from patrolman to sergeant. Over the years, he had refused several opportunities for promotion because he would be less involved in "catching the bad guys." He had never found it necessary to fire his sidearm, but he used his baton, his fists, his taser, and his handcuffs liberally. Sgt. Hightower had the highest rate of closure by confession in the department. He was often asked to be a training officer, where rookie patrolmen would ride along with him and learn the "real" job of being a cop. Late one night, while driving down a busy street with a rookie in the car, Sgt. Hightower saw two men he recognized as neighborhood thugs. They were walking quickly down the sidewalk with a third man between them. The three were walking unusually close together, and Sgt Hightower suspected a shake-down was in progress. He turned his patrol car around, stopped near the curb, got out of the car, and confronted the three men. The rookie also exited the patrol car and stood nearby. Sgt. Hightower asked the three men where they were going and received a mumbled response. He noticed that the man in the middle had been roughed up, as evidenced by a black eye and blood coming from his nose and lower lip. He asked again for identification and received no response. Sgt. Hightower gripped his baton and struck one of the men behind the knee, causing him to fall to the ground. He then kicked the man in the back. The other man attempted to flee, and Sgt. Hightower struck him across the shoulder with the baton, breaking his collar bone. He then kicked the second man in the face, knocking out several teeth. The rookie cop realized that he was witnessing an assault, but he did nothing to intervene.

Chapter 8

Inchoate Crimes

Key Terms and Concepts

Inchoate Crimes	Attempt	Substantial Step
Conspiracy	Solicitation	

8.1 Introduction

What are inchoate crimes? Inchoate crimes are crimes that are categorized based on criminal activity that involves incomplete crimes, preparation to complete crimes, and involvement of others. The most common types of inchoate crimes are attempt, conspiracy, and solicitation. In an inchoate crime, the focus is not on the completion or actual final commission of the crime but on the steps taken to prepare for the crime (attempt) or conversations or urgings to enter into criminal activity (solicitation) or agreement to commit criminal activity (conspiracy). In other words, in inchoate crimes there needs to be some action, some step or steps—it is insufficient for someone to just think about the commission of a crime or criminal activity. There are several typologies in inchoate crimes:

- Attempt—trying to commit a crime.
- Conspiracy—more than one person is involved—an agreement to commit a crime is needed.
- Solicitation—trying to enlist someone else to help in a crime.

All of these typologies involve a specific intent or purpose for attempt. An agreement or solicitation cannot be reached negligently—or recklessly. Several measures of *actus reus* in inchoate crimes can be listed:

- Substantial steps—(What is "substantial"?)
- Physical proximity—how far along were the defendants to completing the crime?

- Indispensable element—have the defendants obtained control of everything they need to complete the crime?
- Unequivocality—if a reasonable person observed the defendants' actions, would he/she believe that a crime was in progress?
- Probable desistance—how far have the defendants progressed towards completing a crime?

8.2 Attempt

"Attempt" is explained under Section 5.01(1) of the MPC:

> A person is guilty of an attempt to commit a crime if, acting with the kind of culpability otherwise required for commission of the crime: (a) purposely engages in conduct that would constitute the crime if the attendant circumstances were as he believes them to be; or (b) when result is an element of the crime, does or omits to do anything with the purpose of causing or with the belief that it will cause such result without further conduct on his part; or (c) purposely does anything that, under the circumstances as he believes them to be, is an act constituting a substantial step in a course of conduct planned to culminate in his commission.

Under Section 5.01(2) of the MPC we learn the definition of a "**substantial step**" and its inherent meaning:

> A Substantial Step must be strongly corroborative of the actor's criminal purpose. The following, if strongly corroborative of the actor's criminal purpose, shall not be held insufficient as a matter of law: (a) lying in wait, searching for or following the contemplated victim of the crime; (b) enticing or seeking to entice the contemplated victim of the crime to go to the place contemplated for its commission; (c) reconnoitering the place contemplated for the commission of the crime; (d) unlawful entry of a structure, vehicle or enclosure in which it is contemplated that the crime will be committed; (e) possession of materials to be employed in the commission of the crime, that are specially designed for such unlawful use or that can serve no lawful purpose of the actor under the circumstances; (f) possession, collection or fabrication of materials to be employed in the commission of the crime, at or near the place contemplated for its commission, if such possession, collection or fabrication serves no lawful purpose of the actor under the circumstances; or (g) soliciting an innocent agent to engage in conduct constituting an element of the crime.

Under Section 5.01(4), it is further explained:

> It is an affirmative defense that he abandoned his effort to commit the crime or otherwise prevented its commission, under circumstances manifesting a complete and voluntary renunciation of his criminal purpose. The establishment of such defense does not affect the liability of an accomplice who did not join in such abandonment or prevention.

Now that we have a general understanding of "attempt," we can review the definition in a few state statutes. In Texas, inchoate offenses, are found in Title 4 and are labeled further as "Preparatory Offenses" in Chapter 15 of Title 4. Criminal attempt is defined in Section 15.01(a) in this way:

> (a) A person commits an offense if, with specific intent to commit an offense, he does an act amounting to more than mere preparation that tends but fails to effect the commission of the offense intended.
>
> (b) If a person attempts an offense that may be aggravated, his conduct constitutes an attempt to commit the aggravated offense if an element that aggravates the offense accompanies the attempt.
>
> (c) It is no defense to prosecution for criminal attempt that the offense attempted was actually committed.

Stop and Engage

Based on this definition in the Texas Penal Code, what is the requisite *mens rea* for the crime of attempt? What "acts" must be committed to prove that a person committed criminal attempt?

We can deconstruct the elements of this crime from the language of the law as follows:

- Specific intent—we cannot negligently stumble into an attempt. We must desire to actually carry out an offense.
- "More than mere preparation"—we will need an interpretation from case law to decide "preparation". The major problem in this element is the word "more." Is 2/3 of an act "more"? How about 50% of an act? It's important to recognize that "mere preparation" is not enough. In this class, we need only to identify the issue.
- "Effect the commission of the offense"—for instance, if a bomb fails to explode, the crime has not been "effected."

In Florida, "attempt," "solicitation," and "conspiracy" are grouped together in Section 777.04. Section 777.04(1) defines the word "attempt":

> A person who attempts to commit an offense prohibited by law and in such attempt does any act toward the commission of such offense, but fails in the perpetration or is intercepted or prevented in the execution thereof, commits the offense of criminal attempt, ranked for purposes of sentencing as provided in subsection (4). Criminal attempt includes the act of an adult who, with intent to commit an offense prohibited by law, al-

lures, seduces, coaxes, or induces a child under the age of 12 to engage in an offense prohibited by law.

Illinois defines attempt in Section 8-4:

(a) Elements of the offense: A person commits the offense of attempt when, with intent to commit a specific offense, he or she does any act that constitutes a substantial step toward the commission of that offense.

(b) Impossibility: It is not a defense to a charge of attempt that because of a misapprehension of the circumstances it would have been impossible for the accused to commit the offense attempted.

Learning Activity

Choose one of the above definitions of attempt or use an internet search engine to find your state's definition of attempt in its criminal or penal code. Then, (a) write a fact pattern for the crime of attempt, and (b) write a model answer that demonstrates how you identify the *mens rea* and the *actus reus* from the actual language of the definition for the crime of attempt.

Case Example: Practice Opportunity

The issue of a "substantial step" is a significant factual determination in cases pertaining to the crime of attempt. Here is a practice opportunity to learn more about how court's decide if there are sufficient facts to prove a particular element of a crime such as a "substantial step." Read the following case excerpt and use a yellow highlighter to identify the material facts of the case; use a blue highlighter to note the relevant statutory language; use a pink highlighter to note the alleged crime; and use a green highlighter to note the court's application of the law to the facts of the case, to highlight the court's analysis.

United States of America v. Jessup

305 F.2d 300 (2002)

Scott William Jessup appeals his conviction for possession of pseudoephedrine with intent to manufacture methamphetamine and his attendant sentence.

A San Antonio police officer on patrol stopped a pickup truck to issue a citation for unlawfully riding in the open bed of the truck. While the officer was questioning the truck's driver about a discrepancy between the license plates and the vehicle registration, the officer noticed that the bed of the truck contained items that he knew were commonly used to manufacture methamphetamine. The officer called for narcotics investigators to respond to the scene. The officers identified the man riding in the open bed of the truck as Jessup. Jessup was arrested on an outstanding warrant for a parole violation.

The driver of the pickup signed a consent to search form. In the course of the search, the officers uncovered a large footlocker containing 27.9 grams of pseudoephedrine (an immediate precursor for the manufacture of methamphetamine) and other items used to make methamphetamine, including a Pyrex dish, a coffee pot with Jessup's fingerprints, filters, funnels, plastic and glass jars, ph paper, and muriatic acid. The officers also found a black gym bag containing a methamphetamine recipe, a chemistry book, a shopping list containing items used to manufacture methamphetamine, and an address book belonging to Jessup. They discovered more methamphetamine ingredients and equipment in the bed of the truck, including iodine crystals, several match boxes (the strike plates on the boxes contain red phosphorous, a methamphetamine ingredient), and a bag containing tubing and hose clamps.

The driver told the officers that the items belonged to Jessup and that he was helping Jessup move. The officers later interviewed Mary Posey, the owner of Jessup's former residence, who said that she had asked Jessup to move out and had packed his belongings. Jessup eventually pleaded guilty to one count of possession of pseudoephedrine with intent to manufacture methamphetamine in violation of 21 U.S.C. §841(d)(1).

On appeal, Jessup challenges the district court's denial of his untimely motion to suppress the evidence found in the pickup truck. Jessup's guilty plea waived any right he might otherwise have had to appeal the denial of the suppression motion.*See United States v. Wise,* 179 F.3d 184, 186 (5th Cir.1999). In *Wise,* we explained that when "a trial court denies a motion to suppress evidence and the defendant subsequently enters an unconditional plea of guilty, the defendant has waived the right to raise further objection to that evidence." *Id.* Here, Jessup's plea did not specify that it was conditional. *See id.* ("Conditional pleas must be made in writing, consented to by the prosecution, and approved by the court."). As such, he has waived any right to challenge the denial of the suppression motion.

Jessup also appeals the district court's sentence on the grounds that, although he *intended* to produce methamphetamine, he did not *attempt* to do so. U.S.S.G. §2D1.11 governs sentencing for, among other offenses, possession of listed chemicals like pseudoephedrine. Section 2D1.11(c) contains a "cross reference." The cross-reference provides that if "the offense involved ... *attempting* to manufacture a controlled substance [like methamphetamine] unlawfully, apply [U.S.S.G.] §2D1.1 ... if the resulting offense level is greater than that determined above" (emphasis added). In order to show that the defendant attempted to manufacture methamphetamine, the government must show that the defendant "(1) acted with the required criminal intent, and (2) engaged in conduct constituting a 'substantial step' toward commission of the substantive offense.'" *United States v. Anderson,* 987 F.2d 251, 255-56 (5th Cir.1993) (setting forth the elements for the crime of attempt to manufacture methamphetamine (explaining that the definition of "attempt" to manufacture methamphetamine for the purposes of the sentencing guidelines is the same as the definition of the substantive offense of attempt to manufacture methamphetamine).

The probation officer determined that Jessup had attempted to manufacture methamphetamine, and therefore applied the cross reference. Jessup objected on the grounds that his actions constituted only "mere preparation," that he had not taken any "substantial step" toward the manufacture of methamphetamine. He also argued that he did not know how to manufacture methamphetamine, even though he had seen it done. The government relied on a Tenth Circuit case, *United States v. Smith,* 264 F.3d 1012 (10th Cir.2001), in which the court upheld a sentence under the §2D1.11(c) cross reference on substantially similar facts. The government also argued that the pseudoephedrine found with Jessup had already been separated into its post-distillate phase. It argued that using pseudoephedrine to make methamphetamine involved a two-step process. The pseudoephedrine first has to be separated into a post-distillate form from cold, sinus, allergy or other similar tablets. The separated pseudoephedrine can then be used to make methamphetamine. According to the government, the pseudoephedrine found with Jessup had already undergone the first step in this process.

The district court sided with the government, holding that "I think in this case there was intent and there was indeed something that went beyond mere preparation and represented a substantial step toward the commission of the offense of manufacture of methamphetamine." It therefore applied the cross reference and sentenced Jessup under the harsher §2D1.1 guideline.

On appeal from sentencing decisions, we review the district court's application of the sentencing guidelines*de novo,* accepting the district court's findings of fact unless clearly erroneous. *United States v. Rodriguez-Guzman,* 56 F.3d 18, 20 (5th Cir.1995). Beyond even the clearly erroneous standard, we are also explicitly required by statute to give "due deference to the district court's *application* of the guidelines to the facts." 18 U.S.C. §3742(e).

Here, the district court correctly identified the governing law: that attempt requires intent and conduct constituting a "substantial step" toward the commission of the offense. We therefore review its application of the rule to the facts of this case with the "due deference" required by the statute.*Cf. Smith,* 264 F.3d at 1016 ("The 'substantial step' question appears to be a factual one, or at least one regarding the application of the guidelines to a particular set of facts."); *United States v. Montanye,* 996 F.2d 190, 191 (8th Cir.1993) ("Whether a defendant's conduct amounts to a substantial step necessarily depends on the facts of each case.")

Applying due deference, we cannot say that the district court erred in concluding that Jessup took a substantial step toward manufacturing methamphetamine. We have described a "substantial step" toward the commission of the crime as a step "strongly corroborative of the firmness of the defendant's criminal intent."*United States v. Mandujano,* 499 F.2d 370, 376 (5th Cir.1974). The affirmative act of collecting a substantial part of the equipment and ingredients for manufacturing methamphetamine can constitute action beyond "mere preparation" sufficient to constitute a substantial step. *See United States v. Fooladi,* 746 F.2d 1027 (5th Cir.1984); *United States v. Anderson,* 987 F.2d 251, 255-56 (5th Cir.1993); *United States v. Stone,* 960 F.2d 426, 433-34 (5th Cir.1992). In *Fooladi,* we upheld Fooladi's conviction for attempt to manufacture amphetamines based on the Drug Enforcement Agency's seizure from Fooladi's residence of P-2-P, an immediate precursor of amphetamines, and several formulas for converting P-2-P into amphetamines. Fooladi also confessed to the agents that he intended to convert the P-2-P to amphetamines. We found that this evidence was sufficient to support a jury verdict for attempt.

Here, Jessup possessed pseudoephedrine, an immediate precursor to methamphetamine, along with a substantial number of other ingredients for producing methamphetamine. Like Fooladi, Jessup possessed a recipe for converting the precursor drug into the final form. Jessup also plead guilty to intent to manufacture methamphetamine, and therefore acknowledged that he intended to finalize the process of converting the pseudoephedrine into methamphetamine. Applying deference, we cannot conclude that the district court erred in finding that Jessup had assembled sufficient equipment, ingredients, and instructions to have crossed the line between "mere preparation" and a "substantial step."

We therefore affirm Jessup's conviction and his sentence.

Stop and Engage

Now that you have highlighted key parts from this case, complete the following activities:

- Identify the main issue(s) in this case.
- Write a concise summary of the material facts.
- Paraphrase the relevant statutory language with precision and accuracy.
- Write a concise summary of the court's reasoning.
- Write a concise explanation as to how and why the court reached its decision—its holding.

8.3 Conspiracy

The crime of conspiracy generally requires that there be an agreement between two or more persons to commit a criminal act or to engage in criminal activity. Under the MPC a person can be charged with conspiracy if the person agrees with another to commit an offense, agrees with another to attempt to commit an offense, agrees with another to solicit others to commit an offense or agrees with another in aiding someone in planning the commission of the offense. You will note that the commonality among these various types of activities is the agreement. You will note some similarities with the concept of "agreement" and "engaging in different types of activities" as we explore the penal and criminal codes of various states.

In Texas, criminal conspiracy is defined in Section 15.02 in the following way:

> (a) A person commits criminal conspiracy if, with intent that a felony be committed:
>
> (1) he agrees with one or more persons that they or one or more of them engage in conduct that would constitute the offense; and
>
> (2) he or one or more of them performs an overt act in pursuance of the agreement.
>
> (b) An agreement constituting a conspiracy may be inferred from acts of the parties.
>
> (c) It is no defense to prosecution for criminal conspiracy that:
>
> (1) one or more of the coconspirators is not criminally responsible for the object offense;
>
> (2) one or more of the coconspirators has been acquitted, so long as two or more coconspirators have not been acquitted;
>
> (3) one or more of the coconspirators has not been prosecuted or convicted, has been convicted of a different offense, or is immune from prosecution;

(4) the actor belongs to a class of persons that by definition of the object offense is legally incapable of committing the object offense in an individual capacity; or

(5) the object offense was actually committed.

How would you write a precise and specific paraphrase of the crime of criminal conspiracy based on the Texas definition? Now we can deconstruct the elements of this crime:

Stop and Engage

- "Intent"—we cannot recklessly enter into conspiracy
- "A felony be committed"—eliminates minor crimes
- "Agrees"—implies discussion and a meeting of the minds about the crime. Raises an issue about the nature of "agreement." The facts must be examined to determine whether we can establish "agreement." Conspiracy is not about participation—the critical issue is about **agreement.**
- "With one or more persons"—the total is two or more; otherwise there cannot be a conspiracy.
- "Engage in conduct"—as soon as agreement is reached, we have a major step in the analysis, but notice at the end of (1) placement of the word "and;" paragraph (2) requires some action. There must be an overt act in the furtherance of the crime. Notice also that not everyone must participate in this act. The language is "he or one or more of them performs." (Raises the issue: must those who do not participate in the overt act at least be present?)
- In (b), the element is this: "agreement ... may be inferred from the acts of the parties." We must examine what the actors do to decide whether an agreement has been reached.

In California, conspiracy is defined in Section 182:

If two or more persons conspire:

(1) To commit any crime.

(2) Falsely and maliciously to indict another for any crime, or to procure another to be charged or arrested for any crime.

(3) Falsely to move or maintain any suit, action, or proceeding.

(4) To cheat and defraud any person of any property, by any means which are in themselves criminal, or to obtain money or property by false pretenses or by false promises with fraudulent intent not to perform those promises.

(5) To commit any act injurious to the public health, to public morals, or to pervert or obstruct justice, or the due administration of the laws.

(6) To commit any crime against the person of the President or Vice President of the United States, the Governor of any state

> or territory, any United States justice or judge, or the secretary of any of the executive departments of the United States.

Further in Section 184 of the California Penal Code it states this:

> No agreement amounts to a conspiracy, unless some act, beside such agreement, be done within this state to effect the object thereof, by one or more of the parties to such agreement.

Stop and Engage

How would you write a precise and specific paraphrase of the crime of conspiracy based on the California definition?

In New York, there are six degrees of conspiracy in Article 105. First degree conspiracy appears in Section 105.17 with this definition:

> When, with intent that conduct constituting a class A felony be performed, he, being over eighteen years of age, agrees with one or more persons under sixteen years of age to engage in or cause the performance of such conduct.

You will note the generality of the definition in relation to the definitions in some other states. However, you will also note some further clarification if you continue to read the headings of the various Articles under 105. Section 105.20 states this:

> A person shall not be convicted of conspiracy unless an overt act is alleged and proved to have been committed by one of the conspirators in furtherance of the conspiracy.

Further, Section 105.30 states the following:

> It is no defense to a prosecution for conspiracy that, owing to criminal irresponsibility or other legal incapacity or exemption, or to unawareness of the criminal nature of the agreement or the object conduct, or of the defendant's criminal purpose or to other factors precluding the mental state required for the commission of conspiracy or the object crime, one or more of the defendant's co-conspirators could not be guilty of conspiracy or the object crime.

Stop and Engage

How would you write a precise and specific paraphrase of the crime of conspiracy based on the New York definition?

In Ohio, conspiracy is defined in Section 2923.01 in this way:

> No person, with purpose to commit or to promote or facilitate the commission of aggravated murder, murder, kidnapping, compelling prostitution, promoting prostitution, aggravated arson, arson, aggravated robbery, robbery, aggravated burglary, burglary, engaging in a pattern of corrupt activity, corrupting another with drugs, a felony drug trafficking, manufacturing, processing, or possession offense, theft of drugs, or illegal processing of drug documents, the commission of a felony offense of unauthorized use of a vehicle, illegally transmitting multiple com-

mercial electronic mail messages or unauthorized access of a computer in violation of section 2923.421 of the Revised Code, or the commission of a violation of any provision of Chapter 3734. of the Revised Code, other than section 3734,18 of the Revised Code, that relates to hazardous wastes, shall do either of the following:

(1) With another person or persons, plan or aid in planning the commission of any of the specified offenses;

(2) Agree with another person or persons that one or more of them will engage in conduct that facilitates the commission of any of the specified offenses.

(B) No person shall be convicted of conspiracy unless a substantial overt act in furtherance of the conspiracy is alleged and proved to have been done by the accused or a person with whom the accused conspired, subsequent to the accused's entrance into the conspiracy. For purposes of this section, an overt act is substantial when it is of a character that manifests a purpose on the part of the actor that the object of the conspiracy should be completed.

(C) When the offender knows or has reasonable cause to believe that a person with whom the offender conspires also has conspired or is conspiring with another to commit the same offense, the offender is guilty of conspiring with that other person, even though the other person's identity may be unknown to the offender.

(D) It is no defense to a charge under this section that, in retrospect, commission of the offense that was the object of the conspiracy was impossible under the circumstances.

(E) A conspiracy terminates when the offense or offenses that are its objects are committed or when it is abandoned by all conspirators. In the absence of abandonment, it is no defense to a charge under this section that no offense that was the object of the conspiracy was committed.

(F) A person who conspires to commit more than one offense is guilty of only one conspiracy, when the offenses are the object of the same agreement or continuous conspiratorial relationship.

(G) When a person is convicted of committing or attempting to commit a specific offense or of complicity in the commission of or attempt to commit the specific offense, the person shall not be convicted of conspiracy involving the same offense.

Stop and Engage

How would you write a precise and specific paraphrase of the crime of conspiracy based on the Ohio definition? Choose two of the above definitions of conspiracy, or choose one and your own state's definition, and, then write an analysis that compares and contrasts the two definitions.

8.4 Solicitation

Solicitation is defined in the MPC Section 5.02 as "commanding or encouraging another person to engage in specific conduct that would constitute a crime or an attempt to commit a crime or that establishes complicity in connection with the commission or attempted commission of the crime. The person must have the purpose of promoting or facilitating the commission of the crime." In order to prove solicitation, the focus is on intent and conduct. Under Section 5.02(3), it is an affirmative defense that the person soliciting the other person persuaded him or her not to do the crime or actually prevented the commission of the crime under circumstances that demonstrate a complete and voluntary renunciation of the criminal purpose. How would you parse out the material elements of the crime from this definition?

- Commanding or encouraging another
- To engage in or attempt to engage in a crime
- With the purpose of promoting or facilitating the commission or attempted commission of the crime.

How are these elements similar to the definition of conspiracy in Virginia? Virginia defines conspiracy in Section 18.2-29 like this:

> Any person who commands, entreats, or otherwise attempts to persuade another person to commit a felony other than murder, shall be guilty of a Class 6 felony. Any person age eighteen or older who commands, entreats, or otherwise attempts to persuade another person under age eighteen to commit a felony other than murder, shall be guilty of a Class 5 felony. Any person who commands, entreats, or otherwise attempts to persuade another person to commit a murder is guilty of a felony punishable by confinement in a state correctional facility for a term not less than five years or more than forty years.

How would you parse the material elements from this definition?

- Commands, entreats or otherwise attempts to
- Persuade another
- To commit a felony

Texas defines solicitation in this way:

> (a) A person commits an offense if, with intent that a capital felony or felony of the first degree be committed, he requests, commands, or attempts to induce another to engage in specific conduct that, under the circumstances surrounding his conduct as the actor believes them to be, would constitute the felony or make the other a party to its commission.
>
> (b) A person may not be convicted under this section on the uncorroborated testimony of the person allegedly solicited and un-

> less the solicitation is made under circumstances strongly corroborative of both the solicitation itself and the actor's intent that the other person act on the solicitation.
>
> (c) It is no defense to prosecution under this section that:
>
> (1) the person solicited is not criminally responsible for the felony solicited;
>
> (2) the person solicited has been acquitted, has not been prosecuted or convicted, has been convicted of a different offense or of a different type or class of offense, or is immune from prosecution;
>
> (3) the actor belongs to a class of persons that by definition of the felony solicited is legally incapable of committing the offense in an individual capacity; or
>
> (4) the felony solicited was actually committed.

How would you parse the material elements from this definition?

- Intent that a capital felony or felony of the first degree be committed
- Requests, commands, or attempts to induce another
- To engage in specific conduct that
- Under the circumstances surrounding his conduct
- He believes them to be
- Would constitute a felony or make the other a party to its commission

Learning Tip

What are some of the factual issues that would need to be established from the facts of the case or the fact pattern hypothetical based on the material elements of the definition?

- How can you use the facts to prove intent?
- How do the facts demonstrate a request, command, or attempt at inducing another?
- What is the specific conduct?
- What does the person soliciting believe the circumstances to be? How do the facts establish that belief?

In New York, five degrees of criminal solicitation are listed. First degree criminal solicitation is defined in Section 100.13 in this way:

> A person is guilty of criminal solicitation in the first degree when, being over eighteen years of age, with intent that another person under sixteen years of age engage in conduct that would constitute a class A felony, he solicits, requests, commands, importunes or otherwise attempts to cause such other person to engage in such conduct.

Stop and Engage

Parse the material elements of this crime. What facts would you need to establish "solicits," "requests," "commands," "importunes," or "otherwise attempts?" Write a fact pattern that has facts that can be used to prove the crime of solicitation in New York without using the words from the actual definition. How does the definition of solicitation in New York compare with the definition of solicitation in Florida (Section 777.04(2))?

> A person who solicits another to commit an offense prohibited by law and in the course of such solicitation commands, encourages, hires, or requests another person to engage in specific conduct which would constitute such offense or an attempt to commit such offense commits the offense of criminal solicitation, ranked for purposes of sentencing as provided in subsection (4).

Case Example: Practice Opportunity

Read the following case excerpt and use a yellow highlighter to identify the material facts of the case, and note in the margin the crime(s) that may be applicable to these facts. Once you have identified the potentially applicable crimes, write out the definition of those crime(s) using Florida law.

Castro v. State of Florida

939 So. 2d 306 (2006)

The State's theory of the case was that Castro was bitter following his divorce and decided to have his ex-wife, Luz Flores, killed to exact revenge for the property she had taken from him in the divorce. The State presented evidence that to accomplish Flores's death; Castro reached out to his employee, Wilson Lopez. Lopez then reached out to Tobias Brown, a friend since childhood. Brown reached out to Seth Bain, a man he knew from work, who, unbeknownst to him, was working as an informant for the FBI. Bain reported the matter to the FBI. Agents put a recording device on Bain and recorded conversations Bain had with Brown and Lopez and had an undercover ATF agent act as the hit-man. The "hit-man" agreed to do the job for $10,000. Lopez told Castro the cost was $20,000, as he, Brown, and Bain were going to split the remaining $10,000. FBI agents contacted Flores and she agreed to allow a make-up artist to apply products to make it look as though she had been shot in the head. These photographs were provided to Brown and Lopez as proof that the job had been completed. Lopez testified that he gave Castro the picture and that Castro responded in the affirmative when he remarked "that's what you wanted." Castro was not a participant in any of the recorded conversations and the evidence introduced by the State established that of all the people involved in the murder for hire scheme, Castro had spoken only to Lopez. Castro's defense was that he had not solicited Lopez to have his ex-wife killed. Rather, Lopez had done this on his own accord in an attempt to impress

Castro and in the hopes of furthering his plans to somehow purchase Castro's deli meat delivery business.

Stop and Engage

Now that you have highlighted key parts from this case, complete the following activities:

- Identify the main issue(s) in this case.
- Write a concise summary of the material facts.
- Paraphrase the relevant statutory language with precision and accuracy.
- Write a model answer of how you would use the material facts to prove the applicable crime(s).

8.5 Summary

Inchoate crimes are crimes that are categorized based on criminal activity that involves incomplete crimes, preparation to complete crimes, and involvement of others. The most common types of inchoate crimes are attempt, conspiracy, and solicitation. Inchoate crimes focus not on the completion or actual final commission of the crime, but instead, on the steps taken to prepare for the crime (attempt) or conversations or urgings to enter into criminal activity (solicitation) or agreement to commit criminal activity (conspiracy). The crime of conspiracy generally requires that there be an agreement between two or more persons to commit a criminal act or engage in criminal activity.

8.6 Chapter Review Activities

Analyze the fact pattern, identifying the relevant facts and elements of a crime and determining what crime would be appropriate for each actor. Be sure to write in clear, well-reasoned sentences. Note as well that you may refer to crimes that you have learned in previous chapters, so think of the crimes of this chapter as well as crimes learned in previous chapters. Reasoning, writing style, and clarity are important factors in this activities.

Hypothetical Fact Pattern I

Anna was in a terrible marriage. For years her husband had enjoyed the company of other women, and when Anna confronted him, he physically and sexually abused her. The emotional abuse occurred almost constantly, but Anna could not bring herself to seek help from professional services, including law enforcement, because she did not want to suffer the humiliation of having her life open to public view. Over the years, the physical abuse worsened until Anna began to fear for her life. In near desperation, Anna decided to end her abuse by killing her husband. Anna began watching reality television shows to help find ways to kill him. This was an especially important decision to Anna because she was a small woman, and her husband could easily overpower her. She decided to purchase a small handgun, learn how to shoot it, and then kill her husband while he slept. Anna went to a flea market and found a gun owner who would sell her a small handgun without asking questions. She bought a weapon and a small supply of ammunition. Over the next several days, Anna spent time at a gun store which had an attached shooting range, and she hired an instructor who would teach her how to use her gun. Soon Anna felt she was ready. On Fridays, her husband went out drinking with friends, and he usually came home very late and extremely intoxicated. On the night Anna decided to act, her husband came home late and went directly to bed. Anna waited until she was sure he had passed out. She entered the bedroom with gun in hand, pressed the gun against his ear, and then lost her nerve. She began crying, ran from the room, and called the police. Discuss the relevant crimes.

Hypothetical Fact Pattern II

The Lucky Pin bowling team had just won second place in the summer league and had claimed a prize of $300. The five members of the team decided to pocket $40 each and spend the remainder on beer in the lounge. After a few minutes of whooping and slapping each other on the back to celebrate their victory, the conversation turned to the economic recession and how three of the five members of the team were out of work. As the beer flowed, the team members grew angry at how unfair it was for some people or businesses to have a lot of money, while they struggled just to pay the rent and buy their beer. Finally, the team hatched a preposterous plan to rob an armored vehicle as it transported cash from the mall. They decided to use pepper spray to disarm the guards, then they would enter the armored vehicle, grab the boxes of cash, and then to flee in a waiting car. They had no pepper spray, so Mike volunteered to go to the sporting goods store and buy several cans. Henry said that since he was out of work anyway, he had the time to watch the mall and decide when and where the armored vehicle stopped at the mall, and what route the guards walked as they picked up cash from merchants. They agreed to meet in a few days to finalize their plans. At the planned future meeting, Mike displayed six cans of pepper spray, and Henry had a chart of the guard's path.

Timothy and Charlie said they had reconsidered and wanted no part of the plan. Carl volunteered to drive the getaway car. Prior to execution of the group's robbery, a local bank opened a branch office in the mall, so individual deposits were made there by employees. Use of the armored car service was discontinued. Discuss the relevant crimes.

Hypothetical Fact Pattern III

Michael's career as a thief was developing nicely. Beginning at age 13, he learned the skill by first shoplifting small items that he could easily sell, then he progressed to stealing larger items from homes and small businesses, and now he had moved on to stealing cars, trucks, and motorcycles. His efforts usually resulted in several hundred dollars a week in earnings. The rare occasions when Michael was arrested, sent to jail, and ordered to make restitution were considered simply a business expense. Michael now believed himself ready to make some real money by robbing banks; he envisioned several thousand dollars in his pocket for just a few minutes of actual work. He realized that banks were more complicated to rob and that he would need some help, so Michael scoured the neighborhood looking for an accomplice. He spoke with friends, acquaintances, and many people that he knew were operating outside the law. None agreed to help until he spoke with Tony. Tony wasn't too bright, but he could park the car near the bank, yell a warning if he heard sirens or saw policemen, and drive the car at a high rate of speed to get away from the scene. Tony agreed to help. Discuss the relevant crimes.

Chapter 9

Selected Defenses

Key Terms and Concepts

Affirmative defenses	Infancy	M'Naghten Rule or Test
Justification defense	Insanity	Durham Rule or Product Test
Self-defense	Excuse defenses	Irresistible Impulse Test
Defense of Others	Castle Doctrine	MPC test or the substantial capacity test

9.1 Introduction

In criminal law, you will recall that the prosecution must prove every element of the crime beyond a reasonable doubt. This means that the prosecutor must establish that the defendant had the requisite culpability state (mental state or *mens rea*), that his or her actions satisfy the specified *actus reus* and that any other circumstances or attendant requirements in the statutory language can also be proven and connected to the defendant. In certain instances, the criminal code or penal code of a particular state may allow the defendant to assert a particular defense to either mitigate a particular charge (for example, in Texas you will recall that in connection with a charge of murder, a defendant "may raise the issue as to whether he caused the death under the immediate influence of sudden passion arising from an adequate cause. If the defendant proves the issue in the affirmative by a preponderance of the evidence, the offense is a felony of the second degree" (Section 19.02(d)), or negate an element of the crime (this is usually referred to as an "affirmative defense") or excuse or justify his or her actions. In most states, you will find general defenses which may be classified as "justifications" or "excuses" as well as "affirmative defenses." Affirmative defenses usually must be asserted by the defendant and proven by the defendant by a preponderance of the evidence (this is the standard for the burden of proof).

When a defendant asserts an affirmative defense, the effort is used to negate a particular element of the crime or avail himself/herself of particular statutory language that allows for the proof of attendant circumstances such as in the Texas murder statute. In the use of a justification defense, a defendant usually asserts that he/she was justified in his/her actions even if his/her actions were criminal in nature, or wrong. A justification defense is usually found in a factual scenario where the defendant faces a no-win situation and must make a choice "between the lesser of two evils"—an example of this would be if a person has to choose between swerving his car and driving on the sidewalk, endangering and potentially killing many pedestrians in order to avoid child in the middle of the street, or hitting and possibly killing the child. Either way, he isn't going to win. Self-defense and the "other" defense-related defenses are usually categorized as justification defenses. Excuse defenses are used by a defendant to argue that there were unusual circumstances or facts that should mandate either no conviction or a lesser punishment. With an excuse, the defendant is not arguing that he/she did not commit the crime, but he/she is saying that there was an excusable reason. Duress is usually an example of an excuse defense. The "heat of passion" defense referenced above in the Texas illustration qualifies as an example of a hybrid between a justification and an excuse defense. Insanity and mental capacity defenses are usually categorized as partial defenses to negate the *mens rea* element of the crime, and they may be used to delay prosecution or lessen the charge.

9.2 General Defenses to Criminal Responsibility

The Texas Penal Code, in general, permits specific defenses to many offenses. These are known as affirmative defenses, and they must be proven by a preponderance of the evidence. See TPC Title 2, Chapter 8. There are two general types of affirmative defenses: (1) justification, excluding culpability because the criminal act can be justified, usually by circumstances and (2) excuse, excluding culpability because an excuse (an acceptable reason) for the criminal act exists. When these defenses are used, the offender does not dispute the facts of the case. He is arguing that he should be relieved of culpability because he has a permissible excuse, arising from one or more of the following circumstances:

> TPC Sec. 8.01. Insanity. (a) It is an affirmative defense to prosecution that, at the time of the conduct charged, the actor, as a

result of severe mental disease or defect, did not know that his conduct was wrong.

(b) The term "mental disease or defect" does not include an abnormality manifested only by repeated criminal or otherwise antisocial conduct.

Several critical concepts are embedded in the insanity defense, and we will discuss more about this defense later in the chapter. The two main issues based on the language of the statute are these: (1) "at the time of the conduct charged"—this is factual determination; in some jurisdictions, "temporary insanity" might be argued, suggesting that the offender was sane prior to the event, and sane after the event (2) "as a result of severe mental disease or defect". Several tests are used to determine whether a mental disease or defect exists. Ignoring the possible exceptions for now, a typical argument could be that the defendant was under a psychiatrist's care. Typically, this argument does not include anomalies; e.g. defendant is not insane—he just enjoys killing.

TPC Sec. 8.02. Mistake of Fact. (a) It is a defense to prosecution that the actor through mistake formed a reasonable belief about a matter of fact if his mistaken belief negated the kind of culpability required for commission of the offense.

(b) Although an actor's mistake of fact may constitute a defense to the offense charged, he may nevertheless be convicted of any lesser included offense of which he would be guilty if the fact were as he believed.

The mistake of fact in this defense pertains to the culpability state; e.g. a mistake of fact might negate "knowingly." For example, an offender might argue that he was charged based upon a fact pattern believed to be true, but the facts were actually different from what he/she believed them to be.

TPC Sec. 8.03. Mistake of Law. (a) It is no defense to prosecution that the actor was ignorant of the provisions of any law after the law has taken effect.

(b) It is an affirmative defense to prosecution that the actor reasonably believed the conduct charged did not constitute a crime and that he acted in reasonable reliance upon:

(1) an official statement of the law contained in a written order or grant of permission by an administrative agency charged by law with responsibility for interpreting the law in question; or

(2) a written interpretation of the law contained in an opinion of a court of record or made by a public official charged by law with responsibility for interpreting the law in question.

(c) Although an actor's mistake of law may constitute a defense to the offense charged, he may nevertheless be convicted of a

> lesser included offense of which he would be guilty if the law were as he believed.

In the mistake of law, you will note that (a) ignorance of the law is not an affirmative defense. The most common use of this defense is when an official quotes or applies it incorrectly.

> TPC Sec. 8.04. Intoxication. (a) Voluntary intoxication does not constitute a defense to the commission of crime.
>
> (b) Evidence of temporary insanity caused by intoxication may be introduced by the actor in mitigation of the penalty attached to the offense for which he is being tried.
>
> (c) When temporary insanity is relied upon as a defense and the evidence tends to show that such insanity was caused by intoxication, the court shall charge the jury in accordance with the provisions of this section.
>
> (d) For purposes of this section "intoxication" means disturbance of mental or physical capacity resulting from the introduction of any substance into the body.

Learning Tip

You will note that in the intoxication defense, voluntary intoxication (having one too many drinks at the bar) is not a defense. Usually, this defense is argued when an offender ingests a legitimate drug (e.g. Benadryl), without knowing that it could cause drowsiness, and an accident occurs. This is a major reason why many over-the-counter medicines carry a warning about operating equipment or driving after taking the drug.

> TPC Sec. 8.05. Duress. (a) It is an affirmative defense to prosecution that the actor engaged in the proscribed conduct because he was compelled to do so by threat of imminent death or serious bodily injury to himself or another.
>
> (b) In a prosecution for an offense that does not constitute a felony, it is an affirmative defense to prosecution that the actor engaged in the proscribed conduct because he was compelled to do so by force or threat of force.
>
> (c) Compulsion within the meaning of this section exists only if the force or threat of force would render a person of reasonable firmness incapable of resisting the pressure.
>
> (d) The defense provided by this section is unavailable if the actor intentionally, knowingly, or recklessly placed himself in a situation in which it was probable that he would be subjected to compulsion.
>
> (e) It is no defense that a person acted at the command or persuasion of his spouse, unless he acted under compulsion that would establish a defense under this section.

When using the defense of duress, the offender argues that he was compelled to engage in criminal acts by threat of *imminent* death or serious bodily injury. This section contains many more circumstances, but we do not need to explore these.

Review the law for duress in New York as defined in Section 40.00; then, compare and contrast it with the law in Texas. New York Law Section 40.00 states this:

> 1. In any prosecution for an offense, it is an affirmative defense that the defendant engaged in the proscribed conduct because he was coerced to do so by the use or threatened imminent use of unlawful physical force upon him or a third person, which force or threatened force a person of reasonable firmness in his situation would have been unable to resist.
>
> 2. The defense of duress as defined in subdivision one of this section is not available when a person intentionally or recklessly places himself in a situation in which it is probable that he will be subjected to duress.

The most common use of entrapment as a defense under the Texas Penal Code pertains to actions by law enforcement officials. In general, the defendant will argue that he was induced to engage in criminal activity by a law enforcement officer. Consider TPC Section 8.06 which states this:

> Sec. 8.06. Entrapment. (a) It is a defense to prosecution that the actor engaged in the conduct charged because he was induced to do so by a law enforcement agent using persuasion or other means likely to cause persons to commit the offense. Conduct merely affording a person an opportunity to commit an offense does not constitute entrapment.
>
> (b) In this section "law enforcement agent" includes personnel of the state and local law enforcement agencies as well as of the United States and any person acting in accordance with instructions from such agents.

Stop and Engage

Compare the Texas statute with the language in New York's statute on entrapment which is defined in the category of "Other Defenses Involving Lack of Culpability" and is found in Section 40.05. This section defines entrapment in this way:

> In any prosecution for an offense, it is an affirmative defense that the defendant engaged in the proscribed conduct because he was induced or encouraged to do so by a public servant, or by a person acting in cooperation with a public servant, seeking to obtain evidence against him for purpose of criminal prosecution, and when the methods used to obtain such evidence were such as to create a substantial risk that the offense would be committed by a person not otherwise disposed to commit it. Inducement or encouragement to commit an offense means active

> inducement or encouragement. Conduct merely affording a person an opportunity to commit an offense does not constitute entrapment.

Note that Article 25 of the Laws of New York is entitled, "Defenses in General," and Section 25 provides some initial guidance regarding the burden of proof:

> § 25.00 Defenses; burden of proof.
>
> 1. When a "defense," other than an "affirmative defense," defined by statute is raised at a trial, the people have the burden of disproving such defense beyond a reasonable doubt.
>
> 2. When a defense declared by statute to be an "affirmative defense" is raised at a trial, the defendant has the burden of establishing such defense by a preponderance of the evidence.

9.3 The Insanity Defense and Other Defenses Lacking Culpability

Defenses which pertain to the negation of an element of a crime such as *mens rea* are often referred to defenses pertaining to culpability. The defendant uses the reasoning that because of a mental defect or impairment, age, involuntary intoxication, or another incapacitating factor, he/she should be able to assert that factor as a defense to mitigate or defeat the charges against him or her. Most states do not consider voluntary intoxication as a defense. Note the language in the Washington State statute, which is fairly representative of many other states:

> No act committed by a person while in a state of voluntary intoxication shall be deemed less criminal by reason of his condition, but whenever the actual existence of any particular mental state is a necessary element to constitute a particular species or degree of crime, the fact of his intoxication may be taken into consideration in determining such mental state.

Stop and Engage

What is the law regarding intoxication as a defense to criminal conduct in your state?

9.3.1 Infancy

Many states have provisions in their penal or criminal codes that require a person to be at or above a certain age in order to be deemed to be capable of forming a culpability state. If the person falls below the statutory age, then he or she may be considered incapable of committing a "crime" for purpose of the criminal or penal code, but there may be other laws that pertain to the person and may be used to hold him or her accountable for his or her actions. California Penal Code, Section 26 in Title 1, entitled "Persons Liable to Punishment for Crime," Section 26 states this:

> All persons are capable of committing crimes except those belonging to the following classes:
>
> One—Children under the age of 14, in the absence of clear proof that at the time of committing the act charged against them, they knew its wrongfulness.
> Two—Persons who are mentally incapacitated.
> Three—Persons who committed the act or made the omission charged under an ignorance or mistake of fact, which disproves any criminal intent.
> Four—Persons who committed the act charged without being conscious thereof.
> Five—Persons who committed the act or made the omission charged through misfortune or by accident, when it appears that there was no evil design, intention, or culpable negligence.
>
> Six—Persons (unless the crime be punishable with death) who committed the act or made the omission charged under threats or menaces sufficient to show that they had reasonable cause to and did believe their lives would be endangered if they refused.

Note that Class One uses age 14 as a "determining point" for criminal culpability in children. Now compare the language in Class One of Section 26 with the language in New York, Section 30:

> §30.00—Infancy.
>
> 1. Except as provided in subdivision two of this section, a person less than sixteen years old is not criminally responsible for conduct.
>
> 2. A person thirteen, fourteen or fifteen years of age is criminally responsible for acts constituting murder in the second degree.... ; and a person fourteen or fifteen years of age is criminally responsible for acts constituting ... kidnapping in the first degree; arson in the first degree; assault in the first degree; manslaughter in the first degree; rape in the first degree; criminal sexual act in the first degree); aggravated sexual abuse in the first degree); burglary in the first degree; burglary in the second degree; arson in the second degree; robbery in the first degree; robbery in the second degree), or where such machine gun or such firearm is possessed on school grounds ... or an attempt to commit murder in the second degree or kidnapping in the first degree, or for such conduct as a sexually motivated felony.
>
> 3. In any prosecution for an offense, lack of criminal responsibility by reason of infancy, as defined in this section, is a defense.

Stop and Engage

What are some of the differences between the California and New York laws on infancy? Note the age requirement in Washington State below which states the following:

> RCW 9A.04.050: Children under the age of eight years are incapable of committing crime. Children of eight and under twelve years of age are presumed to be incapable of committing crime, but this presumption may be removed by proof that they have sufficient capacity to understand the act or neglect, and to know that it was wrong. Whenever in legal proceedings it becomes necessary to determine the age of a child, he may be produced for inspection, to enable the court or jury to determine the age thereby; and the court may also direct his examination by one or more physicians, whose opinion shall be competent evidence upon the question of his age.

Stop and Engage

Why do you think there is such a disparity in the age requirement between Washington and California and New York? What is the age for infancy in Illinois? Under Section 6-1 of the Illinois Criminal Code, the age is 13 "at the time the offense was committed." Use an internet search engine to find the infancy law in your criminal or penal code.

9.3.2 Insanity

One of the most complex defenses involves the insanity defense and related defenses, such as diminished capacity. The issues are quite intricate because there are so many factual and interpretative issues compounded by expert testimony, and the judicial construction of various terms and requirements as interpreted from the numerous definitions of insanity. In this section, you will gain a basic grasp of some of the issues inherent in the insanity defense and become familiar with some of the more common tests and judicial interpretations. Before we consider some of the specific state statutes, it would be helpful to consider some of the definitions and tests that have stemmed from the Model Penal Code. You will recall that the Model Penal Code was originally drafted in 1962 by the American Law Institute as a model statute to provide guidance and direction to the state legislatures so as to promote some uniformity and consistency among the state codes.

MPC or Substantial Capacity Test

Under the Model Penal Code, the notion of an insanity defense is found in Article 4, entitled "Responsibility" and more specifically in Section 4.01, entitled "Mental Disease or Defect Excluding Responsibility" and it states this:

> (1) A person is not responsible for criminal conduct if at the time of such conduct as a result of mental disease or defect he

lacks substantial capacity either to appreciate the criminality of his conduct or to conform his conduct to the requirements of law.

(2) As used in this Article, the terms "mental disease or defect" do not include an abnormality manifested only by repeated criminal or otherwise antisocial conduct.

Based on the language "substantial capacity," some commentators and legal scholars refer to this test as the **MPC test or the substantial capacity test**. What do you think the key issue is in asserting a defense based on the MPC substantial capacity test? The answer is, simply, defining substantial capacity, which is not a simple judicial task. What are some other interpretative concerns? For example, how do you determine "appreciate?" Consider this case from Hawaii for a discussion of these issues.

Stop and Engage

Case Example: Practice Opportunity

Read the following case excerpt, and use a yellow highlighter to identify the material facts of the case; use a blue highlighter to note the relevant statutory language; use a pink highlighter to note the alleged crime; and use a green highlighter to note the court's application of the law to the facts of the case, to highlight the court's analysis.

State of Hawaii v. Byran Uyesugi

60 P.3d 843 (2002)

Defendant-appellant Byran Uyesugi appeals from the judgment of the first circuit court convicting Uyesugi of murder in the first degree in violation of Hawaii Revised Statutes (HRS) §707-701 (1993)1 and attempted murder in the second degree in violation of HRS §§705-500 (1993)2 and 707-701.5 (1993).3 On appeal, Uyesugi argues that: (1) the circuit court erred when it failed to instruct the jury on the legal definition of the terms "appreciate" and "wrongfulness."....

On November 9, 1999, Uyesugi was indicted on one charge of first degree murder for the shooting deaths of seven individuals, seven counts of murder in the second degree, and one count of attempted murder in the second degree. Witnesses testified that Uyesugi was an employee of the Xerox Corporation, and that on November 2, 1999 he arrived at work in time for an 8:00 a.m. "work group" meeting. Two of the seven victims were in the meeting room when witnesses heard a loud explosion, saw the two victims shot, and observed Uyesugi crouched with a gun in his hand. Two other witnesses testified to hearing the loud explosions and discovering the remaining five victims.

Uyesugi surrendered without further incident after a standoff with the police lasting several hours.

Jury instruction number 26, originally proposed by the prosecution, provided that:

> It is an affirmative defense to a criminal charge that, at the time of the offense, the Defendant was not criminally responsible for his conduct. The Defendant is not criminally responsible for his conduct if it is more likely than not or more probable than not that, at the time of the charged offense(s) and as a result of a physical or mental disease, disorder or defect, the Defendant lacked substantial capacity either to appreciate the wrongfulness of his conduct or to conform his conduct to the requirements of the law. A person "lacks substantial capacity" either to appreciate the wrongfulness of his conduct or to conform his conduct to the requirements of the law if his capacity to do so has been extremely limited by physical or mental disease, disorder or defect. The phrase "lack of substantial capacity" does not mean a total lack of capacity. It means capacity which has been impaired to such a degree that only an extremely limited amount remains. The term "physical or mental disease, disorder or defect" does not include an abnormality manifested only by repeated criminal or otherwise antisocial conduct. You must return a verdict of not guilty by reason of physical or mental disease, disorder or defect which excludes criminal responsibility if you find by a preponderance of evidence, that is, that it is more likely or more probable than not, that, at the time of the charged offense, 1) the Defendant was suffering from a physical or mental disease, disorder, or defect, and 2) that as a result of such physical or mental disease, disorder or defect, he lacked substantial capacity either to appreciate the wrongfulness of his conduct or to conform his conduct to the requirements of the law.

Defense counsel withdrew their requested instructions on the affirmative defense of physical or mental disease, disorder, or defect excluding criminal responsibility on June 1, 2000. The withdrawn instructions did not provide definitions of "appreciate" or "wrongfulness." The circuit court also instructed that "[u]nless otherwise provided, the words used in these instructions shall be given their usual sense and in connection with the context in which they appear."

Uyesugi argues that the instructions provided to the jury defining the affirmative defense of mental disease, disorder, or defect excluding penal responsibility (hereinafter "lack of penal responsibility") failed to define "appreciate," thereby depriving him of his right to a fair trial. Because the term was defined differently by the prosecution and defense experts, and because the prosecution argued the wrong definition, Uyesugi asserts that the jurors were left to speculate as to the exact meaning of the term. Uyesugi acknowledges that his trial counsel failed to object to these instructions, but argues that that failure amounted to ineffective assistance of counsel. The jury instructions regarding the defense of lack of penal responsibility could have substantially affected Uyesugi's rights; therefore analysis is appropriate. That analysis reveals that Uyesugi's substantial rights were not affected and that he was not prejudiced by the jury instructions. We hold that the circuit court did not plainly err when it did not define the term "appreciate." Penal Code (MPC), and our own case law. HRS § 704-400(1) employs the phrase "appreciate the wrongfulness of the person's conduct," in place of the original M'Naghten rule that "resolves the problem solely in regard to the capacity of the individual to know what he was doing and to know that it was wrong." MPC, Tentative Drafts Nos. 1-4, Comments § 4.01 at 156 (American Law Institute ed., 1956). The Hawaii legislature was convinced that the M'Naghten rule did not comport with modern medicine and psychiatry and, therefore, adopted the reasoning and language of the MPC. Hse. Stand. Com. Rep. No. 227, in 1971 House Journal, at 785; see also *State v. Moeller*, 50 Haw. 110, 116, 433 P.2d 136, 141 (1967) ("While we agree that the M'Naghten rule should have been discarded with the horse and buggy, it is part of our statutory law and as such, as long as we adhere to the rule that the legislature can prescribe rules of evidence, we must adhere to the statute.") (quoting *State v. Dhaemers*, 150 N.W.2d 61, 66 (Minn. 1967)).

Uyesugi argues that because the standard is no longer whether the defendant knows his act is wrong, the jury instructions should reflect the legislature's concern over the antiquated right/wrong standard and expressly inform the jury that "appreciate conveys a broader sense of understanding than simple cognition." The prosecution generally argues that "appreciate" is commonly used in daily conversation by people of ordinary intelligence and need not be defined.

The prosecution asserts that the fact that the circuit court informed the jury that unless otherwise instructed, words are given their ordinary meaning reinforces its argument that the jury required no specific definition. Defense counsel and the prosecution called experts who testified as to the meaning of the term "appreciate." This testimony was not dissimilar, but it was also not entirely consistent. One defense expert, Park Dietz, M.D., stated:

> I use the word appreciate according to the ordinary dictionary definition, and appreciate in my use of it means to accurately weigh or judge. Now, that means having the capacity to estimate accurately; and in particular, a standard for insanity, the capacity to appreciate wrongfulness, I understand to mean the ability to accurately estimate how wrong the crime was.

The second defense expert, Robert Marvit, M.D., stated that "[t]he word appreciate ... is not simply knowing. Otherwise, why not use the word know. The word appreciate is, in my understanding, the recognition of the greater significance of what's happening." Dr. Marvit then stated that "appreciate means to look beyond some kind of a narrow focus of either or, good or bad, right or wrong, this or that. It's being able to look at the consequence of a behavior." Based upon these definitions, Uyesugi states that the circuit court's instructions failed to convey the meaning of the term "appreciate" as applied to the defense of lack of penal responsibility. The prosecution rebuttal witness defined the term "appreciate" more specifically. For example, the following occurred between the prosecutor and his rebuttal witness, Harold Hall, Ph.D.:

> PROSECUTOR: Can I ask you, in terms of the word appreciate, and when you use that term and when you're using the test in this case or when you're giving your opinions on the test in this case, when you use that word, can it be or do you feel that it's synonymous with know or understand or realize?
>
> WITNESS: Or to know or to realize. During cross-examination of Dr. Hall, defense counsel asked, "Would you agree that to appreciate wrongfulness of conduct, it's different from knowing right from wrong?" Dr. Hall stated, "Well, it goes beyond a simple knowing what's legally right or wrong, yes." The prosecution's questioning of its expert witnesses during its case-in-chief indicated that the prosecution used the term "appreciate" interchangeably with the term "know."

For example, the prosecution asked Thomas Cunningham, Ph.D., "What is the significance of [Uyesugi] having a plan as it relates to the question of whether he knows what he's doing is right or wrong?" The prosecution asked the same witness, "What do you look at to determine whether or not a person knows right from wrong?"

The prosecution asked Tom Greene, Ph.D.:

> PROSECUTION: Do you have an opinion as to whether or not the capacity of the defendant to appreciate the wrong-

fulness of his conduct was substantially impaired by his delusional disorder?

WITNESS: I have an opinion on that.

PROSECUTION: What was your opinion?

WITNESS: No significant impairment.

PROSECUTION: Can you tell us why you had that opinion, why you did not believe that he knew right from wrong?

WITNESS: So the question—are the facts that he appreciated right or wrong behavior basically?

During cross-examination, Dr. Greene was asked whether he was equating "appreciate" with "knowing." Dr. Greene answered affirmatively. The prosecution asked its expert, Leonard Jacobs, M.D., whether the field of medicine, and psychiatry in particular, provides a "scientific basis for making a decision as to whether somebody knows right from wrong?" During cross examination, Dr. Jacobs was asked whether there is a difference between "appreciating" the wrongfulness of conduct and "knowing" the wrongfulness of conduct. Dr. Jacobs answered, "I don't see a difference." During his closing arguments, the prosecution continued to use the term "appreciate" interchangeably with "know."

Defense counsel, in his closing argument, also focused on the term "appreciate" and the meaning that should be ascribed to the term. At the beginning of its instructions, the trial court stated that "[u]nless otherwise provided, the words used in these instructions shall be given their ordinary meaning taken in their usual sense and in connection with the context in which they appear." Because the circuit court did not define the term "appreciate," the jury was left to define the word according to its ordinary usage.11 The circuit court's instructions were consistent with the Hawaii Standard Jury Instructions. See Hawaii Standard Jury Instructions-Criminal, Vol. 1, §7.07 at 93 (1991). The instructions were also consistent with the legislative intent in adopting the ALI/MPC insanity defense. Given the variety of uses and definitions of the term "appreciate," the pivotal question becomes whether the lack of a specific definition during jury instructions denied Uyesugi a fair trial. In its case-in-chief, the prosecution adduced testimony from eyewitnesses, police investigators, and experts, which, if believed, established that: (1) Uyesugi could "appreciate the wrongfulness of his conduct but acted out of anger in spite of that appreciation[,]"; (2) Uyesugi's "major psychiatric disorder" did not "substantially impair [Uyesugi's] capacity to appreciate the wrongfulness of his conduct,"; (3) Uyesugi expressed concern that "everybody was out to get him, that he was going to lose his job. He also had talked about how he was going to let some people down"; (4) the Glock 17 that Uyesugi used carried seventeen rounds of ammunition and was reloaded once during the shooting; (5) three of the victims had died of multiple gunshot wounds; and (6) Uyesugi concealed the weapon when he entered the building.

The defense presented expert testimony that Uyesugi was acting under a delusion that prevented him from acting normally in relation to the individuals who were a part of Uyesugi's delusional framework. According to these experts, Uyesugi could, and did, interact normally with individuals outside of his delusions. When acting within the context of his delusions, Uyesugi argued, he was unable to appreciate the wrongfulness of his actions. One defense expert, Dr. Dietz, testified that:

> In delusional disorder, the individual has ideas that are quite wrong. In lay terms, crazy ideas. And yet at the same time, the person can act normal, look normal, speak normally, think logically about all areas that aren't related to the delusion. And yet at the same time, have very odd whacky wrong ideas about everything connected to the delusions. He went on to state that Uyesugi's delusions had existed for ten to twelve years in relation to particular people at Xerox. These delusions included the belief that particular people he worked with were part of a conspiracy that has purposely, maliciously gone about trying to make him miserable, torment him, make him look bad, gossip about him, ruin his reputation, make it impossible for him to do his work well, make it likely he'll be fired, invade his home and begin to take away any chance of keeping his calm in the face of this repeated, constant day after day, year after year harassment and torment. Dr. Dietz testified that Uyesugi was under the deluded belief that one co-worker was employed by the government, that the FBI and CIA had surveillance equipment in his car and bathtub drain, and that the victims had invaded his home, mutilated his fish, stolen wood working projects, and gone through his private possessions.13 These defense experts agreed that Uyesugi knew killing was wrong, but that in the context of his delusions he could not appreciate the wrongfulness.

Despite the varying uses of the term "appreciate," none was improper. The ordinary meaning of the word is not precise. The jury heard testimony from experts who provided it with definitions, explanations, and examples of the meaning of "appreciate." The thorough and extensive expert testimony gave the jury the tools necessary for it to determine whether Uyesugi could "appreciate" the wrongfulness of his conduct. That testimony also brought forth the inherent subtleties of the term.

The closing arguments of the prosecutor are not evidence and the jury was informed of this. When Uyesugi argues that the standard is more subtle than to simply know the difference between right and wrong, he fails to understand the jury's ability to listen to the judge's instructions and the testimony of the expert witnesses. On the record before us, we hold that the circuit court did not commit plain error in its instructions to the jury.

We hold that: (1) as a matter of plain error analysis, defense counsel having failed to object to the jury instructions in which the term "appreciate" and "wrongfulness" were not defined, Uyesugi has failed to establish that his substantial rights were violated.

Now that you have highlighted key parts from this case, complete the following activities:

- Identify the main issue(s) in this case.
- Write a concise summary of the material facts.
- Paraphrase the relevant statutory language with precision and accuracy.
- Write a concise summary of the court's reasoning.
- Write a concise explanation as to how and why the court reached its decision—its holding.

M'Naghten Test

You may have noticed in this case the reference to the **M'Naghten Test,** or what is also referred to as the M'Naghten Rule. This is another popular test for the defense of insanity. This is perhaps one of the oldest tests, and it is derived from an 1843 British criminal law case. The panel of judges hearing the case developed the M'Naghten rule to determine legal insanity. The test is based on whether the defendant is unable to distinguish between right and wrong at the time of the commission of the crime because of some mental disability or disease of the mind. The essence of the test is whether the defendant knew right from wrong at the time of the crime.

This is a case that applies the M'Naghten rule and provides some interesting analysis. Use a green highlighter to note the court's application of the law to the facts of the case, to highlight the court's analysis.

Case Example: Practice Opportunity

State of Minnesota v. Peterson

764 N.W.2d 816 (2009)

Appellant Timothy James Peterson was convicted of first- and second-degree murder following a bifurcated trial where Peterson pleaded not guilty and not guilty by reason of insanity. In this direct appeal, Peterson asks us to reverse his convictions based on two issues: (1) the district court violated his due process right under the Minnesota Constitution by prohibiting expert psychiatric testimony in the guilt phase of his bifurcated trial, and (2) Peterson presented sufficient evidence to prove his mental illness defense by a preponderance of the evidence in the mental illness phase of his trial. We affirm Peterson's convictions, and we conclude that the statute mandating a sentence of life in prison without the possibility of release does not apply to Peterson's offense.

On March 18, 2005, Howard Hines was shot and killed while seated in the driver's seat of his vehicle, which was parked at his apartment building in Sauk Rapids, Minnesota. A resident of the apartment building discovered Hines inside his car and a number of bullet holes in the windshield. Right before discovering Hines, the resident saw Peterson, another building resident, lean out the window of his third-floor apartment and say, "I'm sorry. I'm sorry. I couldn't handle it anymore." Someone in the apartment building had already called 911.

Peterson also called 911. Disjointedly, he told the operator that he had been having a tough time with people "tunin" his head, he had "lost it," and had shot "one." He said he would be in front of the building when the "cops" came, although the police had already arrived from the earlier 911 call. Peterson came out of the building, where the police immediately handcuffed him. Peterson said that he had "shot him," and that he was "sick of [black people] around here messing with [Peterson]" on the computer. Peterson also told the police that the gun was up in his apartment.

When the police searched Peterson's apartment, they found several shotguns and two rifles. The police also found a chair in front of a bedroom window that faced the apartment parking lot; a large ashtray full of cigarette butts sat on the window ledge. On the floor were four spent gun shell casings, and a fifth spent casing was in the parking lot directly below Peterson's window. These casings were from a .270 caliber rifle, the same type of rifle found in Peterson's apartment.

Interrogations and interviews the same day and shortly after the murder indicated that Peterson had some sort of mental illness. Peterson's answers to police questions often failed to make sense; he talked about things such as being "hooked up" to a system with computers, and people "messing around" with him. But several of Peterson's statements were consistent with other evidence, and Peterson stated several times that he shot the victim. Peterson was charged with first-degree murder, Minn.Stat. §609.185(a)(1) (2008), and second-degree murder, Minn.Stat. §609.19, subd. 1(1) (2008).

In July 2005, Peterson's trial was stayed after the district court found that he was incompetent to stand trial pursuant to Minn. R.Crim. P. 20.01, subd. 2. After a number of reevaluations, Peterson was found competent to proceed on January 3, 2007. Peterson pleaded not guilty and not guilty by reason of insanity; accordingly, the trial would be bifurcated into a guilt phase and a mental illness phase under Minn. R.Crim. P. 20.02.

At a pretrial hearing, Peterson waived his right to a jury trial. At the same hearing, Peterson made a motion in limine on two issues: to allow a diminished capacity defense or, alternatively, to allow expert testimony on his mental illness during the guilt phase of the trial. The motion did not set forth any specific evidence or specific expert testimony that Peterson was trying to admit, but instead relied on the record as a whole. The district court denied the motion for the diminished capacity defense. On the issue of expert testimony, the court found that the offers of proof at that point did not have the "substantial relevance or probative value" to necessitate psychiatric testimony about Peterson's state of mind. The court then said, "[t]hat is not to say that some of that evidence may not be admissible in trial."

The primary contested issue during the guilt phase of the trial was whether Peterson had the intent required for first-degree murder or second-degree murder. Much of the evidence on this issue centered around two interrogations: one done by Officer Eric Norsten the same day as the murder, and the other done two days later by BCA agent Ken McDonald. In the first interrogation, Peterson's answers to Norsten's questions were often disjointed and nonsensical; he spoke most often of himself and others being "hooked up" and "unhooked" from a system. Some of the other themes in his answers included: computers and computer screens, people constantly "playing" and "messing with" Peterson, and Peterson's inability to "stand it" anymore. Peterson spoke of needing to take his aggression out on somebody, and wanting to "take out" his tormentors. Despite the many nonsensical answers to Norsten's questions, Peterson was able to answer some of Norsten's factual questions in a straightforward way.

Peterson was interrogated a few days later by BCA agent Ken McDonald. Again, Peterson's answers were confusing and unclear, with an increase in profanity and confrontational language. Peterson continued to talk about being played with, programmed, and hooked up, and said he shot the victim because he was "the closest one to me." Peterson again was able to answer many of the purely factual questions, but apparently could not respond meaningfully to questions about why he shot Hines.

Peterson did not call any witnesses after the State rested. The interrogating officers' testimony and the transcripts of interviews described above, however, were admitted to show the surrounding circumstances. The district court found Peterson guilty of first- and second-degree murder.

At the mental illness phase of the bifurcated trial, Peterson was the first to testify. On direct examination, his counsel relied solely on the videotape and the transcript of Norsten's interrogation of Peterson. On cross-examination, Peterson said that he was not talking to the officers during the interrogation, but was "looking at people behind them." When asked why he was crying during the interrogation, Peterson said because he had shot someone who had not done anything to Peterson, and he "felt bad that his body was shot and he was dead."

Dr. Gregory Hanson, a forensic psychologist, testified as Peterson's expert witness. Hanson diagnosed Peterson with paranoid schizophrenia, saying that he was exhibiting the typical symptoms in respect to auditory hallucinations, the prominence of paranoia and paranoid delusional beliefs, and mental disorganization. Hanson summarized some of Peterson's most significant delusional beliefs: there were a large number of black-haired individuals, primarily African-Americans, who were controlling and monitoring Peterson through computers and video cameras placed inside flies in his apartment; and he believed that he had been sexually assaulted and that the conspirators could control thoughts and move people's souls from one body to another.

In determining criminal responsibility under the M'Naghten standard, Hanson's opinion was that at the time of the crime, Peterson was not laboring under such defect of reason that he did not know the nature of his actions or the wrongfulness of his conduct. Hanson acknowledged there were strong indicators that Peterson should not be held criminally responsible: Peterson's illness had accelerated to the point that he was in a state of acute crisis, anger, and fear; he had no insight into his mental illness; and he believed Hines was allied with the conspirators. Peterson's statements suggest he saw no alternatives, and that the shooting was "a culmination of his paranoid delusional rage." Ultimately, though, Hanson concluded that the preponderance of the psychological evidence did not support Peterson's M'Naghten defense because Peterson knew the nature of his acts: he knew he was shooting someone, and although some comments suggest that he may not have known Hines would truly die, most statements indicated that he understood the essential nature of his action. Hanson also concluded that Peterson knew the wrongfulness of his conduct: his statements show that he was enraged, and he wanted to vent that hostility and aggression. Peterson's tears, his apologies, and his acknowledgment of the consequences suggest that he knew his actions were wrong.

Dr. Rosemary Linderman, a clinical and forensic psychologist testifying for the State, diagnosed Peterson with schizoaffective disorder. She explained that schizoaffective disorder includes the delusional beliefs of schizophrenia, but with a mood component that includes major depression and manic characteristics-in essence, paranoid schizophrenia with more volatility and emotion. Linderman also concluded that Peterson did not meet the M'Naghten burden of proof: Peterson's 911 call and report, his statements about taking his anger out on somebody, and his comments about the consequences he faced indicate that Peterson knew the nature of his acts. Linderman further concluded that Peterson's numerous apologies, his knowledge of the consequences, and his acknowledgment of alternative behavioral options supported that Peterson knew his conduct was wrong. The district court found that Peterson had not proven his mental illness defense by a preponderance of the evidence. He was sentenced to life in prison without the possibility of release.

We next consider whether there was sufficient evidence to prove Peterson's mental illness defense by a preponderance of the evidence. Minnesota has codified the M'Naghten standard for a mental illness defense at Minn.Stat. §611.026 (2008), which requires the defendant to show that "at the time of committing the alleged criminal act the person was laboring under such a defect of reason as not to know the nature of the act, or that it was wrong." A defendant must prove mental illness at the time of committing the crime by a preponderance of the evidence. *DeMars v. State*, 352 N.W.2d 13, 16 (Minn.1984) (citing *State v. Malley*, 285 N.W.2d 469, 472 n. 3 (Minn.1979)); see Minn.Stat. §611.025 (2008).

When reviewing the record to determine whether a defendant met his burden to prove mental illness, we conduct "a rigorous review of the record to determine whether the evidence, direct and circumstantial, viewed most favorably to support a finding of guilt, was sufficient to permit the trial court to reach its conclusion." *State v. Mytych*, 292 Minn. 248, 252, 194 N.W.2d 276, 279 (1972). We have consistently held that the issue of legal mental illness is a question for the finder of fact, and we have granted the fact finder broad deference in assigning the weight to give to various testimony. See *State v. Wilson*, 539 N.W.2d 241, 244 (Minn.1995); Brom, 463 N.W.2d at 764-65 (listing cases).

Peterson argues that his history of hospitalization, his delusional framework, the nature and severity of his mental illness, and the incomprehensibility of his statements to the police were sufficient proof of legal mental illness. Peterson argues that Hanson, who knew the severity of Peterson's mental illness, applied the M'Naghten standard too strictly to Peterson.

We do not agree with Peterson's characterization of Hanson's findings. Hanson considered all of Peterson's statements and actions, acknowledged that the case presented a close question, and ultimately concluded Peterson knew the nature and wrongfulness of his conduct. Even if Hanson's conclusions are disregarded, Linderman's report still supports a finding that the preponderance of the evidence does not support the M'Naghten standard for mental illness. Both experts concluded that Peterson understood the nature of what he was doing and that his behavior was wrongful, and both gave evidence to support both prongs. The evidence, viewed in a light most favorable to the verdict, was sufficient to permit the district court to find that Peterson had not proved his mental illness defense.

Stop and Engage

Now that you have read a case using the substantial capacity test and the M'Naghten Rule, how would you write a summary of the differences based on the court's analysis in the two cases?

Irresistible Impulse Test

Another test which was formed after the M'Naghten Rule and extends the concepts in the M'Naghten test is the "**Irresistible Impulse Test.**" The irresistible impulse test emphasizes not only whether the defendant knew the difference between right and wrong at the time of crime, but also whether he/she could not control the impulses that drove him/her to commit the "wrong-doing." In *Parsons v. State* 81 Ala 577 (1887), the question emphasized whether the duress of a mental disease impacted the defendant's free agency; the ability to choose between right and wrong. The purpose of the irresistible impulse test would not only be to determine whether a defendant knew right from wrong at the time of the crime, but it would also serve to investigate the defendant's volition, which raises many complex factual determinations. It is important to note that an impulse, for purposes of this test, is not considered a sudden outburst, but it is a festering, lengthy, evolutionary process of an inability to control one's actions. This test has not gained much acceptance and is not used frequently for purposes of the insanity defense.

Durham Rule

The fourth test in this area is known as the **Durham Rule** and was conceived originally in 1871, but it gained notoriety and acceptance in 1954 from the case which bears its name, *Durham v. United States*, 214 F. 2d 862. The Durham Rule is sometimes synonymously referred to as the **Product Test** because the rule states that a person will not be criminally responsible if his criminal act is the product of a mental disease or defect. You can imagine, based on this definition, the number of people who would obtain expert testimony stating that their act was the product of a mental disease. As a result, almost every state has abandoned the use of this test, and the District of Columbia in 1972 in *Brawner v. United States*, 471 F. 2d 969, moved away from the Durham Test towards a modified version of the MPC Test.

Statutory Examples

Now read Section 25 of the California Penal Code which states this:

> (a) The defense of diminished capacity is hereby abolished. In a criminal action, as well as any juvenile court proceeding, evidence concerning an accused person's intoxication, trauma, mental illness, disease, or defect shall not be admissible to show or negate capacity to form the particular purpose, intent, motive, malice aforethought, knowledge, or other mental state required for the commission of the crime charged.
>
> (b) In any criminal proceeding, including any juvenile court proceeding, in which a plea of not guilty by reason of insanity is entered, this defense shall be found by the trier of fact only when the accused person proves by a preponderance of the evidence that he or she was incapable of knowing or understanding the nature and quality of his or her act and of distinguishing right from wrong at the time of the commission of the offense.
>
> (c) Notwithstanding the foregoing, evidence of diminished capacity or of a mental disorder may be considered by the court only at the time of sentencing or other disposition or commitment.

It would appear that Section 25(b) has two prongs:

- The first prong requires a defendant to prove he or she was incapable of knowing or understanding the nature and quality of his or her act.
- The second prong requires the defendant to be able to distinguish between right from wrong at the time of the commission of the offense.

Stop and Engage

How would you label this insanity defense based on the descriptions above? How must this defense be presented based upon the language of the statute? What is the burden of proof, and who has the burden?

How do Sections 25 and 28 relate to one another, if at all?

> 28. (a) Evidence of mental disease, mental defect, or mental disorder shall not be admitted to show or negate the capacity to form any mental state, including, but not limited to, purpose, intent, knowledge, premeditation, deliberation, or malice aforethought, with which the accused committed the act. Evidence of mental disease, mental defect, or mental disorder is admissible solely on the issue of whether or not the accused actually formed a required specific intent, premeditated, deliberated, or harbored malice aforethought, when a specific intent crime is charged.
>
> (b) As a matter of public policy there shall be no defense of diminished capacity, diminished responsibility, or irresistible impulse in a criminal action or juvenile adjudication hearing.
> (c) This section shall not be applicable to an insanity hearing pursuant to Section 1026.
>
> (d) Nothing in this section shall limit a court's discretion, pursuant to the Evidence Code, to exclude psychiatric or psychological evidence on whether the accused had a mental disease, mental defect, or mental disorder at the time of the alleged offense.

New York, Article 40, contains the defenses that pertain to lack of culpability. These defenses include duress, entrapment, renunciation and mental disease or defect. We will review Section 40.15 pertaining to mental disease or defect so that we can compare it to the defense that is defined below in California. Section 40.15 states:

> In any prosecution for an offense, it is an affirmative defense that when the defendant engaged in the proscribed conduct, he lacked criminal responsibility by reason of mental disease or defect. Such lack of criminal responsibility means that at the time of such conduct, as a result of mental disease or defect, he lacked substantial capacity to know or appreciate either:
>
> 1. The nature and consequences of such conduct; or
> 2. That such conduct was wrong.

How would you compare and contrast the California insanity defense and the New York insanity defense? What do you need to prove for each of the defenses? What are some factual questions you will need to pose to apply the language in the statutes?

Stop and Engage

The insanity defense in Florida, found in Section 775.027, is presented as an affirmative defense in the following description:

> (1) All persons are presumed to be sane. It is an affirmative defense to a criminal prosecution that, at the time of the commission of the acts constituting the offense, the defendant was insane. Insanity is established when:
>
> (a) The defendant had a mental infirmity, disease, or defect; and
> (b) Because of this condition, the defendant:
>
> 1. Did not know what he or she was doing or its consequences; or
>
> 2. Although the defendant knew what he or she was doing and its consequences, the defendant did not know that what he or she was doing was wrong.
>
> Mental infirmity, disease, or defect does not constitute a defense of insanity except as provided in this subsection.
>
> (2) Burden of Proof: The defendant has the burden of proving the defense of insanity by clear and convincing evidence.

Stop and Engage

How would you classify the Florida insanity defense based on the four popular defenses discussed above? Explain your reasoning in a summary analysis. What is the burden of proof? How does it differ from a "preponderance of the evidence?" Write a definition for the two different burdens of proof, and then explain the similarities and differences in a summary analysis.

How does Ohio define insanity? In Section 2901.01(14), it states this:

> (14) A person is "not guilty by reason of insanity" relative to a charge of an offense only if the person proves, in the manner specified in section 2901.05 of the Revised Code, that at the time of the commission of the offense, the person did not know, as a result of a severe mental disease or defect, the wrongfulness of the person's acts.

If you were to use a highlighter to identify the material terms in this definition, what would you highlight?

> (14) A person is "not guilty by reason of insanity" relative to a charge of an offense only if the person proves, in the manner specified in section 2901.05 of the Revised Code, that at the time of the commission of the offense, the person did not know, as a result of a severe mental disease or defect, the wrongfulness of the person's acts.

Based on these words, how would you classify this defense using the four classifications discussed earlier in this chapter? What is the trigger word to help you classify this defense?

> The person did not know, as a result of a severe mental disease or defect, the wrongfulness of the person's acts.

How does Illinois define insanity? In 720 ILCS 5/6-2, Section 6-2, the following definition is given:

> (a) A person is not criminally responsible for conduct if at the time of such conduct, as a result of mental disease or mental defect, he lacks substantial capacity to appreciate the criminality of his conduct.
>
> (b) The terms "mental disease or mental defect" do not include an abnormality manifested only by repeated criminal or otherwise antisocial conduct.
>
> (c) A person who, at the time of the commission of a criminal offense, was not insane but was suffering from a mental illness, is not relieved of criminal responsibility for his conduct and may be found guilty but mentally ill.
>
> (d) For purposes of this Section, "mental illness" or "mentally ill" means a substantial disorder of thought, mood, or behavior which afflicted a person at the time of the commission of the offense and which impaired that person's judgment, but not to the extent that he is unable to appreciate the wrongfulness of his behavior.
>
> (e) When the defense of insanity has been presented during the trial, the burden of proof is on the defendant to prove by clear and convincing evidence that the defendant is not guilty by reason of insanity. However, the burden of proof remains on the State to prove beyond a reasonable doubt each of the elements of each of the offenses charged, and, in a jury trial where the insanity defense has been presented, the jury must be instructed that it may not consider whether the defendant has met his burden of proving that he is not guilty by reason of insanity until and unless it has first determined that the State has proven the defendant guilty beyond a reasonable doubt of the offense with which he is charged.

Learning Tip

If you were to use a highlighter to identify the material terms in this definition, what would you highlight?

> A person is not criminally responsible for conduct if at the time of such conduct, as a result of mental disease or mental defect, he lacks substantial capacity to appreciate the criminality of his conduct.

Based on these words, how would you classify this defense using the four classifications discussed earlier in this chapter? What is the trigger word to help you classify this defense?

> A person is not criminally responsible for conduct if at the time of such conduct, as a result of mental disease or mental defect,

> he lacks substantial capacity to appreciate the criminality of his conduct.

Do Ohio and Illinois use the same test based on the four tests discussed earlier in this chapter? What test does Illinois use?

Stop and Engage

9.4 Justification

In a justification defense, the offender is not disputing the facts in the case. He is arguing that he is not culpable because his actions were justified, usually by specific circumstances. In Texas, the two most common defenses in the category of justification are necessity and self-defense, and these are found in Chapter 9 entitled "Justification Excluding Criminal Responsibility." Remember, when reading statutory language, make sure to always determine if there are definitions in the chapter or other chapters or sections that are necessary for you to read and know to fully understand the provisions you are learning. In Chapter 9, the definitions for the chapter are found in Section 9.01, but you may also want to check the general definitions in Section1.07. In the Texas Penal Code, Section 9.02 states this:

> It is a defense to prosecution that the conduct in question is justified under this chapter.

Section 9.22 pertains to the defense of necessity and provides this definition:

> (1) the actor reasonably believes the conduct is immediately necessary to avoid imminent harm;
>
> (2) the desirability and urgency of avoiding the harm clearly outweigh, according to ordinary standards of reasonableness, the harm sought to be prevented by the law proscribing the conduct; and
>
> (3) a legislative purpose to exclude the justification claimed for the conduct does not otherwise plainly appear.

The TPC permits an offender to argue that his actions were *immediately* necessary to avoid *imminent* harm. There is no need to go further in studying this defense, but a good example of this is similar to one we examined earlier. A driver who swerves to avoid children running into his path, but in so swerving, then hits an individual on the sidewalk, causing injury, or death, has attempted to act in an immediate manner to avoid imminent harm. We find the traditional protection of persons defenses in Subchapter C starting with Section 9.31, self-defense which defines the defense in this way:

> (a) Except as provided in Subsection (b), a person is justified in using force against another when and to the degree the actor rea-

sonably believes the force is immediately necessary to protect the actor against the other's use or attempted use of unlawful force. The actor's belief that the force was immediately necessary as described by this subsection is presumed to be reasonable if the actor:

(1) knew or had reason to believe that the person against whom the force was used:

(A) unlawfully and with force entered, or was attempting to enter unlawfully and with force, the actor's occupied habitation, vehicle, or place of business or employment;

(B) unlawfully and with force removed, or was attempting to remove unlawfully and with force, the actor from the actor's habitation, vehicle, or place of business or employment; or

(C) was committing or attempting to commit aggravated kidnapping, murder, sexual assault, aggravated sexual assault, robbery, or aggravated robbery;

(2) did not provoke the person against whom the force was used; and

(3) was not otherwise engaged in criminal activity, other than a Class C misdemeanor that is a violation of a law or ordinance regulating traffic at the time the force was used.

(b) The use of force against another is not justified:

(1) in response to verbal provocation alone;

(2) to resist an arrest or search that the actor knows is being made by a peace officer, or by a person acting in a peace officer's presence and at his direction, even though the arrest or search is unlawful, unless the resistance is justified under Subsection (c);

(3) if the actor consented to the exact force used or attempted by the other;

(4) if the actor provoked the other's use or attempted use of unlawful force, unless:

(A) the actor abandons the encounter, or clearly communicates to the other his intent to do so reasonably believing he cannot safely abandon the encounter; and

(B) the other nevertheless continues or attempts to use unlawful force against the actor; or

(5) if the actor sought an explanation from or discussion with the other person concerning the actor's differences with the other person while the actor was:

(A) carrying a weapon in violation of Section 46.02; or

(B) possessing or transporting a weapon in violation of Section 46.05.

(c) The use of force to resist an arrest or search is justified:

(1) if, before the actor offers any resistance, the peace officer (or person acting at his direction) uses or attempts to use greater force than necessary to make the arrest or search; and

(2) when and to the degree the actor reasonably believes the force is immediately necessary to protect himself against the peace officer's (or other person's) use or attempted use of greater force than necessary.

(d) The use of deadly force is not justified under this subchapter except as provided in Sections 9.32, 9.33, and 9.34.

(e) A person who has a right to be present at the location where the force is used, who has not provoked the person against whom the force is used, and who is not engaged in criminal activity at the time the force is used is not required to retreat before using force as described by this section.

(f) For purposes of Subsection (a), in determining whether an actor described by Subsection (e) reasonably believed that the use of force was necessary, a finder of fact may not consider whether the actor failed to retreat.

Stop and Engage

This is a lengthy and detailed section of statutory language, so it would be helpful to deconstruct and parse the material elements. Take a moment and use a blue highlighter to identify the material elements of this crime based on the statutory language. Is deadly force permissible? Does the person need to "retreat" or find a "way of escape" before using force? What type of force may the person use to defend himself/herself? You will note that the TPC permits an argument that force was necessary for protection. Notice that self-defense must be *immediately necessary*. There are several sub-paragraphs which define when a force is immediately necessary, and we do not need to understand these in detail. Notice also that defensive force cannot be used in response to only verbal provocation.

Now consider Section 9.32 which is entitled, "Deadly Force in Defense of Person":

(a) A person is justified in using deadly force against another:

(1) if the actor would be justified in using force against the other under Section 9.31; and

(2) when and to the degree the actor reasonably believes the deadly force is immediately necessary:

(A) to protect the actor against the other's use or attempted use of unlawful deadly force; or

(B) to prevent the other's imminent commission of aggravated kidnapping, murder, sexual assault, aggravated sexual assault, robbery, or aggravated robbery.

(b) The actor's belief under Subsection (a)(2) that the deadly force was immediately necessary as described by that subdivision is presumed to be reasonable if the actor:

(1) knew or had reason to believe that the person against whom the deadly force was used:

(A) unlawfully and with force entered, or was attempting to enter unlawfully and with force, the actor's occupied habitation, vehicle, or place of business or employment;

(B) unlawfully and with force removed, or was attempting to remove unlawfully and with force, the actor from the actor's habitation, vehicle, or place of business or employment; or

(C) was committing or attempting to commit an offense described by Subsection (a)(2)(B);

(2) did not provoke the person against whom the force was used; and

(3) was not otherwise engaged in criminal activity, other than a Class C misdemeanor that is a violation of a law or ordinance regulating traffic at the time the force was used.

(c) A person who has a right to be present at the location where the deadly force is used, who has not provoked the person against whom the deadly force is used, and who is not engaged in criminal activity at the time the deadly force is used is not required to retreat before using deadly force as described by this section.

(d) For purposes of Subsection (a)(2), in determining whether an actor described by Subsection (c) reasonably believed that the use of deadly force was necessary, a finder of fact may not consider whether the actor failed to retreat.

Stop and Engage

Take a moment and use a blue highlighter to identify the material elements of this crime based on the statutory language. Is deadly force permissible? Does the person need to "retreat" or find a "way of escape" before using force? What type of force may the person use to defend himself/herself? The title of this section implies that deadly force cannot be used to protect property. What about defense of others or a third person? Read Section 9.33.

A person is justified in using force or deadly force against another to protect a third person if:

(1) under the circumstances as the actor reasonably believes them to be, the actor would be justified under Section 9.31 or 9.32 in using force or deadly force to protect himself against the unlawful force or unlawful deadly force he reasonably believes to be threatening the third person he seeks to protect; and

(2) the actor reasonably believes that his intervention is immediately necessary to protect the third person.

The general principle in this section is that if force is appropriate to protect oneself, it is also appropriate to protect someone else. Now we can compare some of these sections in Texas with the laws in New York. In New York, justification is recognized as a defense by the specific language of Section 35.00 which states that the following:

> In any prosecution for an offense, justification, as defined in sections 35.05 through 35.30, is a defense.

The justification defenses identified in Section 35.00 are:

> 35.05—Justification; generally.
>
> 35.10—Justification; use of physical force generally.
> 35.15—Justification; use of physical force in defense of a person.
> 35.20—Justification; use of physical force in defense of premises and in defense of a person in the course of burglary.
> 35.25—Justification; use of physical force to prevent or terminate larceny or criminal mischief.
> 35.27—Justification; use of physical force in resisting arrest prohibited.
>
> 35.30—Justification; use of physical force in making an arrest or in preventing an escape.

Stop and Engage

Based on the above labels, what sections pertain to what is commonly referred to as "self-defense" and "defense of others"? Read Section 35.10(5). May a person use deadly physical force? What else do you need to know to answer this question? Do you need to refer to other sections in the New York Penal Code?

Justification generally is defined in this way:

> Unless otherwise limited by the ensuing provisions of this article defining justifiable use of physical force, conduct which would otherwise constitute an offense is justifiable and not criminal when:
>
> 1. Such conduct is required or authorized by law or by a judicial decree, or is performed by a public servant in the reasonable exercise of his official powers, duties or functions; or
>
> 2. Such conduct is necessary as an emergency measure to avoid an imminent public or private injury which is about to occur by reason of a situation occasioned or developed through no fault of the actor, and which is of such gravity that, according to ordinary standards of intelligence and morality, the desirability and urgency of avoiding such injury clearly outweigh the desirability of avoiding the injury sought to be prevented by the statute defining the offense in issue. The necessity and justifiability of such conduct may not rest upon considerations pertaining only to the morality and advisability of the statute, either in its general application or with respect to its application to a particular class of cases arising there under. Whenever evidence

> relating to the defense of justification under this subdivision is offered by the defendant, the court shall rule as a matter of law whether the claimed facts and circumstances would, if established, constitute a defense.

Stop and Engage

When you read this definition, did a particular factual illustration provided earlier in the chapter come to mind? Can you construct a fact pattern to illustrate the applicability of this defense without using specific words from the statute?

In Florida, "Justifiable Use of Force" is found in Chapter 776, and it includes several different types of justifiable use of force, including defense of person and defense of others. Section 776.012 pertains to "use of force in defense of persons" and states the following:

> A person is justified in using force, except deadly force, against another when and to the extent that the person reasonably believes that such conduct is necessary to defend himself or herself or another against the other's imminent use of unlawful force. However, a person is justified in the use of deadly force and does not have a duty to retreat if:
>
> (1) He or she reasonably believes that such force is necessary to prevent imminent death or great bodily harm to himself or herself or another or to prevent the imminent commission of a forcible felony; or
>
> (2) Under those circumstances permitted pursuant to Section 776.013.

In order to fully understand when a person is justified in the use of deadly force and does not have a duty to retreat, we need to refer to Section 776.013 which is entitled "Home protection; use of deadly force; presumption of fear of death or great bodily harm." This section states this:

> (1) A person is presumed to have held a reasonable fear of imminent peril of death or great bodily harm to himself or herself or another when using defensive force that is intended or likely to cause death or great bodily harm to another if:
>
> (a) The person against whom the defensive force was used was in the process of unlawfully and forcefully entering, or had unlawfully and forcibly entered, a dwelling, residence, or occupied vehicle, or if that person had removed or was attempting to remove another against that person's will from the dwelling, residence, or occupied vehicle; and
> (b) The person who uses defensive force knew or had reason to believe that an unlawful and forcible entry or unlawful and forcible act was occurring or had occurred.
> (2) The presumption set forth in subsection (1) does not apply if:

> (a) The person against whom the defensive force is used has the right to be in or is a lawful resident of the dwelling, residence, or vehicle, such as an owner, lessee, or titleholder, and there is not an injunction for protection from domestic violence or a written pretrial supervision order of no contact against that person; or
> (b) The person or persons sought to be removed is a child or grandchild, or is otherwise in the lawful custody or under the lawful guardianship of, the person against whom the defensive force is used; or
> (c) The person who uses defensive force is engaged in an unlawful activity or is using the dwelling, residence, or occupied vehicle to further an unlawful activity; or
> (d) The person against whom the defensive force is used is a law enforcement officer, as defined in Section 943.10(14), who enters or attempts to enter a dwelling, residence, or vehicle in the performance of his or her official duties and the officer identified himself or herself in accordance with any applicable law or the person using force knew or reasonably should have known that the person entering or attempting to enter was a law enforcement officer.
> (3) A person who is not engaged in an unlawful activity and who is attacked in any other place where he or she has a right to be has no duty to retreat and has the right to stand his or her ground and meet force with force, including deadly force if he or she reasonably believes it is necessary to do so to prevent death or great bodily harm to himself or herself or another or to prevent the commission of a forcible felony.
> (4) A person who unlawfully and by force enters or attempts to enter a person's dwelling, residence, or occupied vehicle is presumed to be doing so with the intent to commit an unlawful act involving force or violence.
> (5) As used in this section, the term:
> (a) "Dwelling" means a building or conveyance of any kind, including any attached porch, whether the building or conveyance is temporary or permanent, mobile or immobile, which has a roof over it, including a tent, and is designed to be occupied by people lodging therein at night.
> (b) "Residence" means a dwelling in which a person resides either temporarily or permanently or is visiting as an invited guest.
>
> (c) "Vehicle" means a conveyance of any kind, whether or not motorized, which is designed to transport people or property.

Learning Tip

Note the factual questions and complexities that are inherent in interpreting this section and applying its requirements to a fact pattern. What factual questions would you need to resolve? What statutory terms and requirements pose interpretative questions? You may want to make a list for practice. You will note that one of the major issues that surfaces in the discussion in the use of force to defend self is that of the "need to" or the " 'requirement' to retreat." A question that has to be answered also is this: What constitutes a "retreat?" The other main issue is whether one can use deadly force to defend self and, if so, what facts should be present based on the requirements of the statutory language. The Supreme Court of the State of Oregon in *State of Oregon v. Sandoval* (2006) reversed an Oregon Court of Appeals decision (204 Or App 457 (2006)) on the issue of "an opportunity to escape."

Case Example: Practice Opportunity

Read the following case excerpt, and use a yellow highlighter to identify the material facts of the case; use a blue highlighter to note the relevant statutory language; use a pink highlighter to note the alleged crime; and use a green highlighter to note the court's application of the law to the facts of the case, to highlight the court's analysis.

State of Oregon v. Sandoval

156 P.3d 60 (2007)

Defendant appealed his conviction after a jury trial on a charge of intentional murder, ORS163.115(1)(a), contending that the trial court improperly instructed the jury to the effect that a person is justified in using deadly force in self defense to defend against imminent use of deadly force by another only if there is no opportunity to escape and no other means of avoiding the combat. A panel of the Court of Appeals affirmed defendant's conviction without opinion. *State v. Sandoval*, 204 Or App 457, 130 P3d 808 (2006). We allowed defendant's petition for review and now conclude that the instruction was an incorrect statement of Oregon law and that the trial court's error in giving the instruction was not harmless. Accordingly, we reverse the decision of the Court of Appeals, reverse defendant's conviction for intentional murder, and remand the case to the circuit court for further proceedings.

Defendant shot and killed his ex-wife's domestic partner, Whitcraft. The two men had a history of combative and sometimes physically violent interactions. The shooting occurred on a road that both men frequently traveled. When the police arrived on the scene, defendant described the following sequence of events: Whitcraft had driven by on the road as defendant was about to turn onto it; after defendant turned onto the road behind Whitcraft, Whitcraft stopped his truck and backed it into defendant's truck; Whitcraft then turned and aimed a pistol at defendant; defendant grabbed a rifle that he was carrying in his own vehicle (both men kept guns in their vehicles), opened the door of his truck and fired a single shot at Whitcraft. Investigators determined that the shot had entered Whitcraft's skull behind his left ear, killing him instantly. Police later found Whitcraft's loaded and cocked pistol under Whitcraft's body.

At trial, the state rejected defendant's version of the events and offered evidence that defendant had essentially ambushed Whitcraft—provoking him until he stopped his truck, training a rifle on him until he reached for his gun, and then shooting him in the head. At the close of trial, the court gave a series of jury instructions that were drawn from Uniform Criminal Jury Instructions:

> "A person is justified in using physical force upon another person to defend himself from what he reasonably believes to be the use or imminent use of unlawful physical force. In defending, a person may only use that degree of force which he reasonably believes to be necessary.
>
> "The burden of proof is on the state to prove beyond a reasonable doubt that the defendant did not act in self-defense.
>
> ... "There are certain limitations on the use of deadly physical force. The defendant is not justified in using deadly physical force against another person in self-defense unless he reasonably believed that the other person was using or about to use unlawful deadly physical force against him and/or committing or attempting to commit a felony involving the use or threatened imminent use of physical force against a person.
>
> "Even in the situation where one of these threatening circumstances is present, the use of deadly physical force is justified only if it does not exceed the degree of force which defendant reasonably believes to be necessary in the circumstances."

Over defendant's objection, the court then gave an additional special instruction that the prosecution had requested:

> "The danger justifying the use of deadly force must be absolute, imminent, and unavoidable, and a necessity of taking human life must be actual, present, urgent and absolutely or apparently absolutely necessary. There must be no reasonable opportunity to escape to avoid the affray and there must be no other means of avoiding or declining the combat."

As we shall explain, that instruction apparently was based, not on the statutes discussed below, but on this court's 1982 opinion in *State v. Charles*, 293 Or 273, 647 P2d 897 (1982). The jury subsequently found defendant guilty of intentional murder with a firearm, apparently rejecting defendant's claim of self defense.

On appeal, defendant assigned error to the trial court's decision to give the special instruction. As noted, the Court of Appeals affirmed without opinion. Petitioner then sought review by this court, and we allowed his petition to consider whether the "duty to retreat" instruction that the trial court gave is a correct statement of Oregon law.

The answer to that question resides in the criminal statutes that define the concept of self-defense for purposes of Oregon law. Two merit discussion. The first, ORS 161.209, describes when the use of physical force for self-defense is "justified" and, thus, lawful:

> "Except as provided in [another statute, not pertinent to this case] and [ORS] 161.219, a person is justified in using physical force upon another person for self-defense or to defend a third person from what the person reasonably believes to be the use or imminent use of unlawful physical force, and the person may use a degree of force which the person reasonably believes to be necessary for the purpose."

The cross-referenced statute, ORS 161.219, deals specifically with the use of *deadly* physical force. It provides:

> "Notwithstanding the provisions of ORS 161.209, a person is not justified in using deadly physical force upon another person unless the person reasonably believes that the other person is: (1) Committing or attempting to commit a felony involving the use or threatened imminent use of physical force against a person; or
>
> (2) Committing or attempting to commit a burglary in a dwelling; or
>
> (3) Using or about to use unlawful deadly physical force against a person."

Our initial task is to determine, from the text and context of the foregoing statutes, whether the legislature intended to limit the availability of the right to use deadly physical force for self-defense to those circumstances in which the person had no opportunity to retreat (or, as the special instruction had it, "no reasonable opportunity to escape to avoid the affray and * * * no other means of avoiding or declining the combat"). *See PGE v. Bureau of Labor and Industries*, 317 Or 606, 610, 859 P2d 1143 (1993) (describing analytical method for construing statutes). If, after that initial examination, the legislature's intent with respect to the existence of a duty to retreat still is unclear, we may proceed to an examination of legislative history. *Id.* at 611-12. On purely textual level, ORS 161.219 contains no specific reference to "retreat," "escape," or "other means of avoiding" a deadly confrontation. Neither, in our view, does it contain any other wording that would suggest a duty of that kind. Instead, it sets out, in straightforward terms, a set of circumstances that justify a person's use of deadly force (a reasonable belief that another person is using or about to use deadly force against a person) and does not purport to interpose any additional requirements beyond those circumstances.

The state contends that a duty to retreat nonetheless is implied by what it describes as a "necessity" concept that it asserts is at the heart of both ORS 161.219 and the basic self-defense statute, ORS 161.209. However, the state does not explain its construction in terms of the specific wording of either ORS 161.209 or 161.219. It simply states, without further elaboration, that the central nature of a concept of necessity is "demonstrate[d]" in "the text of the interrelated statutes," *i.e.*, ORS 161.219 and ORS 161.209.

The state may be relying on the fact that the latter statute contains the word "necessary." However, assuming that ORS 161.209 is relevant to our inquiry, it is clear that the reference to "necessary" in that statute pertains to the *degree* of force which a person threatened with unlawful force reasonably believes to be required for the purpose of self-defense or defense of another. That wording assumes a right to meet unlawful force with *some* level of force and does not suggest that a decision to retreat or otherwise forego the use of the otherwise permissible level of force might be required in some circumstances.

Neither are we persuaded that a duty to retreat may be derived from the requirement in ORS 161.209 that an attacker's use of unlawful physical force be present or "imminent." That requirement speaks solely to the timing of the threat; it is not concerned with the nature of the threatened person's response. In short, nothing in the wording of ORS 161.219 itself, or in its broader counterpart, ORS 161.209, suggests that persons who reasonably believe that another person is about to use deadly physical force against them must calculate whether it is possible to retreat from that threat before they use deadly physical force in self defense.

The state argues that this court's decision in *Charles* is relevant at this stage of our analysis as part of the statute's context. The state asserts, specifically, that *Charles* interpreted ORS 161.219 as imposing a duty of retreat on those who would rely on a self-defense theory to justify their own use of deadly force against another. The state then asserts that *Charles* is precedent that binds us here.

The state's reliance on *Charles* is understandable. In that case, this court rejected a defendant's claim that the trial court had erred in refusing to instruct a jury that a person has no duty to retreat before using deadly force to defend against an imminent use of deadly force by another. The court there stated that such an instruction would be contrary to "the Oregon cases, [which] require a defendant * * * to avoid the threatened danger where it is possible to do so without sacrificing his own safety." 293 Or at 284. The problem with that pronouncement, however, is that the court based that decision entirely on its analysis of "the Oregon cases," while the right of self defense is set out in the two statutes previously discussed.

Indeed, the entire analytical flow of the *Charles* opinion is distinctly odd: The court did not examine the wording of either ORS 161.209 or 161.219 *at all*. Instead, the court set out the wording that the Oregon Criminal Law Commission had *proposed* to the legislature regarding the use of deadly force as part of the final draft of the proposed 1971 Criminal Code, which wording explicitly imposed a duty of retreat to avoid the necessity of using deadly force. Then, after noting that the 1971 legislature had *rejected* that wording, the court cited a view expressed in the Oregon Criminal Law Commission's Commentary to the 1971 Code to the effect that "the statute probably was not necessary" because of existing Oregon case law. 293 Or at 278 (discussing Commentary to Criminal Law Revision Commission Proposed Oregon Criminal Code, Final Draft and Report § 23, at 23-25 (Jul 1970)). Then, without discussing at all the fact that the Oregon legislature had adopted statutes on the subject, the court concluded, inexplicably, that "Oregon case law * * * controls the subject." 293 Or at 277. The court then went on to discuss its prior cases (and to conclude that they did not support the defendant's claim that Oregon does not recognize a "duty of retreat.").

Although, from our present perspective, it seems surprising that this court would attempt to answer the question presented in *Charles* without resort to the controlling criminal statutes that is precisely what the *Charles* court did. The court's analysis did not focus on or even consider the words of the statutes that we now recognize to be pivotal. Neither did the court conclude, as the state suggests, that the drafters of ORS 161.219 had decided to "continue" the "common-law rules" as explicated in the various self-defense cases that preceded the enactment of that statute. *Charles*, therefore, has nothing to contribute to our present effort, which is to discern what the *legislature* intended with respect to the "duty of retreat" question.

Without *Charles*, we are left with our initial impression of the statute: It sets out a specific set of circumstances that justify a person's use of deadly force (that the person reasonably believes that another person is using or about to use deadly force against him or her) and does not interpose any additional requirement (including a requirement that there be no means of escape). That impression is not altered by the requirement in ORS 161.209 that the use of deadly force be present or "imminent," or by the same statute's reference to "the degree of force which the person reasonably believes to be necessary." We conclude, in short, that the legislature's intent is clear on the face of ORS 161.219: The legislature did *not* intend to require a person to retreat before using deadly force to defend against the imminent use of deadly physical force by another. It follows from the foregoing that the trial court erred in giving the instruction in question. The state contends, however, that, even if that is so, the error was harmless, because the facts and legal theories that the parties presented to the jury simply did not involve any question of retreat or whether use of deadly force was unavoidable. Rather, the state argues, the factual dispute before the jury focused solely on the question of whether Whitcraft had resorted to his weapon first. The state contends that, under those circumstances, there was little likelihood that the disputed instruction affected the outcome of the case.

We disagree with the state's assessment. A jury presented with the disputed instruction would assume that it had *some* relevance to the case before it. Even if the state never specifically made the argument, and even if its factual case was not geared to that issue, the jury still would be likely to hear the instruction as requiring it to find that defendant had had no opportunity to retreat from or otherwise "avoid the affray" before it could accept defendant's self-defense theory. With that erroneous impression in mind, the jury may have rejected defendant's self-defense claim based on a finding that defendant could have driven away when he saw Whitcraft backing toward him (or, even better, when he first saw Whitcraft drive by). In short, there is very likelihood that the erroneous instruction affected the verdict. The error was not harmless. The decision of the Court of Appeals is reversed. The judgment of the circuit court is reversed, and the case is remanded to the circuit court for further proceedings.

Stop and Engage

Now that you have highlighted key parts from this case, complete the following activities:

- Identify the main issue(s) in this case.
- Write a concise summary of the material facts.

- Paraphrase the relevant statutory language with precision and accuracy.
- Write a concise summary of the court's reasoning.
- Write a concise explanation as to how and why the court reached its decision—its holding.

You may be familiar with the term "**Castle Doctrine.**" The castle doctrine is a phrase derived from laws that do not require you to retreat before using deadly force when defending yourself in your home (your "castle"). These laws are usually complex, and they require substantive case law to provide an interpretative background for the analysis of a new case or fact pattern. Questions such as these need to be considered: "What constitutes a home?" "What constitutes deadly force?" "What is entry?" "Does there need to be a lethal imminent threat?" These are just a few of the interpretative issues that arise in this complex area. States such as Arizona, Florida, Indiana, and Texas, among others, adhere to the Castle Doctrine. Other states, such as Colorado, Connecticut, Rhode Island, and Wyoming, among others, have some modified form of the Castle Doctrine. What is the law in your state pertaining to the Castle Doctrine?

9.5 Summary

In criminal law, you will recall that the prosecution must prove every element of the crime beyond a reasonable doubt. This means that the prosecutor must establish that the defendant had the requisite culpability state (mental state or *mens rea*), that his or her actions satisfy the specified *actus reus*, and that any other circumstances or attendant requirements in the statutory language can also be proven and connected to the defendant. In most states, you will find general defenses which may be classified as "justifications" or "excuses" as well as "affirmative defenses." Affirmative defenses usually must be asserted by the defendant and proven by the defendant by a preponderance of the evidence (this is the standard for the burden of proof). Defenses which pertain to the negation of an element of a crime such as *mens rea* are often referred to defenses pertaining to culpability. The reasoning is that because of a mental defect or impairment, age, involuntary intoxication, or another incapacitating factor, the defendant should be able to assert the factor as a defense to mitigate or defeat the charges against him or her. Most states do not consider voluntary intoxication as a defense. One of the most complex defenses involves the insanity defense and related defenses, such as diminished capacity. The issues are quite intricate because there are so many factual and interpretative issues compounded by expert testimony and the judicial construction of various terms and requirements as interpreted from the numerous definitions of insanity. In this section you will gain a basic grasp of some of the issues inherent in the insanity defense, and you will become familiar with some of the more common tests and judicial interpretations. In a justification defense, the offender is not disputing the facts in the case. He is arguing that he is not culpable because his actions were justified, usually by specific circumstances. The castle doctrine is a phrase derived from laws that do not require you to retreat before using deadly force when defending yourself in your home (your "castle"). These laws are usually complex, and they require substantive case law to provide an interpretative background for the analysis of a new case or fact pattern.

9.6 Chapter Review Activities

1. What is the main difference between justification defenses and general defenses?
2. Name one material element in self-defense.
3. What is the context for understanding defenses?
4. Name one material element of defense of property.
5. What is the Castle Doctrine?

Chapter 10

Selected Crimes Involving Moral Turpitude

Key Terms and Concepts

Moral Turpitude	Morals	Sensibilities
Mala Prohibita	Malum in se	

10.1 Introduction

In this chapter we will explore those crimes that are focused on societal well-being, decency, and morality. These are crimes that are derived from concepts of social and public duty and which emphasize a certain level of conduct towards one another. Generally, crimes involving moral turpitude are those where acts are base, vile, or depraved, and contrary to the generally accepted mores and norms of societal life. Now that we have a general definition, we can review how certain states in their criminal statutes have defined crimes involving moral turpitude.

10.2 Selected State Statutory Definitions

The Pennsylvania Section 237.9 states:

(a) *Definition.* Moral turpitude includes the following:

(1) That element of personal misconduct in the private and social duties which a person owes to his fellow human beings or to society in general, which characterizes the act done as an act of baseness, vileness or depravity, and contrary to the accepted and customary rule of right and duty between two human beings.

> (2) Conduct done knowingly contrary to justice, honesty or good morals.
>
> (3) Intentional, knowing or reckless conduct causing bodily injury to another or intentional, knowing or reckless conduct which, by physical menace, puts another in fear of imminent serious bodily injury.
>
> (b) *Elements of the crime.* A determination of whether a crime involves moral turpitude will be determined based solely upon the elements of the crime. The underlying facts or details of an individual criminal charge, indictment or conviction are not relevant to the issue of moral turpitude.

Stop and Engage

How would you summarize the Pennsylvania definition of moral turpitude with precision and specificity? What are the required culpability states? What are some of the factual issues posed from the specific wording of this definition? Use an internet search engine to browse through the table of contents of the criminal or penal codes of a few states. Is it easy to find chapters or sections in the criminal code that pertain to crimes involving moral turpitude? Are there chapters or sections that may be analogous and related to crimes involving moral turpitude?

Does your state have a chapter or section for crimes involving moral turpitude?

In The New York Penal Code, Title M includes "Offenses against Public Health and Morals," and Title N includes "Offenses against Public Order, Public Sensibilities and the Right to Privacy." What words in these two title headings are indicators that perhaps those titles include crimes that may be considered those involving moral turpitude?

> "Offenses against Public Health and Morals" and Title N includes "Offenses Against Public Order, Public Sensibilities and the Right to Privacy."

You will note that the crimes listed in Title M include:

- Controlled Substance Offenses
- Offenses involving Marihuana
- Gambling Offenses
- Prostitution Offenses
- Obscenity and Related Offenses

In Title N the crimes include:

- Offenses against Public Order
- Harassment of Rent Regulated Tenants

Learning Activity

Which of these crimes may be considered crimes where the acts are base, vile, or depraved and contrary to the generally accepted mores and norms of societal life? Write a summary analysis explaining your choices, and provide well-supported explanations for your reasons.

10.3 An Attorney General Opinion

The Attorney General of the State of Texas, in Opinion No GA-0299, issued on January 25, 2005, page 2 wrote: "historically, a crime of moral turpitude has been broadly construed to be one that denotes shameful wickedness—so extreme a departure from ordinary standards of honest[y], good morals, justice, or ethics as to be shocking to the moral sense of the community. It has also been defined as an act of baseness, vileness, or depravity in the private and social duties which one person owes to another or to society in general, contrary to the accepted and customary rule of right and duty between people" (Black's Law Dictionary, 1026 (7th ed. 1999). In *Hardeman v. The State of Texas* in the Court of Appeals, Third District of Texas, No. 3-93-363-CR 91993), the Court wrote the following:

> "Moral turpitude has been defined as "[t]he quality of a crime involving grave infringement of the moral sentiment of the community as distinguished from statutory mala prohibita." Black's Law Dictionary 1008-09 (6th ed. 1990). The Court of Criminal Appeals has considered various situations in determining whether a given offense is one that involves moral turpitude. *See, e.g., Holgin v. State*, 480 S.W.2d 405 (Tex. Crim. App. 1972) (prostitution involves moral turpitude); *Stephens v. State*, 417 S.W.2d 286 (Tex. Crim. App. 1967) (driving while intoxicated does not involve moral turpitude); *Bensaw v. State*, 88 S.W.2d 495 (Tex. Crim. App. 1935) (theft involves moral turpitude); *Sherman v. State*, 62 S.W.2d 146 (Tex. Crim. App. 1933) (swindling involves moral turpitude); *Garrison v. State*, 252 S.W. 511 (Tex. Crim. App. 1923) (drunkenness in a public place does not involve moral turpitude); *Miller v. State*, 150 S.W. 635 (Tex. Crim. App. 1912) (gambling does not involve moral turpitude); *Kemper v. State*, 138 S.W. 1025 (Tex. Crim. App. 1911) (simple assault does not involve moral turpitude)."

Stop and Engage

Why do you think some of these crimes (those highlighted in blue) have been classified as involving moral turpitude, and those crimes (printed in blue) have been classified as not involving moral turpitude? Write a summary analysis explaining your choices and provide well-supported explanations for your reasons.

Case Example: Practice Opportunity

Read the following case excerpt to understand how this California case defined moral turpitude. Use a blue highlighter to note any relevant statutory language and references to other cases. Use a pink highlighter to note the alleged crime. Use a green highlighter to underscore the court's reasoning, to highlight the court's analysis.

In re Phong Nguyen Tran

File A28 005 431 (1996)

Moral turpitude is a nebulous concept, which refers generally to conduct which is inherently base, vile, or depraved, contrary to the accepted rules of morality and the duties owed between persons or to society in general. Moral turpitude has been defined as an act which is per se morally reprehensible and intrinsically wrong or *malum in se*, so it is the nature of the act itself and not the statutory prohibition of it which renders the crime one of moral turpitude. *See Matter of Esfandiary*, 16 I&N Dec. 659 (BIA 1979); *Matter of P-*, 6 I&N Dec. 795 (BIA 1955). The essence of moral turpitude is an evil or malicious intent. *Matter of Flores, supra*. The test to determine if a crime involves moral turpitude is whether the act is accompanied by a vicious motive or a corrupt mind. *See Winestock v. INS*, 576 F.2d 234 (9th Cir. 1978); *Matter of Flores, supra*. Where knowing or intentional conduct is an element of a morally reprehensible offense, we have found moral turpitude to be present. *See, e.g., Matter of Danesh, supra*. In *Guerrero de Nodahl v. INS*, 407 F.2d 1405 (9th Cir. 1969), the United States Court of Appeals for the Ninth Circuit determined that the offense of child abuse under section 273d of the California Penal Code is a crime involving moral turpitude. Quoting from the statute, the court found that a person who inflicts on a child "cruel or inhuman corporal punishment or injury" has committed a heinous offense so offensive to American ethics that, when committed willfully, necessarily involves moral turpitude. *Id.* At 1406-07. The Ninth Circuit subsequently relied on the reasoning of *Guerrero* in a case involving spousal abuse under section 273.5(a) of the California Penal Code. *Grageda v. INS*, 12 F.3d 919 (9th Cir. 1993). The court noted there that the statute includes "willfulness" as an element, finding that term to mean that "the person intended to cause the harm." *Grageda v. INS, supra*, at 922. Thus, the court determined that the willful commission of spousal abuse an act of baseness and depravity contrary to accepted moral standards was a crime involving moral turpitude. In our opinion, infliction of bodily harm upon a person with whom one has such a familial relationship is an act of depravity which is contrary to accepted moral standards. *Grageda v. INS, supra*.

> When such an act is committed willfully, it is an offense that involves moral turpitude. *Id.* We will follow the holding in *Grageda v. INS, supra*, that spousal abuse in violation of section 273.5(a) of the California Penal Code is a crime involving moral turpitude. Furthermore, inasmuch as we find that willful infliction of injury upon a cohabitant or parent of the offender's child in violation of the same statute is as reprehensible as spousal abuse, we conclude that such offense also involves moral turpitude. Thus, we hold that any violation of section 273.5(a) of the California Penal Code constitutes a crime involving moral turpitude.

Stop and Engage

Now that you have highlighted key parts from this case, complete the following activities:

- How does this court define moral turpitude?
- Write a concise summary of the court's reasoning.
- How does this court's reasoning of moral turpitude compare with the Attorney General of Texas' opinion?

10.4 Immigration and Visa Issues

Crimes involving moral turpitude also play an important role in immigration status and reasons for deportation. According to Federal Law, 8 U.S.C. §§1182(a)(2)(A)(i) and 1227(a)(2)(A)(i), aliens who have been convicted of crimes involving moral turpitude are subject to removal from the United States. Although the term "crime involving moral turpitude" (CIMT) is not defined specifically in the Federal statute, it has been defined by case law specifically in *Matter of Franklin*, 20 I&N Dec. 867, 868 (BIA 1994), *aff'd*, 72 F.3d 571 (8th Cir. 1995) which states that:

> A crime involving moral turpitude refers generally to conduct which is inherently base, vile, or depraved, and contrary to the accepted rules of morality and the duties owed between persons or to society in general ... Moral turpitude has been defined as an act which is per se morally reprehensible and intrinsically wrong, or *malum in se* so it is the nature of the act itself and not the statutory prohibition of it which renders a crime one of moral turpitude.

According to the United States Department of State Foreign Affairs Manual, Volume 9 (2010), pertaining to Visas, many crimes are committed that have been identified as involving moral turpitude and many that do not involve moral turpitude. Read through the lists below, and think about why some crimes involve moral turpitude and others do not.

9 FAM 40.21(a) N2.2 Defining "Moral Turpitude"

Statutory definitions of crimes in the United States consist of various elements, which must be met before a conviction can be supported. Some of these elements have been determined in judicial or administrative decisions to involve moral turpitude. A conviction for a statutory offense will involve moral turpitude if one or more of the elements of that offense have been determined to involve moral turpitude. The most common elements involving moral turpitude are:

(1) Fraud;

(2) Larceny; and

(3) Intent to harm persons or thing.

9 FAM 40.21(a) N2.3 Common Crimes Involving Moral Turpitude

Categorized below are some of the more common crimes, which are considered to involve moral turpitude. Each category is followed by a separate list of related crimes, which are held not to involve moral turpitude.

a. Most crimes committed against property that involve moral turpitude include the element of fraud. The act of fraud involves moral turpitude whether it is aimed against individuals or government. Fraud generally involves:

(1) Making false representation;

(2) Knowledge of such false representation by the perpetrator;

(3) Reliance on the false representation by the person defrauded;

(4) An intent to defraud; and

(5) The actual act of committing fraud

b. Other crimes committed against property involving moral turpitude involve an inherently evil intent, such as the act of arson. The following list comprises crimes frequently committed against property, which may be held to involve moral turpitude for the purposes of visa issuance:

(1) Arson;

(2) Blackmail;

(3) Burglary;

(4) Embezzlement;

(5) Extortion;

(6) False pretenses;

(7) Forgery;

(8) Fraud;

(9) Larceny (grand or petty);

(10) Malicious destruction of property;

(11) Receiving stolen goods (with guilty knowledge);

(12) Robbery;

(13) Theft (when it involves the intention of permanent taking); and

(14) Transporting stolen property (with guilty knowledge).

c. Crimes against property which do not fall within the definition of moral turpitude include:

(1) Damaging private property (where intent to damage not required);

(2) Breaking and entering (requiring no specific or implicit intent to commit a crime involving moral turpitude);

(3) Passing bad checks (where intent to defraud not required);

(4) Possessing stolen property (if guilty knowledge is not essential);

(5) Joy riding (where the intention to take permanently not required); and

(6) Juvenile delinquency.

9 FAM 40.21(a) N2.3-3 Crimes Committed Against Person, Family Relationship, and Sexual Morality

Crimes committed against the person, family relationship, and sexual morality, which constitute moral turpitude as it relates to visa issuance, include:

(1) Abandonment of a minor child (if willful and resulting in the destitution of the child);

(2) Adultery (see INA 101(f)(2) repealed by Public Law 97-116);

(3) Assault (this crime is broken down into several categories, which involve moral turpitude:

(a) Assault with intent to kill;

(b) Assault with intent to commit rape;

(c) Assault with intent to commit robbery;

(d) Assault with intent to commit serious bodily harm; and

(e) Assault with a dangerous or deadly weapon (some weapons may be found to be lethal as a matter of law, while others may or may not be found factually to be such, depending upon all the circumstances in the case. Such circumstances may include, but are not limited to, the size of the weapon, the manner of its use, and the nature and extent of injuries inflicted.);

(4) Bigamy;

(5) Contributing to the delinquency of a minor;

(6) Gross indecency;

(7) Incest (if the result of an improper sexual relationship);

(8) Kidnapping;

(9) Lewdness;

(10) Manslaughter:

(a) Voluntary, occurs when a person intentionally kills another person after "adequate provocation"; that is, there has been action that was sufficient to incite an "ordinary person" to "sudden and intense passion" such that s/he loses self-control. It should be noted that the time between provocation and the killing should not be long enough for the passion to have cooled off. In most states, "adequate provocation" is defined to be only situations in which there is a threat of deadly force, or in which a person finds his/her spouse in bed with another person. Verbal threats are usually not considered adequate provocation; and

(b) Involuntary, where the statute requires proof of recklessness, which is defined as the awareness and conscious disregard of a substantial and unjustified risk which constitutes a gross deviation from the standard that a reasonable person would observe in the situation. A conviction for the statutory offense of vehicular homicide or other involuntary manslaughter that only requires a showing of negligence will not involve moral turpitude even if it appears the defendant in fact acted recklessly.

(11) Mayhem;

(12) Murder;

(13) Pandering;

(14) Prostitution;

(15) Rape (By statute, a person may be convicted of statutory rape even though the female consents and provided she is under the statutory age at the time of the commission of the act. "Statutory rape" is also deemed to involve moral turpitude.)

b. Crimes committed against the person, family relationship, or sexual morality which do not involve moral turpitude include:

(1) Assault (simple) (i.e., any assault, which does not require an evil intent or depraved motive, although it may involve the use of a weapon, which is neither dangerous nor deadly);

(2) Bastardy (i.e., the offense of begetting a bastard child);

(3) Creating or maintaining a nuisance (where knowledge that premises were used for prostitution is not necessary);

(4) Incest (when a result of a marital status prohibited by law);

(5) Involuntary manslaughter (when killing is not the result of recklessness);

(6) Libel;

(7) Mailing an obscene letter;

(8) Mann Act violations (where coercion is not present);

(9) Riot; and

(10) Suicide (attempted).

9 FAM 40.21(a) N2.4 Attempts, Aiding and Abetting, Accessories and Conspiracy

a. The following types of crimes are held to be crimes involving moral turpitude:

(1) An attempt to commit a crime deemed to involve moral turpitude;

(2) Aiding and abetting in the commission of a crime deemed to involve moral turpitude;

(3) Being an accessory (before or after the fact) in the commission of a crime deemed to involve moral turpitude; or

(4) Taking part in a conspiracy (or attempting to take part in a conspiracy) to commit a crime involving moral turpitude.

b. Conversely, where an alien has been convicted of, or admits having committed the essential elements of, a criminal attempt, or a criminal act of aiding and abetting, accessory before or after the fact, or conspiracy, and the underlying crime is not deemed to involve moral turpitude, then
INA 212(a)(2)(A)(i)(I) would not be applicable.

Learning Activity

Choose two or three crimes that have been categorized above as involving moral turpitude and find those crimes in your state penal or criminal code. Based on the definition of those crimes in your state penal or criminal code, would you classify them as involving moral turpitude? Write a summary analysis that provides a well-reasoned discussion on your thoughts. See if you can find any case law from your state to support your points.

Case Example: Practice Opportunity

Read the following case excerpt and use a yellow highlighter to identify the material facts of the case; use a blue highlighter to note the relevant statutory language; use a pink highlighter to note the alleged crime;

and use a green highlighter to note the court's application of the law to the facts of the case, to highlight the court's analysis.

Ghulam Mehboob v. Attorney General of the United States

549 F.3d 272 (2008)

In this petition for review of the Board of Immigration Appeals' ("BIA") order of removability, we must decide whether a conviction for indecent assault under 18 Pa. Cons. Stat. §3126(a)(8), a strict liability offense, is a crime involving moral turpitude. Because the offense combines a reprehensible act with deliberate conduct, we conclude that indecent assault under Pennsylvania law is a crime involving moral turpitude, and consequently, the petition for review will be denied.

Petitioner, Ghulam Mehboob, is seeking review of the BIA's final order of removal and denial of his application for termination of removal proceedings. Mehboob, a native and citizen of Pakistan, was lawfully admitted to the United States as an immigrant in December, 1997. On December 7, 2001, Mehboob was convicted of a misdemeanor, indecent assault, in violation of 18 Pa. Cons. Stat. §3126(a), for touching the breast of a 15 year old girl, who was a customer in his store. He was sentenced to two years of probation and fined $146.

Following the conviction, the Department of Homeland Security ("DHS") initiated removal proceedings against Mehboob under 8 U.S.C. §1227(a)(2)(A)(*i*), which provides for the deportation of aliens who commit crimes involving moral turpitude. An Immigration Judge ("IJ") determined that Mehboob was removable for having committed a crime involving moral turpitude, and the BIA affirmed. Mehboob then petitioned this Court for review.

Morally turpitudinous conduct is inherently base, vile, or depraved; contrary to the accepted rules of morality and the duties owed other persons, either individually or to society in general. Partyka, 417 F.3d at 413. To determine whether a particular crime involves moral turpitude, we ask whether the criminal act is "accompanied by a vicious motive or a corrupt mind." Id. The general rule that has been culled from the answer to this question is that "evil intent is a requisite element for a crime involving moral turpitude." Id. (citations omitted). Applying this general rule, we have found that, in addition to intentional crimes, serious crimes committed recklessly—that is, "with a conscious disregard of a substantial and unjustifiable risk that serious injury or death would follow"—can be found to involve moral turpitude. This Court, however, has drawn a line at recklessness, and has held that moral turpitude does not inhere in a crime merely requiring a mental state of negligence. Compare Partyka, 417 F.3d at 416 (holding that "negligently inflicted bodily injury lacks the inherent baseness or depravity that evinces moral turpitude") with Knapik, 384 F.3d at 90 (affirming the BIA's decision that first degree reckless endangerment is "a crime involving moral turpitude"). Thus, the "hallmark" of moral turpitude has become "a reprehensible act with an appreciable level of consciousness or deliberation." Partyka, 417 F.3d at 414.

Mehboob was convicted of indecent assault under 18 Pa. Cons. Stat. §3126(a), which contains eight sub-sections. Section 3126(a) is therefore divisible, so we look at the record of conviction. The record of conviction in this case does not specify the sub-section under which Mehboob was convicted. Therefore, we look at the sub-section that requires the least culpability, sub-section (a)(8), to determine whether it is a crime involving moral turpitude. Sub-section (a)(8) is violated when there is "indecent contact with the complainant" when "the complainant is less than 16 years of age and the person is four or more years older than the complainant and the complainant and the person are not married to each other." The term "indecent contact" is defined as "[a]ny touching of the sexual or other intimate parts of the person for the purpose of arousing or gratifying sexual desire, in either person." 18 Pa. Cons. Stat. §3101. Thus, the elements of this offense consist of: (1) purposeful contact; (2) the complainant's age; and (3) the age difference between the defendant and the complainant. There is no *mens rea* element as to the age of the victim; nor has any mental state ever been implied by the Pennsylvania courts. As such, sub-section (a)(8) defines a strict liability offense. The least culpable conduct that would sustain a conviction under §3126(a)(8) would be consensual contact for the purpose of sexual gratification between a 19 year old and a 15 year old. Thus, indecent assault under Pennsylvania law can be a crime involving moral turpitude if such contact between a 19 year old and a 15 year old can be considered inherently base, vile, or depraved or is contrary to the accepted rules of morality. In other words, if it is found to combine "a reprehensible act with an appreciable level of consciousness or deliberation." Partyka, 417 F.3d at 414.

Chevron teaches us to defer to the BIA's determination that a certain crime involves moral turpitude when that determination is reasonable. Knapik, 384 F.3d at 88. In its decision, the BIA distinguished strict liability "morality offenses," which it found to be so manifestly contrary to community mores that they are subject to a presumption of culpability, from other, regulatory "public welfare" offenses, which impose strict liability primarily for policy imperatives and are less directly tied to universal community values. Specifically focusing on 18 Pa. Cons. Stat. §3126(a)(8), the BIA held that, as a classic morality offense, sub-section (a)(8) described a crime involving moral turpitude, despite the fact that the statute does not contain a *mens rea* element as to the complainant's age. We do not find this conclusion to be unreasonable. The absence of a *mens rea* as to a particular element in the statute of conviction does not necessarily connote an absence of moral culpability on the part of the violator. Strict liability morality offenses, like indecent assault under §3126(a)(8), are crimes involving moral turpitude because of the community consensus that such offenses, which are enacted for the protection of the child, are inherently antisocial and depraved.

In this case, the community consensus is that indecent contact between a person less than 16 years of age and another person who is four or more years older is reprehensible and socially unacceptable. The Pennsylvania Supreme Court has found that sub-section (a)(8) serves the legitimate societal purpose of protecting minors from sexual aggressors. See Commonwealth v. Albert, 758 A.2d 1149, 1154 (Pa. 2000) (recognizing that "older, more mature individuals are in a position that would allow them to take advantage of the immaturity and poor judgment of very young minors"). Legislatures often remove *mens rea* elements from sex offenses on the basis of community consensus that certain conduct should not be permitted with children under a certain age. Enacting strict liability offenses such as §3126(a)(8), makes it easier for the state to punish behavior that the community disapproves of because the state is not required to. This presumptive culpability is offset by a mistake of fact defense, which allows a defendant to prove by a preponderance of the evidence that she or he reasonably believed the child to be above the age of 16. 18 Pa. Cons. Stat. §3102. The availability of this defense in a criminal prosecution, however, cannot be used in the immigration context to back into the conclusion that an individual knew the complainant to be under age. Under our immigration precedents, the categorical inquiry is limited to the elements of the offense; it does not encompass separate statutory or common law defenses that are available to a criminal defendant. We cannot presume from the fact of Mehboob's conviction that he knew the child to be under the age of 16. But just because actual knowledge of the victim's age is not an element of the crime does not mean that the perpetrator was not motivated by moral turpitude. Indeed, it would seem impossible to commit an offense, such as the one defined by subsection (a)(8), without violating accepted rules of morality. Thus, the same community consensus that obviates the need to prove knowledge of the actual age of the victim at a criminal trial also categorizes §3126(a)(8) as a crime involving moral turpitude. Accordingly, we hold that the absence of *mens rea* as to a specific element of a crime does not necessarily preclude a finding that a strict liability sex offense involves moral turpitude. It is the nature of the crime, in addition to the particular elements, that determines whether it involves moral turpitude. See Castle v. I.N.S., 541 F.2d 1064, 1066 & n.5 (4th Cir. 1976).

This conclusion does not, as Mehboob suggests, abandon the categorical approach; nor does it remove the evil intent element from the definition of moral turpitude. Mehboob argues that indecent assault under §3126(a)(8) cannot be a crime involving moral turpitude because a person could be convicted without either engaging in inherently base, vile or depraved conduct, or having a vicious motive or corrupt mind. He asserts that the least culpable conduct does not rise to the level of moral turpitude because society would not find a 19 year old's act of touching a 15 year old to be morally reprehensible. Indeed, this is the position of the Court of Appeals for the Ninth Circuit, which held in a recent decision that statutory rape under California law could not be categorized as a crime involving moral turpitude because the least culpable conduct that could support a conviction under the statute might be "socially unacceptable," but was not "inherently base, vile, or depraved." Quintero-Salazar v. Keisler, 506 F.3d 688, 693 (9th Cir. 2007). However, Pennsylvania, as gauged by the enactments of the state legislature, appears to believe that the touching of a person who is less than 16 years of age by a person who is four or more years older for the purpose of arousing or gratifying sexual desire is offensive to public moral values. This view is supported by the fact that the offense is named indecent assault. See Webster's 3d New Int'l Dictionary 1147 (1986) (defining indecent as "altogether unbecoming ... not conforming to generally accepted standards of morality"). A survey of the cases reveals the consensus that moral turpitude inheres in strict liability sex offenses. See, e.g., Sheikh v. Gonzales, 427 F.3d 1077, 1082 (8th Cir. 2005) (concluding that an IJ did not abuse her discretion in finding that the misdemeanor offense of contributing to the delinquency of a minor was a crime involving moral turpitude); Castle v. I.N.S., 541

F.2d 1064, 1066 (4th Cir. 1976) (holding that "a man's carnal knowledge of a fifteen year old girl, not his wife, is so basically offensive to American ethics and accepted moral standards as to constitute moral turpitude per se"); Marinell v. Ryan, 285 F.2d 474, 475-76 (2d Cir. 1961) ("no doubt" that the indecent touching of a child under the age of sixteen involves moral turpitude); Pino v. Nicolls, 215 F.2d 237, 240 (1st Cir. 1954) ("cannot ... be questioned" that assault on a child under sixteen years of age with the intent to unlawfully and carnally know her "belongs in the category of crimes involving moral turpitude"); see also Marciano v. I.N.S., 450 F.2d 1022 (8th Cir. 1971); Ng Sui Wing v. United States, 46 F.2d 755 (7th Cir. 1931); Matter of Dingena, 11 I. & N. Dec. 723 (B.I.A. 1966); Matter of Garcia, 11 I. & N. Dec. 521 (B.I.A. 1966); Matter of R—, 3 I. & N. Dec. 562 (B.I.A. 1949). Moreover, indecent assault, as defined by §3126(a)(8), is not devoid of mens rea. Although it may not require knowledge of the complainant's age, it does require the purposeful conduct, namely the touching of the sexual or other intimate parts of a person in order to arouse or gratify sexual desire. See Model Penal Code §2.02(2). While this type of purposeful conduct on its own might not be viewed as reprehensible, when it is carried out on a person less than 16 years of age by another person who is four or more years older, society's accepted rules of morality are violated. It is the combination of arousing or gratifying sexual desires by touching a child under the age of 16 that is inherently base, vile, and depraved. Drawing a line at penetration, such that statutory rape offenses would be considered morally turpitudinous, but indecent assault offenses would not, as Mehboob has suggested, would not change our conclusion. Not only is penetration somewhat of an arbitrary demarcation between conduct that is socially acceptable and conduct that is not, it is also not supported by case law or the community consensus. Although a majority of the cases in this area have considered statutory rape offenses, several have found crimes not requiring penetration to involve moral turpitude. See, e.g., Marinell, 285 F.2d 474 (indecent touching); Matter of Garcia, 11 I. & N. Dec.521 (taking indecent liberties with a child); Matter of Imber, 16 I. & N. Dec. 256 (sexual misconduct and immoral advances). In addition, the community consensus, as displayed through the enactments of the Pennsylvania legislature, condemns any type of sexual contact between a person less than 16 years of age and another person who is four or more years older, regardless of penetration. Consequently, Mehboob's argument that indecent assault is not a crime of moral turpitude because it only involves touching, and not penetration, is unavailing.

The BIA's determination, that indecent assault under 18 Pa. Cons. Stat. §3126(a)(8) is a crime involving moral turpitude, is not unreasonable. The petition for review will be denied.

Stop and Engage

Now that you have highlighted key parts from this case, complete the following activities:

- Identify the main issue(s) in this case.
- Write a concise summary of the material facts.
- Paraphrase the relevant statutory language with precision and accuracy.
- Write a concise summary of the court's reasoning.
- Write a concise explanation as to how and why the court reached its decision—its holding.

10.5 Summary

Generally, crimes involving moral turpitude are those where acts are base, vile, or depraved, and contrary to the generally accepted mores and norms of societal life. States define crimes involving moral turpitude differently, but essentially, as the attorney general in Texas stated, "they denotes shameful wickedness—so extreme a departure from ordinary standards of honest[y], good morals, justice, or ethics as to be shocking to the moral sense of the community.[1] "

10.6 Chapter Review Activities

1. Use an internet search engine to determine how your state penal or criminal code defines "crimes involving moral turpitude," and using that definition, write a well-reasoned essay on why "crimes" listed as involving moral turpitude should be considered criminal activity subject to punishment (as defined in your state code).
2. How do you determine what is a "departure from ordinary standards of good morals?" How do you define good morals? Write a well-reasoned essay that grapples with these very complex issues.
3. Use an internet search engine to find a case from your state involving moral turpitude. What was the main issue? What was the essence of the court's reasoning? Identify the issue, write a summary of the material facts; write a precise and specific paraphrase

1. Opinion No GA-0299, issued on January 25, 2005, page 2.

of the statutory language; write a summary of the court's reasoning; and then write a well-reasoned analysis of whether you agree or disagree with the court's analysis and holding.

Chapter 11

Selected Crimes Against the State

Key Terms and Concepts

Treason	Sedition	The Patriot Act
Supremacy Clause	Common Law	Seditious Conspiracy
	Terrorism	

11.1 Introduction

The focus of this chapter is on crimes that impact the sovereignty of the state or interfere with governmental operations. The most common crimes found in this category are the crimes of treason, sabotage, espionage, and terrorism. Many states include specific acts against the state as crimes in the state penal or criminal code. We will explore some of the state statutes and see if we can deconstruct and parse the elements of the crimes. We will also explore some of the recent issues associated with terrorism in the United States since September 11, 2001.

11.2 Treason and Sedition

On a federal level, the United States Constitutions states in Article III, Section 3, that treason against the United States:

> Shall consist only in levying War against them or in adhering to their Enemies giving them Aid and Comfort. No Person shall be convicted of Treason unless on the Testimony of two Witnesses to the same over Act or on Confession in open Court.

Can you parse the *mens rea* and *actus reus* from this definition of treason? Treason is also defined in the United States Code, 18 USC Section 2381 as this:

> Whoever, owing allegiance to the United States, levies war against them or adheres to their enemies, giving them aid and comfort within the United States or elsewhere, is guilty of treason and shall suffer death, or shall be imprisoned not less than five years and fined under this title but not less than $10,000; and shall be incapable of holding any office under the United States.

Stop and Engage

How does the federal definition compare with the definition in the Constitution? Some states, such as California, also have laws on treason. In California, Title 3 of the penal code is entitled "Offenses against the Sovereignty of the State" and includes the following crimes:

> 37. (a) Treason against this state consists only in levying war against it, adhering to its enemies, or giving them aid and comfort, and can be committed only by persons owing allegiance to the state. The punishment of treason shall be death or life imprisonment without possibility of parole. The penalty shall be determined pursuant to Sections 190.3 and 190.4.
>
> (b) Upon a trial for treason, the defendant cannot be convicted unless upon the testimony of two witnesses to the same overt act, or upon confession in open court; nor, except as provided in Sections 190.3 and 190.4, can evidence be admitted of an overt act not expressly charged in the indictment or information; nor can the defendant be convicted unless one or more overt acts be expressly alleged therein.
>
> 38. Misprision of treason is the knowledge and concealment of treason, without otherwise assenting to or participating in the crime. It is punishable by imprisonment in the state prison.

Stop and Engage

How would you parse the *mens rea* and *actus reus* of the crime of treason based on the California statute? Now, if we review the Florida Statutes we find that Chapter 876 is entitled "Criminal Anarchy, Treason, and Other Crimes against Public Order" where treason is specifically defined in Section 876.32in this way:

> Treason against the state shall consist only in levying war against the same, or in adhering to the enemies thereof, or giving them aid and comfort. Whoever commits treason against this state shall be guilty of a felony of the first degree.

Stop and Engage

How does the definition of treason in Florida compare to California and the Federal Law? Consider the definition for subversive organization in Section 876.22(2):

> "Subversive organization" means any organization which engages in or advocates, abets, advises, or teaches, or a purpose

> of which is to engage in or advocate, abet, advise, or teach activities intended to overthrow, destroy, or to assist in the overthrow or destruction of the constitutional form of the Government of the United States, the constitution or government of the state, or of any political subdivision of either of them, by revolution, force, violence, or other unlawful means.

Stop and Engage

How does this compare with criminal anarchy as defined in Section 876.01 of the Florida Statutes? What are some of the key similarities and differences between these three Florida crimes?

> "Criminal anarchy," "criminal Communism," "criminal Nazism," or "criminal Fascism" are doctrines that existing form of constitutional government should be overthrown by force or violence or by any other unlawful means, or by assassination of officials of the Government of the United States or of the several states. The advocacy of such doctrines either by word of mouth or writing or the promotion of such doctrines independently or in collaboration with or under the guidance of officials of a foreign state or an international revolutionary party or group is unlawful.

In the General Laws of Massachusetts, Chapter 264 is entitled "Crimes against Governments," and of the crimes listed you will find, among others, these three:

- Treason
- Flag Misuse
- Subversive Organization

The definition for treason is defined in Chapter 264, Section 1, in this way:

> Treason against the commonwealth shall consist only in levying war against it, or in adhering to the enemies thereof, giving them aid and comfort; it shall not be bailable.

Learning Activity

What does the Massachusetts definition have in common with the other state definitions on treason? Can you find treason in your state criminal or penal code? Why do you think there are state laws on treason when the U.S. Constitution and the Federal Laws have provisions regarding treason? Write a well-reasoned essay on this topic and remember to think about the **Supremacy Clause**.

Now, search the United States Constitution and see if you can find a provision on sedition. If you cannot find one, how would you define the crime of sedition? **Common law** defines sedition as conduct directed towards the government which is tantamount to insurrection but which does not rise to the level of treason. In other words, the subtle distinction between sedition and treason is that in treason, the emphasis is on "levying war" against the government or providing "aid and/or comfort" to its enemies whereas sedition emphasizes disturbances that are organized in opposition to governmental authority—an open revolt. The United States Code in 18 USC 2384 defines **seditious conspiracy** as the following:

> If two or more persons in any State or Territory, or in any place subject to the jurisdiction of the United States, conspire to overthrow, put down, or to destroy by force the Government of the United States, or to levy war against them, or to oppose by force the authority thereof, or by force to prevent, hinder, or delay the execution of any law of the United States, or by force to seize, take, or possess any property of the United States contrary to the authority thereof, they shall each be fined under this title or imprisoned not more than twenty years, or both.

Note that the United States Code in 18 USC Section 2385, also has a definition for advocating overthrow of the government and defines it like this:

> Whoever knowingly or willfully advocates, abets, advises, or teaches the duty, necessity, desirability, or propriety of overthrowing or destroying the government of the United States or the government of any State, Territory, District or Possession thereof, or the government of any political subdivision therein, by force or violence, or by the assassination of any officer of any such government; or
>
> Whoever, with intent to cause the overthrow or destruction of any such government, prints, publishes, edits, issues, circulates, sells, distributes, or publicly displays any written or printed matter advocating, advising, or teaching the duty, necessity, desirability, or propriety of overthrowing or destroying any government in the United States by force or violence, or attempts to do so; or
> Whoever organizes or helps or attempts to organize any society, group, or assembly of persons who teach, advocate, or encourage the overthrow or destruction of any such government by force or violence; or becomes or is a member of, or affiliates with, any such society, group, or assembly of persons, knowing the purposes thereof -
> Shall be fined under this title or imprisoned not more than twenty years, or both, and shall be ineligible for employment by the United States or any department or agency thereof, for the five years next following his conviction.
> If two or more persons conspire to commit any offense named in this section, each shall be fined under this title or imprisoned not more than twenty years, or both, and shall be ineligible for employment by the United States or any department or agency thereof, for the five years next following his conviction.

> As used in this section, the terms "organizes" and "organize", with respect to any society, group, or assembly of persons, include the recruiting of new members, the forming of new units, and the regrouping or expansion of existing clubs, classes, and other units of such society, group, or assembly of persons.

Now read a case, and see how these federal definitions are interpreted by the United States Supreme Court.

Case Example: Practice Opportunity

The most famous case on sedition is *Yates v. United States*, 354 US 298 (1957), a United States Supreme Court case in which 14 leaders of the communist party in California were indicted under the Smith Act for conspiring to advocate and teach the duty and necessity of overthrowing the government of the United States by force and violence. In an excerpt from the case we read:

> One object of the conspiracy charged was to violate the third paragraph of 18 U.S.C. §2385, which provides:
>
> > Whoever organizes or helps or attempts to organize any society, group, or assembly of persons who teach, advocate, or encourage the overthrow or destruction of any [government in the United States] by force or violence ... [s]hall be fined not more than $10,000 or imprisoned not more than ten years, or both
>
> The statute does not define what is meant by "organize." Dictionary definitions are of little help, for, as those offered us sufficiently show, the term is susceptible of both meanings attributed to it by the parties here. The legislative history of the Smith Act is no more revealing as to what Congress meant by "organize" than is the statute itself. The Government urges that "organize" should be given a broad meaning, since acceptance of the term in its narrow sense would require attributing to Congress the intent that this provision of the statute should not apply to the Communist Party as it then existed. The argument is that, since the Communist Party as it then existed had been born in 1919 and the Smith Act was not passed until 1940, the use of "organize" in its narrow sense would have meant that these provisions of the statute would never have reached the act of organizing the Communist Party, except for the fortuitous rebirth of the Party in 1945—an occurrence which, of course, could not have been foreseen in 1940. This, says the Government, could hardly have been the congressional purpose, since the Smith Act as a whole was particularly aimed at the Communist Party, and its "organizing" provisions were especially directed at the leaders of the movement.

We find this argument unpersuasive. While the legislative history of the Smith Act does show that concern about communism was a strong factor leading to this legislation, it also reveals that the statute, which was patterned on state anti-sedition laws directed not against Communists but against anarchists and syndicalists, was aimed equally at all groups falling within its scope.

On the other hand, we also find unpersuasive petitioners' argument as to the intent of Congress. In support of the narrower meaning of "organize," they argue that the Smith Act was patterned after the California Criminal Syndicalism Act; that the California courts have consistently taken "organize" in that Act in its narrow sense and that, under such cases as *Willis v. Eastern Trust & Banking Co.,* 169 U. S. 295, 169 U. S. 304, 169 U. S. 309, and *Joines v. Patterson,* 274 U. S. 544, 274 U. S. 549, it should be presumed that Congress in adopting the wording of the California Act intended "organize" to have the same meaning as that given it by the California courts. As the hearings on the Smith Act show, however, its particular prototype was the New York Criminal Anarchy Act, not the California statute, and the "organizing" provisions of the New York Act have never been construed by any court. Moreover, to the extent that the language of the California statute, which itself was patterned on the earlier New York legislation, might be significant, we think that little weight can be given to these California decisions. The "general rule that adoption of the wording of a statute from another legislative jurisdiction carries with it the previous judicial interpretations of the wording ... is a presumption of legislative intention ... which varies in strength with the similarity of the language, the established character of the decisions in the jurisdiction from which the language was adopted and the presence or lack of other indicia of intention."

We are thus left to determine for ourselves the meaning of this provision of the Smith Act, without any revealing guides as to the intent of Congress. In these circumstances, we should follow the familiar rule that criminal statutes are to be strictly construed, and give to "organize" its narrow meaning, that is, that the word refers only to acts entering into the creation of a new organization, and not to acts thereafter performed in carrying on its activities, even though such acts may loosely be termed "organizational." We too think this statute should be read "according to the natural and obvious import of the language, without resorting to subtle and forced construction for the purpose of either limiting or extending its operation."

The Government contends that, even if the trial court was mistaken in its construction of the statute, the error was harmless because the conspiracy charged embraced both "advocacy" of violent overthrow and "organizing" the Communist Party, and the jury was instructed that, in order to convict, it must find a conspiracy extending to both objectives. Hence, the argument is, the jury must, in any event, be taken to have found petitioners guilty of conspiring to advocate, and the convictions are supportable on that basis alone. We cannot accept this proposition for a number of reasons. The portions of the trial court's instructions relied on by the Government are not sufficiently clear or specific to warrant our drawing the inference that the jury understood it must find an agreement extending to*both* "advocacy" and "organizing" in order to convict. Further, in order to convict, the jury was required, as the court charged, to find an overt act which was "knowingly done in furtherance of an object or purpose of the conspiracy charged in the indictment," and we have no way of knowing whether the overt act found by the jury was one which it believed to be in furtherance of the "advocacy", rather than the "organizing" objective of the alleged conspiracy. The character of most of the overt acts alleged associates them as readily with "organizing" as with "advocacy." In these circumstances, we think the proper rule to be applied is that which requires a verdict to be set aside in cases where the verdict is supportable on one ground, but not on another, and it is impossible to tell which ground the jury selected. *Stromberg v. California,* 283 U. S. 359, 283 U. S. 367-368; *Williams v. North Carolina,* 317 U. S. 287, 317 U. S. 291-292; *Cramer v. United States,* 325 U. S. 1, 325 U. S. 36, n. 45.

We conclude, therefore, that, since the Communist Party came into being in 1945, and the indictment was not returned until 1951, the three-year statute of limitations had run on the "organizing" charge, and required the withdrawal of that part of the indictment from the jury's consideration.

Stop and Engage

Now that you have read this excerpt, complete the following activities:

- Identify the main issue(s) in this case.
- Paraphrase the relevant statutory language with precision and accuracy.
- Write a concise summary of the court's reasoning.
- Write a concise explanation as to how and why the court reached its decision—its holding.

11.3 Terrorism

It is difficult to think about the development of the legal concept of terrorism prior to 2001. In fact, terrorism was commonly thought of from an international perspective or attributed to third world or politically tumultuous governments. Since 2001 the concept of domestic terrorism and terrorism targeted towards the United States has permeated every aspect of our daily lives. In 22 USC 2556(f) pertaining to reporting requirements on terrorism are several definitions which are useful for understanding the meaning of various terms related to the discussion on terrorism.

> As used in this section—
>
> (1) the term "international terrorism" means terrorism involving citizens or the territory of more than 1 country;
> (2) the term "terrorism" means premeditated, politically motivated violence perpetrated against noncombatant targets by subnational groups or clandestine agents;
> (3) the term "terrorist group" means any group practicing, or which has significant subgroups which practice, international terrorism;
> (4) the terms "territory" and "territory of the country" mean the land, waters, and airspace of the country; and
> (5) the terms "terrorist sanctuary" and "sanctuary" mean an area in the territory of the country—
> (A) that is used by a terrorist or terrorist organization—
>
> (i) to carry out terrorist activities, including training, fundraising, financing, and recruitment; or
>
> (ii) as a transit point; and
>
> (B) the government of which expressly consents to, or with knowledge, allows, tolerates, or disregards such use of its territory and is not subject to a determination under—
>
> (i) section 2405(j)(1)(A) of the Appendix to title 50;
>
> (ii) section 2371 (a) of this title; or
>
> (iii) section 2780 (d) of this title.

Learning Activity

How would you write a specific and precise definition for the terms "terrorism" and "terrorist group?" What are some interpretative issues that are presented by these definitions? What other words in those definitions would require further clarification for a more complete understanding of the terms? What issues come to mind as you read those definitions that pertain to criminal law?

11.3.1 The Patriot Act and Federal Law

The best-known legislation that has been promulgated since 2001 on terrorism is the Uniting and Strengthening America by Providing Appropriate Tools Required to Intercept and Obstruct Terrorism (USA Patriot Act) Act of 2001. The preamble to the legislation, HR 3162, states "To deter and punish terrorist acts in the United States and around the world, to enhance law enforcement investigatory tools, and for other purposes." The purposes of the Patriot Act are evident from the headings of the various titles in the Act. Some of these titles follow:

- Enhancing Domestic Security Against Terrorism (Title I)
- Enhanced Surveillance Procedures (Title II)
- International Money laundering Abatement and Anti-Terrorist Financing (Title III)
- Protecting the Border (Title IV)
- Removing Obstacles to Investigating Terrorism (Title V)
- Providing for Victims of Terrorism, Public Safety Officers, and their Families (Title VI)
- Increased Information Sharing for Critical Infrastructure Protection (Title VII)
- Strengthening the Criminal Laws against Terrorism (Title VIII)
- Improved Intelligence (Title IX)
- Miscellaneous (Title X)

Section 802 of the Patriot Act amended the definition of domestic terrorism found in 18 USC 2331to read:

> (5) the term "domestic terrorism" means activities that—
>
> (A) involve acts dangerous to human life that are a violation of the criminal laws of the United States or of any State;
> (B) appear to be intended—
>
> (i) to intimidate or coerce a civilian population;
>
> (ii) to influence the policy of a government by intimidation or coercion; or
>
> (iii) to affect the conduct of a government by mass destruction, assassination, or kidnapping; and
>
> (C) occur primarily within the territorial jurisdiction of the United States.

The Patriot Act also amended 18 USC 2339, on harboring or concealing terrorists, to read in this way:

> (a) Whoever harbors or conceals any person who he knows, or has reasonable grounds to believe, has committed, or is about to commit, an offense under section 32 (relating to destruction of aircraft or aircraft facilities), section 175 (relating to biolog-

> ical weapons), section 229 (relating to chemical weapons), section 831 (relating to nuclear materials), paragraph (2) or (3) of section 844 (f) (relating to arson and bombing of government property risking or causing injury or death), section 1366 (a) (relating to the destruction of an energy facility), section 2280 (relating to violence against maritime navigation), section 2332a (relating to weapons of mass destruction), or section 2332b (relating to acts of terrorism transcending national boundaries) of this title, section 236 (a) (relating to sabotage of nuclear facilities or fuel) of the Atomic Energy Act of 1954 (42 U.S.C. 2284 (a)), or section 46502 (relating to aircraft piracy) of title 49, shall be fined under this title or imprisoned not more than ten years, or both.
>
> (b) A violation of this section may be prosecuted in any Federal judicial district in which the underlying offense was committed, or in any other Federal judicial district as provided by law.

In addition, 18 USC 2339A, on providing material support to terrorists, now reads:

> (a) Offense.—Whoever provides material support or resources or conceals or disguises the nature, location, source, or ownership of material support or resources, knowing or intending that they are to be used in preparation for, or in carrying out, a violation of section 32, 37, 81, 175, 229, 351, 831, 842 (m) or (n), 844 (f) or (i), 930 (c), 956, 1114, 1116, 1203, 1361, 1362, 1363, 1366, 1751, 1992, 2155, 2156, 2280, 2281, 2332, 2332a, 2332b, 2332f, or 2340A of this title, section 236 of the Atomic Energy Act of 1954 (42 U.S.C., section 46502 or 60123 (b) of title 49, or any offense listed in section 2332b (g)(5)(B) (except for sections 2339A and 2339B) or in preparation for, or in carrying out, the concealment of an escape from the commission of any such violation, or attempts or conspires to do such an act, shall be fined under this title, imprisoned not more than 15 years, or both, and, if the death of any person results, shall be imprisoned for any term of years or for life. A violation of this section may be prosecuted in any Federal judicial district in which the underlying offense was committed, or in any other Federal judicial district as provided by law.
>
> (b) Definitions.—As used in this section—
>
> (1) the term "material support or resources" means any property, tangible or intangible, or service, including currency or monetary instruments or financial securities, financial services, lodging, training, expert advice or assistance, safehouses, false documentation or identification, communications equipment, facilities, weapons, lethal substances, explosives, personnel (1

or more individuals who may be or include oneself), and transportation, except medicine or religious materials;

(2) the term "training" means instruction or teaching designed to impart a specific skill, as opposed to general knowledge; and

(3) the term "expert advice or assistance" means advice or assistance derived from scientific, technical or other specialized knowledge.

Stop and Engage

Now that you have read some federal statutory language that was created and/or amended because of the promulgation of the Patriot Act, write a summary for each of the three code sections above. Use the internet to find more information on domestic terrorism and prosecutions under the Patriot Act. What issues come to mind as you surf the web that pertain to criminal and/or constitutional law?

11.3.2 Terrorism and State Law

In the Alabama Code, we find the Anti-Terrorism Act of 2002 in Article 7, which provides these dictums specifically in Section 13A-10-152:

(a) A person is guilty of a crime of terrorism when, with intent to intimidate or coerce a civilian population, influence the policy of a unit of government by intimidation or coercion, or affect the conduct of a unit of government by murder, assassination, or kidnapping, he or she commits a specified offense.

In Florida, terrorism is defined in Section 775.30 as:

An activity that:

(1)(a) Involves a violent act or an act dangerous to human life which is a violation of the criminal laws of this state or of the United States; or

(b) Involves a violation of s. 815.06; and

(2) Is intended to:

(a) Intimidate, injure, or coerce a civilian population;

(b) Influence the policy of a government by intimidation or coercion; or

(c) Affect the conduct of government through destruction of property, assassination, murder, kidnapping, or aircraft piracy.

In Arizona, terrorism is defined in Section 13-2301(12) in this way:

"Terrorism" means any felony, including any completed or preparatory offense, that involves the use of a deadly weapon or a weapon of mass destruction or the intentional or knowing infliction of serious physical injury with the intent to either:

(a) Influence the policy or affect the conduct of this state or any of the political subdivisions, agencies or instrumentalities of this state.

(b) Cause substantial damage to or substantial interruption of public communications, communication service providers, public transportation, common carriers, public utilities, public establishments or other public services.

In Pennsylvania, terrorism is defined in Section 2717 in the following way:

(a) General rule.—A person is guilty of terrorism if he commits a violent offense intending to do any of the following:

(1) Intimidate or coerce a civilian population.

(2) Influence the policy of a government by intimidation or coercion.

(3) Affect the conduct of a government.

(b) Grading and penalty.—

(1) If the violent offense is a misdemeanor or a felony of the third or second degree, an offense under this section shall be classified one degree higher than the classification of the violent offense specified in section 106 (relating to classes of offenses).

(2) If the violent offense is a felony of the first degree, a person convicted of an offense under this section shall be sentenced to a term of imprisonment fixed by the court at not more than 40 years and may be sentenced to pay a fine of not more than $100,000.

(c) Definitions.—As used in this section, the following words and phrases shall have the meanings given to them in this subsection:

"Dangerous to human life or property." A violent act or an act which is intended to or likely to cause death, serious bodily injury or mass destruction.

"Mass destruction." An act which is intended to or likely to destroy or cause serious damage to transportation-related infrastructure or facilities, energy-related infrastructure or facilities, public or private buildings, places of public accommodation or public works under circumstances evincing depraved indifference to human life or property.

"Violent offense." An offense under this part, including an attempt, conspiracy or solicitation to commit any such offense, which is punishable by imprisonment of more than one year and involves an act dangerous to human life or property.

In New York, terrorism is defined in Section 490.05(1) like this:

> "Act of terrorism":
>
> (a) for purposes of this article means an act or acts constituting a specified offense as defined in subdivision three of this section for which a person may be convicted in the criminal courts of this state pursuant to article twenty of the criminal procedure law, or an act or acts constituting an offense in any other jurisdiction within or outside the territorial boundaries of the United States which contains all of the essential elements of a specified offense, that is intended to:
>
> (i) intimidate or coerce a civilian population;
>
> (ii) influence the policy of a unit of government by intimidation or coercion; or
>
> (iii) affect the conduct of a unit of government by murder, assassination or kidnapping; or
>
> (b) for purposes of subparagraph (xiii) of paragraph (a) of subdivision one of section 125.27 of this chapter means activities that involve a violent act or acts dangerous to human life that are in violation of the criminal laws of this state and are intended to:
>
> (i) intimidate or coerce a civilian population;
>
> (ii) influence the policy of a unit of government by intimidation or coercion; or
>
> (iii) affect the conduct of a unit of government by murder, assassination or kidnapping.

Learning Activity

Based on the definitions of terrorism in these state statutes, write your own statutory definition of terrorism. What is the *mens rea* and *actus reus*? How would you prove terrorism based on your definition?

Some states have also enacted legislation that pertains to various types of conduct and activities to curtail terrorism. For example, in California, Sections 11415-11419, are entitled "The Hertzberg-Alarcon California Prevention of Terrorism Act," and Section 11416, states this about terrorism:

> The Legislature hereby finds and declares that the threat of terrorism involving weapons of mass destruction, including, but not limited to, chemical, biological, nuclear, or radiological agents, is a significant public safety concern. The Legislature also recognizes that terrorism involving weapons of mass destruction could result in an intentional disaster placing residents of California in great peril. The Legislature also finds it necessary to sanction the possession, manufacture, use, or threatened use of chemi-

> cal, biological, nuclear, or radiological weapons, as well as the intentional use or threatened use of industrial or commercial chemicals as weapons against persons or animals.

In addition, California in Sections 186.20-186.33 of the Penal Code has provisions categorized as "California Street Terrorism Enforcement and Prevention Act." Section 186.22 states:

> 186.22. (a) Any person who actively participates in any criminal street gang with knowledge that its members engage in or have engaged in a pattern of criminal gang activity, and who willfully promotes, furthers, or assists in any felonious criminal conduct by members of that gang, shall be punished by imprisonment in a county jail for a period not to exceed one year, or by imprisonment in the state prison or 16 months, or two or three years.

11.4 Summary

The focus of this chapter is on crimes that impact the sovereignty of the state or interfere with governmental operations. The most common crimes found in this category are the crimes of treason, sabotage, espionage, and terrorism. Many states include specific acts against the state as crimes in the state penal or criminal code. The crimes of treason and sedition have been historically significant since the founding of the United States. It is difficult to think about the development of the legal concept of terrorism prior to 2001. In fact, terrorism was commonly thought of from an international perspective or attributed to third world or politically tumultuous governments. Since 2001, the concept of domestic terrorism and terrorism targeted towards the United States has permeated every aspect of our daily lives. The most well-known legislation that has promulgated since 2001 on terrorism is the Uniting and Strengthening America by Providing Appropriate Tools Required to Intercept and Obstruct Terrorism (USA Patriot Act) Act of 2001. The preamble to the legislation, HR 3162, states this: "To deter and punish terrorist acts in the United States and around the world, to enhance law enforcement investigatory tools, and for other purposes."

11.5 Chapter Review Activities

1. Use the internet to find other states that have enacted various forms of anti-terrorism legislation. Summarize your findings in a table or a chart. Is your state included in your chart?
2. Based on some of the learning activities in this chapter pertaining to terrorism, what other crimes would you categorize as "ter-

rorist activities?" Write a well-reasoned essay that explains your choices.

3. Spend some time reading through The Patriot Act; then, write a well-reasoned essay on your reaction to this legislation. What is missing? What would you change? Think about the practicalities in the implementation of this type of legislation. Please be specific in your discussion.

4. Use an internet search engine to find some well-respected articles on the constitutional issues inherent in the implementation of The Patriot Act. Choose one of these issues and write a well-reasoned essay explaining the constitutional issue and the constitutional concerns. What are some of the "balancing act" realities?

Chapter 12

Selected Issues in Cybercrime

Key Terms and Concepts

Cybercrime	Phishing
Spam	Computer Fraud and Abuse
Identity Theft Protection Act	CAN-SPAM Act of 2003
Computer Fraud and Abuse Act	Theft and Assumption Deterrence Act

12.1 Introduction

In a news release issued on May 26, 2010, by the U.S. Department of Justice, the following information was reported:

> Mitchell L. Frost, age 23, of Bellevue, Ohio, appeared before U.S. Magistrate Judge Nancy A. Vecchiarelli and pleaded guilty to a two-count Information filed on May 14, 2010, which charged Frost with causing damage to a protected computer system and possessing 15 or more unauthorized access devices. According to court documents, Frost admitted that between August 2006, and March 2007, while enrolled as a student at the University of Akron, he used the University's computer network to access IRC channels on the Internet to control other computers and computer networks via computers intentionally infected and taken over, known as "BotNet" zombies, which were located throughout the United States and in other countries. Frost also admitted gaining access to other computers and computer networks by various means, including scanning the Internet searching for computer networks which were vulnerable to attack or unauthorized intrusion, gaining unauthorized access to and con-

> trol over such computers, and fraudulently obtaining user names and passwords for users on such systems. Frost admitted using the compromised computers to spread malicious computer codes, commands and information to even more computers, all for the purpose of harvesting and obtaining information and data from the compromised computer networks, including user names, passwords, credit card numbers, and CVV security codes, and for the purpose of launching Distributed Denial of Service (DDoS) attacks on computer systems and Internet websites. Frost admitted that between August 2006 and March 2007, Frost initiated DDoS attacks on numerous computers connected to the Internet hosting various websites temporarily interrupting operation of the websites, which required the site owners to intervene and repair their computer systems. Frost also admitted initiating denial of service attacks against the University of Akron computer server on or about March 14, 2007, which caused the entire University of Akron computer network to be knocked offline for approximately 8½ hours, preventing all students, faculty and staff members from accessing the network. This denial of service attack required the University of Akron to employ diagnostic and remedial measures to restore computer service causing losses in excess of $10,000.

In another press release issued by the Department of Justice on May 6, 2010, this was reported:

> Rodolfo Rodriguez Cabrera, 43, a Cuban national, and Henry Mantilla, 35, of Cape Coral, Fla., pleaded guilty to one count of conspiracy to produce and sell counterfeit International Game Technology (IGT) video gaming machines, commonly known as slot machines, and counterfeit IGT computer programs. Cabrera and Mantilla were indicted by a federal grand jury in Las Vegas on April 22, 2009, on one count of conspiracy, two counts of trafficking in counterfeit goods, two counts of trafficking in counterfeit labels and two counts of criminal copyright infringement. According to court documents, Cabrera and Mantilla conspired between August 2007 and April 15, 2009, to make and sell unauthorized copies of computer programs designed for IGT video slot machines and counterfeit IGT video slot machines bearing IGT's registered trademarks, all without the permission of IGT. The defendants also agreed to forfeit any and all counterfeit items in their possession and any illegal proceeds from their criminal activity.

These are just two examples from hundreds of thousands of cases pertaining to various forms of cybercrime. **Cybercrime** has been broadly defined to include computer and internet-related crime, crime pertaining to password trafficking, child exploitation on the internet, copyright piracy, and other online activities. Consider the following reported by the U.S. Department of Justice on January 26, 2006:

> A California man was arrested this morning on federal charges that allege he sent thousands of e-mails to America Online users that appeared to be from AOL's Billing Department and prompted the subscribers to send personal and credit card information, which was later used by the defendant to make unauthorized credit and debit card purchases. Jeffrey Brett Goodin, 45, was charged in a criminal complaint filed yesterday with operating a sophisticated "phishing" scheme—an Internet-based scam designed to obtain personal information by tricking people into believing that they are providing their information to a legitimate business. Goodin is specifically charged with wire fraud and the unauthorized use of an access device (credit card). According to the affidavit in support of the criminal complaint Goodin used several email accounts to send e-mails to AOL users. Those e-mails appeared to be from AOL's billing department, urged the subscribers to "update" their AOL billing information or lose service, and referred them to one of several fraudulent Internet websites where they could input personal information, including name, address, AOL account information, and credit or debit card data. Goodin, who allegedly controlled those websites, used the fraudulently obtained information to make unauthorized charges on the credit or debit cards belonging to the duped AOL subscribers.

Stop and Engage

What are the specific criminal charges stated in this report? Can you find these crimes in the California Penal Code? Write a summarized, precise, and specific definition for each of these crimes. What is the required *mens rea* and *actus reus*? What facts, in addition to those above, would you need to successfully prove these crimes? Check the code in your state, and then find a section that pertains to cybercrime and write a fact pattern that illustrates that crime without using the specific words in the statutory definition of the crime.

12.2 Federal Laws on Cybercrime

One of the best resources for information on federal laws related to cybercrime is the Department of Justice, Computer Crime and Intellectual Property Section Website found at http://www.justice.gov/criminal/cybercrime. On this website is a list of "Federal Criminal Code Related to Computer Intrusions" which includes these codes:

- 18 U.S.C. § 1029. Fraud and Related Activity in Connection with Access Devices

- 18 U.S.C. §1030. Fraud and Related Activity in Connection with Computers
- 18 U.S.C. §1362. Communication Lines, Stations, or Systems
- 18 U.S.C. §2510 et seq. Wire and Electronic Communications Interception and Interception of Oral Communications
- 18 U.S.C. §2701 et seq. Stored Wire and Electronic Communications and Transactional Records Access
- 18 U.S.C. §3121 et seq. Recording of Dialing, Routing, Addressing, and Signaling Information

In addition to the federal legislation on cybercrime, there are also well-recognized categories of cybercrime that include, among others:

- Cybersquatting
- Domain Hijacking
- E-mail
- Hacking
- Identity Theft
- Obscenity
- Pharming
- Phishing
- Privacy
- Spam
- Spyware

Stop and Engage

Use an internet search engine to find reliable and accurate definitions for the above listed categories of cybercrime. There are also federal laws related to other areas of cybercrime such as the Identity Theft Enforcement and Restitution Act of 2008 which amended language in the Computer Fraud and Abuse Act found in 18 USC 1030 which states this:

> (a) Whoever—
>
> (1) having knowingly accessed a computer without authorization or exceeding authorized access, and by means of such conduct having obtained information that has been determined by the United States Government pursuant to an Executive order or statute to require protection against unauthorized disclosure for reasons of national defense or foreign relations, or any restricted data, as defined in paragraph y. of section 11 of the Atomic Energy Act of 1954, with reason to believe that such information so obtained could be used to the injury of the United States, or to the advantage of any foreign nation willfully communicates, delivers, transmits, or causes to be communicated, delivered, or transmitted, or attempts to communicate, deliver, transmit or cause to be communicated, delivered, or transmitted the same to any person not entitled to receive it, or willfully retains the same

and fails to deliver it to the officer or employee of the United States entitled to receive it;

(2) intentionally accesses a computer without authorization or exceeds authorized access, and thereby obtains—

(A) information contained in a financial record of a financial institution, or of a card issuer as defined in section 1602 (n) of title 15, or contained in a file of a consumer reporting agency on a consumer, as such terms are defined in the Fair Credit Reporting Act (15 U.S.C. 1681 et seq.);

(B) information from any department or agency of the United States; or

(C) information from any protected computer;

(3) intentionally, without authorization to access any nonpublic computer of a department or agency of the United States, accesses such a computer of that department or agency that is exclusively for the use of the Government of the United States or, in the case of a computer not exclusively for such use, is used by or for the Government of the United States and such conduct affects that use by or for the Government of the United States;

(4) knowingly and with intent to defraud, accesses a protected computer without authorization, or exceeds authorized access, and by means of such conduct furthers the intended fraud and obtains anything of value, unless the object of the fraud and the thing obtained consists only of the use of the computer and the value of such use is not more than $5,000 in any 1-year period;

(5)

(A) knowingly causes the transmission of a program, information, code, or command, and as a result of such conduct, intentionally causes damage without authorization, to a protected computer;

(B) intentionally accesses a protected computer without authorization, and as a result of such conduct, recklessly causes damage; or

(C) intentionally accesses a protected computer without authorization, and as a result of such conduct, causes damage and loss.

(6) knowingly and with intent to defraud traffics (as defined in section 1029) in any password or similar information through which a computer may be accessed without authorization, if—

(A) such trafficking affects interstate or foreign commerce; or

(B) such computer is used by or for the Government of the United States;

(7) with intent to extort from any person any money or other thing of value, transmits in interstate or foreign commerce any communication containing any—

(A) threat to cause damage to a protected computer;

(B) threat to obtain information from a protected computer without authorization or in excess of authorization or to impair the confidentiality of information obtained from a protected computer without authorization or by exceeding authorized access; or

(C) demand or request for money or other thing of value in relation to damage to a protected computer, where such damage was caused to facilitate the extortion; shall be punished as provided in subsection (c) of this section.

(b) Whoever conspires to commit or attempts to commit an offense under subsection (a) of this section shall be punished as provided in subsection (c) of this section.

Case Example: Practice Opportunity

Read the following case excerpt, and use a yellow highlighter to identify the material facts of the case; use a blue highlighter to note the relevant statutory language; use a pink highlighter to note the alleged crime; and use a green highlighter to note the court's application of the law to the facts of the case:, to highlight the court's analysis.

United States of America v. Lori Drew

United States District Court, Central District of California,
No. CR 08-0582-GW (2009)

This case raises the issue of whether (and/or when will) violations of an Internet website's terms of service constitute a crime under the Computer Fraud and Abuse Act ("CFAA"), 18 U.S.C. § 1030.

Drew, a resident of O'Fallon, Missouri, entered into a conspiracy in which its members agreed to intentionally access a computer used in interstate commerce without (and/or in excess of) authorization in order to obtain information for the purpose of committing the tortious act of intentional infliction of emotional distress upon "M.T.M.," subsequently identified as Megan Meier ("Megan"). Megan was a 13 year old girl living in O'Fallon who had been a classmate of Drew's daughter Sarah. Pursuant to the conspiracy, on or about September 20, 2006, the conspirators registered and set up a profile for a fictitious 16 year old male juvenile named "Josh Evans" on the www.MySpace.com website ("MySpace"), and posted a photograph of a boy without that boy's knowledge or consent. Such conduct violated MySpace's terms of service. The conspirators contacted Megan through the MySpace network (on which she had her own profile) using the Josh Evans pseudonym and began to flirt with her over a number of days. On or about October 7, 2006, the conspirators had "Josh" inform Megan that he was moving away. On or about October 16 2006, the conspirators had "Josh" tell Megan that he no longer liked her and that "the world would be a better place without her in it." Later on that same day, after learning that Megan had killed herself, Drew caused the Josh Evans MySpace account to be deleted.

As Jae Sung (Vice President of Customer Care at MySpace) ("Sung") testified at trial, MySpace is a "social networking" website where members can create profiles" and interact with other members. Anyone with Internet access can go onto the MySpace website and view content which is open to the general public such as a music area, video section, and members' profiles which are not set as "private." However, to create a profile, upload and display photographs, communicate with persons on the site, write "blogs," and/or utilize other services or applications on the MySpace website, one must be a "member." Anyone can become a member of MySpace at no charge so long as they meet a minimum age requirement and register.

In 2006, to become a member, one had to go to the sign-up section of the MySpace website and register by filling in personal information (such as name, email address, date of birth, country/state/postal code, and gender) and creating a password. In addition, the individual had to check on the box indicating that "You agree to the MySpace Terms of Service and Privacy Policy." The terms of service did not appear on the same registration page that contained this "check box" for users to confirm their agreement to those provisions. In order to find the terms of service, one had (or would have had) to proceed to the bottom of the page where there were several "hyperlinks" including one entitled "Terms." Upon clicking the "Terms" hyperlink, the screen would display the terms of service section of the website. A person could become a MySpace member without ever reading or otherwise becoming aware of the provisions and conditions of the MySpace terms of service by merely clicking on the "check box" and then the "Sign Up" button without first accessing the "Terms" section. As used in its website, "terms of service" refers to the "MySpace.com Terms of Use Agreement" ("MSTOS"). The MSTOS in 2006 stated, inter alia:

> This Terms of Use Agreement ("Agreement") sets forth the legally binding terms for your use of the Services. By using

> the Services, you agree to be bound by this Agreement, whether you are a "Visitor" (which means that you simply browse the Website) or you are a "Member" (which means that you have registered with Myspace.com). The term "User" refers to a Visitor or a Member. You are only authorized to use the Services (regardless of whether your access or use is intended) if you agree to abide by all applicable laws and to this Agreement. Please read this Agreement carefully and save it. If you do not agree with it, you should leave the Website and discontinue use of the Services immediately. If you wish to become a Member, communicate with other Members and make use of the Services, you must read this Agreement and indicate your acceptance at the end of this document before proceeding.
>
> By using the Services, you represent and warrant that (a) all registration information you submit is truthful and accurate; (b) you will maintain the accuracy of such information; (c) you are 14 years of age or older; and (d) your use of the Services does not violate any applicable law or regulation.

The MSTOS prohibited the posting of a wide range of content on the website including (but not limited to) material that: a) "is potentially offensive and promotes racism, bigotry, hatred or physical harm of any kind against any group or individual"; b) "harasses or advocates harassment of another person"; c) "solicits personal information from anyone under 18"; d) "provides information that you know is false or misleading or promotes illegal activities or conduct that is abusive, threatening, obscene, defamatory or libelous"; e) "includes a photograph of another person that you have posted without that person's consent"; f) "involves commercial activities and/or sales without our prior written consent"; g) "contains restricted or password only access pages or hidden pages or images"; or h) provides any phone numbers, street addresses, last names, URLs or email addresses...." MySpace also reserved the right to take appropriate legal action (including reporting the violating conduct to law enforcement authorities) against persons who engaged in "prohibited activity" which was defined as including, inter alia: a) "criminal or tortious activity", b) "attempting to impersonate another Member or person", c) "using any information obtained from the Services in order to harass, abuse, or harm another person", d) "using the Service in a manner inconsistent with any and all applicable laws and regulations", e) "advertising to, or solicitation of, any Member to buy or sell any products or services through the Services", f) "selling or otherwise transferring your profile", or g) "covering or obscuring the banner advertisements on your personal profile page...." The MSTOS warned users that "information provided by other MySpace.com Members (for instance, in their Profile) may contain inaccurate, inappropriate, offensive or sexually explicit material, products or services, and MySpace.com assumes no responsibility or liability for this material."

Further, MySpace was allowed to unilaterally modify the terms of service, with such modifications taking effect upon the posting of notice on its website. Thus, members would have to review the MSTOS each time they logged on to the website, to ensure that they were aware of any updates in order to avoid violating some new provision of the terms of service. Also, the MSTOS provided that "any dispute" between a visitor/member and MySpace "arising out of this Agreement must be settled by arbitration" if demanded by either party. At one point, MySpace was receiving an estimated 230,000 new accounts per day and eventually the number of profiles exceeded 400 million with over 100 million unique visitors worldwide. "Generally speaking," MySpace would not monitor new accounts to determine if they complied with the terms of service except on a limited basis, mostly in regards to photographic content. Sung testified that there is no way to determine how many of the 400 million existing MySpace accounts were created in a way that violated the MSTOS. The MySpace website did have hyperlinks labelled "Safety Tips" (which contained advice regarding personal, private and financial security vis-a-vis the site) and "Report Abuse" (which allowed users to notify MySpace as to inappropriate content and/or behavior on the site). MySpace attempts to maintain adherence to its terms of service. It has different teams working in various areas such as "parent care" (responding to parents' questions about this site), handling "harassment/cyberbully cases, imposter profiles," removing inappropriate content, searching for underage users, etc. As to MySpace's response to reports of harassment:

> It varies depending on the situation and what's being reported. It can range from ... letting the user know that if they feel threatened to contact law enforcement, to us removing the profile, and in rare circumstances we would actually contact law enforcement ourselves.

Once a member is registered and creates his or her profile, the data is housed on computer servers which are located in Los Angeles County. Members can create messages which can be sent to other MySpace members, but messages cannot be sent to or from other Internet service providers such as Yahoo! All communications among MySpace members are routed from the sender's computer through the MySpace servers in Los Angeles. Profiles created by adult MySpace members are by default available to any user who accesses the MySpace website. The adult members can, however, place privacy settings on their accounts such that only pre-authorized "friends" are able to view the members' profile pages and contents. For members over 16 but under 18, their profiles are by default set at "private" but can be changed by the member. Members under 16 have a privacy setting for their profiles which cannot be altered to allow regular public access. To communicate with a member whose profile has a privacy setting, one must initially send a "friend" request to that person who would have to accept the request. To become a "friend" of a person under 16, one must not only send a "friend" request but must also know his or her email address or last name. According to Sung, MySpace owns the data contained in the profiles and the other content on the website. MySpace is owned by Fox Interactive Media which is part of News Corporation.

In 2006, the CFAA (18 U.S.C. §1030) provided in relevant part that:

> (a) Whoever—(2) intentionally accesses a computer without authorization or exceeds authorized access, and thereby obtains –
>
> (A) information contained in a financial record of a financial institution, or of a card issuer as defined in section 1602(n) of title 15, or contained in a file of a consumer reporting agency on a consumer, as such terms are defined in the Fair Credit Reporting Act (15 U.S.C. 1681 et seq.); (B) information from any department or agency of the United States; or (C) information from any protected computer if the conduct involved an interstate or foreign communication; shall be punished as provided in subsection (c) of this section.
>
> (c) The punishment for an offense under subsection (a) or (b) of this section is –
>
> (2)(A) except as provided in subparagraph (B), a fine under this title or imprisonment for not more than one year, or both, in the case of an offense under subsection (a)(2), (a)(3), (a)(5)(A)(iii), or (a)(6) of this section which does not occur after a conviction for another offense under this section, or an attempt to commit an offense punishable under this subparagraph; ...
>
> (B) a fine under this title or imprisonment for not more than 5 years, or both, in the case of an offense under subsection (a)(2), or an attempt to commit an offense punishable under this subparagraph, if –

(i) the offense was committed for purposes of commercial advantage or private financial gain;

(ii) the offense was committed in furtherance of any criminal or tortious act in violation of the Constitution or laws of the United States or of any State; or

(iii) the value of the information obtained exceeds $5,000....

As used in the CFAA, the term "computer" "includes any data storage facility or communication facility directly related to or operating in conjunction with such device...." 18 U.S.C. § 1030(e)(1). The term "protected computer" "means a computer—(A) exclusively for the use of a financial institution or the United States Government ... ; or (B) which is used in interstate or foreign commerce or communication...." Id. § 1030(e)(2). The term "exceeds authorized access" means "to access a computer with authorization and to use such access to obtain or alter information in the computer that the accesser is not entitled so to obtain or alter ..." Id. § 1030(e)(6). During the relevant time period herein,12 the misdemeanor 18 U.S.C. § 1030(a)(2)(C) crime consisted of the following three elements:

First, the defendant intentionally [accessed without authorization] [exceeded authorized access of] a computer;

Second, the defendant's access of the computer involved an interstate or foreign communication; and

Third, by [accessing without authorization] [exceeding authorized access to] a computer, the defendant obtained information from a computer ... [used in interstate or foreign commerce or communication]....

In this case, a central question is whether a computer user's intentional violation of one or more provisions in an Internet website's terms of services (where those terms condition access to and/or use of the website's services upon agreement to and compliance with the terms) satisfies the first element of section 1030(a)(2)(C). If the answer to that question is "yes," then seemingly, any and every conscious violation of that website's terms of service will constitute a CFAA misdemeanor.

Initially, it is noted that the latter two elements of the section 1030(a)(2)(C) crime will always be met when an individual using a computer contacts or communicates with an Internet website. Addressing them in reverse order, the third element requires "obtain[ing] information" from a "protected computer"—which is defined in 18 U.S.C. § 1030(e)(2)(B) as a computer "which is used in interstate or foreign commerce or communication...." "Obtain[ing] information from a computer" has been described as "'includ[ing] mere observation of the data. Actual aspiration ... need not be proved in order to establish a violation....'" As for the "interstate or foreign commerce or communication" component, the Supreme Court in Reno v. American Civil Liberties Union, 521 U.S. 844, 849 (1997), observed that: "The Internet is an international network of interconnected computers." See also Brookfield Communications v. West Coast Entertainment Corp., 174 F.3d 1036, 1044 (9th Cir. 1999) ("The Internet is a global network of interconnected computers which allows individuals and organizations around the world to communicate and to share information with one another."). The Ninth Circuit in United States v. Sutcliffe, 505 F.3d 944, 952 (9th Cir. 2007), found the Internet to be "similar to—and often using—our national network of telephone lines." Thus, the third element is satisfied whenever a person using a computer contacts an Internet website and reads any response from that site.

As to the second element (i.e., that the accessing of the computer involve an interstate or foreign communication), an initial question arises as to whether the communication itself must be interstate or foreign (i.e., it is transmitted across state lines or country borders) or whether it simply requires that the computer system, which is accessed for purposes of the communication, is interstate or foreign in nature (for example, akin to a national telephone system). "[T]he plain language of section 1030(a)(2)(C) requires that the conduct of unlawfully accessing a computer, and not the obtained information, must involve an interstate or foreign communication." It has been held that "[a]s a practical matter, a computer providing a 'web-based' application accessible through the internet would satisfy the 'interstate communication' requirement."

This interpretation is consistent with the legislative history of the CFAA. Therefore, where contact is made between an individual's computer and an Internet website, the second element is per se established. As to the first element (i.e. intentionally accessing a computer without authorization or exceeding authorized access), the primary question here is whether any conscious violation of an Internet website's terms of service will cause an individual's contact with the website via computer to become "intentionally access[ing] ... without authorization" or "exceeding authorization." Initially, it is noted that three of the key terms of the first element (i.e., "intentionally," "access a computer," and "without authorization") are undefined, and there is a considerable amount of controversy as to the meaning of the latter two phrases.

Under § 1030(a)(2)(C), the "requisite intent" is "to obtain unauthorized access of a protected computer." United States v. Willis, 476 F.3d 1121, 1125 (10th Cir. 2007) ("The government need not also prove that ... the information was used to any particular ends."); ("[T]he crux of the offense under subsection 1030(a)(2)(C) ... is abuse of a computer to obtain the information."). As to the term "accesses a computer," one would think that the dictionary definition of verb transitive "access" would be sufficient. That definition is "to gain or have access to; to retrieve data from, or add data to, a database...." Webster's New World Dictionary, Third College Edition, 7 (1988) (henceforth "Webster's New World Dictionary"). Most courts that have actually considered the issue of the meaning of the word "access" in the CFAA have basically turned to the dictionary meaning. As to the term "without authorization," the courts that have considered the phrase have taken a number of different approaches in their analysis. Within the breach of contract approach, most courts that have considered the issue have held that a conscious violation of a website's terms of service/use will render the access unauthorized and/or cause it to exceed authorization.

In this particular case, as conceded by the Government, the only basis for finding that Drew intentionally accessed MySpace's computer/servers without authorization and/or in excess of authorization was her and/or her co-conspirators violations of the MSTOS by deliberately creating the false Josh Evans profile, posting a photograph of a juvenile without his permission and pretending to be a sixteen year old O'Fallon resident for the purpose of communicating with Megan. Therefore, if conscious violations of the MySpace terms of service were not sufficient to satisfy the first element of the CFAA misdemeanor violation as per 18 U.S.C. §§ 1030(a)(2)(C) and 1030(b)(2)(A), Drew's Rule 29(c) motion would have to be granted on that basis alone. However, this Court concludes that an intentional breach of the MSTOS can potentially constitute accessing the MySpace computer/server without authorization and/or in excess of authorization under the statute.

There is nothing in the way that the undefined words "authorization" and "authorized" are used in the CFAA (or from the CFAA's legislative history which indicates that Congress intended for them to have specialized meanings. As delineated in Webster's New World Dictionary at 92, to "authorize" ordinarily means "to give official approval to or permission for...." It cannot be considered a stretch of the law to hold that the owner of an Internet website has the right to establish the extent to (and the conditions under) which members of the public will be allowed access to information, services and/or applications which are available on the website. Nor can it be doubted that the owner can relay and impose those limitations/restrictions/conditions by means of written notice such as terms of service or use provisions placed on the home page of the website. While issues might be raised in particular cases as to the sufficiency of the notice and/or sufficiency of the user's assent to the terms, and while public policy considerations might in turn limit enforcement of particular restrictions, the vast majority of the courts (that have considered the issue) have held that a website's terms of service/use can define what is (and/or is not) authorized access vis-a-vis that website.

Here, the MSTOS defined "services" as including "the MySpace.com Website..., the MySpace.com instant messenger, and any other connection with the Website. It further notified the public that the MSTOS "sets forth the legally binding terms for your use of the services." Id. Visitors and members were informed that "you are only authorized to use the Services ... if you agree to abide by all applicable laws and to this Agreement." Id. Moreover, to become a MySpace member and thereby be allowed to communicate with other members and fully utilize the MySpace Services, one had to click on a box to confirm that the user had agreed to the MySpace Terms of Service. Clearly, the MSTOS was capable of defining the scope of authorized access of visitors, members and/or users to the website.

As discussed above, terms of service which are incorporated into a browsewrap or clickwrap agreement can, like any other type of contract, define the limits of authorized access as to a website and its concomitant computer/server(s). However, the question is whether individuals of "common intelligence" are on notice that a breach of a terms of service contract can become a crime under the CFAA. Arguably, they are not. First, an initial inquiry is whether the statute, as it is written, provides sufficient notice. Here, the language of section 1030(a)(2)(C) does not explicitly state (nor does it implicitly suggest) that the CFAA has "criminalized breaches of contract" in the context of website terms of service. Normally, breaches of contract are not the subject of criminal prosecution. Thus, while "ordinary people" might expect to be exposed to civil liabilities for violating a contractual provision, they would not expect criminal penalties. Id. This would especially be the case where the services provided by MySpace are in essence offered at no cost to the users and, hence, there is no specter of the users "defrauding" MySpace in any monetary sense. Second, if a website's terms of service controls what is "authorized" and what is "exceeding authorization"—

which in turn governs whether an individual's accessing information or services on the website is criminal or not, section 1030(a)(2)(C) would be unacceptably vague because it is unclear whether any or all violations of terms of service will render the access unauthorized, or whether only certain ones will. For example, in the present case, MySpace's terms of service prohibits a member from engaging in a multitude of activities on the website, including such conduct as "criminal or tortious activity," "gambling," "advertising to ... any Member to buy or sell any products," "transmit[ting] any chain letters," "covering or obscuring the banner advertisements on your personal profile page," "disclosing your password to any third party," etc. The MSTOS does not specify which precise terms of service, when breached, will result in a termination of MySpace's authorization for the visitor/member to access the website.

Treating a violation of a website's terms of service, without more, to be sufficient to constitute "intentionally access[ing] a computer without authorization or exceed[ing] authorized access" would result in transforming section 1030(a)(2)(C) into an overwhelmingly overbroad enactment that would convert a multitude of otherwise innocent Internet users into misdemeanant criminals. Utilizing a computer to contact an Internet website by itself will automatically satisfy all remaining elements of the misdemeanor crime in 18 U.S.C. §§ 1030(a)(2)(C) and 1030(c)(2)(A). Where the website's terms of use only authorizes utilization of its services/applications upon agreement to abide by those terms (as, for example, the MSTOS does herein), any violation of any such provision can serve as a basis for finding access unauthorized and/or in excess of authorization. One need only look to the MSTOS terms of service to see the expansive and elaborate scope of such provisions whose breach engenders the potential for criminal prosecution. Obvious examples of such breadth would include: 1) the lonely-heart who submits intentionally inaccurate data about his or her age, height and/or physical appearance, which contravenes the MSTOS prohibition against providing "information that you know is false or misleading"; 2) the student who posts candid photographs of classmates without their permission, which breaches the MSTOS provision covering "a photograph of another person that you have posted without that person's consent"; and/or 3) the exasperated parent who sends out a group message to neighborhood friends entreating them to purchase his or her daughter's girl scout cookies, which transgresses the MSTOS rule against advertising to, or solicitation of, any Member to buy or sell any products or services through the Services." See Exhibit 3 at 4. However, one need not consider hypotheticals to demonstrate the problem. In this case, Megan (who was then 13 years old) had her own profile on MySpace, which was in clear violation of the MSTOS which requires that users be "14 years of age or older." Id. at 2. No one would seriously suggest that Megan's conduct was criminal or should be subject to criminal prosecution. Given the incredibly broad sweep of 18 U.S.C. §§ 1030(a)(2)(C) and 1030(c)(2)(A), should conscious violations of a website's terms of service be deemed sufficient by themselves to constitute accessing without authorization or exceeding authorized access, the question arises as to whether Congress has "establish[ed] minimal guidelines to govern law enforcement." Kolender, 461 U.S. at 358; see also City of Chicago v. Morales, 527 U.S. 41, 60 (1999). Section 1030(a)(2)(C) does not set forth "clear guidelines" or "objective criteria" as to the prohibited conduct in the Internet/website or similar contexts. See generally Posters 'N' Things, Ltd., 511 U.S. at 525-26. For instance, section 1030(a)(2)(C) is not limited to instances where the website owner contacts law enforcement to complain about an individual's unauthorized access or exceeding permitted access on the site.29 Nor is there any requirement that there be any actual loss or damage suffered by the website or that there be a violation of privacy interests.

Here, the Government's position is that the "intentional" requirement is met simply by a conscious violation of a website's terms of service. The problem with that view is that it basically eliminates any limiting and/or guiding effect of the scienter element. It is unclear that every intentional breach of a website's terms of service would be or should be held to be equivalent to an intent to access the site without authorization or in excess of authorization. This is especially the case with MySpace and similar Internet venues which are publically available for access and use. However, if every such breach does qualify, then there is absolutely no limitation or criteria as to which of the breaches should merit criminal prosecution. All manner of situations will be covered from the more serious (e.g. posting child pornography) to the more trivial (e.g. posting a picture of friends without their permission). All can be prosecuted. Given the "standardless sweep" that results, federal law enforcement entities would be improperly free "to pursue their personal predilections." In sum, if any conscious breach of a website's terms of service is held to be sufficient by itself to constitute intentionally accessing a computer without authorization or in excess of authorization, the result will

> be that section 1030(a)(2)(C) becomes a law "that affords too much discretion to the police and too little notice to citizens who wish to use the [Internet]."

Stop and Engage

Now that you have highlighted key parts from this case, complete the following activities:

- Identify the main issue(s) in this case.
- Write a concise summary of the material facts.
- Paraphrase the relevant statutory language with precision and accuracy.
- Write a concise summary of the court's reasoning.
- Write a concise explanation as to how and why the court reached its decision—its holding.

Learning Tip

You can see from reading this statutory language the complexities that arise in connection with the application of the rules of law to a particular factual scenario. Another piece of legislation is the CAN-SPAM Act of 2003, 15 U.S.C. §§7701–13 (Supp. IV 2004) the purpose of which is described in the following paragraph:

> (i) prohibit senders of electronic mail (e-mail) for primarily commercial advertisement or promotional purposes from deceiving intended recipients or Internet service providers as to the source or subject matter of their e-mail messages; (ii) require such e-mail senders to give recipients an opportunity to decline to receive future commercial e-mail from them and to honor such requests; ... and (iv) prohibit businesses from knowingly promoting, or permitting the promotion of, their trade or business through e-mail transmitted with false or misleading sender or routing information (S. REP. NO. 108-102, at 1).

The Act defined spam in 15 USC 7702(2)(A) as:

> Any electronic mail message the primary purpose of which is the commercial advertisement or promotion of a commercial product or service (including content on an Internet website operated for a commercial purpose.

12.2.1 Phishing and Identity Theft

Phishing is a cybercrime that is not *per se* illegal under a particular federal law, but it is prosecuted as a crime under the Computer Fraud and Abuse Act as well as the CAN-SPAM Act, among others. **Phishing** is commonly used in identity theft as a means for obtaining personal information through the dissemination of fraudulent e-mail messages. In addition to prosecution for phishing under federal statutes, several states have enacted crimes related to the material elements of phishing. For example, Virginia Code Section 18.2-152.5:1(A) states:

> It is unlawful for any person, other than a law-enforcement officer, as defined in §9.1-101, and acting in the performance of his official duties, to use a computer to obtain, access, or record, through the use of material artifice, trickery or deception, any identifying information, as defined in clauses (iii) through (xiii) of subsection C of §18.2-186.3.

New Mexico Code Section 30-16-24.1 states, in part, that:

> A. Theft of identity consists of willfully obtaining, recording or transferring personal identifying information of another person without the authorization or consent of that person and with the intent to defraud that person or another.
>
> B. Obtaining identity by electronic fraud consists of knowingly and willfully soliciting, requesting or taking any action by means of a fraudulent electronic communication with intent to obtain the personal identifying information of another.
>
> C. As used in this section:
>
> (1) "fraudulent electronic communication" means a communication by a person that is an electronic mail message, web site or any other use of the internet that contains fraudulent, false, fictitious or misleading information that depicts or includes the name, logo, web site address, email address, postal address, telephone number or any other identifying information of a business, organization or state agency, to which the person has no legitimate claim of right; and
>
> (2) "personal identifying information" means information that alone or in conjunction with other information identifies a person, including the person's name, address, telephone number, driver's license number, social security number, place of employment, maiden name of the person's mother, demand deposit account number, checking or savings account number, credit card or debit card number, personal identification number, passwords or any other numbers or information that can be used to access a person's financial resources.
>
> D. Whoever commits theft of identity is guilty of a fourth degree felony.
>
> E. Whoever commits obtaining identity by electronic fraud is guilty of a fourth degree felony.
>
> F. Prosecution pursuant to this section shall not prevent prosecution pursuant to any other provision of the law when the conduct also constitutes a violation of that other provision.

> G. In a prosecution brought pursuant to this section, the theft of identity or obtaining identity by electronic fraud shall be considered to have been committed in the county:
>
> (1) where the person whose identifying information was appropriated, obtained or sought resided at the time of the offense; or
>
> (2) in which any part of the offense took place, regardless of whether the defendant was ever actually present in the county.

California has its law in the Business and Professions Code rather than the penal code. Section 22948.2 states:

> It shall be unlawful for any person, by means of a Web page, electronic mail message, or otherwise through use of the Internet, to solicit, request, or take any action to induce another person to provide identifying information by representing itself to be a business without the authority or approval of the business.

Section 22948.1 of the California Business and Professions Code provides the necessary definitions for a proper interpretation of Section 22948.2:

> For the purposes of this chapter, the following terms have the following meanings:
>
> (a) "Electronic mail message" means a message sent to a unique destination, commonly expressed as a string of characters, consisting of a unique user name or mailbox (commonly referred to as the "local part") and a reference to an Internet domain (commonly referred to as the "domain part"), whether or not displayed, to which an electronic message can be sent or delivered.
>
> (b) "Identifying information" means, with respect to an individual, any of the following:
>
> (1) Social security number.
>
> (2) Driver's license number.
>
> (3) Bank account number.
>
> (4) Credit card or debit card number.
>
> (5) Personal identification number (PIN).
>
> (6) Automated or electronic signature.
>
> (7) Unique biometric data.
>
> (8) Account password.
>
> (9) Any other piece of information that can be used to access an individual's financial accounts or to obtain goods or services.

> (c) "Internet" shall have the meaning as defined in paragraph (6) of subdivision (f) of Section 17538.
>
> (d) "Web page" means a location that has a single uniform resource locator or other single location with respect to the Internet.

Stop and Engage

Does your state have a law on phishing and/or identity theft? If so, write a paraphrased definition with specificity and precision. Remember to check other codes in your state since California is a reminder that you may not find what you need in the criminal code, and remember to search for definitions. Do not use your own understanding or definitions to interpret statutory language. Note further that if the law is not in the criminal code, then it will likely carry civil penalties, not incarceration. The penalties for violation of Section 22948.2 in California are found in Section 22948.3 and are civil in nature.

What are the commonalities in the definitions for Virginia, New Mexico, and California? What are some of the differences?

On the federal level, the Identity Theft and Assumption Deterrence Act, 18 USC 1028, was passed in 1998 and states this, in part:

> (a) Whoever, in a circumstance described in subsection (c) of this section—
>
> (1) knowingly and without lawful authority produces an identification document, authentication feature, or a false identification document;
>
> (2) knowingly transfers an identification document, authentication feature, or a false identification document knowing that such document or feature was stolen or produced without lawful authority;
>
> (3) knowingly possesses with intent to use unlawfully or transfer unlawfully five or more identification documents (other than those issued lawfully for the use of the possessor), authentication features, or false identification documents;
>
> (4) knowingly possesses an identification document (other than one issued lawfully for the use of the possessor), authentication feature, or a false identification document, with the intent such document or feature be used to defraud the United States;
>
> (5) knowingly produces, transfers, or possesses a document-making implement or authentication feature with the intent such document-making implement or authentication feature will be used in the production of a false identification document or another document-making implement or authentication feature which will be so used;
>
> (6) knowingly possesses an identification document or authentication feature that is or appears to be an identification docu-

> ment or authentication feature of the United States or a sponsoring entity of an event designated as a special event of national significance which is stolen or produced without lawful authority knowing that such document or feature was stolen or produced without such authority;
>
> (7) knowingly transfers, possesses, or uses, without lawful authority, a means of identification of another person with the intent to commit, or to aid or abet, or in connection with, any unlawful activity that constitutes a violation of Federal law, or that constitutes a felony under any applicable State or local law; or
>
> (8) knowingly traffics in false or actual authentication features for use in false identification documents, document-making implements, or means of identification; shall be punished as provided in subsection (b) of this section.

Stop and Engage

Note the *mens rea* requirements associated with the different *actus reus* in this statute; why do you think the *mens rea* is the same? Is the *mens rea* a higher or lower culpability mental state in the hierarchy of culpable mental states? Write a precise and specific paraphrase of this statute that captures the material elements for the various crimes stated therein.

In 2004, Congress passed the Identity Theft Protection Act, 18 USC 1028A, to amend some of the language above in 18 USC 1028, so as to provide more stringent penalties for more serious identity theft-related crimes among other changes.

Learning Tip

You may want to note that in most states, identity theft is a felony. For example, Arizona in 13-2008, classifies the taking of the identity of another as a Class 4 felony. In Arkansas, financial identity fraud in 5-37-227, is a Class C felony. In Colorado in 18-5-901, identity theft is a Class 4 felony. In the California Penal Code, Sections 530.5(b), (c)(1), and (c)(2) it states this:

> Every person who willfully obtains personal identifying information, as defined in subdivision (b) of Section 530.55, of another person, and uses that information for any unlawful purpose, including to obtain, or attempt to obtain, credit, goods, services, real property, or medical information without the consent of that person, is guilty of a public offense, and upon conviction therefore, shall be punished by a fine, by imprisonment in a county jail not to exceed one year, or by both a fine and imprisonment, or by imprisonment in the state prison.
>
> Every person who, with the intent to defraud, acquires, transfers, or retains possession of the personal identifying information of another person is guilty of a public offense, and upon conviction therefore, shall be punished by a fine, by imprisonment in a county jail not to exceed one year, or both a fine and

> imprisonment. Every person who, with the intent to defraud, acquires or retains possession of the personal identifying information of another person, and who has previously been convicted of a violation of this section upon conviction therefore shall be punished by a fine, by imprisonment in a county jail not to exceed one year, or by both a fine and Imprisonment, or by imprisonment in the state prison.
>
> Every person who, with the intent to defraud, acquires or retains possession of the personal identifying information of 10 or more other persons is guilty of a public offense, and upon conviction therefore, shall be punished by a fine, by imprisonment in a county jail not to exceed one year, or by both a fine and imprisonment, or by imprisonment in the state prison.
>
> Every person who, with the intent to defraud, sells, transfers, or conveys the personal identifying information of another person is guilty of a public offense, and upon conviction therefore, shall be punished by a fine, by imprisonment in a county jail not to exceed one year, or by both a fine and imprisonment, or by imprisonment in the state prison.
>
> Every person who, with actual knowledge that the personal identifying information, of a specific person will be used to commit a violation of subdivision (a), sells, transfers, or conveys that same personal identifying information is guilty of a public offense, and upon conviction therefore, shall be punished by a fine, by imprisonment in the state prison, or by both fine and imprisonment.
>
> Every person who commits mail theft, as defined in §1705 of Title 18 of the United States Code, is guilty of a public offense, and upon conviction therefore shall be punished by a fine, by imprisonment in a county jail not to exceed one year, or by both a fine and imprisonment. Prosecution under this subdivision shall not limit or preclude prosecution under any other provision of law, including, but not limited to subdivisions (a) to (c), inclusive, of this section.

Florida Section 817.568 states:

> Any person who willfully and without authorization fraudulently uses, or possesses with intent to fraudulently use, personal identification information concerning an individual without first obtaining that individual's consent, commits the offense of fraudulent use of personal identification information, which is a felony of the third degree.

In New York Penal Code Sections 190.77-190.84, identity theft in the first and second degree constitute felonies, whereas identity theft in the third degree is a Class A misdemeanor. In the Texas Penal Code Section 32.51, the fraudulent use of possession of identifying information is a state jail felony.

Learning Activity

In September 2008, the President's Identity Theft Task Force issued a report with recommendations pertaining to data protection, data misuse, victim assistance, and deterrence. Use an internet search engine to find this report, read it, choose a few recommendations, and write an action plan for the implementation of those chosen recommendations. How would your plan work in connection with the laws in your state on identity theft?

12.3 Selected State Laws on Cybercrime

In the Texas Penal Code, computer crimes are grouped in Title 7 under "Offenses against Property" with the definition section commencing in Section 33.01. The two crimes in this section are "breach of computer security" (Section 33.02), and "online solicitation of a minor" (Section 33.021). Telecommunications crimes are found in Title 7 as well beginning in Section 33A.01 and include "Unauthorized use of telecommunications service" (Section 33A.02), "manufacture, possession, or delivery of unlawful telecommunications device" (Section 33A.03), "theft of telecommunications service," (Section 33A.04), and "publication of telecommunications access device" (Section 33A.05). In addition, there are several crimes that pertain to cybercrime related issues in the Fraud Section, Chapter 32 as well.

Learning Activity

Use an internet search engine to find Chapter 32 of the Texas Penal Code and read through the list of crimes in that chapter; then identify which ones have cybercrime related implications. Write a list of those crimes, and then write a well-reasoned discussion of why you chose those particular crimes.

California Penal Code Section 630 states:

> The Legislature hereby declares that advances in science and technology have led to the development of new devices and techniques for the purpose of eavesdropping upon private communications and that the invasion of privacy resulting from the continual and increasing use of such devices and techniques has created a serious threat to the free exercise of personal liberties and cannot be tolerated in a free and civilized society.
>
> The Legislature by this chapter intends to protect the right of privacy of the people of this state.

> The Legislature recognizes that law enforcement agencies have a legitimate need to employ modern listening devices and techniques in the investigation of criminal conduct and the apprehension of lawbreakers. Therefore, it is not the intent of the Legislature to place greater restraints on the use of listening devices and techniques by law enforcement agencies than existed prior to the effective date of this chapter.

The following Sections 631-638 in Title 15, Chapter 1.5, further define crimes related to the "invasion of privacy." In the preceding Chapter 1.4 entitled, "interception of wire, electronic digital pager, or electronic cellular telephone communications," sections 629.50-629.98, describe a variety of definitions and crimes. Wire communication is defined in Section 629.51(a) in this way:

> "Wire communication" means any aural transfer made in whole or in part through the use of facilities for the transmission of communications by the aid of wire, cable, or other like connection between the point of origin and the point of reception (including the use of a like connection in a switching station), furnished or operated by any person engaged in providing or operating these facilities for the transmission of communications.

Stop and Engage

Could this definition be a component in a cybercrime? Investigate this further using an internet search engine, and then write an essay with an in-depth substantive discussion supported by credible sources as to your findings.

Article 156 of the Laws of New York is entitled "Offenses Involving Computers" and includes the crimes of "unauthorized use of a computer" (Section 156.05), "computer trespass" (Section 156.10), "computer tampering" in the first to fourth degree (Sections 156.20-156.27), "unlawful duplication of computer related material" in the first and second degree (Sections 156.29 and 156.30), and "criminal possession of computer related material" (Section 156.35). Computer tampering in the first degree is defined in Section 156.27:

> A person is guilty of computer tampering in the first degree when he commits the crime of computer tampering in the fourth degree and he intentionally alters in any manner or destroys computer data or a computer program so as to cause damages in an aggregate amount exceeding fifty thousand dollars.

Stop and Engage

What words require interpretation in this definition?

> A person is guilty of computer tampering in the first degree when he commits the crime of computer tampering in the fourth degree and he intentionally alters in any manner or destroys computer data or a computer program so as to cause damages in an aggregate amount exceeding fifty thousand dollars.

Where can you find definitions for these words? See Sections 156.00 and 156.20, which state:

> A person is guilty of computer tampering in the fourth degree when he or she uses, causes to be used, or accesses a computer, computer service, or computer network without authorization and he or she intentionally alters in any manner or destroys computer data or a computer program of another person.

Stop and Engage

You will need to refer to Section 156.00 for the general definitions of the same words printed in blue in Section 156.27 that are found in this definition. What is the *mens rea* for this crime? Where can you find the definition for the requisite culpable mental state? (Hint, see Section 15.05). What are some factual questions you will need to resolve based on the definition of this crime? The highlighted terms present factual interpretative issues that would need to be resolved when composing a well-reasoned analysis to a hypothetical fact pattern scenario.

> A person is guilty of computer tampering in the fourth degree when he or she uses, causes to be used, or accesses a computer, computer service, or computer network without authorization and he or she intentionally alters in any manner or destroys computer data or a computer program of another person.

Hypothetical Fact Pattern Exercise

- Read the case once, and then read it again using a yellow highlighter to identify the material facts of the case noting any potentially applicable crimes while you highlight the material facts.

Susan and Steve share a cubicle at Wiley Network Systems. Susan works the morning shift from 6 A.M. to 1 P.M., and Steve works from 1 P.M. to 9 P.M. They each have their own computer in the cubicle as well as individually authorized passwords and access codes. They also share a computer which allows them to access highly sensitive company data through personal encrypted password access devices. One afternoon as Susan was preparing to leave for the day and was logging-out of her computer, she received a phone call on her office landline. As she was finishing her conversation, Steve came into the cubicle to begin his work day since it was 1:03 P.M. Upon seeing Steve enter the cubicle, Susan ended her call and gathered her belongings, saying goodbye to Steve. After Susan left, Steve logged onto his computer and began working. One of his assignments required him to use the shared computer to access some highly sensitive company data. When he started to log into the computer, he noticed that Susan had failed to log off, and he decided to use it to complete his assignment since that computer usually took a very long time to restart for a new login. As he was working, he noticed that Susan had made some errors on a previous assignment and decided to correct the errors by deleting certain files and re-inserting the correct files. When Steve was finished with his assignment and correcting Susan's work, he logged-off for the day and went home. Is Steve guilty of a crime under California law?

- After you identify the potentially applicable crimes, write a precise and specific definition for the crime based on the statutory language. Based on the definition of the crime, what *mens rea* and *actus reus* do you need to find in the facts? What facts will you use to prove each element of the crime? Once you have developed a strategy, write a well-reasoned analysis that answers the call of the question.

In Florida, computer-related crimes are found in Chapter 815 of Title XLVI; pertaining to crimes in the Florida Statutes, Section 815.016 states:

(1) Whoever willfully, knowingly, and without authorization:

(a) Accesses or causes to be accessed any computer, computer system, or computer network;

(b) Disrupts or denies or causes the denial of computer system services to an authorized user of such computer system services, which, in whole or part, is owned by, under contract to, or operated for, on behalf of, or in conjunction with another;

(c) Destroys, takes, injures, or damages equipment or supplies used or intended to be used in a computer, computer system, or computer network;

(d) Destroys, injures, or damages any computer, computer system, or computer network; or

(e) Introduces any computer contaminant into any computer, computer system, or computer network, commits an offense against computer users.

Stop and Engage

What is the required *mens rea*(s) for this crime in Florida? What are the required *actus reus*(s)? Does Section 815.03 help you in identifying and interpreting the required *actus reus*(s) for this crime? Write an analysis to the fact pattern above based on Florida Statute Section 815.016.

In Illinois Part C of the Criminal Code identifies "Offenses directed against Property" and includes computer crimes (Article 16D), wireless service theft (Article 16F), and Online Property Offenses (Article 16J), among others. Article 16J includes a number of crimes, such as these:

Sec. 16J 10. Online sale of stolen property. A person commits the offense of online sale of stolen property when he or she uses or accesses the Internet with the intent of selling property gained through unlawful means.

> Sec. 16J 15. Online theft by deception. A person commits the offense of online theft by deception when he or she uses the Internet to purchase or attempt to purchase property from a seller with a mode of payment that he or she knows is fictitious, stolen, or lacking the consent of the valid account holder.
>
> Sec. 16J 20. Electronic fencing. A person commits the offense of electronic fencing when he or she sells stolen property using the Internet, knowing that the property was stolen. A person who unknowingly purchases stolen property over the Internet does not violate this Section.

The Maryland Criminal Code, Title 7, pertaining to "Theft and Related Crimes" in Subtitle 3 lists crimes involving "Telecommunications and Electronics." Section 7-302 states:

> (1) A person may not intentionally, willfully, and without authorization:
>
> (i) access, attempt to access, cause to be accessed, or exceed the person's authorized access to all or part of a computer network, computer control language, computer, computer software, computer system, computer service, or computer database; or
>
> (ii) copy, attempt to copy, possess, or attempt to possess the contents of all or part of a computer database accessed in violation of item (i) of this paragraph.
>
> (2) A person may not commit an act prohibited by paragraph (1) of this subsection with the intent to:
>
> (i) cause the malfunction or interrupt the operation of all or any part of a computer, computer network, computer control language, computer software, computer system, computer service, or computer data; or
>
> (ii) alter, damage, or destroy all or any part of data or a computer program stored, maintained, or produced by a computer, computer network, computer software, computer system, computer service, or computer database.
>
> (3) A person may not intentionally, willfully, and without authorization:
>
> (i) possess, identify, or attempt to identify a valid access code; or
>
> (ii) publicize or distribute a valid access code to an unauthorized person.

Learning Activity

Use an internet search engine to find some of the computer and computer-related crimes in your state. Make a list of the crimes, and then choose a few to explore further, writing the definitions of those crimes in your own words using precision and specificity.

12.4 Summary

Cybercrime has been broadly defined to include computer and internet-related crime, crime pertaining to password trafficking, child exploitation on the internet, copyright piracy, and other online activities. One of the best resources for information on federal laws related to cybercrime is the Department of Justice, Computer Crime and Intellectual Property Section Website found at http://www.justice.gov/criminal/cybercrime. Phishing is a cybercrime that is not *per se* illegal under a particular federal law, but it is prosecuted as a crime under the Computer Fraud and Abuse Act as well as the CAN-SPAM Act, among others.

12.5 Chapter Review Activities

Analyze the fact pattern, identifying the relevant facts and elements of a crime, and determining what crime is appropriate for each actor. Be sure to write in clear, well-reasoned sentences. Note as well that you may need to refer to crimes that you have learned in previous chapters, so think of the crimes of this chapter as well as crimes learned in previous chapters. Reasoning, writing style, and clarity are important factors in these activities.

Hypothetical Fact Pattern

John, Mary, and Sue attend a seminar on decrypting secured wireless access point passwords. The seminar is offered in connection with an Internet Security conference. The FBI has a demonstration showing how they can decrypt such passwords in three minutes or less. After the conference, John and Sue decide to try out their newly acquired skills, and they meet in Sue's backyard where they use Sue's wireless laptop to find wireless connections in the neighborhood. They find several unsecured networks and two secured (WAP password) networks. They use their skills and spend about an hour unable to break the WAP passwords. Frustrated and hungry, they decide to order a Papa John's pizza and log-into the website by using one of the unsecured wireless connections. When the pizza arrives, Tony the pizza dude, says "Hey dudes, didn't I see you at the Internet Security Conference?" Sue and John respond, "Don't remember, but we attended the decrypting seminar and have been trying to break some passwords with no success." Tony responds, "Dudes, watch this," and he whips out his computer, shows them the secured wireless connections in the neighborhood, picks one, and breaks the password in seven minutes. Astounded, John and Sue ask Tony to show them how to access the neighbor's network and see what documents the neighbor has on his computer. Just as Tony begins to show them, Sue's dad comes home, and Tony closes the computer. Is there any criminal activity? Discuss any and all crimes.

Chapter 13

Identifying Applicable Rules of Criminal Procedure Within the Criminal Law Frame

Key Terms and Concepts

Investigation
Miranda Rights
Probable Cause
Fourth Amendment
Terry Stop
Hot Pursuit
Suggestiveness
Fifth Amendment
Sixth Amendment
Eighth Amendment
Fourteenth Amendment
Fishing Expedition
Plain View Doctrine
Fruit of the Poisonous Tree Doctrine
Search
Seizure
Curtilage
Knock and Announce Rule
Reasonable suspicion
Exclusionary Rule

13.1 Introduction

The purpose of this chapter is to introduce you to certain important concepts in criminal procedure so that you can begin to think about how criminal procedure fits within a criminal law frame. Remember from the first and second chapters of this book that it is easier to learn when you have a context for the information you are learning and when the ideas have some relevance to you. In most law and criminal justice programs, Criminal Law and Criminal Procedure are separate courses, so in this chapter we will reference many cases, but this chapter will not provide detailed explanations. We will also highlight the more important concepts and terms in criminal procedure but not explain them in detail. The detail and the depth will come when you take a specific course in Criminal Procedure. At the end of this chapter, however, you will have a foundational understanding of the names and general principles of the more important concepts:

- Constitutional provisions related to Criminal Procedure
- Cases in Criminal Procedure
- Substantive and Interpretative Issues
- Major Concepts

As you have learned so far in your course in Criminal Law—the emphasis is on substantive law. In criminal procedure, the emphasis is primarily on the process and procedure for the collection of evidence, making an arrest, questioning a suspect, etc. In other words, you learn the steps that must be followed and how these steps are connected to the other frames in the integrative frame model. In criminal procedure, there are carefully defined and specific steps necessary to achieve success in a criminal prosecution. The frame for criminal procedure is through an examination of concepts, statutory rules, and cases pertaining to the process. These regulations are connected to the penal or criminal code in criminal law where the elements of the crime are defined, and where each element must be proven using a precise process since the prosecutor must prove each element beyond a reasonable doubt, and if procedure is violated, that could impact the admission of evidence, a confession, etc., and the success of the prosecution.

Another frame that is closely interrelated to both criminal law and criminal procedure is evidence, and we will discuss that frame in the next chapter. This frame is concerned with developing evidence/facts (which can be admitted) that will prove each element of a crime. Generally, evidence is either physical evidence or testimony from credible witnesses who saw or heard what happened. The goal is for the prosecutor to have enough evidence to prove each element of a crime so that a conviction can be obtained. If the evidence is corrupted by faulty processes, then proof will be impacted. Typical issues in both the criminal process and the evidence include: chain of custody, probable cause, interrogation of suspects, and contamination of crime scene.

Procedural issues also impinge on constitutional rights, and, therefore, the constitutional frame is ever important in criminal procedure. The constitutional frame focuses the spotlight on issues usually related to rights where the penalty for violation may be the exclusion of important evidence. For instance, the probable cause issues that are embodied in the Fourth Amendment (probable cause and warrants), if violated, can destroy the prosecutor's case, and the penalties may influence and shape the behavior, words, conduct, and actions of law enforcement. In other words, many of the procedures that are studied in a course on Criminal Procedure are derived from a need to protect constitutional rights, including such amendments as the Fourth, Fifth, Sixth, and Eighth Amendments, among others.

13.2 Parties in the Criminal Justice System

In the discussion of an introduction to criminal procedure through a criminal law lens, it is necessary to have a basic understanding of the parties or players in our criminal justice system. The primary parties include the following:

1. The Defendant
2. Defense Attorney
3. Prosecutor
4. Victims
5. Law Enforcement
6. Magistrates/Judges
7. Jurors
8. Witnesses
9. The Public
10. The Media
11. Corrections Officers
12. Courtroom Personnel
13. Others

Concerns regarding the parties in the criminal justice process are usually centered in the issues these actors confront such as these: (a) constitutional protections; (b) rules of evidence; and (c) forensics. Several issues arise early in the process:

Law enforcement must be careful when confronting and evaluating notions of suspicious criminal activity. For example, someone who appears to be breaking into a vehicle may only have lost his/her keys, and the actions are innocent. Rarely do law enforcement officers actually witness a crime; rather, their suspicions are aroused by other people—like witnesses. The credibility of witnesses is a major issue for law enforcement. For example, if a professor and studenst at a university all report the same suspicious criminal activity; then law enforcement might attach more credibility to the report than if a known drug dealer in the university parking lot reported the suspicious activity.

When law enforcement is notified of suspicious activity, the officer will usually investigate to determine if there is any merit to the reports. Investigation is a process that triggers many different procedural steps and the protection of individual rights. For example, in an investigation, how much questioning is appropriate before it becomes unwarranted or an invasion of privacy? What other investigative tools may an officer use, and at what stage in the process? For example, may an officer "pat down" a suspect? May a suspect be detained without an arrest and for how long? The rules of criminal procedure and case law provide answers to these types of questions. The permissible actions of the officer vary with, among other things, the level of suspicion (e,g., reasonable suspicion, probable cause, etc.) Any violation (or perceived violation) of a procedure may open the door for the defense attorney to ask for the evidence to be excluded or dismissed. Prosecutors and defense attorneys often have opposing perspectives of the events and the evidence and, therefore, the acts of investigators and the procedures they employed or followed may be major issues at trial. Because of trial cost, workloads, and a variety of other factors, prosecutors and defense attorneys may try to plea bargain a case to reach a speedy conclusion and avoid a lengthy trial. The strength of the evidence, therefore, is a major negotiating tool, and its strength is often directly related to how the evidence was obtained and its admissibility at trial.

Investigation is primarily related to the gathering and collection of evidence, and there are several issues related to this activity which may become important at trial. For instance, what is the chain of custody of the evidence? What were the laboratory procedures? If procedures are not followed, there may be a contamination of evidence leading to its exclusion at trial. Veteran law enforcement officers often develop a sense of when sufficient evidence has been obtained to support a particular charge or charges. Prosecutors may not agree, and they may want law enforcement to obtain more evidence before they will file charges or seek an indictment. This situation is difficult for law enforcement and may tempt some to find shortcuts or even rules of procedure to obtain the necessary evidence.

A critical step in law enforcement procedure is placing a suspect under arrest. When an arrest is made, or, if there is a custodial interrogation, then there are concerns related to *Miranda* rights which will be discussed later in this chapter. If there is a violation of *Miranda,* testimony or confessions can be excluded from trial. Law enforcement may try to delay an arrest and engage only in "conversation" with suspects and witnesses so as to avoid "custodial interrogation" or "arrest" that will trigger *Miranda.* If, duringthese "conversations," officers develop enough information to justify an arrest, they must then inform the suspect of his/her *Miranda* rights and of the charge(s) against him.

13.3 Common Issues in the Process

The process or procedure is critical to law enforcement. If violations occur, defense counsel will petition that the evidence obtained by a flawed process be excluded from trial. If critical physical evidence is excluded because of a chain of custody error, and critical testimony is excluded because of Miranda violations, then the prosecutor will usually not have a case, and the charges against the defendant will be dropped for failure to have sufficient evidence to prove each element of the crime beyond a reasonable doubt. Law enforcement uses several tools to identify and develop evidence—each with a specific objective of avoiding exclusion and obtaining a conviction. Some of these tools are heavily dependent upon the experience and skill of the officer. An issue then arises as to whether the officer has sufficient skill to identify or determine suspicious acts, words, or conducts. What events or behaviors will raise the suspicion of the officer? Will an experienced officer react to more subtle cues than a rookie? Questions, such as "What are the differences between a 'hunch,' 'intuition,' and 'suspicion?'" become important questions when discussing the requisite standard for stopping, questioning, detaining, or arresting a suspect. These determinations become factual issues as well, in that a thirty-year veteran officer will likely have good intuitions while a rookie might not yet have developed the ability to distinguish a hunch or intuition from his/her own desire to make an arrest.

A major concept in criminal procedure is the **Fourth Amendment** and the notion of **probable cause,** both of which will be briefly and generally discussed in this chapter. When does a law enforcement officer need probable cause? What is probable cause? How is probable cause different from reasonable suspicion? If a law enforcement officer does not have probable cause, can he still engage a suspect? Are there exceptions to the probable cause requirements, such as the ***Terry* stop**? (What does a *Terry* stop allow?). How may probable cause be developed? One technique might be a pat down, but how much "patting" is permitted in a pat down? How much force or pressure can be applied? May the officer squeeze the contents of a pants pocket in an attempt to identify it? Must the "patting" be applied to only external garments, or may the officer reach inside a jacket? May an officer interrogate to develop probable cause? What is the extent of permissible questioning? When can a suspect be taken into custody? What is Miranda? What is plain view? Also embodied in the Fourth Amendment is the idea of arbitrary arrest and unreasonable search and seizure. From a historical perspective, the Founding Fathers were concerned about excessive government controls. If the processes which protect us from these unreasonable controls are violated, then evidence obtained by the poisoned process will be excluded at trial, and the prosecution's case will be damaged, and possibly even lost.

Other issues arise from the Code of Criminal Procedure. For example, Article 14.01 of the Texas Code of Criminal Procedure states:

> Art. 14.01. Offense within view. (a) A peace officer or any other person, may, without a warrant, arrest an offender when the offense is committed in his presence or within his view, if the offense is one classed as a felony or as an offense against the public peace.
>
> (b) A peace officer may arrest an offender without a warrant for any offense committed in his presence or within his view.

Although the language appears to be straightforward, there are many issues that need further interpretive clarification. For instance, an officer may arrest an offender without a warrant if an offense is "committed in his presence". What is "in his presence"? May the officer appoint an agent? If an offense is committed in the agent's presence, has proper procedure been followed? Similarly, what is "in his view"? Are there limitations on where the officer may stand for the offense to be in his view? Or, if the offense occurred at night, was it in the officer's "view"? The case excerpts which follow the language of the law provide valuable illustrations of principle. In each excerpt, identify the distinguishing fact which makes this case unique.

All of these are issues related to procedure and these are the types of questions that we will briefly and generally address in this chapter, and which you will explore in more detail in a course in Criminal Procedure.

13.4 Selected Constitutional Amendments Other Than the Fourth Amendment

In addition to the Fourth Amendment there are other amendments which appear frequently in a course in Criminal Procedure; these include, among others, the Fifth Amendment, the Sixth Amendment, the Eighth Amendment, and the Fourteenth Amendment.

Fifth Amendment

> No person shall be held to answer for a capital, or otherwise infamous crime, unless on a presentment or indictment of a Grand Jury, except in cases arising in the land or naval forces, or in the Militia, when in actual service in time of War or public danger; nor shall any person be subject for the same offence to be twice put in jeopardy of life or limb; nor shall be compelled in any criminal case to be a witness against himself, nor be deprived of life, liberty, or property, without due process of law; nor shall private property be taken for public use, without just compensation.

The Fifth Amendment is known generally as the self-incrimination amendment, but it has several other clauses. Notice that the self-incrimination protection applies only in a *criminal* case; it does not apply in a civil case or to a traffic case. The amendment states that no individual may be compelled to be a witness against himself. At trial, one of the forms of evidence is testimony of witnesses (another is physical evidence). This protection means that a defendant may offer testimony, but cannot be compelled to do so. Another clause in this amendment requires that a grand jury indict a suspect in a *capital* or *infamous* case (but not in all cases). The amendment also offers protection from double jeopardy—an individual cannot be tried for the same offense twice. Keep in mind that offenses are specific—manslaughter is not the same as second-degree murder. Finally, the Fifth Amendment requires due process in criminal proceedings. (See also the Fourteenth Amendment). Specifically, an individual cannot be deprived of life or liberty without due process of law. Some of the elements of due process include (a) notice of charge, (b) access to information and (c) right of defense. This clause minimizes the risk or arbitrary enforcement—e.g. the university cannot arbitrarily reduce everyone's grade by a letter.

Sixth Amendment

> In all criminal prosecutions, the accused shall enjoy the right to a speedy and public trial, by an impartial jury of the State and district wherein the crime shall have been committed, which district shall have been previously ascertained by law, and to be informed of the nature and cause of the accusation; to be confronted with the witnesses against him; to have compulsory process for obtaining witnesses in his favor, and to have the Assistance of Counsel for his defense.

The Sixth Amendment provides a right to a speedy and public trial. However, note the need for judicial interpretation for some of these words. For example, what is considered "speedy"? Also, how do you define "public?"—does it mean that anyone and everyone can attend a trial; are there limitations? According to case law, judges may exclude some people from attending a trial for (usually) privacy concerns—especially where children are the victims. Other provisions of this amendment include a right to know what charges have been filed against you (after an arrest has occurred), a right to be faced by an accuser (this might occur in chambers, especially where children are involved), and a right to counsel in criminal cases.

Eighth Amendment

> Excessive bail shall not be required, nor excessive fines imposed, nor cruel and unusual punishments inflicted.

There are two important clauses in this relatively brief amendment: (a) excessive bail may not be imposed; but this raises interpretative issues, such as what is "excessive"? Usually, the defendant's ability to pay is not a factor considered by the courts, but severity of the crime and flight risk is two of the major variables that a court takes into consideration; (b) cruel and unusual punishment. Obviously, "cruel" and "unusual" are concepts that require judicial interpretation as well, and there is an abundance of case law on the meaning of these words.

Fourteenth Amendment

> Section 1: All persons born or naturalized in the United States and subject to the jurisdiction thereof are citizens of the United States and of the State wherein they reside. No State shall make or enforce any law which shall abridge the privileges or immunities of citizens of the United States; nor shall any State deprive any person of life, liberty, or property, without due process of law; nor deny to any person within its jurisdiction the equal protection of the laws.

The Fourteenth is relevant to a course in Criminal Procedure because it allows for an incorporation of the federal due process requirements into state law. Notice that this amendment also contains an equal protection clause.

13.5 The Fourth Amendment

Generally, the Fourth Amendment provides citizens protection against unreasonable invasion of privacy by the government. The language is broad, and, therefore, extensive study is required to understand the meaning of each word in this amendment which states:

Fourth Amendment

> The right of the people to be secure in their persons, houses, papers, and effects, against unreasonable searches and seizures, shall not be violated, and no Warrants shall issue, but upon probable cause, supported by Oath or affirmation, and particularly describing the place to be searched, and the persons or things to be seized.

Stop and Engage

Use a yellow highlighter to identify those words that may be most relevant to a discussion of Fourth Amendment concerns in criminal procedure and determining the propriety of the actions of law enforcement officers. What are the two most important warrants from a law enforcement perspective? Use a pink highlighter to highlight these two words.

When you deconstruct and parse the words and phrases in this amendment, you should ask questions. For example, what is "unreasonable"? What is "search"? What is "seizure"? It is crucial to your success in a course in Criminal Procedure to memorize this amendment and focus on the key words and concepts. Since the language of the amendment is very broad, it is essential that you consult case law and judicial interpretation to determine the meaning of the words and how to correctly apply the requirements of the amendment to individual fact patterns and cases. One of the most important concepts from a law enforcement conduct perspective is "probable cause." The amendment clearly states that "no warrant shall issue but upon probable cause" which raises a crucial interpretative question: What constitutes probable cause? Especially law enforcement needs to understand this concept in detail, because without probable cause, a warrant cannot be issued.

Also, notice that in the constitutional language, there is a requirement for an "oath or affirmation," which you will learn from case law in Criminal Procedure "particularly describes" the places or persons to be searched and the items to be seized. While the notion of "particularly describes" may seem straightforward, you can infer that questions such as "how particular?" begin to surface in this interpretative discussion. For example, if the search warrant uses the word "house," does this include the garage, or other buildings, or surrounding land? A warrant cannot be authorization to engage in a **fishing expedition** (obtaining a warrant in the hope that once you gain entry or access to the place or person you will find some evidence of illegal activity), and therefore, the warrant cannot be general and open to interpretation as to the purpose of the search and/or seizure. Remember that for the amendment to be applicable to a particular set of facts, there must be a "search" and/or a "seizure."

A general search can be thought of as a fishing expedition, which will *invade privacy*. For example, officers cannot just randomly search 100 acres to see what can be discovered. If an individual's privacy is to be invaded, there must be a justifiable reason for it; a reason that can be discussed with particularity. Notice however, that a balance between the person's right to privacy and the needs of law enforcement must be reached in this discussion. *Groh v. Ramirez*, 540 US 551 (2004), examined the issue of accurate information in an officer's affidavit when the warrant did not contain the necessary "specifics." The general rule is that the officer must be able to articulate probable cause—e.g. "search living room to determine whether stolen TVs are present." If this degree of specificity is not present in the warrant, the court may rule as they did in *Groh* that the warrant violated the Fourth Amendment, and, therefore, the search was unreasonable. The key distinction is that the warrant must contain the particular and specific information, not the affidavit. If you use an internet search engine to find and then read the case, you will note that Justice Thomas, who wrote that the search was reasonable in spite of a defective warrant, dissented. In *Muehler v. Mena*, 544 US 93 (2005), the court held that a person who just happens to be present when the warrant is executed cannot be searched if that person is not referenced in the warrant. This is another example of the balance that must be found between the right to privacy and the needs of law enforcement.

Learning Tip

There are numerous landmark cases which help you to understand the requirements of this amendment. Actually, there are hundreds of cases that provide judicial interpretation, and in this chapter you will be introduced to a few of these cases. For your success in a criminal procedure course, it is important to know the case name and to be able to provide a relatively brief summary of the illustrative concepts of the case. Remember, the focus of the Fourth Amendment is unreasonable search and seizure, and probable cause. One of these landmark cases is *Katz v. U.S*,

389 US 347 (1967). This case is important because it provides it explores a fundamental issue related to the concept of "the right of the people to be secure in their persons, houses, papers, and effects, against unreasonable searches and seizures" (Fourth Amendment). Implicit and inherent in "the right of the people to be secure in their persons, houses, etc. against unreasonable searches and seizures" is the concept of **right to privacy**. In *Katz v. United States* the United States Supreme Court used a two-pronged test for privacy: (1) is there an expectation of privacy *and* (2) is this expectation reasonable? The Court held in part that:

> The Government's eavesdropping activities violated the privacy upon which petitioner justifiably relied while using the telephone booth, and thus constituted a "search and seizure" within the meaning of the Fourth Amendment and the Fourth Amendment governs not only the seizure of tangible items, but extends as well to the recording of oral statements.

Stop and Engage

Use an internet search engine to find and read this United States Supreme Court case and write a short summary of the material facts and the Court's reasoning and analysis. Now, think about what you learned from *Katz* in the context of the following question: Is there an expectation of privacy in your classroom? May a law enforcement officer enter the classroom without a warrant and conduct a search? In order to answer these questions, you must determine the implicit related issues since there are several layers of required analysis before you can form your answer. For example, an officer may have the right to enter the classroom because it is generally accessible to faculty, students, administrators, staff, etc., and there may be no expectation of privacy in that place (as contrasted with a phone booth where you enter and close the door for the purpose of making a private phone call). Once the officer is in the classroom, can he/she conduct a search of your book bag or your other personal effects? In order to answer this question, you must reason through whether an expectation of privacy in those places or regarding those items exists. Similarly, if someone is jogging on a public street, there is no expectation of privacy, but his personal items may not be searched.

The second test in *Katz* is that the expectation must be reasonable. An individual's personal expectation is not sufficient; society must recognize that the expectation is reasonable, as determined by (among other things) location and cultural norms. For example, there is no question that, in American cultural society, we have a reasonable expectation of privacy in our home, but what constitutes a "home"? What is a home for a homeless person living in a cardboard box on the street? Is the cardboard box a home, and can the notion of reasonable expectation of privacy be extended to that "home?" This just one example of many that arise in the discussion of a reasonable expectation of privacy; these are very complex issues with numerous cases providing interpretative guidance. Note that as you read cases, you need to understand how the court is defining certain terms. Also, remember to develop an understanding of the larger issues in these cases. In *Katz*, the issue was expectation of privacy, and the decision was related to a reasonable expectation of privacy. Notice that the ruling focused on the person, not the privacy itself which raises the question of what is a "reasonable expectation?" To answer this question, an analysis of the term "search" must occur since the concepts in the case are closely related; if there is no expectation of privacy, then an unreasonable search is not the issue.

It is important to understand that if probable cause exists, then a warrant is not needed. Many law enforcement officers will obtain a warrant anyway, to provide proof for the probable cause and to provide a safety net for law enforcement. To receive a warrant, law enforcement must present to the magistrate facts which are sufficient to enable the magistrate or judicial officer to reach a conclusion regarding the existence of probable cause. If there are sufficient facts to support a claim for probable cause, then an independent magistrate will usually issue a warrant to for the search/seizure. One of the underlying concepts of whether probable cause exists is whether a "reasonable and prudent" man would believe that a crime had occurred or that evidence exists in a particular location or with a particular person. The broader the scope of search, the stronger the argument must be for the necessity of the breadth—it is always easier to support a claim for probable cause with specificity than with generality. Generally, probable cause must be determined by factual and practical considerations that occur in everyday life.

One way that law enforcement can support a claim of probable cause is based on their personal knowledge of particular facts and circumstances. Another way for law enforcement to gain access to information is through other people, such as informants. In *Aguilar v. Texas*, 378 U.S. 108 (1964), an affidavit given by police officers to obtain a state search warrant stated that: "Affiants have received reliable information from a credible person and do believe that heroin ... and other narcotics ... are being kept at the above described premises for the purpose of sale and use contrary to the provisions of the law."

The affidavit provided no further information concerning either the undisclosed informant or the reliability of the information. The warrant was issued, a search made, and the evidence obtained was admitted at the trial at which petitioner was found guilty of possessing heroin.

The court held that:

1. The standard of reasonableness for obtaining a search warrant is the same under the Fourth and the Fourteenth Amendments.

Stop and Engage

2. Although an affidavit supporting a search warrant may be based on hearsay information and need not reflect the direct personal observations of the affiant, the magistrate must be informed of some of the underlying circumstances relied on by the person providing the information and some of the underlying circumstances from which the affiant concluded that the informant, whose identity was not disclosed, was creditable or his information reliable.

Note that in *Aguilar*, the Court held that information provided by an informant, in and of itself, does not establish probable cause. The informant must be reliable and must provide credible information. Note the following from the Court's decision:

- The point of the Fourth Amendment, which often is not grasped by zealous officers, is not that it denies law enforcement the support of the usual inferences which reasonable men draw from evidence. Its protection consists in requiring that those inferences be drawn by a neutral and detached magistrate instead of being judged by the officer engaged in the often competitive enterprise of ferreting out crime." *Johnson v. United States*, 333 US 10, at 13-14.
- Under the Fourth Amendment, an officer may not properly issue a warrant to search a private dwelling unless he can find probable cause therefor from facts or circumstances presented to him under oath or affirmation. Mere affirmance of belief or suspicion is not enough." *Nathanson v. United States*, 290 U.S. 41, at 47.
- Although an affidavit may be based on hearsay information and need not reflect the direct personal observations of the affiant, *Jones v. United States*, 362 U.S. 257, the magistrate must be informed of some of the underlying circumstances from which the informant concluded that the narcotics were where he claimed they were, and some of the underlying circumstances from which the officer concluded that the informant, whose identity need not be disclosed, see *Rugendorf v. United States*, 376 U.S. 528, was "credible" or his information "reliable."

In order to obtain a warrant, law enforcement must establish the following: (a) the informant's basis for the knowledge; (b) and the circumstances from which the informant made his/her determinations; and (c) that the informant is credible and the information is reliable.

Review

What are the two clauses in the Fourth Amendment that are relevant to a class in Criminal Procedure? Use complete sentences to answer this review question.

1. The Fourth Amendment protects against unreasonable (not "illegal") searches and seizures.
2. The Fourth Amendment requires (or states that) no warrant shall issue but upon probable cause.

13.5.1 Other Issues Related to the Expectation of Privacy

There are numerous issues related to a discussion of whether an individual has an expectation of privacy. In *Katz,* the issue pertained to expectations of privacy in a phone booth. In *Hester v. U.S.*, 265 US 57 (1924), the Court held that there is no expectation of privacy in open fields, which raises questions such as what constitutes an open field? In *Oliver v. U.S.*, 466 US 170 (1984), the central issue in the case arose when this occurred:

> Acting on reports that marihuana was being raised on petitioner's farm, narcotics agents of the Kentucky State Police went to the farm to investigate. Arriving at the farm, they drove past petitioner's house to a locked gate with a "No Trespassing" sign, but with a footpath around one side. The agents then walked around the gate and along the road and found a field of marihuana over a mile from petitioner's house. The District Court in applying *Katz* held that petitioner had a reasonable expectation that the field would remain private and that it was not an "open" field that invited casual intrusion. The Court of Appeals reversed, holding that *Katz* had not impaired the vitality of the open fields doctrine of *Hester v. United States* which permits police officers to enter and search a field without a warrant. The United States Supreme Court explained Since *Katz,* the touchstone of Fourth Amendment analysis has been whether a person has a "constitutionally protected reasonable expectation of privacy." *Id.* at 360. The Amendment does not protect the merely subjective expectation of privacy, but only those "expectation[s] that society is prepared to recognize as 'reasonable.'" *Id.* at 361. Because open fields are accessible to the public and the police in ways that a home, office, or commercial structure would not be, and because fences or "No Trespassing" signs do not effectively bar the public from viewing open fields, the asserted expectation of privacy in open fields is not one that society recognizes as reasonable. Analysis of the circumstances of the search of an open field on a case-by-case basis to determine whether reasonable expectations of privacy were violated would not provide a workable accommodation between the needs of law enforcement and the interests protected by the Fourth Amendment. Steps taken to protect privacy, such as planting the marihuana on secluded land and erecting fences and "No Trespassing" signs around the property, do not establish that expectations of privacy in an open field are legitimate in the sense required by the Fourth Amendment. The test of legitimacy is not whether the individual chooses to conceal assertedly "private" activity, but

> whether the government's intrusion infringes upon the personal and societal values protected by the Amendment.

Rather than open field, the issue could be related to the notion of **curtilage.** *Dunn v. U.S.*, 480 U.S. 294 (1987), provides some insights into the issue of curtilage as it relates to expectations of privacy and the Fourth Amendment. An excerpt from *Dunn* follows:

> In 1980, Drug Enforcement Administration agents, having discovered that one Carpenter had bought large quantities of chemicals and equipment used to make controlled substances, placed tracking "beepers" in some of the equipment and one of the chemical containers, which, when transported in Carpenter's truck, led the agents to respondent's ranch. Aerial photographs of the ranch showed the truck backed up to a barn behind the ranch house. The ranch was completely encircled by a perimeter fence, and contained several interior barbed wire fences, including one around the house approximately 50 yards from the barn, and a wooden fence enclosing the front of the barn, which had an open overhang and locked, waist-high gates. Without a warrant, officers crossed the perimeter fence, several of the barbed wire fences, and the wooden fence in front of the barn. They were led there by the smell of chemicals, and, while there, could hear a motor running inside. They did not enter the barn but stopped at the locked gate and shined a flashlight inside, observing what they took to be a drug laboratory. They then left the ranch, but entered it twice the next day to confirm the laboratory's presence. They obtained a search warrant and executed it, arresting respondent and seizing chemicals and equipment, as well as bags of amphetamines they discovered in the house. After the District Court denied respondent's motion to suppress all evidence seized pursuant to the warrant, respondent and Carpenter were convicted of conspiracy to manufacture controlled substances and related offenses. However, the Court of Appeals reversed, holding that the barn was within the residence's curtilage and therefore within the Fourth Amendment's protective ambit. The area near the barn is not within the curtilage of the house for Fourth Amendment purposes. Extent-of-curtilage questions should be resolved with particular reference to the following four factors, at least to the extent that they bear upon whether the area claimed to be curtilage is so intimately tied to the home itself that it should be placed under the home's "umbrella" of protection: (1) the proximity of the area to the home; (2) whether the area is within an enclosure surrounding the home; (3) the nature and

> uses to which the area is put; and (4) the steps taken by the resident to protect the area from observation by passersby. Applying the first factor to the instant case, the barn's substantial distance from the fence surrounding the house (50 yards) and from the house itself (60 yards) supports no inference that it should be treated as an adjunct of the house. Second, the barn did not lie within the fence surrounding the house, which plainly demarks the area that is part and parcel of the house, but stands out as a distinct and separate portion of the ranch. Third, it is especially significant that the officers possessed objective data indicating that the barn was not being used as part of respondent's home, in that the aerial photographs showed that Carpenter's truck was backed up to the barn, apparently to unload its contents which included the chemical container, and the officers detected strong chemical odors coming from, and heard a motor running in, the barn. Fourth, respondent did little to protect the barn area from observation by those standing outside, the ranch's fences being of the type used to corral livestock, not to ensure privacy.

In other words, the Fourth Amendment based on the facts in *Dunn* since "the barn did not lie within the fence surrounding the house, which plainly demarks the area that is part and parcel of the house, but stands out as a distinct and separate portion of the ranch." The implications of these cases provide guidance as to the constitutional limitations, or the lack thereof, on law enforcement's rights to search.

Stop and Engage

Does marijuana growing in a flower box attached to a person's home have the same constitutional protection from search as a crop growing in an open field located a hundred or more yards from the home? How would you develop a well-reasoned analysis to answer this question? Still another issue in the expectation of privacy is aerial searches—are these types of searches unreasonable? Courts have held that aerial searches are not unreasonable (see, *Dow Chemical Co. v. United States*, 476 U.S. 227 (1986). What about thermal imaging of homes—is this technique a search? In *Kyllo v. U.S.*, 533 U.S. 27 (2001), the court held that a person can retreat into his home with an expectation of privacy, and that a thermal image violates this expectation, and, therefore, a thermal image constitutes a search. How is this different from an aerial search? The question could be extended to TSA searches at airports, where images can be produced of a person's body. Does this activity violate an expectation of privacy?

See *California v. Greenwood*, 486 US 35 (1988), for another issue regarding the expectation of privacy pertaining to the disposition of trash. The issue in this case was whether when a person places trash on the street to be collected, does that person have an expectation of privacy regarding its contents? The court ruled that there is no such expectation of privacy, and the trash is not protected by the Fourth Amendment. In this case, the respondent knowingly exposed the trash to the public, and, therefore, had no expectation of privacy (see *Katz* test). The general concept is that whatever someone knowingly exposes to the public, regardless of where it is located, it cannot be protected from search. The central idea in *California v. Greenwood* was that the trash was on the curb which was outside the curtilage, which raises another issue—what about trash placed next to the front door of the house or next to the garage? You may want to spend some time using an internet search engine to explore some of the issues in more depth in preparation for a course in Criminal Procedure.

13.6 Search and Seizure

The meaning of words continues to be a fundamental issue in criminal procedure because of the broad meaning of words, such as "search" and "seizure" in the United States Constitution. How do you define these words? What constitutes a search or a seizure? Based on *Katz,* you know that there must be a reasonable expectation of privacy before one can claim there was an unreasonable violation of that right through a search. According to the United States Supreme Court decision in *United States v. Mendenhall*, 446 US 544 (1980), seizure is defined as:

> A person has been "seized" within the meaning of the Fourth Amendment only if, in view of all of the circumstances surrounding the incident, a reasonable person would have believed that he was not free to leave, and as long as the person to whom questions are put remains free to disregard the questions and walk away, there has been no intrusion upon that person's liberty or privacy as would require some particularized and objective justification.

A seizure may be described as a meaningful interference with an individual's movement by submission to authority. Notice that this is not necessarily a physical restraint. So, what is "meaningful interference"?

Learning Tip

On exams or other assessments, it may not be necessary to answer questions like these, but it is necessary to recognize the issue, raise it, identify tests, and discuss the implications. Seizure of property has similar issues. Usually a warrant or probable cause is needed, but the concept is similar: meaningful interference with possession of property where the owner had a reasonable expectation of privacy. Notice how various concepts are beginning to work in these issues.

Case Example: Practice Opportunity

Read the following case excerpt and use a yellow highlighter to identify the material facts of the case; use a blue highlighter to note the relevant statutory language; use a pink highlighter to note the alleged crime; and use a green highlighter to note the court's application of the law to the facts of the case, to highlight the court's analysis.

Illinois v. Caballes

543 U.S. 405 (2005)

Illinois State Trooper Daniel Gillette stopped respondent for speeding on an interstate highway. When Gillette radioed the police dispatcher to report the stop, a second trooper, Craig Graham, a member of the Illinois State Police Drug Interdiction Team, overheard the transmission and immediately headed for the scene with his narcotics-detection dog. When they arrived, respondent's car was on the shoulder of the road and respondent was in Gillette's vehicle. While Gillette was in the process of writing a warning ticket, Graham walked his dog around respondent's car. The dog alerted at the trunk. Based on that alert, the officers searched the trunk, found marijuana, and arrested respondent. The entire incident lasted less than 10 minutes. The question on which we granted certiorari, 541 U.S. 972 (2004), is narrow: "Whether the Fourth Amendment requires reasonable, articulable suspicion to justify using a drug-detection dog to sniff a vehicle during a legitimate traffic stop." Pet. for Cert. i. Thus, we proceed on the assumption that the officer conducting the dog sniff had no information about respondent except that he had been stopped for speeding. Here, the initial seizure of respondent when he was stopped on the highway was based on probable cause, and was concededly lawful. It is nevertheless clear that a seizure that is lawful at its inception can violate the Fourth Amendment if its manner of execution unreasonably infringes interests protected by the Constitution. *United States* v. *Jacobsen,* 466 U.S. 109, 124 (1984). A seizure that is justified solely by the interest in issuing a warning ticket to the driver can become unlawful if it is prolonged beyond the time reasonably required to complete that mission. The Illinois Supreme Court held that the initially lawful traffic stop became an unlawful seizure solely as a result of the canine sniff that occurred outside respondent's stopped car. That is, the court characterized the dog sniff as the cause rather than the consequence of a constitutional violation. In its view, the use of the dog converted the citizen-police encounter from a lawful traffic stop into a drug investigation, and because the shift in purpose was not supported by any reasonable suspicion that respondent possessed narcotics, it was unlawful. In our view, conducting a dog sniff would not change the character of a traffic stop that is lawful at its inception and otherwise executed in a reasonable manner, unless the dog sniff itself infringed respondent's constitutionally protected interest in privacy. Our cases hold that it did not. Accordingly, the use of a well-trained narcotics-detection dog—one that "does not expose non-contraband items that otherwise would remain hidden from public view," *Place*, 462 U.S., at 707—during a lawful traffic stop, generally does not implicate legitimate privacy interests. In this case, the dog sniff was performed on the exterior of respondent's car while he was lawfully seized for a traffic violation. Any intrusion on respondent's privacy expectations does not rise to the level of a constitutionally cognizable infringement. This conclusion is entirely consistent with our recent decision that the use of a thermal-imaging device to detect the growth of marijuana in a home constituted an unlawful search. *Kyllo* v. *United States*, 533 U.S. 27 (2001). Critical to that decision was the fact that the device was capable of detecting lawful activity—in that case, intimate details in a home, such as "at what hour each night the lady of the house takes her daily sauna and bath." *Id.*, at 38. The legitimate expectation that information about perfectly lawful activity will remain private is categorically distinguishable from respondent's hopes or expectations concerning the non-detection of contraband in the trunk of his car. A dog sniff conducted during a concededly lawful traffic stop that reveals no information other than the location of a substance that no individual has any right to possess, does not violate the Fourth Amendment.

Stop and Engage

Now that you have highlighted key parts from this case, complete the following activities:

- Identify the main issue(s) in this case.
- Write a concise summary of the material facts.
- Paraphrase the relevant statutory language with precision and accuracy.
- Write a concise summary of the court's reasoning.
- Write a concise explanation as to how and why the court reached its decision— its holding.
- Do you agree with the holding; why or why not?

Learning Tip

Here is another way to approach this case. In thinking beyond the court case, it is important to learn to frame an issue. In this case, the issue was whether there was reasonable suspicion or probable cause for the officer to use a drug-sniffing dog to conduct an outside search of the vehicle (if in fact, it was a search since the person had been stopped for a minor traffic violation). In applying applicable law, such as the Fourth Amendment, make sure that a governmental authority was conducting the search—otherwise the Fourth Amendment does not apply. Since clearly, state troopers are government authorities, this is a non-issue, but it is useful to point it out when writing an analysis answer to a fact pattern. The next step is to determine if there was reasonable suspicion or probable cause for the second officer (Graham) to walk his drug dog around the car. This is a contentious issue that must be argued from the facts. The traffic stop was minor, and the original officer was in the process of writing a warning ticket, when Graham arrived with his dog. Graham's assistance had not been requested by the first officer. Graham let his dog out of the car, without apparent suspicion of the presence of illegal materials. (The defendant was seated in the back of the patrol car when Graham arrived. It is unknown whether this is relevant, so do not read facts into the case which are not stated). Based on the dog's alert, the defendant's car was searched, and illegal drugs were found in the trunk. This raises an ancillary issue of: On what basis did Graham decide to walk his dog around the car? More to the point: Why was the dog even in the vicinity of the car? What was the probable cause (or at least a reasonable suspicion)? (Based on the dog's alert, there might have been probable cause for a search, but this does not mitigate the original issue of the reason for the dog's activity.) After the marijuana was found, the defendant was arrested. The trial judge denied a motion to suppress based upon an unreasonable search argument from the defense. On appeal, the Illinois Supreme Court ruled that there was no reasonable suspicion (or probable cause) for the search during the traffic stop. Note that the Court addressed a narrow issue. (For example, whether there is a difference between the trunk of a car and a home as related to expectation of privacy was not addressed by the Court). You may want to argue that there was no reasonable suspicion or probable cause for the drug-dog to even be on the scene, never mind sniffing around the car.

Learning Tip

When reading text materials or cases, keep in mind that these are component parts which are related and which fit together. Assembly of these component parts will lead you to raise issues and to form an intelligent analysis. It is important to identify material facts (facts which will help you analyze important elements), but avoid becoming bogged down in facts which do not help you to determine how the pieces fit together. Frame the issues first, define applicable law, and then discuss procedures.

The general concept that developed from *Wilson v. Arkansas*, 514 US 927 (1995), is commonly known as the **Knock and Announce rule**. Read the facts and use a yellow highlighter to highlight what you perceive to be the material facts:

> During November and December 1992, petitioner Sharlene Wilson made a series of narcotics sales to an informant acting at the direction of the Arkansas State Police. In late November, the informant purchased marijuana and methamphetamine at the home that petitioner shared with Bryson Jacobs. On December 30, the informant telephoned petitioner at her home and arranged

> to meet her at a local store to buy some marijuana. According to testimony presented below, petitioner produced a semiautomatic pistol at this meeting and waved it in the informant's face, threatening to kill her if she turned out to be working for the police. Petitioner then sold the informant a bag of marijuana. The next day, police officers applied for and obtained warrants to search petitioner's home and to arrest both petitioner and Jacobs. Affidavits filed in support of the warrants set forth the details of the narcotics transactions and stated that Jacobs had previously been convicted of arson and firebombing. The search was conducted later that afternoon. Police officers found the main door to petitioner's home open. While opening an unlocked screen door and entering the residence, they identified themselves as police officers and stated that they had a warrant. Once inside the home, the officers seized marijuana, methamphetamine, valium, narcotics paraphernalia, a gun, and ammunition. They also found petitioner in the bathroom, flushing marijuana down the toilet. Petitioner and Jacobs were arrested and charged with delivery of marijuana, delivery of methamphetamine, possession of drug paraphernalia, and possession of marijuana.

Based on these facts, form an issue statement and read the Court's phrasing; then use a pink highlighter to highlight the issue statement in the wording below:

> The Arkansas Supreme Court noted that "the officers entered the home *while they were identifying themselves,*" but it rejected petitioner's argument that "the Fourth Amendment requires officers to knock and announce prior to entering the residence." Finding "no authority for [petitioner's] theory that the knock and announce principle is required by the Fourth Amendment," the court concluded that neither Arkansas law nor the Fourth Amendment required suppression of the evidence. We granted certiorari to resolve the conflict among the lower courts as to whether the common law knock and announce principle forms a part of the Fourth Amendment reasonableness inquiry.

Now note the Court's reasoning and analysis:

> Our own cases have acknowledged that the common law principle of announcement is "embedded in Anglo American law," *Miller* v. *United States,* 357 U.S. 301, 313 (1958), but we have never squarely held that this principle is an element of the reasonableness inquiry under the Fourth Amendment. We now so hold. Given the longstanding common law endorsement of the practice of announcement, we have little doubt that the Framers of the Fourth Amendment thought that the method of an offi-

> cer's entry into a dwelling was among the factors to be considered in assessing the reasonableness of a search or seizure. Contrary to the decision below, we hold that in some circumstances an officer's unannounced entry into a home might be unreasonable under the Fourth Amendment. This is not to say, of course, that every entry must be preceded by an announcement. The Fourth Amendment's flexible requirement of reasonableness should not be read to mandate a rigid rule of announcement that ignores countervailing law enforcement interests. As even petitioner concedes, the common law principle of announcement was never stated as an inflexible rule requiring announcement under all circumstances.

Based on this case, it is logical that law enforcement should identify itself and state the purpose of its presence prior to entering a person's residence to execute a warrant. This rule is based on a constitutional provision that persons must be secure in their house, persons, papers, etc. Police cannot just knock down the door. One key exception is the notion of **exigent circumstances**, such as a toilet flush that can destroy evidence, or someone firing a weapon, or noises that indicate that someone is escaping out a window. Are there categorical exceptions to the "Knock and Announce" rule? *Richards v. Wisconsin,* 520 US 385 (1997), the Supreme Court states this:

> In *Wilson* v. *Arkansas,* 514 U.S. 927 (1995), we held that the Fourth Amendment incorporates the common law requirement that police officers entering a dwelling must knock on the door and announce their identity and purpose before attempting forcible entry. At the same time, we recognized that the "flexible requirement of reasonableness should not be read to mandate a rigid rule of announcement that ignores countervailing law enforcement interests," *id.,* at 934, and left "to the lower courts the task of determining the circumstances under which an unannounced entry is reasonable under the Fourth Amendment." In this case, the Wisconsin Supreme Court concluded that police officers are *never* required to knock and announce their presence when executing a search warrant in a felony drug investigation. In so doing, it reaffirmed a pre-*Wilson* holding and concluded that *Wilson* did not preclude this *per se* rule. We disagree with the court's conclusion that the Fourth Amendment permits a blanket exception to the knock and announce requirement for this entire category of criminal activity. We recognized in *Wilson* that the knock and announce requirement could give way "under circumstances presenting a threat of physical violence," or "where police officers have reason to believe that evidence would likely be destroyed if advance notice were given." It is indisputable that felony drug investigations may frequently involve

> both of these circumstances. In order to justify a "no knock" entry, the police must have a reasonable suspicion that knocking and announcing their presence, under the particular circumstances, would be dangerous or futile, or that it would inhibit the effective investigation of the crime by, for example, allowing the destruction of evidence. This standard—as opposed to a probable cause requirement—strikes the appropriate balance between the legitimate law enforcement concerns at issue in the execution of search warrants and the individual privacy interests affected by no knock entries. Cf. *Maryland* v. *Buie,* 494 U.S. 325, 337 (1990) (allowing a protective sweep of a house during an arrest where the officers have "a reasonable belief based on specific and articulable facts that the area to be swept harbors an individual posing a danger to those on the arrest scene"); *Terry* v. *Ohio,* 392 U.S. 1, 30 (1968) (requiring a reasonable and articulable suspicion of danger to justify a pat down search). This showing is not high, but the police should be required to make it whenever the reasonableness of a no knock entry is challenged.

Terry v. Ohio, 392 US 1 (1967), is one of the most important cases in this area, and it raises fundamental questions concerning the role of the Fourth Amendment. The issue in *Terry v.* Ohio was whether an officer can stop someone without probable cause. The Court found that a brief stop was reasonable; this ruling became known as a "**Terry Stop**." To understand the important concepts derived from this case we need to review the facts:

> A Cleveland detective (McFadden), on a downtown beat which he had been patrolling for many years, observed two strangers (petitioner and another man, Chilton) on a street corner. He saw them proceed alternately back and forth along an identical route, pausing to stare in the same store window, which they did for a total of about 24 times. Each completion of the route was followed by a conference between the two on a corner, at one of which they were joined by a third man (Katz) who left swiftly. Suspecting the two men of "casing a job, a stick-up," the officer followed them and saw them rejoin the third man a couple of blocks away in front of a store. The officer approached the three, identified himself as a policeman, and asked their names. The men "mumbled something," whereupon McFadden spun petitioner around, patted down his outside clothing, and found in his overcoat pocket, but was unable to remove, a pistol. The officer ordered the three into the store. He removed petitioner's overcoat, took out a revolver, and ordered the three to face the wall with their hands raised. He patted down the outer clothing of Chilton and Katz and seized a revolver from Chilton's outside overcoat pocket. He did not put his hands under the

> outer garments of Katz (since he discovered nothing in his pat-down which might have been a weapon), or under petitioner's or Chilton's outer garments until he felt the guns. The three were taken to the police station. Petitioner and Chilton were charged with carrying concealed weapons.

Review of the material facts and issues:

Stop and Engage

There was a confrontation on the street between a citizen and a policeman. The policeman was investigating suspicious circumstances (what are these?—remember to define terms). This is the entire focus of the case in this specific, factual scenario. Factually, Terry was convicted of carrying two weapons. Two revolvers and ammunition were seized and introduced into evidence. Was there an unreasonable search? The officer was wearing plain clothes, at 2:30 in the afternoon. The officer had not seen the men before, meaning that he had no prior knowledge of their behaviors. This calls into question the basis for the officer's suspicions, because "suspicious" means "out of the ordinary." The officer could not have known what "ordinary" is for these men. Further, the officer testified that he did not know what attracted his attention to the men. On the other hand, the officer had 39 years experience, sufficient to develop credible "hunches." He observed activity which led him to believe that the men were "casing" one or more stores on the block. The men walked past the stores 5–6 times, conferring often. The officer's suspicions were growing. He also believed that the men might be armed (why?).

The officer approached the men and identified himself as an officer. The "out of uniform" issue was resolved when he identified himself. The officer asked for the men's name, but could not understand their mumbled answer. The officer then grabbed the men and patted down the outside of their clothing. He reached inside the outer garment, and felt a gun. (These are critical facts. What are the limits of a pat down? Is this a search? The officer was patting down external clothing for presence of weapons—this is critical. At what point does the Fourth Amendment become relevant? At what point did search and seizure occur? Is a stop and frisk the same as a search and seizure? This is critical: if they are not the same, then the Fourth Amendment does not apply. Generally, a Terry Stop is for identification alone—other factors might further raise an officer's suspicion. There are two key elements in this case: (1) suspicion which led to the stop was based upon the officer's experience alone and (2) a pat down of external clothing is permissible to determine whether there are weapons. What are the limits of a stop and frisk if there is no probable cause? E.g. when is only reasonable suspicion enough? Generally, if the officer believes that there is a safety issue because of the presence of weapons, he may pat down external clothing for weapons. If drugs are found during this pat down they will not be admissible without probable cause.

Now read the Court's findings:

> The Fourth Amendment applies to "stop and frisk" procedures such as those followed here. Whenever a police officer accosts an individual and restrains his freedom to walk away, he has "seized" that person within the meaning of the Fourth Amendment. A careful exploration of the outer surfaces of a person's clothing in an attempt to find weapons is a "search" under that Amendment. Where a reasonably prudent officer is warranted in the circumstances of a given case in believing that his safety or that of others is endangered, he may make a reasonable search for weapons of the person believed by him to be armed and dangerous regardless of whether he has probable cause to arrest that individual for crime or the absolute certainty that the individual is armed. Though the police must, whenever practicable, secure a warrant to make a search and seizure, that procedure cannot be followed where swift action based upon on-the-spot observations of the officer on the beat is required. The reasonableness of any particular search and seizure must be assessed in light of the particular circumstances against the standard of whether a man of reasonable caution is warranted in believing that the action taken was appropriate. The officer here was performing a legitimate function of investigating suspicious conduct when he decided to approach petitioner and his companions. An officer justified in believing that an individual whose suspicious behavior he is investigating at close range is armed may, to neutralize the threat of physical harm, take necessary measures to determine whether that person is carrying a weapon. A search for weapons in the absence of probable cause to arrest must be strictly circumscribed by the exigencies of the situation. An officer may make an intrusion short of arrest where he has reasonable apprehension of danger before being possessed of information justifying arrest. The officer's protective seizure of petitioner and his companions and the limited search which he made were reasonable, both at their inception and as conducted. The actions of petitioner and his companions were consistent with the officer's hypothesis that they were contemplating a daylight robbery and were armed. The officer's search was confined to what was minimally necessary to determine whether the men were armed, and the intrusion, which was made for the sole purpose of protecting himself and others nearby, was confined to ascertaining the presence of weapons. The revolver seized from petitioner was properly admitted into evidence against him, since the search which led to its seizure was reasonable under the Fourth Amendment.

One of the issues associated with a Terry stop is "suspicious behavior." What is this? The factual context leads to application of different rules. For example, a stop for arrest must be supported by probable cause—not reasonable suspicion. Remember, the Fourth Amendment is the umbrella beneath which all procedures must operate and function. If a person is arrested, then a warrantless search may be performed "incident to arrest." (This is discussed in the next section of this chapter). If a person is stopped without an intention of arrest, then a search may not be performed—only a frisk of the external clothing to discover a weapon. Remember, the basis for this frisk is reasonable suspicion. Typical topics related to this issue include these: (1) authority to stop and frisk; (2) distinction between a stop and an arrest; (3) permissible actions of law enforcement when they conduct a stop; and (4) necessities for a stop.

Learning Tip

- *Authority to stop and frisk*: both a stop and an arrest are seizures where freedom of movement is restrained. The issue is whether a seizure is reasonable. As mentioned earlier, an arrest must be supported by probable cause, and stops require only reasonable suspicion. There is not a bright line separating the two concepts. One attempt to differentiate the two is that an arrest involves "sustained interrogation" (but what is "sustained interrogation"—interrogation for 15 minutes? An hour? A full day? This is a key concept for purposes of Fourth Amendment compliance. Look at the total circumstances and determine whether they lead to a conclusion of probable cause.
- *Some events are clearly an arrest*: if a suspect is handcuffed and transported to the station house, it is clear than an arrest has occurred. See *Florida v. Royer*, 460 US 491 (1983), where the Court stated:

  > When the detectives identified themselves as narcotics agents, told respondent he was suspected of transporting narcotics, and asked him to accompany them to the police room, while retaining his airline ticket and driver's license and without indicating in any way that he was free to depart, respondent was effectively seized for purposes of the Fourth Amendment. At the time respondent produced the key to his suitcase, the detention to which he was then subjected was a more serious intrusion on his personal liberty than is allowable on mere suspicion of criminal activity. What had begun as a consensual inquiry in a public place escalated into an investigatory procedure in a police interrogation room, and respondent, as a practical matter, was under arrest at that time? Moreover, the detectives' conduct was more intrusive than necessary to effectuate an investigative detention otherwise authorized by the Terry line of cases.

- *Permissible actions of law enforcement when they conduct a stop*:—See *Hibel v. Sixth Judicial District Court of Nevada*, 542 US 177 (2004), where in a *Terry* stop it is reasonable for an officer to require an individual to identify him/herself without implicating the Fourth Amendment. (A properly executed *Terry* stop does not constitute a seizure and therefore does not violate the Fourth Amendment.) Also, the stop must be brief and must be limited. It is important to understand that the stop must be justified at its inception by the circumstances—the stop cannot be a fishing expedition. Almost any reason will suffice in traffic enforcement—tail light out, no stickers, etc.—even in an arbitrary roadblock in a known drug corridor is usually sufficient for a stop.

- *Necessities for a stop*: What circumstances are sufficient for reasonable suspicion? There is not a precise definition, nor is there a bright line. The circumstances are factually driven and contextually based. Typical actions that will produce reasonable suspicion in law enforcement: (1) trying to evade a roadblock; (2) informant tip; or (3) profiling. There are numerous constitutional issues in profiling.
- General comments about seizure: individual movement is limited, and the person is not free to leave.
- General comments about arrest: an arrest must be based on probable cause—reasonable suspicion is not enough. Reasonable suspicion is sufficient for a stop and frisk, but the stop must be for investigatory purposes only, and a frisk is limited to a pat down to uncover weapons only—this is an officer safety issue. The standard is higher for an arrest.

Review

Is a warrant necessary for an arrest? In *U.S. v. Watson*, 423 US 411 (1976), a written warrant is not needed if there is probable cause. It follows that a warrant cannot be issued without probable cause, so the critical need in arrest is probable cause, with or without a warrant. In other words, a warrantless arrest is permissible if the arresting officer has probable cause. Some of the facts in *Watson* which led to probable cause include these were:

- The informant had stolen credit cards in his possession.
- The informant informs a postal inspector (building credibility as an informant).
- The informant delivers a stolen credit card and informs the inspector that he can obtain more. (At this point, it is clear that reasonable suspicion has developed, and further facts will lead to probable cause.)

This information prompted a search of Watson's car. Watson consented to the search, even after officers warned him that anything found could be used against him. Stolen cards were found in the search, leading officers to believe that criminal activity had occurred. Based upon this probable cause, Watson was arrested. At trial, Watson petitions for suppression of the search and evidence found based upon a lack of probable cause. The Court of Appeals ruled that arrest was permissible because Watson consented to the search (removing the need for a warrant), and the evidence found in the search established probable cause.

Success Tip

On exams, written assignments, and other assessments, writing only 2–3 sentences to explain an issue is not enough. A major part of an assessment in these law-related courses is to demonstrate depth of substantive and analytical reasoning to your professor. For example, simply writing that an officer may seize any evidence which is in plain view is not sufficient, since this sentence presents only a conclusion and does not demonstrate any integration of the rules with the facts—no reasoning or analysis.

13.7 Exceptions to the Warrant Requirements for Searches

Generally a warrantless search is presumptively unreasonable. If there is probable cause but no warrant, can an officer still take action? Notice that the Fourth Amendment does not require a warrant for search and seizure—only probable cause is needed. However, there are specific situations where an officer can conduct a search without probable cause. Some of these situations include the following:

- Incident to arrest—evaluate the facts to determine whether the search was reasonable
- In hot pursuit—this situation is a favorite of TV shows
- In plain view—what is plain view?
- Automobile
- Search by customs/immigration at a U.S. border
- Exigent circumstances

More than one of these can apply in a single incident or case.

Incident to Arrest

A key case in the "incident to arrest" exception is *Chimel v. California*, 395 US 752 (1969). Read an excerpt from the case:

> Police officers, armed with an arrest warrant but not a search warrant, were admitted to petitioner's home by his wife, where they awaited petitioner's arrival. When he entered he was served with the warrant. Although he denied the officers' request to "look around," they conducted a search of the entire house "on the basis of the lawful arrest." At petitioner's trial on burglary charges, items taken from his home were admitted over objection that they had been unconstitutionally seized. His conviction was affirmed by the California appellate courts, which held, despite their acceptance of petitioner's contention that the arrest warrant was invalid, that since the arresting officers had procured the warrant "in good faith," and since in any event

they had had sufficient information to constitute probable cause for the arrest, the arrest was lawful. The courts also held that the search was justified as incident to a valid arrest. Held: Assuming the arrest was valid, the warrantless search of petitioner's house cannot be constitutionally justified as incident to that arrest.

Stop and Engage

Note that one of the most important factors is that the search must take place at the time of arrest, not later. What are some of the material facts of the case? Use a yellow highlighter to identify them in the excerpt above, and then note some issues that arise based on the facts. Did you highlight and think about these issues?

- The officers had an arrest warrant but not a search warrant. This raises the issue of whether a search of the entire house (more than the surrounding area) can be conducted based upon an arrest warrant.
- The search required 45 minutes to an hour. Is this within the scope of "incident to arrest?" An officer may search a person and the immediate area for weapons and for evidence that might be destroyed or concealed, but conducting an exhaustive search requiring an extended period of time may be beyond the scope of "incident to arrest."

The defendant argued to have the evidence excluded because it was obtained in an unreasonable search (no warrant). The Court agreed. The important factor to recognize is that, at the time of arrest, a search may be performed of the person and of the immediate surrounding areas. If a more extensive search is needed, a search warrant is required.

Hot Pursuit

An important case in the "hot pursuit" exception is *Warren v. Hayden*, 387 US 294 (1967). When police enter a home in pursuit of a suspect, the Knock and Announce doctrine does not apply. The Fourth Amendment does not require officers to delay entry (possibly allowing the suspect to escape or to take hostages) while a warrant is obtained. Similar to the incident to arrest exception, the entry must be made at the time of pursuit, not later. See also *Payton v. New York*, 445 US 573 (1980).

Plain View Doctrine

The "plain view" doctrine is quite complex, and there are several issues associated with this exception. First, the officer must be in a permissible location (must have a reason for intrusion) when the evidence was observed in plain view. Otherwise, plain view cannot apply. Secondly, the officer is permitted to use all of his senses to detect evidence—not just sight. For instance, he can seize marijuana if he can smell it. Thirdly, even if evidence is unrelated (e.g. a search for child pornography which uncovered marijuana also), it can be seized. An important limitation to this situation is that the discovery of unrelated evidence must be inadvertent. See *Horton v. California*, 496 US 128 (1990), for an example of inadvertent discovery. It is important to recognize that seizure in these cases is not by warrant, but by a recognized exception to a warrant. These exceptions cannot be used to conduct a fishing expedition (an open search). Also, the "plain view" exception cannot be stretched. For example, if, while conducting a search for drugs in a dilapidated apartment, an officer sees an expensive TV which he believes to be stolen, he cannot move the TV to read a serial number. The serial number was not only out of plain view, but it was not inadvertent. It was not apparent that the TV was contraband, even though it might have been in a deplorable environment.

Now read an excerpt from *Horton v. California*:

> A California policeman determined that there was probable cause to search petitioner Horton's home for the proceeds of a robbery and the robbers' weapons. His search warrant affidavit referred to police reports that described both the weapons and the proceeds, but the warrant issued by the Magistrate only authorized a search for the proceeds. Upon executing the warrant, the officer did not find the stolen property but did find the weapons in plain view and seized them. The trial court refused to suppress the seized evidence, and Horton was convicted of armed robbery. The California Court of Appeal affirmed. Since the officer had testified that while he was searching Horton's home for the stolen property he was also interested in finding other evidence connecting Horton to the robbery, the seized evidence was not discovered "inadvertently." The Fourth Amendment does not prohibit the warrantless seizure of evidence in plain view even though the discovery of the evidence was not inadvertent. Although inadvertence is a characteristic of most legitimate plain-view seizures, it is not a necessary condition. In order for a warrantless seizure of an object in plain view to be valid, two conditions must be satisfied in addition to the essential predicate that the officer did not violate the Fourth Amendment in arriving at the place from which the object could be plainly viewed. First, the object's incriminating character must be "immediately apparent." Second, the officer must have a lawful right of access to the object itself.

Now write a definition for the plain view doctrine.

Write a Definition

Case Studies

Use an internet search engine to find the following cases and answer the specific questions in a well-developed substantive analysis.

1. *Illinois v. Wardlow*, 528 US 119 (2000). (1) What actions may an officer take during a stop? (2) Does an officer have reasonable suspicion permitting him to stop a fleeing suspect? Note, the Court held that reasonable suspicion is enough for an investigatory stop—probable cause is not needed.
2. *U.S. v. Sokolow*, 490 US 1 (1989). Is the issue whether reasonable suspicion is the standard to support a stop based on profiling? Note, the Court held that totality of circumstances and material facts in aggregate was sufficient to raise reasonable suspicion.
3. Compare *Florida v. J.L.*, 529 US 266 (2000), and *Illinois v. Gates*, 462 US 213 (1983), and write a summary that explains the contrast. In *Florida*, the issue is whether an officer can have reasonable suspicion arising from an anonymous tip, justifying a stop and frisk of a suspect. The Court held that an anonymous tip is not enough because the tipster's credibility cannot be investigated. In *Gates*, the issue was whether a detailed letter to law enforcement informing them of drug activity was sufficient for reasonable suspicion. The Court held that letter, by itself, was not enough. This is a totality of circumstances issue.

Success Tip

Before you answer, read the case and questions carefully; determine whether the question is a "what" or a "why" determination. In your answers, do not write in vague generalities. Know the facts and the context of the relevant cases. The issues should be framed specifically. Take the time to write in complete sentences, and be sure to include key (trigger) words. Avoid general, vague language, and be sure to integrate the material facts with the material legal principles and rules of law to develop detailed, substantive, in-depth analytical reasoning.

13.8 Exclusionary Rule

Why is the Exclusionary Rule important? The primary importance of the Exclusionary Rule is to deter law enforcement officers from seizing evidence or obtaining testimony in violation of the Fourth Amendment. (Or, alternatively—to deter law enforcement from obtaining evidence in violation of the law.) As you have learned, there is an expectation of privacy issue embedded in the Fourth Amendment. The Fourth Amendment serves as an incentive to law enforcement to act in accordance with the law (e.g. requiring probable cause or a warrant to conduct a search). (In some cases, law enforcement is completely focused on making an arrest, and might accomplish an arrest without concern for the law. Only by acting in accordance with law will the arrest be valid and constitutional.). For example, if a search is carried out in violation of the law, the results of the search will be excluded from trial under the exclusionary rule and the prosecutor's case will be damaged.

Deterrence of improper and illegal conduct by law enforcement is a key purpose of the Exclusionary Rule. Notice that the Rule is not in the Constitution—it arises from case law. One of the first and the most important cases is *Weeks v. U.S*, 232 US 383 (1914). A review of the facts in this case should reveal a variety of Fourth Amendment issues. The facts are as follows:

> The defendant was arrested by a police officer, so far as the record shows, without warrant, at the Union Station in Kansas City, Missouri, where he was employed by an express company. Other police officers had gone to the house of the defendant, and being told by a neighbor where the key was kept, found it and entered the house. They searched the defendant's room and took possession of various papers and articles found there, which were afterwards turned over to the United States marshal. Later in the same day police officers returned with the marshal, who thought he might find additional evidence, and, being admitted by someone in the house, probably a boarder, in response to a rap, the marshal searched the defendant's room and carried away certain letters and envelops found in the drawer of a chiffonier. Neither the marshal nor the police officer had a search warrant.

Stop and Engage

What are some of the issues that arise based on the facts? (1) Was there a seizing and taking possession of papers and other materials? (2) Did taking a door key from under the mat constitute a legal entry? (3) What authority does a boarder have to grant access? (4) Is access limited to only common areas of an apartment, and possibly the boarder's bedroom? (5) Does the boarder have authority to grant access to a roommate's bedroom? These are the kind of questions that should arise from a reading of the facts. Notice that the facts do not indicate whether the police had a search warrant. If not, it is not a case-breaking issue if probable cause existed. If neither probable cause nor a warrant existed, and if recognized exceptions to the warrant requirement did not exist, then the search and seizure would likely constitute a violation of the Fourth Amendment. Use an internet search engine to find and read the Court's analysis and holding.

An extension of the Exclusionary Rule is found in a concept known as the "fruit of the poisonous tree" doctrine. This doctrine holds that if, for example, a confession is obtained as a result of an unreasonable arrest, then the confession will also be excluded because it is considered to be "tainted fruit." More generally, the "poisonous tree" is the act which originally violated the Fourth Amendment, and the "fruit" is any evidence or testimony which is obtained as a result of the original unconstitutional act (anything which is related to it).

Exceptions to the Exclusionary Rule

Recall that the purpose of the Exclusionary Rule is to deter law enforcement misconduct. This Rule does not apply in some situations; these situations must be justified and must not undercut the purpose of the rule. Some of the situations in which the Exclusionary Rule does not apply include these:

(1) Independent source: the evidence must have been obtained independent of police misconduct. If the police did not engage in misconduct, there would be no exclusionary rule issue.

(2) Inevitable discovery: Law enforcement must demonstrate that even without a violation of the Fourth Amendment, discovery of the evidence was probable (using proper procedures). The burden of proof is on law enforcement to demonstrate inevitable discovery, even though the process might have been flawed.

(3) Inadequate causal connection: Causation is critical in law, and this exception discusses an attenuation of taint—notice the specific language. The Exclusionary Rule applies if there is a substantial connection between illegal police activity and the evidence. If so, then the fruit of the poisonous tree doctrine could also apply, and all evidence obtained as a result of the illegal actions would be excluded. In other words, if the link is attenuated (less substantial) the evidence may be admissible.

(4) Reasonable reliance on an invalid warrant: This is sometimes known as the "good faith" exception. *U.S. v. Leon*, 468 US 897 (1984), is an important case in this area.

13.9 Fifth and Sixth Amendment Issues and *Miranda*

There is often much confusion when discussing the invocation of certain rights under the Fifth Amendment and Sixth Amendment particularly in light of the "right to counsel" that was established in *Miranda v. Arizona*, 384 US 436 (1966), which will be discussed in Section 13.9.3 below. Generally, the Fifth Amendment applies when a defendant is called upon to provide testimony which is potentially incriminating and compulsory. When on the witness stand, a witness cannot refuse to answer only some questions—e.g. refuse to answer questions only in cross-examination. If the witness brings the Fifth Amendment into play, and then continues to talk, he/she has effectively waived his/her Fifth Amendment rights. The legislative intent behind the Sixth Amendment right to counsel is to have a capable person (an attorney) who can mount a meaningful defense. The emphasis as you will see in Section 13.9.2 below is on "formulation of a defense," and it provides the primary reason that the Sixth Amendment can be used only when formal charges have been filed; since prior to that point, there is technically nothing to defend. This is where the Sixth Amendment becomes confusing with the *Miranda* rights attributable to the Fifth Amendment since one under *Miranda* is entitled to the assistance of counsel once her/she is in a "custodial interrogation." You will learn below that the Fifth Amendment does not provide a right to counsel; but *Miranda* (which is derived from an interpretation of the Fifth Amendment) provides this right. You will also learn that the intent of *Miranda* was to prevent self-incrimination during custodial interrogation. Since most investigative questioning occurs prior to the filing of charges, *Miranda* is the appropriate concept at this stage, not the Sixth Amendment. One of the most important distinctions is that the protections of the Sixth Amendment occur in response to a specific criminal charge (so that an attorney can assist in preparing a defense).

13.9.1 Fifth Amendment Issues

> **Fifth Amendment:** No person shall be held to answer for a capital, or otherwise infamous crime, unless on a presentment or indictment of a Grand Jury, except in cases arising in the land or naval forces, or in the Militia, when in actual service in time of War or public danger; nor shall any person be subject for the same offence to be twice put in jeopardy of life or limb; nor shall be compelled in any criminal case to be a witness against himself, nor be deprived of life, liberty, or property, without due process of law; nor shall private property be taken for public use, without just compensation.

Fifth Amendment

The Fifth Amendment applies to police interrogation during a criminal (not civil) case, where a defendant could potentially be a witness against himself. Notice that this protection includes the interrogation process. If a suspect invokes his Fifth Amendment privilege, he must stop talking to the police once he invokes his rights under the Fifth Amendment. At trial, whether to invoke the Fifth Amendment protections is a strategic decision made by the defendant and his counsel to determine whether to take the stand and put his/her testimony at issue.

13.9.2 Sixth Amendment Issues

> **Sixth Amendment:** In all criminal prosecutions, the accused shall enjoy the right to a speedy and public trial, by an impartial jury of the State and district wherein the crime shall have

Sixth Amendment

> been committed, which district shall have been previously ascertained by law, and to be informed of the nature and cause of the accusation; to be confronted with the witnesses against him; to have compulsory process for obtaining witnesses in his favor, and to have the Assistance of Counsel for his defense.

Sixth Amendment Right to Counsel

Recall that *Miranda* activates when a person has been taken into custody (e.g. seized). You will note from the constitutional language that "in all criminal prosecutions the accused shall ... have the assistance of counsel for his defense." The foundational question in the inquiry as to when this right commences is found in the words "defense." So the question may be phrased, when does prosecution begin? The trigger point is usually when adversarial proceedings have begun. Note that initial questioning by law enforcement might not be adversarial; for instance, the questioning might arise from a Terry stop for identification purposes. Usually, the proceedings become adversarial when formal charges have been filed or an indictment occurs. In *Powell v. Alabama*, 287 US 45 (1932), the Court held that the most critical juncture in the proceedings begins with arraignment, and, therefore, under the Sixth Amendment an attorney must be present. The Sixth Amendment prevents law enforcement from speaking with an accused after adversarial proceedings have begun with the accused attorney's present.

13.9.3 *Miranda* Issues

Two critical cases on the topic of custodial interrogation and the right to an attorney are *Miranda v. Arizona* and *Dickerson v. U.S.* It is important to note that prior to *Miranda*, the emphasis on whether a confession was admissible was related to the right to counsel derived from the Sixth Amendment (See *Escobedo v. Illinois*, 378 US 478 (1964), whereas in *Miranda* the emphasis shifted to the Fifth Amendment privilege against self-incrimination and the right to counsel to protect that particular right. *Miranda* represents a consolidation of several cases all involving the same facts; read an excerpt:

> In each of these cases the defendant while in police custody was questioned by police officers, detectives, or a prosecuting attorney in a room in which he was cut off from the outside world. None of the defendants was given a full and effective warning of his rights at the outset of the interrogation process. In all four cases the questioning elicited oral admissions, and in three of them signed statements as well, which were admitted at their trials. All defendants were convicted and all conviction. In No. 759, Miranda v. Arizona, the police arrested the defendant and

> took him to a special interrogation room where they secured a confession.

Now read an excerpt of the opinion delivered by Chief Justice Warren:

> More specifically, we deal with the admissibility of statements obtained from an individual who is subjected to custodial police interrogation and the necessity for procedures which assure that the individual is accorded his privilege under the Fifth Amendment to the Constitution not to be compelled to incriminate himself.
>
> The constitutional issue we decide in each of these cases is the admissibility of statements obtained from a defendant questioned while in custody or otherwise deprived of his freedom of action in any significant way. In each, the defendant was questioned by police officers, detectives, or a prosecuting attorney in a room in which he was cut off from the outside world. In none of these cases was the defendant given a full and effective warning of his rights at the outset of the interrogation process. In all the cases, the questioning elicited oral admissions, and in three of them, signed statements as well which were admitted at their trials. They all thus share salient features—incommunicado interrogation of individuals in a police-dominated atmosphere, resulting in self-incriminating statements without full warnings of constitutional rights.
>
> The prosecution may not use statements, whether exculpatory or inculpatory, stemming from custodial interrogation of the defendant unless it demonstrates the use of procedural safeguards effective to secure the privilege against self-incrimination. By custodial interrogation, we mean questioning initiated by law enforcement officers after a person has been taken into custody or otherwise deprived of his freedom of action in any significant way. As for the procedural safeguards to be employed, unless other fully effective means are devised to inform accused persons of their right of silence and to assure a continuous opportunity to exercise it, the following measures are required. Prior to any questioning, the person must be warned that he has a right to remain silent, that any statement he does make may be used as evidence against him, and that he has a right to the presence of an attorney, either retained or appointed. The defendant may waive effectuation of these rights, provided the waiver is made voluntarily, knowingly and intelligently. If, however, he indicates in any manner and at any stage of the process that he wishes to consult with an attorney before speaking there can be no questioning. Likewise, if the individual is alone and indicates in any manner that he does not wish to be interrogated, the police may not question him. The mere fact that he

may have answered some questions or volunteered some statements on his own does not deprive him of the right to refrain from answering any further inquiries until he has consulted with an attorney and thereafter consents to be questioned.

From the foregoing, we can readily perceive an intimate connection between the privilege against self-incrimination and police custodial questioning. It is fitting to turn to history and precedent underlying the Self-Incrimination Clause to determine its applicability in this situation. At the outset, if a person in custody is to be subjected to interrogation, he must first be informed in clear and unequivocal terms that he has the right to remain silent. For those unaware of the privilege, the warning is needed simply to make them aware of it—the threshold requirement for an intelligent decision as to its exercise. More important, such a warning is an absolute prerequisite in overcoming the inherent pressures of the interrogation atmosphere. It is not just the subnormal or woefully ignorant who succumb to an interrogator's imprecations, whether implied or expressly stated, that the interrogation will continue until a confession is obtained or that silence in the face of accusation is itself damning and will bode ill when presented to a jury. Further, the warning will show the individual that his interrogators are prepared to recognize his privilege should he choose to exercise it.

The Fifth Amendment privilege is so fundamental to our system of constitutional rule and the expedient of giving an adequate warning as to the availability of the privilege so simple, we will not pause to inquire in individual cases whether the defendant was aware of his rights without a warning being given. Assessments of the knowledge the defendant possessed, based on information as to his age, education, intelligence, or prior contact with authorities, can never be more than speculation; a warning is a clear cut fact. More important, whatever the background of the person interrogated, a warning at the time of the interrogation is indispensable to overcome its pressures and to insure that the individual knows he is free to exercise the privilege at that point in time.

The warning of the right to remain silent must be accompanied by the explanation that anything said can and will be used against the individual in court. This warning is needed in order to make him aware not only of the privilege, but also of the consequences of forgoing it. It is only through an awareness of these consequences that there can be any assurance of real understanding and intelligent exercise of the privilege. Moreover, this warning may serve to make the individual more acutely aware that he is faced with a phase of the adversary system—

that he is not in the presence of persons acting solely in his interest.

The circumstances surrounding in-custody interrogation can operate very quickly to overbear the will of one merely made aware of his privilege by his interrogators. Therefore, the right to have counsel present at the interrogation is indispensable to the protection of the Fifth Amendment privilege under the system we delineate today. Our aim is to assure that the individual's right to choose between silence and speech remains unfettered throughout the interrogation process. A once-stated warning, delivered by those who will conduct the interrogation, cannot itself suffice to that end among those who most require knowledge of their rights. A mere warning given by the interrogators is not alone sufficient to accomplish that end. Prosecutors themselves claim that the admonishment of the right to remain silent without more "will benefit only the recidivist and the professional." Brief for the National District Attorneys Association as amicus curiae, p. 14. Even preliminary advice given to the accused by his attorney can be swiftly overcome by the secret interrogation process. Cf. Escobedo v. Illinois. Thus, the need for counsel to protect the Fifth Amendment privilege comprehends not merely a right to consult with counsel prior to questioning, but also to have counsel present during any questioning if the defendant so desires.

The presence of counsel at the interrogation may serve several significant subsidiary functions as well. If the accused decides to talk to his interrogators, the assistance of counsel can mitigate the dangers of untrustworthiness. With a lawyer present the likelihood that the police will practice coercion is reduced, and if coercion is nevertheless exercised the lawyer can testify to it in court. The presence of a lawyer can also help to guarantee that the accused gives a fully accurate statement to the police and that the statement is rightly reported by the prosecution at trial.

An individual need not make a pre-interrogation request for a lawyer. While such request affirmatively secures his right to have one, his failure to ask for a lawyer does not constitute a waiver. No effective waiver of the right to counsel during interrogation can be recognized unless specifically made after the warnings we here delineate have been given. The accused who does not know his rights and therefore does not make a request may be the person who most needs counsel.

Stop and Engage

As is evident from the case excerpts above, a key concept in *Miranda* is the determination of custodial interrogation. According to the Court's decision, law enforcement must administer *Miranda* warnings prior to a custodial interrogation. There are at least three issues contained in this concept: (1) When is a person in custody? (2) What is interrogation? (3) What are the necessary steps to ensure that law enforcement properly administers *Miranda* warnings? Remember, *Miranda* warnings are a procedural safeguard to secure the privilege against self-incrimination under the Fifth Amendment.

Prior to questioning, a person must be warned of several things: (1) to remain silent (to avoid self-incrimination); (2) that statements made can and will be used as evidence; and (3) that he/she has a right to an attorney. The person may waive his right to an attorney—and then change his mind. If an attorney is requested at any stage in questioning, the questioning must stop. If questioning does not stop, any evidence obtained after the request will be excluded. Also, the person must waive the right to an attorney: (1) voluntarily (2) knowingly and (3) intelligently. Language, drugs, or mental defect might impact any of these requirements.

Stop and Engage

What is interrogation? Notice that if a person volunteers information without questioning, interrogation has not occurred and *Miranda* warnings are not necessary. This is a crucial element in determining whether a confession should be admitted.

Learning Activity

An important case is *Rhode Island v. Innis*, 446 US 291 (1980), where the defendant was in custody and received three Miranda warnings on three separate occasions. The suspect requested an attorney, and questioning stopped. Soon after, the suspect interrupted a conversation between two officers, offering to show them where a weapon was located (to assure the safety of children). At this point, the issue was whether the defendant waived his *Miranda* rights when he interrupted the conversation. The weapon was located with the assistance of the defendant. The defense argued the weapon should be excluded because a waiver was not properly given by the defendant? What do you think? Use an internet search engine to find the case and then:

- Write a concise summary of the material facts.
- Paraphrase the relevant constitutional language.
- Write a concise summary of the court's reasoning and analysis.
- Write a concise explanation as to how and why the court reached its decision—its holding.
- Compare/contrast it with *Brown v. Mississippi*, 297 US 278 (1936).

How does *Spano v. New York*, 360 US 315 (1959), pertain to the issue of whether a confession is voluntary? What is the totality of circumstances test enunciated in *Spano*?

13.10 Lineups and Identification

On the topic of line-ups and identification, it must be remembered that one of law enforcement's jobs is to gather evidence—not just arrest suspected criminals. Once an arrest is made, a prosecutor uses that evidence to establish and to prove guilt. This proof must be based on the evidence, which can be either physical or testimonial. One of the issues implicit in identification is that testimonial evidence is provided by eyewitness accounts of an accused's identity, actions, words, and conduct. Unfortunately, eyewitnesses usually get it wrong. Elizabeth Loftus is a pioneering psychologist who conducted numerous empirical studies on eyewitness testimony, and she established that much of the time, eyewitnesses displayed errors in reporting what they witnessed at the scene of a crime. One of the products of these mistakes is skepticism and stereotypes. Another danger inherent in identification is the notion of law enforcement's attempt to "help" an eyewitness identify a suspect because of concerns related to suggestiveness, whether in identification or in a line-up. **Suggestiveness** can be thought of as creating a "leading" environment, context, or situation; such as in a line-up or in "planting" ideas or suggests related to the accused or the events of the crime which will direct the eyewitness's attention to a particular individual. For example, constructing a lineup of four Hispanic women and one blond woman is suggestive and prejudicial because the construction increases the likelihood that the blond will be identified by the witness. See *Stovall v. Denno*, 388 US 293 (1967), and *Foster v. California*, 394 US 440 (1969), both of which affirmed that unnecessarily suggestive lineups violate due process.

Among the protections that the Supreme Court has developed to guard against suggestiveness is an accused or defendant's right to counsel. Defendants have a right to counsel in some identification situations, usually when a line-up occurs after indictment. In *U.S. v. Wade*, 388 US 218 (1967), the Court ruled that there is no right to counsel prior to indictment. The constitutional concern with proper line-up procedures is one of due process since a suggestive situation infringes upon a defendant's due process rights. The issue in *U.S. v. Wade* was whether identification may be excluded because the suspect did not have counsel at a pre-indictment line-up. Recall that the Fifth Amendment does not apply in this case because there is no issue of self-incrimination; this is a Sixth Amendment issue. Also, notice that a suspect cannot refuse to stand in a line-up because the evidence obtained is not testimonial—without testimony, there can be no self-incrimination so the Fifth Amendment does not protect against failure to present for a lineup. Also, notice that, in addition to a right of counsel at trial, the suspect must have counsel at any stage of prosecution. The Court in *Wade* held that pre-indictment is not part of the prosecutorial process. In *Illinois v. Kirby*, 406 US 682

(1972), the Court ruled that law enforcement cannot manipulate a situation to develop sufficient evidence because of due process concerns.

13.11 Summary

The purpose of this chapter is to introduce you to certain important concepts in criminal procedure so that you can begin to think about how criminal procedure fits within a criminal law frame. In criminal procedure the emphasis is primarily on the process and procedure for the collection of evidence, making an arrest, questioning a suspect, etc. In other words, what steps must be followed and how are these steps connected to the other frames in the integrative frame model? In criminal procedure, there are carefully defined and specific steps necessary to achieve success in a criminal prosecution. In the discussion of an introduction to criminal procedure through a criminal law lens, it is necessary to have a basic understanding of the parties or players in our criminal justice system. A major concept in criminal procedure is the Fourth Amendment and the notion of probable cause. The meaning of words continues to be a fundamental issue in criminal procedure because of the broad meaning of words, such as "search" and "seizure" in the United States Constitution. Generally, a warrantless search is presumptively unreasonable. The primary importance of the exclusionary rule is to deter law enforcement officers from seizing evidence or obtaining testimony in violation of the Fourth Amendment. On the topic of line-ups and identification, it must be remembered that one of law enforcement's jobs is to gather evidence—not just arrest suspected criminals. Once an arrest is made, a prosecutor uses that evidence to establish and to prove guilt. This proof must be based on the evidence, which can be either physical or testimonial.

13.12 Chapter Review Activities

1. What are the essential clauses in the Fourth Amendment as they pertain to criminal procedure?
2. When do you need probable cause?
3. Define the seizure of a person?
4. What is the importance of *Katz v. United States*?
5. What is the importance of *Terry v. Ohio*?
6. Identify three exceptions to the warrant requirement.
7. What is the distinction between cartilage and open fields? Why is it important?
8. Does a person have a reasonable expectation of privacy in trash? Why or why not? What are some of the criteria that must be examined to answer this question?

9. What is the *Aguilar-Spinelli* two-part test? What does it pertain to?
10. Is probable cause based on an objective or subjective standard?
11. Why is the warrant requirement a crucial aspect of the Fourth Amendment?
12. When is a person "seized" (*U.S. v. Mendenhall*)?
13. How does the exception of "hot pursuit" pertain to entering a home?
14. What is the authority for "stop and frisk?"
15. Define the "plain view doctrine" with specificity (make sure to mention the cases of *Coolidge* and *Horton*).
16. Why is *Minnesota v. Dickerson* important?
17. Discuss "reasonable suspicion" as it pertains to an informant.
18. What are the consequences if the police violate the Fourth Amendment (be specific and focused)?
19. Discuss the main issue and holding of *Weeks v. United States*, and then discuss the main issue and holding of *Mapp v. Ohio*. How do these two cases relate to one another; how are they similar and how are they different? Please write in complete well-reasoned sentences and paragraphs that develop a logical flow and progression of your answer to the question. Please make sure to demonstrate your specific and focused thinking—do not write in generalities.

Fact Pattern Hypothetical

Officer A was told by an informant that the informant had suspicions that C, the apartment next door, was selling drugs from her (C's) apartment. During the next three nights, Officer A surveilled C's apartment and saw people of all kinds going in and out. Officer A stopped one of them who, upon being stopped, threw away what she had in her hand, which, upon examination, turned out to be crack cocaine. Officer A entered the apartment without a warrant and found more cocaine on the living room table. Officer A seized the drugs. Was there anything invalid about what Officer A did? Identify issues, state applicable rules of procedure, and then explain your reasoning before you reach a conclusion.

Chapter 14

Identifying Applicable Rules of Evidence Within the Criminal Law Frame

Key Terms and Concepts

Prosecutor	Reasonable Doubt	The Federal Rules of Evidence
Judicial Notice	Relevancy	Character Evidence
Expert Testimony	Hearsay	Authentication

14.1 Introduction

In studying Criminal Law, the emphasis is on learning the types of crimes, the definitions of crimes and parsing those crimes so as to prove each element of the crime based on a particular set of facts. Learning the types of crimes and their material elements is a very important first step in the criminal trial process. Law enforcement must have a solid grasp of what constitutes a crime and what elements must be established in order to prove that crime so that they can identify criminal activity and take appropriate action. As you learned in the last chapter on criminal procedure, there are very specific constitutional concerns that impact how law enforcement questions a suspect, investigates a crime, and even makes an arrest or collects evidence so that a **Prosecutor** can successfully prove each element of the crime beyond a **reasonable doubt** and obtain a conviction. Criminal procedure and evidence are intertwined in that any item seized by law enforcement or any testimony of the accused or a witness, if not obtained in accord with the rules, process, and constitutional concerns attributable to criminal procedure will result in the exclusion of the evidence under the **Exclusionary Rule** and all tainted evidence under the **Fruit of the Poisonous Tree Doctrine.** The **Federal Rules of**

Evidence also provide guidance as to the admissibility of evidence pretrial, during trial, and post trial. In this chapter you will gain a basic familiarity with some of the major categories and principles pertaining to the types of and admissibility of evidence so that you can frame a discussion of criminal law within a broader contextual frame that includes what you have learned in the chapter on criminal procedure and what you will learn in this chapter.

14.2 Federal Rules of Evidence

The Federal Rules of Evidence govern the rules, procedure, and process related to the introduction or admission of "evidence" in criminal and civil proceedings. The purpose of this section is to introduce you to some of the categories in the Federal Rules of Evidence so that you can become familiar with some of the issues that may confront law enforcement, forensics, and attorneys in the criminal trial process.

General Provisions

Article I is entitled "General Provisions" and contains rules related to the purpose and scope of the Federal Rules of Evidence. Rule 104 pertains to "Preliminary Questions" and states in 104(a) and (d):

> (a) Questions of admissibility generally.—Preliminary questions concerning the qualification of a person to be a witness, the existence of a privilege, or the admissibility of evidence shall be determined by the court, subject to the provisions of subdivision (b). In making its determination it is not bound by the rules of evidence except those with respect to privileges.
>
> (d) Testimony by accused.—The accused does not, by testifying upon a preliminary matter, become subject to cross-examination as to other issues in the case.

Why is 104(a) important? Remember that in criminal procedure the credibility of the informant is important for determining probable cause in the issuance of a warrant. In the Federal Rules of Evidence, attorneys from either side may have issues pertaining to the qualifications of a witness, or the admissibility of certain evidence (there may be assertions that the collection of the evidence violated Fourth Amendment considerations or other Rules of criminal procedure) and Rule 104(a) allows these disputes to be determined by the Court before the trial. Rule 104(d) is important because it allows an accused who may testify before a judge on the facts surrounding the collection of a piece of evidence, for example, without subjecting him/herself to cross-examination as to other issues in the case. It provides an opportunity for the accused to present testimony without opening him/herself up to questions on other matters which may be damaging to the case of the accused.

Judicial Notice

Article II pertains to "Judicial Notice" and allows the Court to "take notice"—that is, acknowledge certain undisputed facts without one side or the other having to prove the fact. For example, if a crime was committed at City Hall in a small town in which there is one City Hall and the location is well-known, the Court could take judicial notice of the location of City Hall without the attorneys having to introduce evidence to establish its location. If you think about a trial as each side having to introduce sufficient evidence to prove each statement, point, and proposition, then you can see how without judicial notice a trial could become not only unnecessarily long but burdened with trivial matters, such as the location of City Hall in Town A. It is important to note that in Rule 201(a), judicial notice may only be of adjudicative facts —that is factual matters (such as whether it is a fact that City Hall in Town A is located at Maple and Vine). Rule 201(b) states this:

> A judicially noticed fact must be one not subject to reasonable dispute in that it is either (1) generally known within the territorial jurisdiction of the trial court or (2) capable of accurate and ready determination by resort to sources whose accuracy cannot reasonably be questioned.

Judicial notice is an important concept because it allows the Court to recognize undisputed facts without one side having to prove the accuracy and veracity of these facts; such as the location of City Hall. What would be some other examples of when a Court could take judicial notice?

Relevancy

Relevancy is found in Article IV and is a very significant concept. We have discussed in the previous chapters of this book the importance of "materiality." You have learned how to identify the material elements of a crime and the material facts in a hypothetical fact pattern. Relevancy is a legal term that is crucial to the admissibility of evidence. Relevancy is related to "pertinence" to how it bears upon or relates to the "matter at hand." Evidence which is not relevant has no usefulness in proving the underlying claim, and, therefore, Rule 402 states that:

> All relevant evidence is admissible, except as otherwise provided by the Constitution of the United States, by Act of Congress, by these rules, or by other rules prescribed by the Supreme Court pursuant to statutory authority. Evidence which is not relevant is not admissible.

In light of this statement, it is important to know how to define "relevant evidence," and Rule 401 provides a definition:

> "Relevant evidence" means evidence having any tendency to make the existence of any fact that is of consequence to the determination of the action more probable or less probable than it would be without the evidence.

Learning Tip

This concept of relevance is very useful in deconstructing a hypothetical fact pattern. When you identify the material facts, you are searching for facts that are "of consequence"—that will either make it more probable or less probable to prove each element of the crime, based on definition of the crime.

Note, however, in Rule 403 that even if evidence is relevant, it can be excluded at trial based on other concerns. These concerns can include the following:

- Its probative value is substantially outweighed by the danger of unfair prejudice,
- Confusion of the issues, or
- Misleading the jury, or
- Considerations of undue delay, waste of time, or needless presentation of cumulative evidence.

This allows the Court discretion in determining the admissibility of relevant evidence based on other considerations which may be prejudicial to the overall case or the proper functioning of the Court.

Character Evidence

The admissibility of character evidence is quite complex and is discussed in Rule 404. Note that generally these definitions apply:

> Evidence of a person's character or a trait of character is not admissible for the purpose of proving action in conformity therewith on a particular occasion ...

But there are exceptions. One of the exceptions is that if the accused "puts his/her character in issue" that is the "evidence of a pertinent trait of character is offered by an accused" (401(a)(1)), it may be admitted for purposes of proving or disputing "action in conformity therewith" (401(a)). The same rule is also applicable to an alleged victim, and the provisions are found in 401(1)(2). But how do we prove character? Rule 405 states:

> (a) Reputation or opinion.—In all cases in which evidence of character or a trait of character of a person is admissible, proof may be made by testimony as to reputation or by testimony in the form of an opinion. On cross-examination, inquiry is allowable into relevant specific instances of conduct.
>
> (b) Specific instances of conduct.—In cases in which character or a trait of character of a person is an essential element of a charge, claim, or defense, proof may also be made of specific instances of that person's conduct.

Stop and Engage

Based on the language of this Rule what are the two methods for proving character? Is there a different method if character is an essential element of the charge? If so, what is it?

Remember, if the prosecutor must prove each element of the crime beyond a reasonable doubt, then it is often useful to establish the accused's propensity towards such a crime by prior crimes or acts. Rule 401(b) states that:

> Evidence of other crimes, wrongs, or acts is not admissible to prove the character of a person in order to show action in conformity therewith. It may, however, be admissible for other purposes, such as proof of motive, opportunity, intent, preparation, plan, knowledge, identity, or absence of mistake or accident, provided that upon request by the accused, the prosecution in a criminal case shall provide reasonable notice in advance of trial, or during trial if the court excuses pretrial notice on good cause shown, of the general nature of any such evidence it intends to introduce at trial.

Learning Activity

Can you write a precise and specific paraphrase of this Rule? Use a highlighter to highlight the key words in this definition. Use a pink highlighter to highlight the main rule. What are the exceptions under this Rule?

There are other provisions in Article IV; use an internet search engine to find the Federal Rules of Evidence and then take some time to read the remaining Rules in that Article.

Witnesses

The testimony of witnesses is crucial to establishing the facts surrounding the activities of the accused. Witnesses are used to provide information that attorneys can use to prove or disprove material and relevant facts related to the material elements of the crime(s). Rule 602 is very important in that it provides that criteria:

> A witness may not testify to a matter unless evidence is introduced sufficient to support a finding that the witness has personal knowledge of the matter. Evidence to prove personal knowledge may, but need not, consist of the witness' own testimony.

In other words, if a witness does not have "personal knowledge," then the witness may not testify on that specific matter. Since a witness who has personal knowledge may testify, and the credibility and veracity of that testimony is largely a function of the character of the witness, there are rules that apply to attacking the credibility of a witness. Rule 608 states some of the rules:

> (a) Opinion and reputation evidence of character.—The credibility of a witness may be attacked or supported by evidence in the form of opinion or reputation, but subject to these limitations: (1) the evidence may refer only to character for truthfulness or untruthfulness, and (2) evidence of truthful character is admissible only after the character of the witness for truthfulness has been attacked by opinion or reputation evidence or otherwise.
>
> (b) Specific instances of conduct.—Specific instances of the conduct of a witness, for the purpose of attacking or supporting the witness' character for truthfulness, other than conviction of crime as provided in rule 609, may not be proved by extrinsic evidence. They may, however, in the discretion of the court, if probative of truthfulness or untruthfulness, be inquired into on cross-examination of the witness (1) concerning the witness' character for truthfulness or untruthfulness, or (2) concerning the character for truthfulness or untruthfulness of another witness as to which character the witness being cross-examined has testified.
>
> The giving of testimony, whether by an accused or by any other witness, does not operate as a waiver of the accused's or the witness' privilege against self-incrimination when examined with respect to matters that relate only to character for truthfulness.

Stop and Engage

Use a yellow highlighter to highlight the key words in this definition. Can you write a precise and concise paraphrase of this Rule?

There are many Rules in Article XI, but among them is another Rule that pertains to "refreshing recollection." Have you ever forgotten when you said to someone yesterday or last week? Often in a trial, a witness will provide statements that are recorded and then transcribed into a writing prior to trial and then is questioned about those statements at trial; but the witness may have forgotten what he or she said previously. Rule 612 allows for a "Writing to be used to Refresh Memory" and states this:

> If a witness uses a writing to refresh memory for the purpose of testifying, either—
>
> (1) while testifying, or
> (2) before testifying, if the court in its discretion determines it is necessary in the interests of justice,
>
> an adverse party is entitled to have the writing produced at the hearing, to inspect it, to cross-examine the witness thereon, and to introduce in evidence those portions which relate to the testimony of the witness.

There is a similar rule pertaining to the "Prior Statements of Witnesses" in Rule 613, which states the following:

> (a) Examining witness concerning prior statement.—In examining a witness concerning a prior statement made by the witness, whether written or not, the statement need not be shown nor its contents disclosed to the witness at that time, but on request the same shall be shown or disclosed to opposing counsel.
>
> (b) Extrinsic evidence of prior inconsistent statement of witness.—Extrinsic evidence of a prior inconsistent statement by a witness is not admissible unless the witness is afforded an opportunity to explain or deny the same and the opposite party is afforded an opportunity to interrogate the witness thereon, or the interests of justice otherwise require.

What is the purpose of Rules 612 and 613? Why are they important? Think about the practicalities of the criminal trial process, and then write a well-reasoned answer to these two questions. **Stop and Engage**

Opinions and Expert Testimony

We all know that everyone has an opinion (well numerous opinions). We also know that opinions are often based on unsubstantiated fact or are just a belief not derived from any concrete proof or any certain information. Opinions can, therefore, be prejudicial and damaging when presented by a lay witness at trial. Rule 701 addresses this concern by stating the following:

> If the witness is not testifying as an expert, the witness' testimony in the form of opinions or inferences is limited to those opinions or inferences which are (a) rationally based on the perception of the witness, and (b) helpful to a clear understanding of the witness' testimony or the determination of a fact in issue, and (c) not based on scientific, technical, or other specialized knowledge within the scope of Rule 702.

Rule 702 states that:

> If scientific, technical, or other specialized knowledge will assist the trier of fact to understand the evidence or to determine a fact in issue, a witness qualified as an expert by knowledge, skill, experience, training, or education, may testify thereto in the form of an opinion or otherwise, if (1) the testimony is based upon sufficient facts or data, (2) the testimony is the product of reliable principles and methods, and (3) the witness has applied the principles and methods reliably to the facts of the case.

What is the purpose of Rules 701 and 702? Why are the important? Think about the practicalities of the criminal trial process, and then write a well-reasoned answer to these two questions. **Stop and Engage**

Hearsay

Remember the Rule about a witness testifying from personal knowledge (what Rule is this?) well, what if a witness tries to testify about something he/she heard from another person, or one which was made by someone else that the witness is now trying to testify to at trial? These types of testimony fall under the rules on hearsay—so what is hearsay? Hearsay is defined in Rule 801(c) as this:

> A statement, other than one made by the declarant while testifying at the trial or hearing, offered in evidence to prove the truth of the matter asserted

What other words do we have to define to understand this definition? Does the Rule also provide a definition for "Statement" and "Declarant?" In Rule 801(a) and (b), these terms are defined in this way:

> (a) A "statement" is (1) an oral or written assertion or (2) nonverbal conduct of a person, if it is intended by the person as an assertion.
>
> (b) Declarant.—A "declarant" is a person who makes a statement.

Since you know what hearsay is, under Rule 801(c); what statements are not hearsay? Rule 801(d) states this:

> (d) Statements which are not hearsay.—A statement is not hearsay if—
>
> (1) Prior statement by witness.—The declarant testifies at the trial or hearing and is subject to cross-examination concerning the statement, and the statement is (A) inconsistent with the declarant's testimony, and was given under oath subject to the penalty of perjury at a trial, hearing, or other proceeding, or in a deposition, or (B) consistent with the declarant's testimony and is offered to rebut an express or implied charge against the declarant of recent fabrication or improper influence or motive, or (C) one of identification of a person made after perceiving the person; or
>
> (2) Admission by party-opponent.—The statement is offered against a party and is (A) the party's own statement, in either an individual or a representative capacity or (B) a statement of which the party has manifested an adoption or belief in its truth, or (C) a statement by a person authorized by the party to make a statement concerning the subject, or (D) a statement by the party's agent or servant concerning a matter within the scope of the agency or employment, made during the existence of the relationship, or (E) a statement by a coconspirator of a party dur-

ing the course and in furtherance of the conspiracy. The contents of the statement shall be considered but are not alone sufficient to establish the declarant's authority under subdivision (C), the agency or employment relationship and scope thereof under subdivision (D), or the existence of the conspiracy and the participation therein of the declarant and the party against whom the statement is offered under subdivision (E).

Learning Activity

Can you write a concise and precise paraphrase of Rule 801(d)? What is the purpose of this Rule and why is it important? Think about the practicalities of the criminal trial process, and then write a well-reasoned answer to this question.

It is important to note that there are several exceptions to the hearsay rule, and they are enumerated and defined in Rule 803. Note, these are exceptions that allow testimony even if the declarant is available as a witness:

Stop and Engage

- Present sense impressions
- Excited utterance
- Then existing mental, emotional, or physical condition
- Statements for purposes of medical diagnosis or treatment
- Recorded recollection
- Records or regularly conducted activity
- Absence of entry in records
- Public records and reports
- Records of vital statistics
- Absence of public record or entry
- Records of religious organizations
- Marriage, baptismal, and similar certificates
- Family records
- Records of documents affecting an interest in property
- Statements in ancient documents
- Market reports, commercial publications
- Learned Treatises
- Reputations concerning personal or family history
- Reputation concerning boundaries or general history
- Reputation as to character
- Judgment of previous conviction
- Judgment as to personal, family, or general history, or boundaries

There are also exceptions in the event that the declarant is unavailable which are specifically defined in Rule 804. Remember, do not use your own definition of "unavailable;" the Rule has a specific definition for "unavailability as a witness."

Stop and Engage

Use an internet search engine to find Rule 804 and make a list, like the one above, of the noted exceptions. Why do you think these are exceptions? Why is it important to have these as exceptions? Write a well-reasoned essay in response to these two questions.

Authentication and Identification

Since success for a prosecutor or a defense counsel is based on the ability to admit credible, material, and relevant evidence, and evidence can be in the form of testimony or tangible evidence, such as documents, it is easy to see why issues of authentication and identification are important in the rules of evidence. Article IX of the Federal Rules of Evidence address these issues. Rule 901 states:

> (a) General provision.—The requirement of authentication or identification as a condition precedent to admissibility is satisfied by evidence sufficient to support a finding that the matter in question is what its proponent claims.
>
> (b) Illustrations.—By way of illustration only, and not by way of limitation, the following are examples of authentication or identification conforming with the requirements of this rule:
> (1) Testimony of witness with knowledge.—Testimony that a matter is what it is claimed to be.
> (2) Nonexpert opinion on handwriting.—Nonexpert opinion as to the genuineness of handwriting, based upon familiarity not acquired for purposes of the litigation.
> (3) Comparison by trier or expert witness.—Comparison by the trier of fact or by expert witnesses with specimens which have been authenticated.
> (4) Distinctive characteristics and the like.—Appearance, contents, substance, internal patterns, or other distinctive characteristics, taken in conjunction with circumstances.
> (5) Voice identification.—Identification of a voice, whether heard firsthand or through mechanical or electronic transmission or recording, by opinion based upon hearing the voice at any time under circumstances connecting it with the alleged speaker.
> (6) Telephone conversations.—Telephone conversations, by evidence that a call was made to the number assigned at the time by the telephone company to a particular person or business, if (A) in the case of a person, circumstances, including self-identification, show the person answering to be the one called, or (B) in the case of a business, the call was made to a place of business and the conversation related to business reasonably transacted over the telephone.
> (7) Public records or reports.—Evidence that a writing authorized by law to be recorded or filed and in fact recorded or filed

in a public office, or a purported public record, report, statement, or data compilation, in any form, is from the public office where items of this nature are kept.
(8) Ancient documents or data compilation.—Evidence that a document or data compilation, in any form, (A) is in such condition as to create no suspicion concerning its authenticity, (B) was in a place where it, if authentic, would likely be, and (C) has been in existence 20 years or more at the time it is offered.
(9) Process or system.—Evidence describing a process or system used to produce a result and showing that the process or system produces an accurate result.

(10) Methods provided by statute or rule.—Any method of authentication or identification provided by Act of Congress or by other rules prescribed by the Supreme Court pursuant to statutory authority.

Stop and Engage

Do all documents or other forms of tangible evidence require authentication or identification? Note that Rule 902 references certain types of documents that are "self-authenticating." Use an internet search engine to find this Rule and see what types of documents fall into this category.

Contents of Writings, Recordings, Photographs

As you can imagine with technological advances, serious concerns exist with the authenticity and veracity of writings, recordings, and photographs which are so easily altered with technology tools. Article V addresses this topic and provides definitions for these terms in Rule 1001. In order to avoid opportunities for tampering and alteration, Rule 1002, requires that an original be presented into evidence:

> To prove the content of a writing, recording, or photograph, the original writing, recording, or photograph is required, except as otherwise provided in these rules or by Act of Congress.

What is the obvious next question? What happens if there is no original? Look at Rule 1003:

> A duplicate is admissible to the same extent as an original unless (1) a genuine question is raised as to the authenticity of the original or (2) in the circumstances it would be unfair to admit the duplicate in lieu of the original.

How is duplicate defined? Is it the same as a copy? Rule 1001(4) defines duplicate this way:

> A "duplicate" is a counterpart produced by the same impression as the original, or from the same matrix, or by means of photography, including enlargements and miniatures, or by mechanical or electronic re-recording, or by chemical reproduction,

> or by other equivalent techniques which accurately reproduces the original.

Are there instances when an original is not required? Rule 1004 states:

> The original is not required, and other evidence of the contents of a writing, recording, or photograph is admissible if—
>
> (1) Originals lost or destroyed.—All originals are lost or have been destroyed, unless the proponent lost or destroyed them in bad faith; or
> (2) Original not obtainable.—No original can be obtained by any available judicial process or procedure; or
> (3) Original in possession of opponent.—At a time when an original was under the control of the party against whom offered, that party was put on notice, by the pleadings or otherwise, that the contents would be a subject of proof at the hearing, and that party does not produce the original at the hearing; or
>
> (4) Collateral matters.—The writing, recording, or photograph is not closely related to a controlling issue.

Stop and Engage

So back to the question above, what happens if the original is not available? Do you use Rule 1003 or 1004? Write an answer to this question, but be sure to provide a substantive explanation based on the rules not just a conclusion.

14.3 State Rules of Evidence

Each state also has its own rules of evidence which are often similar to the Federal Rules of Evidence. For example, the California Evidence Code has provisions on Judicial Notice, Expert Witnesses, and Hearsay, among others. California defines "hearsay evidence" in Section1200 in this way:

> (a) ... [E]vidence of a statement that was made other than by a witness while testifying at the hearing and that is offered to prove the truth of the matter stated.
>
> (b) Except as provided by law, hearsay evidence is inadmissible.
>
> (c) This section shall be known and may be cited as the hearsay rule.

How does this definition compare with the Federal Rule definition in the previous section of this chapter?

In the Florida Evidence Code in Title VII, Chapter 90, there are similar categories of rules to both the Federal Rules and California. For example, how is character evidence admissible according to the Federal Rules above? How is it admissible in California or Florida? Florida Section 90.404 states this:

(1) CHARACTER EVIDENCE GENERALLY.—Evidence of a person's character or a trait of character is inadmissible to prove action in conformity with it on a particular occasion, except:
(a) *Character of accused.*—Evidence of a pertinent trait of character offered by an accused, or by the prosecution to rebut the trait.
(b) *Character of victim.*—
1. Except as provided in s. 794.022, evidence of a pertinent trait of character of the victim of the crime offered by an accused, or by the prosecution to rebut the trait; or
2. Evidence of a character trait of peacefulness of the victim offered by the prosecution in a homicide case to rebut evidence that the victim was the aggressor.
(c) *Character of witness*—Evidence of the character of a witness, as provided in ss. 90.608-90.610.

Case Example: Practice Opportunity

Read the following case excerpt and use a yellow highlighter to highlight the material facts of the case; use a blue highlighter to note the relevant statutory language; use a pink highlighter to note the alleged crime; and use a green highlighter not note the court's application of the law to the facts of the case, to highlight the court's analysis. Remember this is a case regarding the application of a Florida Rule of Evidence so focus on the issue and reasoning pertaining to the evidence issue.

Alisha Nicole Vice v. State of Florida

In the District Court of Appeal, Case No. 1D08-5622 (2010)

On this direct appeal from convictions and sentences for aggravated child abuse and child neglect, Alisha Nicole Vice argues the trial court erred in allowing the state to introduce "similar fact evidence" on the purported authority of section 90.404(2)(a), Florida Statutes (2006). We reverse and remand for a new trial.

Dr. Alexa Canady, the pediatric neurosurgeon called to the Intensive Care Unit to treat then three-month-old J.C.H. upon his admission to the hospital on April 5, 2007, described the baby's injuries as the result of "classic non-accidental trauma," of a type formerly said to characterize Shaken Baby Syndrome. The jury heard evidence that J.C.H. sustained a subdural hematoma along with hemorrhaging in the back of his eyes; that blood and bruising were found in the right frontal portion of his brain; and that the bleeding appeared to have occurred at different times: some apparently occurred no earlier than three days before he was brought in, while some could have originated any time between March 31 and April 5, 2007.

By all accounts, during the period between March 31 and April 5, 2007, only three individuals were alone with the baby at any one time: Ms. Vice, the baby's mother; Chris H., the baby's father; and a next door neighbor who was an occasional babysitter.

On April 5, Chris H. picked up the baby from the babysitter around midday. Later, after Ms. Vice joined them at home and heard the sleeping baby inhale "raspy breaths," Ms. Vice and Chris H. took him to the hospital, where his injuries were diagnosed and treated.

Alerted by the medical authorities to apparent child abuse, the police questioned all three caregivers: Mr. H., the babysitter and Ms. Vice. After Ms. Vice voluntarily submitted to lengthy interrogation, she was charged—despite her consistent denials—with aggravated child abuse (and child neglect).

Evidence of two prior shaking incidents allegedly perpetrated by this defendant upon an infant not the victim in the case w[as] presented. Those two incidents are relevant and probative insofar as issues of identity, opportunity, intent and absence of mistake or accident. When the state filed notice of its intent to rely on evidence of other crimes, wrongs, or acts, as permitted under Williams v. State, 110 So. 2d 654 (Fla. 1959), to prove Ms. Vice was the perpetrator, she filed a motion in limine seeking to exclude such evidence. After an evidentiary hearing, the court denied the motion, stating conclusorily:

> Evidence of two prior shaking incidents allegedly perpetrated by this defendant upon an infant not the victim in the case w[as] presented. Those two incidents are relevant and probative insofar as issues of identity, opportunity, intent and absence of mistake or accident. Barber v. State, 781 So. 2d 425 ([Fla.] 5th DCA 2001); Washington v. State, 737 So. 2d 1208 ([Fla.] lst DCA 1999).

Specifically, the state sought to prove that six years earlier Ms. Vice's then-husband and then-mother-in-law witnessed her shaking—but not injuring—a child born of that marriage. In the course of what proved to be a four-day trial, the state put this evidence on to show that it was Ms. Vice—not Mr. H. (or the babysitter)—who was responsible for J.C.H.'s injury.

The Williams rule evidence consisted of testimony by Daniel Cooper (Ms. Vice's former husband) and Melissa Lindsey (Daniel Cooper's mother). Mr. Cooper (who acknowledged he had been an abusive husband whose abuse contributed to the dissolution of his marriage to Ms. Vice) testified at trial that, when he arrived home from work one day in early 2001, Ms. Vice "had [the child] up in the air, like, in front of her face, about like this, and was shaking him rapidly, screaming at him to shut up while he was crying." Mr. Cooper did not report the incident to the authorities and testified that the child did not suffer any harm.

Ms. Lindsey testified at trial that, one day in the spring of 2001 when she approached their apartment, she saw Ms. Vice through the curtains "sitting with [the infant] on the couch and she was shaking him violently" close to her face while yelling at him to shut up. Ms. Lindsey did not report the incident to the authorities at the time, and testified that the child did not require medical attention.

"A trial court's decision to admit collateral crime or Williams rule evidence is reviewed for an abuse of discretion. However, '[t]he admission of improper collateral crime evidence is presumed harmful error because of the danger that a jury will take the bad character or propensity to commit the crime as evidence of guilt of the crime charged.' For the harmless error rule to apply, the State must prove that there is " 'no reasonable possibility that the error contributed to the conviction.' " ... "Similar fact evidence of other crimes, wrongs, or acts is admissible when relevant to prove a material fact in issue, including, but not limited to, proof of motive, opportunity, intent, preparation, plan, knowledge, identity, or absence of mistake or accident, but it is inadmissible when the evidence is relevant solely to prove bad character or propensity." §90.404(2)(a), Fla. Stat. (2006). See Williams, 110 So. 2d at 659-60 ("Our view of the proper rule simply is that relevant evidence will not be excluded merely because it relates to similar facts which point to the commission of a separate crime. The test of admissibility is relevancy. The test of inadmissibility is a lack of relevancy." The evidence in the present case was "relevant solely to prove bad character or propensity." §90.404(2)(a), Fla. Stat. (2006).

Evidence that does not logically tend to prove a fact in issue (other than propensity) is irrelevant and inadmissible. See Williams, 110 So. 2d at 662 ("[W]e emphasize that the question of the relevancy of this type of evidence should be cautiously scrutinized before it is determined to be admissible."). Before admitting Williams rule evidence, it is incumbent upon the trial court to make multiple determinations, including whether the defendant committed the prior crime, whether the prior crime meets the similarity requirements necessary to be relevant as set forth in our prior case law, whether the prior crime is too remote so as to diminish its relevance, and finally, whether the prejudicial effect of the prior crime substantially outweighs its probative value.

The trial court allowed the state to put on evidence of prior shakings to prove "identity, opportunity, intent and absence of mistake or accident," without any explanation of how the Williams rule evidence would logically tend to prove anything properly at issue to do with the events of March 31 through April 5, 2007. The trial court made no finding as to whether Ms. Vice shook the other baby; as to whether what occurred was sufficiently similar. The present case does not involve any allegation of sexual molestation. Although the law governing Williams rule evidence has been altered in the context of child sexual molestation cases, see §90.404(2)(b)1., Fla. Stat. (2006) ("In a to be somehow relevant to the charged offense; as to whether the conduct with another baby six years earlier was too remote to be relevant; or, as Robertson also requires, as to whether the prejudicial nature of the evidence of prior abuse outweighed its probative value, if any, in the present case.

The threshold issue in the present case is relevance. ("Evidence which is admissible under this theory is frequently called 'similar fact evidence.' However, evidence of collateral crimes or acts is admissible under section 90.404(2)(a) not because it is similar to the crime or act in issue, but because it is relevant to prove a material fact or issue in the instant case other than the defendant's propensity or bad character. Thus, it can be misleading to refer to this evidence as 'similar fact evidence' because the similarity of the facts involved in the collateral act or crime does not ensure relevance or admissibility. Similarly, evidence of collateral crimes may be relevant and admissible even if it is not similar."

The probative value comes from the fact that the collateral crimes were committed with a unique modus operandi which was the same as that used in the crime in question; therefore, it may be inferred that the same person committed both crimes. When that evidence is coupled with an identification of the defendant as the person who committed the prior crime, the evidence is relevant. Evidence that the defendant has committed prior crimes, without evidence of a similar unique modus operandi, does not raise the same inference. Only when the court can find that modus operandi is so unusual so that it is reasonable to conclude that the same person committed both crimes is the evidence of the prior crime admissible to prove identity.

In the present case, there are no "points of similarity" that "when taken as a whole are 'so unusual as to point to the defendant.'" Barber v. State, 781 So. 2d.The jury was instructed that to prove the crime of aggravated child abuse the state had to show two elements beyond a reasonable doubt: (1) that Ms. Vice "knowingly or willfully committed child abuse upon J.C.H. and in so doing caused great bodily harm, permanent disability, or permanent disfigurement" and (2) "J.C.H. was under the age of 18 years." The jury was instructed that "willfully" means "knowingly, intentionally, and purposely." The jury was informed that "child abuse" means "the intentional infliction of physical or mental injury upon a child or an intentional act that could reasonably be expected to result in physical or mental injury to a child."

In fact, the state was unable to establish how the injury occurred. In contrast to the charged offense, the shakings of the other child did not cause any injury or result in any need for medical attention. This is not a case where two infants sustained "strikingly similar" injuries and symptoms within the same short period of time. Compare Barber, 781 So. 2d at 428. Six years separated the prior incidents and the offense charged. Intent and the absence of a mistake or accident are also material facts at issue in the present case. To convict Ms. Vice of aggravated child abuse, the jury had to find that she acted "willfully," or "knowingly, intentionally, and purposely." "Evidence of similar acts that contradict an innocent explanation of the defendant's act is admissible. The more frequently an act is done, the less likely it is that it is innocently done." But, as our supreme court has made clear, "substantial similarity of crimes is a requirement when the evidence is sought to be admitted for the specific purpose of establishing absence of mistake or accident." Robertson, 829 So. 2d at 909.

Evidence that Ms. Vice shook a different child six years earlier without injuring him does not meet this similarity requirement. In the absence of any evidence of injury or the need for medical treatment attributable to the two shakings six years earlier, the "similar fact evidence" adduced below was not relevant to show intent or absence of mistake or accident. The fact that Ms. Vice shook a baby six years earlier without injuring the baby would, if anything, tend to prove any shaking of J.C.H. was not intended to injure and that no injury was anticipated. Because the "similar fact evidence" did not "contradict an innocent explanation" of J.C.H.'s injury, Ehrhardt, supra, §404.12, at 246, or share any "substantial similarity" with the charged offense, Robertson, 829 So. 2d at 909, the trial court abused its discretion in admitting the similar fact evidence to prove the absence of mistake or accident.

Finally, opportunity was not in issue. As his mother, Ms. Vice spent a lot of time with J.C.H., according to the evidence. The evidence was also uncontroverted that she was alone with J.C.H. more than once during the five-day period in which he was injured. See Thomas v. State, 599 So. 2d 158, 162 (Fla. 1st DCA 1992) ("If there is no bona fide dispute over a material fact

> that the similar fact evidence is offered to prove, then the probative value of such evidence necessarily has significantly less importance than its prejudicial effect, and the evidence should be excluded....”). With clear and undisputed evidence on the point, the trial court abused its discretion by allowing the state to introduce evidence of events six years in the past to prove opportunity, even if it viewed such evidence as somehow probative.
>
> In sum, the testimony of appellant's ex-husband and his mother about shaking another baby six years earlier was not relevant to any material fact properly in issue, and the trial court erred by allowing the state to adduce the testimony. Error of this kind is presumed harmful. It may be considered harmless only if the state demonstrates there is no reasonable possibility that it affected the jury's verdict. Given the paucity of probative evidence, there is a reasonable possibility that admission of the similar fact evidence contributed to the conviction. The state has not demonstrated otherwise. Reversed and remanded.

Stop and Engage

Now that you have highlighted key parts from this case, complete the following activities:

- Identify the main issue(s) in this case.
- Write a concise summary of the material facts.
- Paraphrase the relevant statutory language with precision and accuracy.
- Write a concise summary of the court's reasoning.
- Write a concise explanation as to how and why the court reached its decision—its holding.

Is this a relevancy case or is it a character evidence case or both? Remember these cases often contain more than one issue combined with applicable rules of law.

In Texas, the general categories in the Rules of Evidence are similar to the Federal Rules. You will note Articles on Judicial Notice, Relevancy, Witnesses, etc. Section 401 of the Texas Rules of Evidence defines “relevant evidence” in this way:

> All relevant evidence is admissible, except as otherwise provided by Constitution, by statute, by these rules, or by other rules prescribed pursuant to statutory authority. Evidence which is not relevant is inadmissible.

How does this compare to the language in the Federal Rules? If you use an internet search engine to find the rules of evidence for different states, you may notice some similarities. For example, in Ohio “relevant evidence” is also defined in Rule 401 as like this:

> Relevant evidence means evidence having any tendency to make the existence of any fact that is of consequence to the determination of the action more probable or less probable than it would be without the evidence.

Is this language similar or different from that in the Federal Rules and in Texas?

Notice in Texas Rule 405, the stated "methods for proving character:"

> (a) Reputation or Opinion. In all cases in which evidence of a person's character or character trait is admissible, proof may be made by testimony as to reputation or by testimony in the form of an opinion. In a criminal case, to be qualified to testify at the guilt stage of trial concerning the character or character trait of an accused, a witness must have been familiar with the reputation, or with the underlying facts or information upon which the opinion is based, prior to the day of the offense. In all cases where testimony is admitted under this rule, on cross-examination inquiry is allowable into relevant specific instances of conduct.
>
> (b) Specific Instances of Conduct. In cases in which a person's character or character trait is an essential element of a charge, claim or defense, proof may also be made of specific instances of that person's conduct.

How does this compare to the language in the Federal Rules? In Ohio the rules are stated in Rule 405 (notice how the numbering of the Rules is similar in the states to the federal numbering?) as:

Learning Tip

> (A) Reputation or opinion. In all cases in which evidence of character or a trait of character of a person is admissible, proof may be made by testimony as to reputation or by testimony in the form of an opinion. On cross-examination, inquiry is allowable into relevant specific instances of conduct.
>
> (B) Specific instances of conduct. In cases in which character or a trait of character of a person is an essential element of a charge, claim, or defense, proof may also be made of specific instances of his conduct.

How does the Ohio rule compare/contrast with the Texas rule? Use an internet search engine to find the evidentiary rules for the methods of proving character in your state, and then note some similarities and differences.

14.4 Summary

It is important to remember the context for your learning in any subject. When studying Criminal Law, the emphasis is on learning the definitions and material elements of the crimes so that you can use them to identify criminal activity for the purpose of determining whether there is sufficient evidence to prove the elements of the crime (or the lack thereof) and further whether such evidence is admissible based not only on rules of evidence but on rules of criminal procedure. If there is insufficient evidence, or there is insufficient admissible evidence, then all the "guilt" in the world will not be adequate for a prosecutor to file charges and seek an indictment. This is why it is so important to understand the rules of criminal procedure as well as the rules of evidence when studying criminal law. Since the prosecutor must prove each element of the crime beyond a reasonable doubt, the prosecutor must be able to admit evidence, such as testimony, tangible evidence, and other forms of evidence in order to prove the elements of the crime. Issues such as relevancy and the competency of witnesses are foundational to the admission of evidence. If a witness can only testify as to what someone else has said to the witness or to facts that are not known personally to the witness, there may be hearsay issues. When learning about the different crimes and their material elements in criminal law, remember that this is a "bigger picture"—and that "picture" is to prove or defend against elements of the crime through the proper collection of that evidence for its use at trial.

14.5 Chapter Review Activities

Please make sure to answer each question thoroughly with fully-developed reasoning, support for your answers and a demonstration of your knowledge of the subject matter. Please write in fully developed paragraphs.

1. Identify ten objections that you as a prosecutor or defense attorney would raise at trial. Explain why you would raise these objections, and make sure to frame your answers in the context of your state's Rules of Evidence.

2. Use an internet search engine to find two Supreme Court cases that pertain to relevancy and Rule 401. Extract from the Court's reasoning in both cases the focal points for the case decision and then compare/contrast these two cases.

3. Choose a rule from your state's Rules of Evidence, and, in one paragraph and in your own words, summarize the substantive content of this rule; then identify and discuss the procedural mechanisms; and finally, in 1–2 pages, present a well-reasoned discussion using sources of Criminal Law, Criminal Procedure, and Constitutional Law, a public policy argument for or against this rule.

4. Define and discuss how direct evidence is different from circumstantial evidence. Provide an example of each.
5. Why is judicial notice important in the evidentiary process?
6. What is the prosecutor's burden of proof? What is the defense's burden of proof?
7. What are some reasons for the "beyond a reasonable standard" requirement in criminal cases? How has it been defined? Who has this burden?
8. Define relevant evidence, material evidence, and competent evidence? Why are these three terms so important?

Chapter 15

Applied Learning—A Collaborative Activity: The Mock Trial

15.1 Introduction

The purpose of this chapter is to provide you with an opportunity to apply your learning in a collaborative activity. You have learned through this course that developing a context for your learning is important, and that using your knowledge develops reinforcement and a sustained understanding of the course content. In this collaborative activity, you will work in groups to present a case within the criminal trial process using your knowledge of criminal law, criminal procedure, constitutional law, and evidence. You will have the opportunity to serve as part of the prosecuting attorney team, as part of the defense attorney team, as a witness, or as a member of the jury. Each role is important to the success of the overall activity, and this will require your commitment and dedication to the process. The attorney teams will have a heavier workload, but they will have the chance to present their case before the court. The witnesses will have to memorize scripts and to be prepared to answer questions that may be unexpected—this may require some "acting and impromptu" abilities. The jury will listen to the evidence presented in the trial and will then deliberate and reach a verdict. The professor will serve as the "judge" so that he/she can rule on any pre-trial and trial motions as well as provide instructions to the jury and maintain order in the "Courtroom." This mock criminal trial is a fun way to implement your learning and gain exposure to and experience in the integrative frames that comprise the criminal trial process.

15.2 Logistics

Your professor will determine how the prosecuting team, defense team, witnesses, and jury members are selected for this collaborative activity. Since the purpose is to engage the whole class, it is necessary to take some liberties with the mock criminal trial. Whereas in a real criminal trial there are usually 1–2 attorneys on each side, there may be 3–4 depending upon the size of the class. More than 4–5 attorneys per team can become unyielding and difficult. There are usually 12 jurors, but, again, depending on the size of the class and the number of witnesses, there may be more or less jurors; but the jury should consist of an even number of members. During the mock trial, the attorneys on each team should focus on different issues or arguments as they work through the prosecuting and defense strategy for the case so that each attorney team member has a chance to question witnesses and present in the mock criminal trial. One attorney from each team should be chosen by the team for purposes of presenting the opening and closing statements. Another important difference in the mock criminal trial is that there are time constraints based on class schedules and other course logistics. This may require that examination and cross-examination of witnesses be limited, and that 2–3 class sessions (depending upon the length of the class session) be allocated to this collaborative activity. The attorney teams, in particular, will need to spend significant amounts of time outside of class preparing their motions and strategies, witness preparation, and evidence gathering. The witnesses will also have to spend time outside of class meeting with the attorneys and memorizing their scripts. The jurors have the least amount of work outside of the classroom.

Most of the preparation for the mock criminal trial will require time outside of scheduled class time and should be thought of as time you would use to prepare for several assignments or examinations. In fact, your professor may want to use the mock criminal trial as a final exam substitute or an end-of-the semester final activity. If you are on an attorney team, you should be prepared to schedule time to meet with your team members and your witnesses, and if you are a witness, you will need to meet with an attorney from an attorney team, depending upon whether you are a witness for the prosecution or the defense. The attorney teams will also have to coordinate with the professor for rulings on any pre-trial motions and individual team strategies. Your professor will not only serve as the "judge" but also as a consultant to assist the attorney teams with preparation and trial strategies.

The actual trial is very straightforward and where possible, the classroom should be set up as a courtroom, or another room, if that is possible, can be used where you can set it up to simulate a courtroom. There need to be a table and chairs for the prosecuting attorneys, a table and chairs for the defense attorneys, a chair for the testifying witness, chairs for the members of the jury, and a desk and chair for the judge. Witnesses will need to stay outside of the courtroom (classroom) until they are called to testify since witnesses are not allowed to hear the testimony of other witnesses prior to providing their testimony to the court. Once a witness has testified and is dismissed, he/she may stay in the courtroom to hear the remainder of the trial. Witnesses and jury members should not speak to one another or to members of the attorney teams during this collaborative mock criminal trial. The only exception is that a witness for the defense may speak with the defense attorney team (but not the prosecuting attorney team), and a witness for the prosecution may speak to the prosecuting attorney team (but not to the defense attorney team).

When the mock criminal trial begins, the attorneys will be seated and the clerk of the court will call the court to order and all will rise and the judge will enter the room. The judge will then call the jury to enter the room and be seated. The judge will ask the attorneys if they are ready to begin and if the prosecution will present its opening statement. The defense then presents its opening statement. After the opening statements, the prosecution will present its case—that is, call its witnesses and offer its evidence into trial (this will require familiarity with the Rules of Evidence—since the defense team may object based on proper objections within the Rules of Evidence and the judge will rule on any objections). When a witness is called, the prosecutor asks his/her questions, and the witness responds (it is best if this is done without reading from a script but rather based on memory). When the prosecution is finished asking his/her questions, the defense attorney team may cross-examine the witness by asking questions related to the testimony. This is another opportunity for objections based on the Rules of Evidence. This continues until the prosecution has called all of its witnesses and rests its case. Then the defense team follows the same procedure: calls each witness for direct examination with the prosecution having the opportunity for cross-examination until the defense team rests its case. The prosecution will present its closing argument, and then the defense team will present its closing argument. The judge will then present instructions to the jury, and the jury will be dismissed for deliberations. When the jury has reached its decision, the clerk of court will call the court back to order and the jury will enter; the jury foreman will hand its decision to the clerk of the court, who will hand it to the judge, and then the jury foreman will pronounce the findings of the jury.

Remember, due to time constraints, class schedules, and other logistics there may be time limits on direct and cross-examination. These time limits should be determined prior to the mock criminal trial once each attorney team has had a chance to write the witness script, meet with the witness, and determine its strategy. The time limits should be agreed to in advance with the professor's consent, and then held to during the trial by the clerk of the court who can also serve as the timekeeper. There should also be a time limit on the jury deliberations so that you can plan course time accordingly.

15.3 Hypothetical Case

The following is the hypothetical case that will be used for the mock criminal trial. It is important for the attorney teams to read the case several times, identify the applicable crimes, identify the relevant state statutes (using the penal or criminal code of your state, or using the Texas Penal Code as is used in the model documents presented in this chapter), identify the relevant witnesses, and then think about not only their own strategy but how the opposing attorney team will approach the hypothetical case to present its arguments to the Court.

Facts

Gladewaterville was selected to host a three-day food festival for the region known as the "FoodieFest Festival" from January 11–14, 2011. Prior to 2010, Gladewaterville was a little Piney woods town with few outside visitors and little unusual activities. However, since retirees and young professionals started purchasing lake property, the population and economy of Gladewaterville is growing and many "city folk" are moving and visiting Gladewaterville. The small downtown village which has several antique ice cream and fudge shops as well as several vacant buildings and lots mixed among local real estate, insurance, and auto lots is undergoing revitalization by the Gladewaterville Chamber of Commerce. Some of the local residents and the local officials are in disagreement over the revitalization plans and are resentful towards the many "city folk" who are "invading" the peace and quiet of historic Gladewaterville. However, local officials decided that holding the FoodieFest Festival in Gladewaterville would aid with its economic revitalization.

Some of the older local residents have formed a group to protest and rally against the revitalization and have solicited support from some staunch veterans who have turned to Paul Popular for insights and guidance for their protests and rallies which include attending town meetings and voicing their opinions as well as throwing rocks at some of the homeless pets. There are several other local groups, "Leave Gladewaterville Alone" and

"We must Grow" that have their various agendas and are at odds with the various policies and changes facing Gladewaterville in its revitalization. "Leave Gladewaterville Alone" is organized by Stan Leverly who is particularly concerned about the impact of the revitalization on Gladewaterville's homeless pet population; specifically those who have taken shelter with several homeless people in the abandoned lot next to the new fudge factory, "FudgeCo" which is owned by Freddie Fudge the organizer of "We must Grow." Stan is known for providing food to the homeless as well as teaching them how to cook outside and has conducted workshops on starting fires with sticks and stones.

When Freddie Fudge saw that Gladewaterville was desperate for revitalization and a fire had destroyed his main factory in TylerTown he decided Gladewaterville would be a great location for the new factory and had issued numerous press releases and had made statements to his office staff that Gladewaterville would be ideal and he needed to make sure the locals "were on board" and that he was willing to do "whatever it takes" to make sure Gladewaterville grew so that he would make lots of money and that he "knew exactly how to do it." Many in TylerTown had been suspicious of the fire that destroyed the main factory and the significant insurance money that FudgeCo received which Freddie was contributing to Gladewaterville's revitalization.

Since the economy was in a downturn and many of the surrounding employers had closed factories and laid off people, there was a significant homeless population in Gladewaterville and they had taken refuge with the local homeless pets in the vacant lot next to FudgeCo, which had tried to run off the people and the animals numerous times creating significant tensions and verbal outburst between Freddie and Stan. In fact Freddie had been seen throwing rocks ate Stan on two occasions. In addition, FudgeCo had to hire a security team which was owned by Paul, who was also a volunteer firefighter for Gladewaterville. Paul had seen Stan watching FudgeCo at night from his car parked across the street and sometimes chatting with Sarah Jane and dimwitted Billy.

It was well known that Stan and the homeless population were avid in their disdain for FudgeCo and its failure to provide fudge to the homeless people and pets. The "Leave Gladewaterville Alone" Organization had published many articles in the local newspaper accusing FudgeCo of cruelty to persons and animals for their failure to provide free fudge. One of the more notorious homeless was Sarah Jane who has been accused in the past of selling narcotics to the local teens in Gladewaterville and who has been in and out of jail on assault, drug, and theft charges. When Sarah Jane had money she would usually use it to but the homeless pets' food and go out drinking and binging on drugs. Because she had a phobia of uncooked or raw food, of any kind, she would often make a fire outside her cardboard box in the lot next to FudgeCo to cook her food and the food for the animals. She would often share her food with her dimwitted and mentally deranged friend, Billy who liked to sleep under the rear entrance awnings at FudgeCo and howl at the moon.

There were rumors that Billy was the half-brother of Paul and that Paul had associations with several anti-fudge groups. In fact, a long time anti-candy advocate and pro-homeless animal crusader, Olivia had been seen with Billy, Paul, and Stan by some local residents after dinner on January 11th near the homeless lot smoking cigarettes and chatting with some of the homeless. In addition, some had seen Paul and Billy drinking coffee at the Mama Miaz Latte Parlor at 11:00 pm on January 11th owned by Mama Mia who heard them talking about the fire in TylerTown and Freddie Fudge's "tossing money around town."

On January 11, the first night of the FoodFest Festival, at around 11:00 pm, Fat Frankie was seen by Paul, who was driving home from the Festival, outside the entrance to FudgeCo smoking cigarettes and vomiting on the front door. Paul called the police who came and found Frankie roaming around with a handful of rocks and acting suspiciously, so the officer questioned him and took him to the police station for further questioning. He was detained for over 6 hours until he was sober enough to go home. The next morning when Freddie arrived at FudgeCo he found the factory had been set on fire but not destroyed, windows smashed by rocks, and Sarah Jane was dead under FudgeCo's rear entrance awning.

You may find that you need to revise or clarify the fact pattern based on laws in your state or other strategic decisions. Your professor can provide guidance on whether there needs to be any revisions or changes to the fact pattern and whether as part of collaborative activity, he/she would suggest that both the prosecution and the defense propose any changes, mutually agree to them, and then use a consolidated revised fact pattern.

Next Steps

Based on the hypothetical, each attorney team—the prosecution and the defense—should independently, with their team members, deconstruct the case and agree on the material facts. In addition, the prosecution needs to determine if there are additional crimes or charges that it wants to file, and then present those to the defense team. Remember, you only want to bring charges for which you have sufficient evidence to prove each element at trial beyond a reasonable doubt.

15.4 Statutory Provisions

Based on the hypothetical case you know, and the "Next Steps" above, you now need to determine what statutory provisions are applicable based on the definitions of the crimes you have identified in your state criminal or penal code. You know that according to the hypothetical case, that one Sarah Jane is dead, but is it murder or another form of homicide?

Learning Activity

Once the prosecution has clearly identified the crimes and the parties it is charging for those crimes, the prosecution needs to make a list of those crimes with the associated offenders (defendants)—the **Crime and Offender Worksheet.**

The prosecution should use its state penal or criminal code to find the definitions for those crimes, and then parse the material elements of the crimes. Once the prosecution has the definitions and the parsed elements prepared in a well-organized document, submit this **Statutory Worksheet** to your professor for his/her review and then upon his/her approval, to the defense team so that both teams know what party is charged with what crime and the relevant state law that applies.

Now the prosecution needs to begin to build its case by determining how it will apply the material facts to prove beyond a reasonable doubt each element of the crime against the appropriate party.

The defense also needs to begin to build its defense and to think about what evidence and witness statements it will need to negate any possible evidence presented by the prosecution, and to see if there are any applicable defenses for each party charged with a crime.

15.5 Witness Scripts and Evidence Lists

Witness Lists

Based on the hypothetical case or a revised version if you are using one, make a list of who you will call as a witness based on the facts of the case. There should be a **Prosecution Witness List** and a **Defense Witness List.** You may need to make-up some names and identify some of those people mentioned in the hypothetical case more specifically. You may also need witnesses (such as expert witnesses or crime scene investigators), who are not specifically mentioned in the facts. It is important to think about all of the witnesses you will need to prove or defend against the criminal charges. Remember, your witness list should only contain those witnesses whom you can use to support or defend the facts related to the elements of the crime and the party accused of committing that crime.

Once each team has identified the name of the witness, the occupation (or lack thereof) of the witness, then each team should submit its appropriate Witness List to your professor for review. If there are duplicate names on each list, then your professor will need to meet with you to determine the appropriate list for that particular witness.

Witness Script

Once the Prosecution Witness List and the Defense Witness List have been approved, your professor will assign a witness to a particular member of your class. That person is now responsible for writing the script for the witness based on the facts of the case. **The Witness Script** should include some background on the witness, what the witness knows or has seen, and what the witness intends to say at trial based on the facts of the hypothetical case. The Witness Script should not be more than a few pages, and it should be specifically sufficient so that the appropriate attorney team can formulate direct examination questions based on the script. The Witness Script should only be seen by the professor and the prosecution team if it is a prosecution witness or the defense team if it is a defense witness.

Evidence List

If the prosecution or defense intends to use any tangible evidence based on the hypothetical case or a revised version, then the team or teams using such evidence, such as a rock found at the scene, should prepare an **Evidence List.** If both teams list the same item, it will default to the prosecution team since the prosecution will introduce it into evidence first in proving its case, and then the defense team can refer to the evidence when making its case. The Evidence List should be submitted to your professor for review when it is completed, and then each piece of physical or tangible evidence should be placed in a clear bag and marked as either Prosecution Exhibit A, B, C, etc. or Defense Exhibit A, B, C, etc. You will need to consult with your State Rules of Evidence to determine the proper procedure for introducing evidence at trial. Remember relevancy, authentication, an identification are part of the "laying the foundation" for the introduction to evidence at trial.

15.6 Motions and Stipulations

As you begin to prepare to formulate the questions, you will ask your witnesses based on the Witness Scripts and you think about the order in which you want to present information you may realize that there are undisputed facts, or items that are appropriate for judicial notice, or issues of admissibility of certain evidence or testimony for which you need a pre-trial ruling. These matters will be handled by way of stipulations between the prosecution and defense teams and pre-trial motions. Pre-trial motions are most commonly used to exclude evidence, compel or exclude the testimony of a witness, compel a witness or the defendant to an examination, etc.

There are also specific rules that apply to pre-trial motions. The Federal Rules of Criminal Procedure (Rule 12) states:

(a) Pleadings.

The pleadings in a criminal proceeding are the indictment, the information, and the pleas of not guilty, guilty, and nolo contendere.
(b) Pretrial Motions.
(1) *In General.*
Rule 47 applies to a pretrial motion.
(2) *Motions That May Be Made Before Trial.*
A party may raise by pretrial motion any defense, objection, or request that the court can determine without a trial of the general issue.
(3) *Motions That Must Be Made Before Trial.*
The following must be raised before trial:
(A) a motion alleging a defect in instituting the prosecution;
(B) a motion alleging a defect in the indictment or information—but at any time while the case is pending, the court may hear a claim that the indictment or information fails to invoke the court's jurisdiction or to state an offense;
(C) a motion to suppress evidence;
(D) a Rule 14 motion to sever charges or defendants; and
(E) a Rule 16 motion for discovery.
(4) *Notice of the Government's Intent to Use Evidence.*
(A) *At the Government's Discretion.*
At the arraignment or as soon afterward as practicable, the government may notify the defendant of its intent to use specified evidence at trial in order to afford the defendant an opportunity to object before trial under Rule 12(b)(3)(C).
(B) At the Defendant's Request.
At the arraignment or as soon afterward as practicable, the defendant may, in order to have an opportunity to move to suppress evidence under Rule 12(b)(3)(C), request notice of the government's intent to use (in its evidence-in-chief at trial) any evidence that the defendant may be entitled to discover under Rule 16.
(c) Motion Deadline.
The court may, at the arraignment or as soon afterward as practicable, set a deadline for the parties to make pretrial motions and may also schedule a motion hearing.

(d) Ruling on a Motion.

The court must decide every pretrial motion before trial unless it finds good cause to defer a ruling. The court must not defer ruling on a pretrial motion if the deferral will adversely affect a party's right to appeal. When factual issues are involved in deciding a motion, the court must state its essential findings on the record.

Stop and Engage

What are the rules in your state? Find the equivalent of Federal Rule 12 in your state rules of criminal procedure.

Learning Activity

Use an internet search engine to find a reputable website that has information on how to draft stipulations and pre-trial motions for criminal cases. Find some samples, and then both teams should work together to produce one model form that both teams will use for the format of any pre-trial motions submitted to the judge (your professor). Note as well that when one side files a motion, for example, to suppress evidence, the other side may need to file a response to that motion, setting forth its legal argument and reasons why the motion should not be granted.

15.7 Suggested Strategies

Your professor will guide you and counsel you in this process, but you may want to take note of the following suggestions for success:

- This is a collaborative activity that will require time management, organization, and administrative skills.
- Once you deconstruct the fact pattern, make sure you have a good grasp of the issues and the relevant crimes.
- If you are the prosecution team, make sure the parties you charge for specific crimes can be proven based on the facts at trial.
- Make sure you have an excellent knowledge of the elements of the crimes and the facts you will use to prove them.
- Make sure the Witness Script is viable and covers the information you need to formulate the appropriate questions at trial.
- Remember you want to use pre-trial motions and stipulations to resolve issues before trial.
- Make sure you use the Rules of Evidence to make objections during the trial and that you introduce evidence at trial in accord with these Rules.
- Make sure you call your witnesses in a logical order—if you are the prosecution, you have the burden of proof to prove each element of the crime beyond a reasonable doubt, so you want to "build

a narrative—tell a story" through the order in which you call witnesses and present evidence.

- Both teams and the witnesses want to make sure they are speaking to the jury; remember it is the Jury that is the trier of fact and issues the verdict.
- The jury will receive jury instructions (that are probably drafted in a collaborative effort by both the prosecution and defense teams and submitted to your professor in advance for approval), and the jury must use the law and instructions to decide the facts presented to it and the evidence submitted at trial.

Suggested Timeframe

The collaborative mock trial activity is great fun when approached with commitment and dedication. It is a great way to receive some practical application experience, but it does require time outside of the classroom and significant effort. Depending on the number of weeks that your Criminal Law course meets, and the number of meetings per week, if your professor is using this mock criminal trial as an end-of-the semester activity or assessment, then it is probably advisable to begin thinking about this activity mid-way through the course when you have read and been exposed to Chapters 1–6 so that you have an understanding of how to deconstruct a fact pattern, identify issues, parse the elements of a crime, and think about developing well-reasoned analysis for a hypothetical fact pattern (which is similar to analyzing a case and formulating strategies for a mock criminal trial). It is probably useful to allocate a week or two to working with the mock trial hypothetical case facts, identifying applicable crimes and parties to be charged, and parsing the applicable state criminal or penal code based on the identified crimes. Once this has been accomplished, it is best to start working on identifying witnesses and evidence and completing Witness Lists so that Witness Scripts can be completed within a week or so and then witness questions can be formulated so witnesses can prepare for the courtroom and attorney teams can develop their trial strategy. These steps can be completed in one month so that 2–3 class sessions at the end of the semester or into final exam week can be used to actually hold the mock criminal trial. One suggested approach it to have one class period for the prosecution's case and one class period for the defense's case with the final class period for closing arguments and jury deliberations. This way the jury can come back before the end of class with its verdict.

15.8 Summary

The mock criminal trial is a meaningful way to integrate many of the skills and much of the information you learn in a course on Criminal

Law. It is also helpful for those who are thinking about law school or working in the judicial system to have an opportunity to develop and practice some viable skills necessary for success in careers in these fields. Serving as a witness or a jury member also provides experience in learning how to answer questions and think about how arguments are structured and presented for resolution. This type of critical thinking is an important skill for anyone who wants to work in the criminal justice, legal, or associated professions. Regardless of your role in the mock criminal trial, you will need to "think outside the box" and learn to find gaps, anticipate issues and questions, develop flexibility, and learn to work effectively with others. Hopefully, this activity will not only be a great applied learning tool, but a great experience you will remember for many years.

Index